A Fan's Guide

FOOTBALL GROUNDS

England & Wales

DUNCAN ADAMS

First published 2007
Reprinted 2008

ISBN (10) 0 7110 3268 8
ISBN (13) 978 0 7110 3268 2

Published by Ian Allan Publishing

an imprint of Ian Allan Publishing Ltd, Hersham, Surrey KT12 4RG.
Printed in England by Ian Allan Printing Ltd, Hersham, Surrey KT12 4RG.

Code: 0810/A1

Visit the Ian Allan Publishing website at
www.ianallanpublishing.com

Front cover: Millwall.

Contents

Introduction

Welcome to the 2007/08 edition of 'A Fan's Guide: Football Grounds – England & Wales'. This book covers every ground in the Premier League and Coca-Cola Football Leagues, plus the Cup Finals venue, the new Wembley Stadium. Inside you will find a host of information useful to the travelling supporter. Not only are there practical details, such as directions to the grounds, but other information to make your day more enjoyable, such as pub recommendations. There are also a number of excellent colour photos of all the grounds themselves.

Well, the new Wembley Stadium has finally arrived. It was great to hear again last season at some football grounds the chants of 'We're going to Wembley' for those fans who were looking forward to attending the FA Cup or play-off finals. I personally think it is a superb venue and one that is worthy of the tag 'the home of football'. Other fans have not been so enthusiastic about the stadium, but the bottom line is that it is bigger and better than any other stadium that we currently have in Britain and one which supporters will enjoy for many years to come.

Two other new stadiums are opening this season. After 97 years at their Gay Meadow ground, Shrewsbury Town will embark on a new era at their new 10,000 capacity stadium on the outskirts of town, whilst MK Dons have shown that they are a club who are here to stay and have big ambitions, with their new 22,000 capacity stadium, which can be easily expanded to around 30,000. The Football League also welcomes two new clubs in Morecambe, plus Dagenham & Redbridge, both of whom have never previously been in the Football League, so history will be created for both of them.

The biggest change though for football grounds this season is the introduction of the ban on smoking in enclosed work and public places. Although some may argue that football grounds are not enclosed spaces the legislation makes it clear that anywhere that has a roof is considered to be affected and hence grounds will become no smoking. For a lot of fans this is going to be quite a culture shock as many have smoked at grounds for years. But I guess it is a sign of the times and for many other fans the ban will be welcomed.

The Guide has been compiled based on not only my personal visits to the grounds but the feedback of thousands of supporters who have visited them in recent seasons, giving an all-round independent view of each of them. Without this feedback this book would not have been possible, so a big thank you to everyone who has contributed.

Although I have striven to make sure that every detail is as up-to-date as it can be, things can change over the course of a season; for example, a pub will close or another open, so please bear this in mind. I hope you find this guide useful and informative. But remember this is only a guide and should be treated as such. If you find that things have changed, or you feel that you can give better directions or provide useful additional information then please feel free to e-mail me at duncan@footballgrounds.net. Remember this guide is for football fans by football fans, so feel free to have your say. Wherever possible I'll strive to include your comments in future editions. To see the latest updates to the Guide remember to visit www.footballgroundguide.co.uk on the Internet.

Author

As a member of the Campaign For Real Ale (CAMRA), I like nothing more than enjoying a good pint of real ale or traditional cider before a game. CAMRA produce a 'Good Beer Guide' each year. If there is a pub near to a particular football ground that is listed within the CAMRA Guide, that I have visited, then I have endeavoured to mention it, in the 'Where To Drink' Section.

The Guide does not cover disabled facilities within the grounds as I feel that currently such information is better covered by other sources. This is something that I will look to address in future editions. Most wheelchair places need to be booked in advance of the match with the individual clubs concerned, whose telephone numbers are listed within the Guide.

I hope you enjoy the book and that it will improve your away trips, as well as perhaps whetting the appetite to visit a ground that you hadn't thought about visiting before.

Duncan Adams
July 2007

Special Thanks

To Ian Dewar, an exiled Nottingham Forest fan in Canada, for rewriting parts of the Guide so that it became immensely more readable. To Owen Pavey for providing a number of great photographs, plus thanks to Colin Peel, John Cowen, Tim Rigby and Richard Hooper for their photos of Leyton Orient and MK Dons, Brighton & Hove Albion, Shrewsbury Town and Gillingham.

Also special thanks to Tim Rigby, Neil Shenton, Chris Bax, Mark Sugar, Gary Bond & Tony Kavanagh for their contributions. To Thomas Mapfumo of European Football Statistics for providing the average attendance information; please visit his website at www.european-football-statistics.co.uk. I am also indebted to Simon Inglis and his book 'The Football Grounds Of Great Britain' for some of the historical information contained within this Guide.

Legal Notice:

Arsenal

Emirates Stadium

Ground Name: Emirates Stadium
Capacity: 60,432 (all seated)
Address: Highbury House,
75 Drayton Park
London, N5 1BU
Telephone No: 0207-704-4000
Fax No: 0207-704-4001
Ticket Office: 0207-704-4040
24 Hour Ticket Info: 0207-704-4242
Club Nickname: The Gunners
Year Ground Opened: 2006

Official Website:
www.arsenal.com

Unofficial Websites:
Arsenal Land - www.arsenal-land.co.uk
Arseweb - www.arseweb.com
Arsenal World - www.arsenal-world.net
German Gunners - www.arsenalfc.de
Tipperary Gunners - www.tipperary-gunners.freeservers.com

■ What's The Ground Like?

After 93 years of playing at one of the most historic grounds in the country, Arsenal have moved a short distance away to their new super-modern home.
The stadium, designed by HOK Sport (who also designed Stadium Australia in Sydney, which was used for the Olympics) and built by Sir Robert McAlpine Ltd, cost £390m to build. Unlike the new Wembley Stadium, the new Arsenal Stadium, was built on time and within budget. It has been named the Emirates Stadium in a ten-year corporate sponsorship deal.

With a capacity of over 60,000, the stadium is huge in comparison to Highbury and is the largest football ground in London. It is the only stadium that I know of in this country that is four-tiered. The lower tier is large and shallow, set well back from the playing surface as a cinder track surrounds the playing area. A small second tier, which is called the Club tier, has seating and a row of executive boxes at the rear; this Club tier slightly overhangs the bottom tier. 150 executive boxes in total are located within the stadium. The third tier is even smaller, being only eight rows deep and fits entirely under the large fourth tier. This fourth tier, known as the upper tier, has been designed in a semi-circular fashion and is topped by an impressive-looking roof that includes a lot of visible white tubular steelwork and perspex panels to allow more light to get to the pitch. The roofs, though, do not follow the semi-circular shape of the stands but in fact run across the top of them and even dip down towards them giving them a strange look. Two excellent-looking large video screens situated in the North West & South East corners, below the roof line, complete the stadium. For those that have been to Benfica's Stadium of Light in Portugal, the Emirates is very similar, both having been designed by HOK Sport.

■ What Is It Like For Visiting Supporters?

Away fans are housed in the lower tier of the South East corner of the stadium. The normal allocation for away fans will be 3,000 tickets, but this can be increased for cup games. Although fans will have big padded seats and plenty of leg room, the lower tier of the stadium is quite shallow (unlike the upper tiers which have plenty of height between rows), meaning that the view might not be as good as you would expect from a new stadium.

Entrance to the stadium is by a 'smart ticket', whereby rather than giving your ticket to a turnstile operator, you enter it into a ticket reader to gain entry. This always confuses the away fans and a number of club staff have to be on hand to help out (as well of course trying to spot adults using the cheaper child tickets!). Once inside you'll find spacious concourses and a number of food outlets, each selling different items. Although pricey there is a wide range on offer including; Fish and chips (£5.90), Pie, mash & gravy (or liquor instead of gravy, £6.50), Scottish Cheeseburger (£4), Hot Dog (£3.50), Balti Pie (£4), Minced Beef & Onion Pie (£4), Roasted vegetables and cauliflower pie (£4) and probably the best value, a slice of pizza for £2.50. Alcohol is available in the form of Fosters or John Smiths at £3.20 per pint. Even at half time the queues were bearable, but it would have been nice if a proper queuing system had been put in place. There are plenty of flat-screen televisions on the concourse to keep you entertained, although the volume on some was so loud that you would almost think for a moment that you are queuing inside a UCI cinema rather than a football ground. There are also Ladbrokes betting facilities available.

The stadium is simply stunning. Is it the best in the League? Is it better than Old Trafford? Well, the Emirates certainly gets my vote of yes to both questions!

Where To Drink?

The traditional pub for away supporters at Highbury was the Drayton Arms, which is located near to Arsenal tube station and Drayton Park railway station. This Courage pub overlooks the new stadium and is only a few minutes walk away. However, with the move to the new stadium it is unclear whether this pub will still welcome away fans.

Mark Long recommends the Twelve Pins (formerly the Finsbury Park Tavern) near Finsbury Park Tube Station. 'Normally a good mix of home and away fans and about a ten minute walk from the ground'. Whilst Guy McIntyre adds; 'The Blackstock opposite The Twelve Pins, also welcomes away fans, plus it has a big screen showing Sky Sports'.

Alcohol is available inside the stadium (Fosters, John Smith's & Strongbow) and hopefully (unlike Highbury) this will be made available to away supporters before the match and at half time. The Club are installing a new system for dispensing beer called Ultra-Flow, which apparently can pour four pints in five seconds and will also ensure that the beer is served at the correct temperature. Let's hope we can get to the front of the queue to sample it!

How To Get There & Where To Park?

Leave the M1 at Junction 2 and onto the A1, following the signs for City (Central London). Keep going on the A1 for around six miles, until you see Holloway Road Tube Station on your right. Take the next left at the traffic lights into Hornsey Road and the stadium is about a quarter of a mile further down this road.

There is little parking at the stadium itself or in nearby streets. An extensive residents-only parking scheme operates around the stadium on matchdays. It's probably better to park further out of London around a tube station such as Cockfosters and get the tube to the ground.

By Tube/Train

The nearest underground station to the stadium is Holloway Road on the Piccadilly Line. However, this will be closed on matchdays as it relies mostly on lifts to transport passengers to and from street level and this could cause problems when large crowds are in attendance. Fans should therefore alight at the next stop

on the Piccadilly Line which is Arsenal tube station. It is only a few minutes walk from here to the stadium. On exiting the station turn right and follow Drayton Park Road around to the left. Then take one of the large bridges over the railway line to the stadium. Other tube stations in walking distance of the stadium are Finsbury Park on the Piccadilly Line and Highbury & Islington on the Victoria Line.

Otherwise you can take an overland train to Finsbury Park Railway Station from London Kings Cross. It is then about a 10 to 15-minute walk from Finsbury Park to the stadium. Drayton Park Station, which is situated right by the stadium, is closed at weekends.

Local Rivals
Tottenham Hotspur.

Admission Prices
The club operate a category system for ticket prices (A+B), whereby the most popular games cost more to watch. Category A games are: Chelsea, Liverpool, Manchester United, Tottenham Hotspur and West Ham United. Category B prices are shown in brackets.

Home Fans:

Centre Upper: £94 (£66)
Centre Upper Back £70 (£49)
Next to Centre Upper £70 (£49)
Next to Centre Upper Back £61 (£43)
Wing Upper £60 (£42)
Wing Upper Back £55 (£38)
Corner Upper £60 (£42)
Goal Upper £66 (£46)
Goal Upper Back £55 (£38)
Centre Lower £51 (£35)
Wing Lower £46 (£32)
Corner Lower £46 (£32)
Goal Lower £46 (£32)

Family enclosure:

Adult £46
Senior Citizen £20 (£14)
Junior Gunner £18 (£13)

Away Fans

Adults (£46) £32, Over 65's (£23) £16

Programme & Fanzines
Official Programme £3.
The Gooner Fanzine £2.
Up The A**e Fanzine £1.

Stadium Tours
Daily tours are available of the stadium, dependent on fixtures. The tour which also includes a visit to the Club Museum costs £12 for adults and £6 for concessions (senior citizens and under 16's).
Tours can be booked by calling 0207-704-4504.

Record Attendance
At The Emirates:
60,132 v Reading
Premier League, March 3rd, 2007.

At Highbury:
73,295 v Sunderland
Division One, March 9th, 1935.

Average Attendance
2006-2007: 60,046 (Premier League)

Did You Know?
Arsenal tube station was originally opened as Gillespie Road tube station in 1906. It was renamed in 1932. Apparently it is the only tube station to have been totally renamed.

Aston Villa

Villa Park

Ground Name: Villa Park
Capacity: 42,573 (all seated)
Address: Villa Park, Trinity Rd, Birmingham, B6 6HE
Main Telephone No: 0121-327-2299
Main Fax No: 0121-322-2107
Ticket Office: 0121-327-5353
Ticket Office Fax: 0121-328-5575
Stadium Tours: 0121-327-5353
Club Nickname: The Villans
Year Ground Opened: 1897
Pitch Size: 115 x 72 yards
Home Kit Colours: Claret & Blue

Official Website:
www.avfc.co.uk

Unofficial Websites:
Heroes & Villans - www.heroesandvillans.net
Villa Talk - www.villatalk.com
Holteenders.com - www.holteenders.com (Rivals Network)
Aston Villa Blog – www.astonvilla.biz
A Villa Fan – www.avillafan.com
Vital Villa – www.astonvilla.vitalfootball.co.uk

■ What's The Ground Like?

Three sides of the ground have been rebuilt in recent years, making it one of the better in the League. The Holte End is a large two-tiered structure, opened in the 1994/95 season and holding 13,500 supporters. The other end, the North Stand, is older (built in the late 1970s), but still modern-looking. This is two-tiered, with a double row of executive boxes running across the middle. On one side of the pitch is the Doug Ellis stand, which again is two-tiered and is roughly the same height as the other two stands. Opposite is the three-tiered Trinity Road Stand, complete with a row of executive boxes. Although many fans were disappointed to see the old Trinity Road Stand go, I think its replacement gives the ground a more balanced look overall, because the new stand, although the largest at Villa Park, has roughly the same roof level as the other three sides. There are also two large video screens installed in opposite corners of the ground. An unusual feature is that between the Trinity Road & Holte End Stands is a pavilion-type structure that was built at the same time as the Trinity Road. This three-tiered building is used for corporate hospitality. On the other side of the Holte End is another similar-looking structure that is used for police control. The only disappointment with Villa Park is that the corners of the ground are open; however, there are plans to fill in the corners at the North Stand end of the ground (see Future Ground Developments).

■ Future Ground Developments

The Club have received planning permission to redevelop the North Stand. This would involve building a new stand that would extend around the current open corners at that end of the stadium. However, there is currently no firm timescale as to when this will take place. When completed the capacity of Villa Park will be increased to 51,000.

■ What Is It Like For Visiting Supporters?

Away supporters are housed in the lower tier of the North Stand where up to 3,000 fans can be accommodated. If demand requires it, then part of the Doug Ellis Stand can also be allocated to away fans. A visit to Villa Park is normally an enjoyable experience with a good atmosphere being generated within the ground. Please note that most fans tend to frequent the refreshment area and toilets that are right by the turnstile entrance to the away end.

There is, in fact, another refreshment area and toilet block at the back on the other side of the North Stand (on the new Trinity Road Stand side), which tends to be quieter. The delicious 'Football's Famous Chicken Balti Pie' (£2.50) is available inside the ground. Also just inside the entrance there is a programme 'hut' from which not only the current match programme is available, but also a selection of older programmes, normally including a number involving the away side. The Club operate a 'no smoking' policy throughout the ground.

Now, as I support the other team in Birmingham (and no, it isn't Solihull Moors!), it has been suggested that I am biased against Villa Park. Well, all I can say that I have been to the ground on a number of occasions; in fact I can now claim to have sat in every stand, so that just shows you how unbiased I really am!

■ Where To Drink?

There are a number of pubs in the vicinity of Villa Park, but on match days most of them are either members only or have bouncers on the door. However, Dave Cooper recommends the following for away fans; 'The Cap and Gown (formerly The Witton Arms), is not a bad pub, to which half the pub is given to away fans (there is even a separate entrance for visiting fans). It is only two minutes walk from the away entrance, right on Witton Island, however it does charge £2 per person to gain entry. Otherwise there is the Harriers, which is on Broadway, near to the school of the same name. It is ten minutes walk from the ground and you can usually find street parking in this area'. If you arrive a bit earlier then you may wish to visit the historic Barton Arms, located about a 15 minute walk away on High Street Aston (A34). This Grade II listed building is one of Birmingham's finest pubs, with superb Victorian decor, serving Oakham ales and Thai food is also on offer. It was awarded the Birmingham CAMRA pub of the year award for 2004. Please note that alcohol is **not** available in the away end.

■ How To Get There & Where To Park?

The ground can be seen from the M6, if you are coming from the North side of Birmingham. Leave the M6 at Junction 6 and take the slip road signposted Birmingham (NE). Turn right at the island (the fourth exit), the ground is well signposted from here. However to be on the safe side, turn right at the second set of traffic lights (there is the King Edward VII pub on the corner) on to Aston Hall Road. This road will take you down to the ground. Mostly street parking (don't be surprised though if you are approached by kids wanting to 'mind your car'), although this is not as plentiful as it once was due to a local residents-only parking scheme now in place in the streets around the Witton Island area.

■ By Train

Take the short train journey from Birmingham New Street (around 10-15 minutes) to either Aston or Witton station. Witton station is nearer to the away end and is only a few minutes walk from the ground. Turn left out of the station exit and continue down to a roundabout. Turn left at the roundabout into Witton Lane and the entrance to the away section is down this road on the first corner of the ground that you reach. Aston station is a ten-minute walk away from the ground. Extra trains are laid on to the ground on matchdays.

■ Local Rivals

Birmingham City, West Bromwich Albion & Wolverhampton Wanderers.

Aston Villa

■ Admission Prices

Like a number of other clubs a category scheme for ticket prices is in operation (A, B & C), whereby the most popular games cost more to watch. Category B & C prices are shown in brackets below:

Trinity Road Stand (Upper & Middle Centres):
Doug Ellis Stand (Upper Centre):
Adults £35 (B £33) (C £31),
Students & Armed Forces £30 (B £28) (C £26),
Under 21's £28 (B £26) (C £24),
Over 65's £21 (B £19) (C £17),
Under 16's £19 (B £17) (C £15).

Trinity Road Stand (Upper & Middle Wings):
Doug Ellis Stand (Upper Wings):
Holte End (Upper Centre):
Adults £32 (B £30) (C £28),
Students & Armed Forces £29 (B £27) (C £26),
Under 21's £25 (B £23) (C £21),
Over 65's £20 (B £18) (C £16),
Under 16's £19 (B £17) (C £15).

Trinity Road Stand (Lower Centre):
Doug Ellis Stand (Lower Centre):
Holte End (Upper Wings):
Adults £30 (B £28) (C £26),
Students & Armed Forces £27 (B £26) (C £24),
Under 21's £24 (B £22) (C £20),
Over 65's & Under 16's £19 (B £17) (C £15).

Doug Ellis Stand (Lower Wings):
Holte End (Lower Centre):
Adults £32 (B £30) (C £25),
Students & Armed Forces £29 (B £27) (C £23),
Under 21's £24 (B £23) (C £19),
Over 65's & Under 16's £19 (B £17) (C £15).

Trinity Road Stand (Lower Wings):
Holte End (Lower Wings):
Adults £29 (B £27) (C £25),
Students & Armed Forces £26 (B £25) (C £23),
Under 21's £23 (B £20) (C £19),
Over 65's & Under 16's £19 (B £17) (C £15).

North Stand (Upper Tier):
Adults £20 (B £19) (C £15),
Students, Under 21's & Armed Forces £30 (B £28) (C £26),
Over 65's £12 (B £10) (C £5),
Under 16's £10 (B £9) (C £5).

Away Fans:

North Stand (Lower Tier):
Adults £29 (B £27) (C £25),
Under 21's £2 (B £20) (C £19),
Over 65's £19 (B £17) (C £15),
Under 16's £19 (B £17) (C £15).
Doug Ellis Stand (Lower Tier):
Adults £32 (B £30) (C £28),
Under 21's £24 (B £23) (C £19),
Over 65's £19 (B £17) (C £15),
Under 16's £19 (B £17) (C £15).

■ Programme & Fanzines

Official Programme £2.50
Heroes & Villans Fanzine £1.20
Holy Trinity Fanzine £1

■ Record Attendance

76,588 v Derby County
FA Cup 6th Round, March 2nd, 1946

Modern All Seated Attendance Record:
42,632 v Manchester United
Premier League, August 26th, 2001.

■ Average Attendance

2006-2007: 36,214 (Premier League)

■ Stadium Tours

Tours are available daily except matchdays and public holidays. The cost for the tour only (except Sundays) is £6.95 for adults and £4.50 concessions. There is also the option to take lunch in the Corner Flag restaurant overlooking the pitch (except Saturdays when the restaurant is closed). The cost of the tour plus lunch is; Adults £19.95 and £8.95 for concessions. On Sundays the Club offer a combined tour and Sunday lunch package for £19.95 adults and £9.95 concessions. Family tickets are also available. Tours can be booked on 0121-327-5353 (and then selecting the events option).

■ Did You Know?

That Villa Park used to have a set of four floodlights, the bulbs of which were arranged to outline the letters A & V. Alas, they were taken down when the stadium was redeveloped.

Birmingham City

St Andrews

Ground Name: St Andrews
Capacity: 30,016 (all seated)
Address: St Andrews Ground, Birmingham B9 4NH
Main Telephone No: 0871-226-1875
Fax No: 0121-766-7866
Ticket Office No: 0871-226-1875
Pitch Size: 115 x 75 yards
Club Nickname: The Blues
Year Ground Opened: 1906
Home Kit Colours: Royal Blue & White

Official Website:
www.bcfc.com

Unofficial Websites:
Keep Right On – www.keeprighton.co.uk
Birmingham City Fanzine - www.bcfcfanzine.com
Singing The Blues – www.singingtheblues.co.uk (Footy Mad Network)
Planet Blues - http://birminghamcity.rivals.net/default.asp?sid=902 (Rivals Network)

What's The Ground Like?

Approximately three quarters of the ground have been rebuilt since the mid 90's. One large single-tiered stand, incorporating the Tilton Road End & Spion Kop, completely surrounds half the pitch and has replaced a former huge terrace. At the back of the Spion Kop Stand, which runs along one side of the pitch, is a row of executive boxes, as well as a central seated executive area which also incorporates the Directors' box. The other new stand, the Railway End, was opened in February 1999. It is a large two-tiered stand, unusual in having quite a small top tier, called 'The Olympic Gallery', which overhangs the lower tier. Again there is a row of executive boxes in this stand, housed at the back of the lower tier. Only one 'old' stand (it was built in 1952), the Main Stand, now remains of the former St Andrews. This is a two-tier stand running along one side of the pitch, with a row of executive boxes across its middle.

Future Ground Developments

The Club are still weighing up the options as to the possibility of moving to new stadium or whether to further redevelop St Andrews. If the latter option was chosen then this would involve the rebuilding of the Main Stand. This would increase the overall capacity of St Andrews to around 36,500 at a cost of around £12m.

What Is It Like For Visiting Supporters?

Away supporters are housed on one side of the Railway Stand's lower tier where the normal allocation is 3,000 tickets, but this can be increased to around 4,500 for cup games. There are Birmingham fans housed above the away supporters, as well as to the other side of the stand (fans are separated by plastic netting). The facilities and the view from this stand are pretty good. There is an array of food on offer; burgers (£2.80) and rollover hot dogs (£2.70), plus a range of Shire Foods pasties, sausage rolls & pies including the delicious 'Football's Famous Chicken Balti Pie' (£2.30). The Club catering is supplemented by a burger van. It is worth bearing in mind that a certain section of Birmingham fans are particularly passionate about their club and this can make for an intimidating atmosphere for away supporters. I would advise as a precaution to keep your club colours covered around the ground or in the city centre.

John, a visiting Burnley fan, informs me; 'The beer inside the ground was drinkable and the Balti pies were delicious! On the downside, the seat I had been allocated was in Row 21 seat 002 which was right up against the wall. I've had more legroom on a package tour flight to the Canaries! What really annoyed me were a small section of the City fans who spent the entire game screaming abuse and gesturing to the away fans'.

Alan Sexton, a visiting West Ham supporter adds; 'The ground itself is three-quarters of the way to being a top-class stadium but desperately needs a new Main Stand. If this is built, joining with the Tilton Road and Railway Stands then St Andrews will be one of the best if not the best ground in the Midlands. Atmosphere-wise it was the best I have visited all season for sheer volume before and during the game. As for the concourses they left little to be desired and were extremely crowded; the scrum to try and get a pie was not for the faint-hearted'.

Well, having watched the Blues since 1972, I can honestly say that I have almost seen it all. The good, the bad and the ugly. The atmosphere at some games can be electric, at others virtually non existent. The club itself has come on a great deal under the ownership of David Sullivan and the Gold brothers and the stadium has been transformed. The crowd, when on form, can still give a great rendition of the Blues anthem 'Keep Right On To The End Of The Road'.

■ Where To Drink?

Most of the pubs near to the ground can be quite intimidating for away supporters and are not recommended. However there is the Brighton pub on the Coventry Road which does tolerate away fans in small numbers. This pub is about a ten-minute walk away, going past Woolworths & Morrisons on your left. Otherwise it may be best to drink in the city centre and get a taxi to the ground (about £5). If you are walking to the ground from the city centre, then you may care to stop at the Anchor Pub on Bradford Street, renowned for its range of real ales on offer, and named Birmingham 'CAMRA Pub Of The Year' on more than one occasion. Although there are a number of Blues fans that frequent the pub they tend to be of the CAMRA bearded variety and therefore as long as you don't turn up mob-handed, you should be okay. The pub is situated just behind Digbeth coach station. Otherwise alcohol is served within the ground.

If you're coming by train or decide to drink in the city centre beforehand, if you like your real ale, then you can't do much better than visit the Wellington Pub on Bennetts Hill. With 15 real ales on tap, including 12 guest ales, this is somewhat of a mecca for real ale drinkers. In 2005 alone, the pub served over 2,600 different beers! To find this pub, assuming that you are coming into New Street Station by train, then as you come onto the passenger concourse at the station, so straight up the escalators in front of you. At the top of the escalators turn left and then proceed towards the 'Foot Locker' outlet. Turn left at this store and then right and proceed down the ramp past McDonalds. At the bottom of the ramp turn left into New Street and walk along the pedestrian area. Bennetts Hill is the fourth turning on the right (there is a Barclays Bank is on the corner). The Wellington pub is about two thirds of the way up Bennetts Hill on the right hand side. There is also a handy Wetherspoons outlet called the Briar Rose (which is no smoking) on Bennetts Hill as well. The Wellington does not provide food, but has no objections to you bringing in your own. There are a couple of taxi ranks nearby that you can use if you wish to get you to the ground.

■ How To Get There & Where To Park?

Leave the M6 at Junction 6 and take the A38(M) (known locally as the Aston Expressway) for Birmingham City Centre. Continue past the first turn off (Aston, Waterlinks) and then take the next turn off, for the Inner Ring Road. Turn left at the island at the top of the slip road and take the Ring Road East, sign posted Coventry/Stratford. Continue along the ring road for two miles, crossing straight across three islands. At the fourth island (there is a large McDonalds on the far left hand corner) turn left towards Small Heath. Birmingham City's ground is about a quarter of a mile up this road on your left. The ground is well signposted on the Inner Ring Road.
There is a small car park directly outside the entrance to the away end, but availability of space for cars is determined by how many away coaches are expected as they park in the same car park, which may mean for certain games that there is no space available for cars at all. There is though plenty of street parking off the left hand side of the ring road. Either around the small park at the third island you cross or along the road next to and behind the BP garage before the fourth island. Bear in mind that if you arrive after 1.30pm these areas are likely to be already full. There are some local schools and businesses that offer parking facilities for around £4-£5.

■ By Train

The nearest station is Bordesley, which is about a ten-minute walk away from the ground, but is only served by trains from Birmingham Snow Hill and the service is not very frequent on Saturdays. If you arrive at New Street Station in the city centre, either walk to Snow Hill (ten minutes) take a taxi (about £5) or embark on the 20-minute walk to the ground.

As you come onto the concourse of New Street, bear to the left of the escalators and through the glass doors. Walk down towards to the end of the Station Service Road. Cross to the other side of the road at the bottom (where there is a new shopping centre) turn right and follow the purple pedestrian signs for Digbeth Coach Station. These will see you descending a flight of stairs at the side of the shopping centre on your left and then going down a road with the Markets on your right and a large church on your left. Follow this road around to the right and then take the next left to take you up to the main dual carriage way. Turn right along the dual carriageway, passing Digbeth Coach Station on your right and the impressive-looking Crown Pub on your left. Cross over the dual carriageway to the Crown pub side of the road and continue walking away from the City Centre.

You will come to a fork in the road where you want to bear left going underneath a railway bridge. Passing the Clements Arms on your left just continue straight down this road, crossing a large roundabout (with a McDonalds over on one corner). The entrance to the away section is further up the road on your left.

Otherwise you can take the following buses from the city centre; Nos 96, 97, 58 & 60. The 97 & 98 can be found in Carrs Lane in the city centre. As you come off the platform and onto the station concourse, go straight up the escalators in front of you. At the top the escalators turn left and keep in that direction so that you leave the shopping centre by going down a long ramp. Turn right at the bottom the ramp into New Street and continue to the bottom. Then turn left into the High St and just past Marks & Spencers on the right is Carrs Lane. Turn into Carrs Lane and the bus stops are down on the left by the church.

Local Rivals

Aston Villa, West Bromwich Albion & Wolverhampton Wanderers.

Admission Prices

At the time of going to press, the matchday ticket prices for the 2007/08 season had yet to be announced. Prices for last season are shown below:

Like a number of clubs, Birmingham City operate a category policy (A, B & C) whereby the ticket prices cost more for the most popular games.

Home Fans:

Spion Kop Club Class Seats:
Adults £35 (B £30) C £25),
Concessions £19 (B £17 (C £14)

Main Stand Centre:
Adults £30 (B £27) C £25),
Concessions £18 (B £15 (C £12.50)
Under 12's £10 (B £7.50) (C £5)

Other Areas of the Ground:
Adults £29 (B £25) C £20),
Concessions £15 (B £13 (C £10)
Under 12's £10 (B £7.50) (C £5)

Railway End Lower Tier:
Adults £30 (B £27) C £25),
Concessions £18 (B £15 (C £12.50)
Under 12's £10 (B £7.50) (C £5)

Away Fans

Railway End Lower Tier:
Adults £30 (B £27) C £25),
Concessions £18 (B £15 (C £12.50)
Under 12's £10 (B £7.50) (C £5)

Programme & Fanzines

Official Programme £3
Made In Brum Fanzine - £1
Tired & Weary Fanzine - £1

Record Attendance

66,844 v Everton
FA Cup 5th Round, February 11th, 1939.

Modern All Seated Attendance Record:
29,588 v Arsenal
Premier League, November 22nd, 2003.

Average Attendance

2005-2006: 21,738 (Championship)

Did You Know?

That the Club was formed in 1875 as Small Heath Alliance. The Club's first pitch was across the road from St Andrews in Arthur Street.

Blackburn Rovers

Ewood Park

Ground Name:	Ewood Park
Capacity:	31,367 (all seated)
Address:	Blackburn, Lancashire, BB2 4JF
Main Telephone No:	08701-113-232
Fax No:	01254-671-042
Ticket Office:	08701-123-456
Pitch Size:	115 x 76 yards
Club Nickname:	Rovers
Year Ground Opened:	1890
Home Kit Colours:	Blue & White

Official Website:
www.rovers.co.uk

Unofficial Websites:
BRFC Supporters - www.brfcs.co.uk
Rovers Mad - www.blackburnrovers-mad.co.uk (Footy Mad Network)
Rovers Net – www.roversnet.co.uk (Rivals Network)

■ What's The Ground Like?

The ground is quite impressive, having had three new large stands built during the 1990s. These stands are at both ends and at one side of the ground. They are of the same height and of roughly similar design, being two-tiered and having a row of executive boxes and similar roofs. The ends are particularly impressive, both having large lower tiers. The only downside is the open corners, although there is a superb Sony Jumbotron screen at one corner by the away end, which shows an excellent pre-match programme and the teams emerging from the dressing rooms and onto the pitch. There is also an electric scoreboard at the Darwen End of the ground. The Riverside is the only undeveloped stand, running down one side of the pitch. This is a smaller single-tiered stand and is not as pleasing to the eye as its modern counterparts. It also contains a fair number of supporting pillars and is partly covered (to the rear). Just to highlight how much the ground has changed, this was at one time the 'best' stand at Ewood Park. One other interesting feature of the ground, is the fact that the pitch is raised. This means that players have to run up a small incline, whilst taking throw-ins and corners. Outside the stadium behind the Blackburn End there is a statue of former club owner Jack Walker.

■ Future Ground Developments

There are plans to redevelop the Riverside Stand, but there are no firm timescales as to when this is likely to take place. The proposed new stand will increase the capacity at Ewood park to around 40,000.

■ What Is It Like For Visiting Supporters?

Away fans are housed at the Darwen End, where the facilities provided are good. However, the spacing between the rows of seats leaves a lot to be desired, being quite tight. The Darwen End is shared with home supporters, but if demand requires the whole of the stand can be made available. Normally the away allocation is for three-quarters of the stand, at just under 4,000 tickets, which are split between the whole of the upper tier and part of the lower tier (with the lower tier being allocated first). If you have not bought a ticket in advance, then you need to buy one from the away supporters ticket office at the ground as you can't pay on the turnstiles. The ticket office is located on the corner of the Darwen End & the Jack Walker Stand.

Alcohol is available on the concourse as well as the normal range of pies (including the delicious 'Football's Famous Chicken Balti Pie' at £1.90), burgers, hot dogs and chips. If you are looking to eat something prior to entering the ground, then there is a baker in Bolton Road selling hot pies from one of its windows. Across the Bolton Road by the home end is a McDonalds, which I noticed had a walk through service for fans! I found the Blackburn fans both friendly and helpful, which coupled with the relaxed stewarding, has made it so far for me, four pleasant visits to Ewood Park.

Where To Drink?

The Fernhurst is really known as the 'away supporters pub'. It is on the Bolton Road (A666) just across from the ground at the away supporters end (Darwen End). You can also park at the Fernhurst pub for £3, but you will be delayed in getting away after the game. It is a large pub with Sky Sports being shown on a large screen and has a restaurant area to its rear and a large function room upstairs. On my last visit the pub had even put up a number of signs welcoming the fans of the visiting team, which was a nice touch. The Fernhurst also offers reasonably-priced accommodation. Most other pubs that I came across in the area had large signs outside showing that they were for home fans only. Alcohol is also served within the ground.

Andrew Kennedy, a visiting Sunderland supporter, adds; 'I would also recommend the Golden Cup pub just up Bolton Road from the Fernhurst (going away from the ground). It is on the small side but had a good mix of home and away supporters on my visit'. This pub is a good 15-minute walk away from the Fernhurst going uphill. A little closer but in the same direction is the Bear Hotel which also has a bar.

If you are arriving at Mill Hill station, then you might want to give the Navigation pub a try. It is a Thwaites pub which sits on one side of a canal and on my visit had a good mix of home and away supporters. It is about a five-minute walk way from the station. As you exit the station turn left and just keep straight on up the road in front of you. As you approach a bridge going over the canal, the pub can be seen just over on the right.

How To Get There & Where To Park?

From The North

Use Motorway M6 to junction 30, to the M61 - leave junction 9 then onto the M65 towards Blackburn - leave the M65 at Junction 4 (A666) and follow signs towards Blackburn. Ewood Park is about 1 mile down the road on the right hand side.

From The South

Use Motorway M6 to junction 29, then onto the M65 towards Blackburn - leave the M65 at Junction 4 (A666) and follow signs towards Blackburn. Turn right at the first set of traffic lights and Ewood Park is about 1 mile down the road on the right hand side.

From The East

Use Motorway M62 onto M66/A56, then onto the M65, head towards Blackburn - leave the M65 at Junction 4 (A666) and follow signs towards Blackburn. Turn right at the first set of traffic lights and Ewood Park is about 1 mile down the road on the right hand side.

Various private Car Parks are available around the ground, costing in the region of £3. If you want to get away reasonably quickly after the game (the roads immediately around Ewood are closed off for crowd safety for around 30mins after the game) then as you come down the hill on the A666, you will pass a Total garage on your left. Turn right at the next traffic lights and down on your left there are some industrial units where you can park for £3. After the game turn left out of the car park, so that you are going away from Ewood, turn right at the second mini roundabout and this will take you back up to the M65.

By Train

Blackburn station is at least a couple of miles from the ground and hence a good 20-25-minute walk away. Perhaps grab a taxi instead, or as Dave Grest suggests; 'get a Darwen-bound bus from stand M, outside of the railway station. It costs £1 one way and you really can't miss the ground'. Blackburn station is served by trains from Manchester & Leeds.

Tony Durkin adds; 'The main doors to the railway station face the bus station, from where you can take a either a Number 1, 3 or 225 bus (the latter goes from Stand N) bus to Ewood. To walk it to the ground instead, turn left at those main doors and go straight on towards Darwen Street. Turn left and you will reach a major junction over which runs a railway bridge (Darwen Street Bridge), which is impossible to miss. Crossing over the road as soon as you turn left onto Darwen Street will be a help, as when you get to the junction you need to follow the road towards Bolton and Blackburn Royal Infirmary. It is called Great Bolton Street after the bridge and then becomes Bolton Road. Follow this straight along for just over a mile (passing the Infirmary on your left and the canal on the right). After you go under another railway bridge and pass Kwik-Save supermarket on your right, the ground is on your left just after you pass the Aqueduct pub (for home fans only)'.

Tony Hughes informs me; 'Closer to the ground is the small station of Mill Hill, which is a 10-15 minute walk away. Blackburn station is only a three minute ride away from Mill Hill. Walk up the steps from the platform and turn left onto New Chapel Street continue along the street past the shopping area and park. (If you need any money, there is a Lloyds TSB bank with 2 cash machines on this street.) With the Spar supermarket on the opposite side of the road from you, turn left into New Wellington Street. Continue down New Wellington Street until you come to a small bridge that crosses over the Leeds-Liverpool canal. You are now on Albion Street there is a large mill building on the left and a small school on the right. Walk along Albion Street to the end, and you will find yourself on Livesey Branch Road. Turn left onto this road, and you will be able to see the football stadium in front of you at the foot of the hill'.

Local Rivals

Burnley, Bolton, Preston, Manchester United, Manchester City.

Blackburn Rovers

Admission Prices

Like a number of Clubs, Blackburn operate a match category policy (1 & 2) whereby the ticket prices cost more for the most popular games. Category 1 games for the 2007/08 season are: Manchester United, Liverpool, Chelsea and Arsenal. Category 2 prices are shown below in brackets:

Home Fans:

Jack Walker Stand (Centre):
Adults £35 (£25)
OAPs/Under-21s £25 (£15)
Juniors £20 (£15)

Jack Walker Stand (Wings):
Adults £30 (£20)
OAPs/Under-21s £20 (£10)
Juniors £15 (£7)

CIS Riverside Stand:
Adults £25 (£15)
OAPs/Under-21s £15 (£10)
Juniors £15 (£7)

Blackburn End:
Adults £30 (£20)
OAPs/Under-21s £20 (£10)
Juniors £15 (£7)

Darwen End
Adults £30 (£20)
OAPs/Under-21s £20 (£10)
Juniors £15 (£7)

Away Fans:

Darwen End:
Adults £30 (£20),
OAPsUnder-21s £20 (£10),
Juniors £15 (£7).

Programme & Fanzine

Official Programme £3.
4000 Holes Fanzine £1.

Record Attendance

62,522 v Bolton Wanderers,
FA Cup 6th Round, March 2nd, 1929.

Average Attendance

2006-2007: 21,275 (Premier League)

Stadium Tours

The club offer 90-minute tours of the ground, which are run on weekdays all year round. The tour costs: Adults £3.50 and Concessions £2. There is also a family ticket available, priced at £10 for two adults and two children. Tours can be booked on 08701-123-456.

Did You Know?

That the Blackburn Rovers versus West Bromwich Albion match on February 5th, 1898 was the first ever football league match to be captured on movie film.

Bolton Wanderers

Reebok Stadium

Ground Name: Reebok Stadium
Capacity: 28,723 (all seated)
Address: Burnden Way, Horwich, Bolton, BL6 6JW
Main Telephone No: 01204-673-673
Main Fax No: 01204-673-773
Ticket Office: 0871-871-2932
Ticket Office Fax: 0871-871-8183
Stadium Tours: 01204-673-650
Team Nickname: The Trotters
Year Ground Opened: 1997
Pitch Size: 105 x 68 metres
Home Kit Colours: White With Navy Trim

Official Website:
www.bwfc.co.uk

Unofficial Websites:
Wanderers Way - www.wanderersway.com
London Whites - www.londonwhites.co.uk
The Wanderer - www.thewanderer.co.uk
Walking Down The Manny Road - www.sportnetwork.net/main/s474.htm (Sport Network)
Bolton Wanderers Mad - www.boltonwanderers-mad.co.uk (Footy Mad Network)
World Wide Wanderers - http://boltonwanderers.rivals.net/default.asp?sid=1018 (Rivals Network)
BWFC24 - www.bwfc24.co.uk
Bolton Banter - www.boltonbanter.com/forum/

■ What's The Ground Like?

The Reebok Stadium, which was opened in 1997 and built by Birse Construction, is simply stunning and can be seen for miles around. The design is space-age in appearance and is unlike anything else in the country. Each stand has a conventional rectangular lower tier, with a semi-circular upper tier above. This is then topped with some diamond-shaped floodlights that sit above the supporting tubular steel supporting structure. The ground is completely enclosed and has a large video screen in one corner, which replays goals from the game. This gives you an opportunity to cheer a goal at least three more times after it has been scored. One unusual feature of the ground is that the teams emerge from separate tunnels at either side of the halfway line.

■ What Is It Like For Visiting Supporters?

Away fans are housed in the two-tiered South Stand at one end of the ground, where up to 5,000 supporters can be accommodated, although the normal allocation is nearer 3,000. The lower tier is shared with home supporters, but the upper tier is given entirely to away fans. The leg room and facilities within this stand are good and the atmosphere is boosted in the home end by the presence of a drummer. Alex Smith adds; 'away fans should note that the bottom rows of the lower tier are not covered by the roof and therefore you may get wet if it rains'. Whilst Paul Kelly warns; 'the stewards at the Reebok can be a bit over-zealous, often throwing out fans for little reason. My advice to away fans is do not even think about celebrating a goal by going further forward than the front row. They'll have you even if you're just on the bit of track behind the adverts. Also you may be told to sit down during the game, take heed and do so. Fans have been removed who persistently stand up during the game'.

I was particularly impressed with the stadium and for the first time in this country, I felt I could have easily been sitting in a comparable stadium in the United States. The refreshment facilities are good (albeit queuing times can be long on occasion) and I wish that other clubs would copy the way that supporters in the Reebok are served. There are proper queuing barriers and exit lanes. One person takes the order and deals with the money, whilst another prepares your order at the same time. Simple when you think about it; it is just a pity that other clubs seem to think that supporters enjoy the lottery of being in the scrum that develops around the refreshment kiosk. The stadium is certainly one of the best in England, although a capacity of under 30,000 means that by Premiership standards it is on the small side. A 125-room hotel has been built behind the away end of the ground, 19 of which have views of the pitch. I just wonder if hotel guests occupying these rooms may at some time put on their own half-time show!

■ Where To Drink?

Steve Openshaw recommends the Bromilow Arms; "from the M61, go past the stadium on your left, move into the right-hand filter lane and turn right at the traffic lights into Lostock Lane, go past the Barnstormers pub on your right and the Bromilow Arms is further down on left. Good ale, friendly atmosphere, free car parking. Ten minutes walk away from ground". I personally visited this pub before a game and I was well impressed with the warm welcome and the good mix of home and away fans. The small pub has a country feel, serves good real ale from the local Bank Top Brewery and food from a lunchtime snack menu. All in all it was a gem!

Darren Brown, a visiting Manchester City fan, adds; 'The Barnstormers pub on the same road as the Bromilow Arms does have a sign up saying 'No away fans', but they will let you in if you don't look like you will cause any bother'. There is also the Beehive Pub near to the ground where you can also park your car (see below). Otherwise alcohol is served within the ground, although for some games such as local derbies, the Club opt not to sell any. Or on my last visit alcohol was available to away supporters before the game but not at half time, much to the annoyance of the travelling fans.

There are a number of bars on the nearby Middlebrook Retail Park (Reebok Stadium is on the Middlebrook Retail estate). However most of these have bouncers on the doors that only admit home fans on production of a matchday or season ticket, There are, however, plenty of eating outlets on the Retail Park; KFC, Burger King, Pizza Hut and a Bolton Wanderers-themed McDonalds as well as several other themed restaurants, whilst inside the stadium there is the usual array of pies, rollover hot dogs & burgers on sale.

■ How To Get There & Where To Park?

From The South:
M6 to Junction 21a, take eastbound M62 leaving at Junction 12. Follow signs for M61 (Bolton/Preston) and leave the M61 motorway at Junction 6. The ground is visible from this junction and is clearly signposted.

■ From The North:

M6 to Junction 29 and take the M65 towards Blackburn. Leave the M65 at junction two and join the M61 towards Manchester. Leave the M61 at junction six. The ground is visible from this junction and is clearly signposted. John Walsh adds; 'Because of traffic congestion on the M60 (formerly M62) caused by the Trafford Centre, I would recommend that those supporters travelling from the South should take the North directions above. It is about 10 miles further but can save 30 minutes and a lot of frustration!'

There is a car park at the ground, but wait for this, it costs £6! Plus, on my last visit the cars in the away section of the car park were packed in like sardines, meaning that away fans leaving early (my team had just been stuffed!) couldn't make a quick getaway as cars were blocking them in. However a lot of the surrounding industrial estate units offer cheaper parking, usually around the £3 mark. Some of these are located on either side of Lostock Lane. From the M61, go past the stadium on your left, move into the right-hand filter lane and turn right at the traffic lights into Lostock Lane. If you continue down Lostock Lane and take a left hand turn before to the Bromilow Arms, then I noticed on my last visit that there was some street parking to be had at the bottom of this road.

Gary Lovatt adds 'On the parking front, a handy little idea is to park at the Beehive pub which is on the roundabout (half a mile past the stadium coming from the motorway) where you pay £5 per car but get it all back at the bar. I also recommend the cajun chicken baguette there!' To get to the Beehive leave the M61 at Junction 6 and drive down towards the stadium. Then continue straight on past the stadium and the Beehive pub is situated at the next roundabout, on Chorley New Road.

■ By Train

Horwich Parkway railway station serves the stadium, with regular trains from Bolton's main station. Horwich Parkway is only a few minutes walk from the stadium.

■ Local Rivals

Manchester United, Manchester City, Bury, Blackburn, Wigan, Preston and from a little further afield, Tranmere Rovers.

■ Admission Prices

Bolton operate a four-category system of ticket pricing (A+, A, B, C) whereby the most popular matches will cost more to watch than the least popular ones. The highest category (A+) ticket prices are shown below, with the lowest category (C) ticket prices shown in brackets.

Home Fans*:

North, East & West Stands (Upper Tier):
Adults £39 (£29),
Senior Citizens & Students £28 (£20),
Juniors £21 (£14)

East & West Stands (Lower Tier):
Adults £36 (£25),
Senior Citizens & Students £26 (£17),
Juniors £16 (£10)

North & South Stands (Lower Tier):
Adults £31 (£21),
Senior Citizens & Students £24 (£16),
Juniors £16 (£10)

Family Area:
1 Adult + 1 Junior £44 (£26),
2 Adults + 2 Juniors £88 (£52)

Away Fans:

South Stand (Upper Tier):
Adults £39 (£29),
Senior Citizens & Students £28 (£20),
Juniors £21 (£14)

South Stand (Lower Tier):
Adults £31 (£21),
Senior Citizens & Students £24 (£16),
Juniors £16 (£10)

* Club members can receive substantial discounts on some of these ticket prices. The senior citizen concessions apply to over 65's.

■ Programme & Fanzines

Official Programme: £3.
White Love Fanzine £1.
Tripes & Trotters Fanzine £1.

■ Record Attendance

At The Reebok:
28,353 v Leicester City
Premier League, December 28th, 2003.

At Burnden Park:
69,912 v Manchester City
FA Cup 5th Round, February 18th, 1933.

■ Average Attendance

2006-2007: 23,606 (Premier League)

■ Stadium Tours

The club offer regular tours of the stadium on most days. The cost of the tours is Adults £2.50 and £1.50 for concessions or £6 for a family ticket (2 adults & 2 children). Tours must be pre-booked at the Club Shop, or by calling the Club on 01204-673650.

■ Did You Know?

That prior to moving to the Reebok in 1997, Bolton spent 102 years at their previous ground, Burnden Park.

Chelsea

Stamford Bridge

Ground Name: Stamford Bridge
Capacity: 42,449 (all seated)
Address: Fulham Road,
London, SW6 1HS
Main Telephone No: 0870-300-2322
Fax No: 020-7381-4831
Ticket Bookings: 0870-300-2322
(Outside UK: 00-44-207-915-2900)
Ticket Enquiries: 020-7915-2951
Stadium Tours: 0870-603-0005
Pitch Size: 113 x 74 yards
Club Nickname: The Blues
Year Ground Opened: 1905*
Home Kit Colours: Royal Blue With White Trim

Official Website:
www.chelseafc.co.uk

Unofficial Websites:
Blue And White Army – www.chelsea.rivals.net (Rivals Network)
CFC Net - www.cfcnet.co.uk

■ What's The Ground Like?

The ground has been transformed in recent years with three sides of the ground being rebuilt. The completion, at one side of the pitch, of the attractive-looking West Stand in 2001, means that Stamford Bridge is now an impressive sight. A far cry from the Stamford Bridge of old, which was largely open with one huge three-tiered stand, the East Stand, being at one side of the pitch. This stand, opened in 1973, has been retained and the developers have taken advantage of the fact that the 'old' Stamford Bridge was oval-shaped by stretching the new stands right around the ground to fill the corners, so that the ground is totally enclosed. The team dug-outs are located on this side of the stadium. Both ends are two-tiered, with the North Stand now renamed the Matthew Harding Stand in memory of the man who did so much to transform the club. Below the roof of the Shed End, is a Police Control Box, which keeps a look out over proceedings. The new West Stand is a superb three-tiered affair with a row of executive boxes running across its middle, the type of which you are able to sit outside. Its roof is virtually transparent, allowing more light to reach the pitch and gives it a unique look.

■ Future Developments

The Club have announced that they are looking into the feasibility of building a new 55,000-capacity stadium in West London. The Club are unable to significantly redevelop Stamford Bridge any further, so to increase capacity would mean building a new stadium.

■ What Is It Like For Visiting Supporters?

Away fans are located in the South East corner of the Shed End, rather, where the normal allocation for league games is 3,000 tickets, with fans located in a portion of the upper tier of the Shed End Stand and the whole of the lower tier. If clubs elect to take only 1,500 tickets then fans will be located on the East side of the stand in both the upper and lower tiers. For cup games the whole of the Shed End can be allocated. The view from this area of the ground is pretty good and the refreshment areas and concourses were modern and new-looking. There are televisions on the concourses, showing amongst other things at half time, highlights from the first half. A range of Shire Foods and pasties is on offer, including the delicious 'Football's Famous Chicken Balti Pie' (£2.50) and roll-over hot dogs (£3). Alcohol is also available with bottles of Budweiser on offer at £3.

On the whole I found Stamford Bridge a pleasurable day out. There was a good atmosphere within the ground and even though there wasn't a lot of space between the home and away fan sections, it didn't feel intimidating. The stewards were pretty laid back. The only 'hassle' I had was trying to get through two lines of stewards to gain entrance to the away turnstiles as they seemed to assume that I was a Chelsea fan and kept ushering me towards the home end. Only after showing my ticket for the away section for a third time did I finally make it inside! I was seated in the upper tier and I found a little difficult to go up and down the steps of the stand as they were quite small and there were steps between each row. Considering that the stand is quite steep then they seemed quite awkward or do you think it may have been something to do with the few beers that I had consumed beforehand? Please also note that the whole stadium has now been made a no smoking one, this includes the concourses as well as the seating areas. There is a Harry Ramsden's fish and chip shop located just outside the entrance to the away end, which was doing a brisk trade on my last visit.

Where To Drink?

The pubs near the ground can be quite partisan, so I would recommend getting a drink somewhere on the journey there. Gordon, a visiting Newcastle fan, adds 'there are quite a few pubs on the Kings Road that are okay as long as you don't break into a chorus about your team!'. Ross Mooring adds; The best (well, least partisan) pub for away fans is the Slug and Lettuce outside Fulham Broadway train station situated a few minutes walk from the ground. It's an upmarket pub with a good security and police presence outside on matchdays. Very full but rarely any trouble. Away fans though should avoid the Sofa Bar. Alcohol (Budweiser) is available inside the ground but it is a bit pricey, even for Londoners!'. About a ten-minute walk away from the ground near Parsons Green tube station is the White Horse. A large comfortable pub which sells good food and a range of real ales including Harveys Ales from Sussex. To find this pub with the new West Stand behind you turn right (up past where the away coaches are parked) up Fulham Road and into Fulham Broadway, passing the tube station on your right. Continue to follow Fulham Road around to the left and then take a left hand turn into Parsons Green Road. Go under the bridge passing Parsons Green tube station on your right and you will reach the White Horse pub on your left.

How To Get There & Where To Park?

Leave the M25 at Junction 15 and take the M4 towards London, which then becomes the A4 up to Hammersmith. Carry on over the Hammersmith flyover and after a further one and half miles, take the turning for Earls Court. Continue past Earls Court station and down the one-way system until you reach the junction with Fulham Road. At this junction, turn right at the traffic lights and after about half a mile, you will see the ground on your right. A number of local resident schemes are in operation around the ground, so you may well end up having to park some way from the ground itself. Thanks to Andy Harris for providing the directions.

By Tube/Train

The nearest tube station is Fulham Broadway which is on the District Line. Take a tube to Earls Court and if necessary, change for a Wimbledon bound tube.
The nearest overground train station is West Brompton, which is served by trains from Clapham Junction (which is in turn served by trains from London Waterloo and Victoria stations). It is around a 15-minute walk to the ground from West Brompton station. Turn right outside the station past the Tournament Pub, then right again into Brompton Cemetery. Walk on through the Cemetery (just follow the crowd) and Stamford Bridge is soon visible to the right. If it is a night game then turn right after the cemetery into Finborough Road. After half a mile, turn right onto the Fulham Road. Thanks to Jim Millington for providing the directions.

Local Rivals

Fulham, Arsenal, Tottenham, West Ham and from a little further afield Leeds & Manchester United.

Admission Prices

Home Fans*:

West Stand Upper & Middle Tiers:
£60 - No Concessions

West Stand Lower Tier:
Adults £48 - No Concessions

Shed End Stand Upper Tier:
Adults £48 - No Concessions

Shed End Stand Lower Tier:
Adults £45 - No Concessions

Matthew Harding Upper Tier:
Adults £48 - No Concessions

Matthew Harding Lower Tier:
Adults: £45 - No Concessions

East Stand Upper Tier:
Adults: £48,
Senior Citizens/Under 16's £20,
Young Adults (16-21) £35

East Stand Middle Tier:
Season Tickets Only

East Stand Lower Tier (Family Area):
Adults: £35,
Senior Citizens/Under 16's £15

Chelsea

Away Fans:

Shed End Stand Upper Tier:
Adults £48,
Senior Citizens/Under 16's £20

Shed End Stand Lower Tier:
Adults £45,
Senior Citizens/Under 16's £20

* Prices quoted are for club members. Non-members are charged up to £5 more per ticket.

Programme & Fanzines
Official Programme £3.
Chelsea Independent Fanzine: £1.50.
CFCUK Fanzine: £1.

Record Attendance
82,905 v Arsenal
Division One, October 10th, 1935.

Modern All Seated Attendance Record:
42,328 v Newcastle United
Premier League, December 4th, 2002.

Average Attendance
2006-2007: 41,543 (Premier League)

Stadium Tours & Museum
The club offer tours of the ground, which are available three times a day, except match days & bank holidays. The tour lasts for around 75 minutes and is coupled with a visit to the new Chelsea Museum. It costs; Adults £14 & Concessions £8. To book your tour, call Chelsea World Of Sport on 0870-603-0005. If you wish you can just visit the museum. This costs; Adults £5 & Concessions £3 and does not need to be pre-booked.

Did You Know?
That Stamford Bridge hosted the FA Cup Final on three occasions between 1920 & 1922.

* This date was when the ground was developed to house football and the year that Chelsea first played there. The site had been used previously since 1877 as home to the London Athletics Club.

Derby County

Pride Park

Ground Name: Pride Park Stadium
Capacity: 33,597 (all seated)
Address: Pride Park Stadium, Derby, DE24 8XL
Main Telephone No: 0870-444-1884
Fax No: 01332-667540
Pitch Size: 105 x 68 metres
Club Nickname: The Rams
Year Ground Opened: 1997
Home Kit Colours: Black & White

Official Website:
www.dcfc.co.uk

Unofficial Websites:
The Rams - www.therams.co.uk
Popside Message Board - www.popside.com
Ram Zone - http://derbycounty.rivals.net/default.asp?sid=886 (Rivals Network)

■ What's The Ground Like?

The ground is a big, handsome change from the old Baseball Ground, which was the former home of the Club since 1895. The new stadium, opened by Her Majesty the Queen in 1997, is totally enclosed with all corners being filled. One corner is filled with executive boxes, giving the stadium a continental touch. The large Toyota West Stand which runs down one side of the pitch is two-tiered, complete with a row of executive boxes. The rest of the ground is smaller in size than the West Stand, as the roof drops a tier to the other sides, making it look unbalanced. It is a pity that the West Stand could not be replicated throughout the rest of the stadium as this would have made it truly magnificent.

■ What Is It Like For Visiting Supporters?

Away fans are located at one end of the stadium in the Cawarden (South) Stand, where the allocation is normally 3,000, although this can be increased to 4,800, if demand requires it. I have thoroughly enjoyed my visits to Pride Park. The stadium and the facilities within it are superb. The PA system is almost better than you would experience in a cinema and queuing for a beer behind the stands reminded me of being at a theme park, as you are able to watch television screens as you wait. The Derby supporters are passionate about their team and this coupled with the stadium design makes for a great noisy atmosphere. I found the Derby supporters friendly and did not experience any problems at all. The delicious 'Football's Famous Chicken Balti Pie' (£2) is available inside the ground, as well as burgers, hot dogs and chips. The game is shown live on these screens, with commentary, so that you don't have to miss anything while waiting for your half time cuppa. There is also a Ladbrokes betting outlet too. Please note that you have to buy a match ticket before entering the stadium from the lottery office adjacent to the away turnstiles.
George Donovan, a visiting Ipswich Town supporter adds; 'In my opinion Pride Park is the best ground in the Championship - yes, even better than Portman Road! - thanks to its location, proximity to the train station,

Derby County

best pub I've been to on the way to the ground (The Brunswick - over a dozen real ales always on tap including my fave Timmy Taylors Landlord), superb catering with no queues, fantastic view, friendly home fans and great PA'.

■ Where To Drink?

There are a couple of pubs opposite the station, such as the Merry Widows, that tend to be the favourite haunts of away supporters. However, unless you are going to arrive mob handed, then it is probably best to turn right out of the station and make your way down to The Brunswick or Alexandra Hotel. Both these pubs have a railway theme, serve a great range of real ales and offer a selection of filled rolls. Although they both have bouncers on the doors away fans are normally let in as long as there is no singing. There are bars at the back of the Stands (£2.50 a pint), however they do get quite crowded.

■ How To Get There & Where To Park?

From the M1, exit at Junction 25 and take the the A52 towards Derby. The ground is signposted off the A52 after about seven miles. There is not a great deal of parking available around the stadium so it may be an idea to park in the centre of town and then walk out to the ground. Kenny Lyon suggests; 'perhaps a better place to park for all fans is the cattle market car park. This costs £2 and is about 5-10 minutes walk from the ground and is just off the A52. To get there, go past the normal turning for the stadium and go up to the 'pentagon roundabout'; take the first turning off there and then take the next left - you then drive about 300 yards back on yourself, passing it on your left as you drive along the A52'.

Steve Hallam informs me; 'A stretch of the A52 between Nottingham and Derby has been named Brian Clough Way in honour of the great man's achievements with both Derby and Forest. Signs have recently been erected along this stretch of the A52 to show this'.

■ By Train

The ground is about fifteen minutes walk from Derby railway station and is signposted. As you exit, turn right and at the bottom of the road turn right again and follow the crowd.

■ Local Rivals

Nottingham Forest, Leicester City.

■ Admission Prices

At the time of going to press ticket prices for the 2007-2008 season had yet to be announced.

■ Programme

Official Programme £2

■ Record Attendance

At Pride Park;
33,597 England v Mexico,
Friendly, May 25th, 2001.

For a Derby game at Pride Park:
33,475 v Glasgow Rangers
Friendly, May 1st, 2006.

At the Baseball Ground;
41,826 v Tottenham Hotspur,
Division One, September 20th, 1969.

■ Average Attendance

2006-2007: 25,945 (Championship)

■ Did You Know?

That the first ever league game to be played at Pride Park had to be abandoned because of a floodlight failure. Derby were leading Wimbledon 2-1 when the floodlights went out on 56 minutes.

Everton

Goodison Park

Ground Name:	Goodison Park
Capacity:	40,569 (all seated)
Address:	Goodison Road, Liverpool, L4 4EL
Main Telephone No:	0870-442-1878
Fax No:	0151-286-9112
Ticket Office:	0870-442-1878
Ground Tours:	0151-330-2305
Pitch Size:	112 x 78 yards
Club Nickname:	The Toffees
Shirt Sponsors:	Chang
Kit Manufacturers:	Umbro
Home Kit Colours:	Royal Blue & White

Official Website:
www.evertonfc.com

Unofficial Websites:
Toffee Web - www.toffeeweb.com
Blue Kipper - www.bluekipper.com
When Skies Are Grey - www.whenskiesaregrey.com (Rivals Network)

What's The Ground Like?

Looking from the outside, Goodison, with its tall stands seems huge. The crowds filling the narrow streets around the ground on matchday make you feel that you are going back in time, to when the outside of every football ground appeared like this. However, that's Goodison's problem. Apart from the newish Park Stand (which has an electric scoreboard on its roof), the rest of the ground looks tired. Yes the ground is still large, but it needs modernising. For example there are lots of supporting pillars (at least the club don't sell tickets directly behind them) and the ground just looks as if it has seen better days. Nevertheless unlike some new grounds, Goodison oozes character and the three-tiered Main Stand is still an impressive sight. There are two large video screens at opposite corners of the ground. If you are a home/neutral fan who is not scared of heights then try and get a ticket for the top balcony of the Main Stand. Not only do you get a 'bird's-eye' view of the game, but also views across Stanley Park, with Anfield in the distance. Now thinking about it if you were an Everton fan you probably wouldn't want to see Anfield during the game, so this advice is for neutrals!

A unique feature of the stadium is a church called St Luke's, which sits just beyond one corner of the ground (selling teas & snacks at reasonable prices, plus upstairs it normally hosts a small programme fair on matchdays). If you have time before the game look out for the statue behind the Park Stand; a tribute to the legend that was Dixie Dean. After all these years, the Everton team still come out to the theme tune of the old police series, Z-Cars.

Future Ground Developments

The Club have announced plans to build a new 55,000 all+seated stadium at Kirkby. The development would also include a large Tesco's outlet. The proposed move has infuriated some Everton fans as the stadium would be located outside Liverpool, as Kirkby lies beyond the city boundary.

What Is It Like For Visiting Supporters?

Away fans are located in one corner of the two-tiered, Bullens Road Stand which is at the side of the pitch, where just over 3,000 away fans can be accommodated. If you can, try to get tickets for the upper tier, as the view from the lower tier can be quite poor. In the rear of the lower tier there are a number of supporting pillars that can hinder your view, the seating is of the old wooden type and the gap between rows is tight. The front of the lower tier is a lot better, having newer seats and no supporting pillars to contend with. Some visiting clubs elect to take a lower allocation than the 3,000 on offer; if this applies then only the lower tier is given to away fans. The facilities within the stand are basic and it is really showing its age. However, away fans can generate some noise from this stand, making for a great atmosphere. The catering includes amongst other things; a Scouse Pie (£2), Steak Pie (£2.10), Chicken & Chilli Pie (£2.10) and Sausage Rolls (£1.90).

I have enjoyed a couple of good days out at Goodison. The atmosphere was relaxed and friendly, with both sets of fans mixing freely before the game. Neil Thompson, a visiting Preston supporter adds; 'The stewards inside the ground were superb and the best I have seen at any ground;. they just ran things with a sensible head and communicated with people, first class. There are lot of grounds that can learn from the Everton stewarding'.

On a poignant note, if you do happen to notice some flowers lying around the perimeter of the pitch, this is because the ashes of a number of supporters (over 800) have been interred around it.

■ Where To Drink?

I found a moderately busy pub called the Anfield Hotel. I guess with a name like that a lot of Evertonians boycott the place! To find this pub, walk up to Walton Lane (the A580 dual carriageway) from the ground. Turn left and take a ten minute walk down Walton Lane, passing Walton police station. As you go under a bridge the pub is a short distance down the next road on your left. Tom Hughes adds 'The city centre is usually the best bet for a pre-match drink, There are hundreds of pubs available ranging from designer types to real ale and sawdust bars. The pubs nearest to Lime Street Station are best avoided with the exception of the big-House (the Vines) next to the Adelphi which is worth a visit. Nearer Goodison,The Hermitage (a friendly pub, 5/10 minutes walk up Walton Lane and under the bridge) on Queens Drive is also okay'.

Peter Bennett suggests the following; 'Pubs on Walton Lane or The Spellow and Wilnslow Hotel outside Goodison are recommended. The only pub that away fans should avoid is The Royal Oak.' Otherwise alcohol is served in the away section of the ground, including beer from the Club's sponsors Chang.

■ How To Get There & Where To Park?

Follow the M62 until you reach the end of the motorway (beware of a 50mph speed camera about a quarter of a mile from the end of the motorway). Then follow the A5058 towards Liverpool. After three miles turn left at the traffic lights into Utting Avenue (there is a McDonalds on the corner of this junction). Proceed for one mile and then turn right at the corner of Stanley Park into Priory Road. Goodison is at the end of this road.

If you arrive early (around 1pm) then there is street parking to be found around Walton Lane. Otherwise park over towards Anfield or in Stanley Park itself (the entrance to the car park which costs £6, is in Priory Road). Randy Coldham adds; 'If you approach from the M57 (to join the M57, leave the M62 at Junction 6), and then leave the M57 at Junction 4. Take the A580 towards Liverpool, and on the the right you will reach the Warton Sports Centre where you can park for £3. It is then a 15 minute walk to the ground with a very good Chinese Chippy on the way. By parking there you are well away from the traffic jams that you tend to get at Stanley Park after the match and only a five minute drive from the motorway system.

■ By Train

Kirkdale station is the closest to the ground (just under a mile away). However, it may be more advisable to go to Sandhills station as this has the benefit of a bus service to the ground, which runs for a couple of hours before the game and around 50 minutes after the final whistle. The bus drops you off within easy walking distance of Goodison.

Gary Beaumont adds; 'The best route for away fans from the city centre if they want to use public transport is definitely the Merseyrail Northern Line to Sandhills where they alight and catch the special Soccerbuses; trains can be caught from Liverpool Central. If fans are buying their train tickets in Liverpool, ask for a return to Goodison Park as opposed to Sandhills even though that's where you're getting off. The advantage of doing this is that the train ticket is valid also for the Soccerbus and the additional fare is only £1 return as opposed to £1.50 that you'd have to pay on the bus if you only bought your ticket to Sandhills. Both Sandhills & Kirkdale stations can be reached by first getting a train from Liverpool Lime Street to Liverpool Central and then changing there for Kirkdale.

On exiting from Kirkdale Station turn right and then cross the railway bridge, you will see a pub opposite called the 'Melrose Abbey', which is a recommended watering hole. Walk up Westminster Road, alongside the pub, for about 400yds and you'll see the Elm Tree pub. Turn left at the pub into Goodall Street and walk up to end of the road, crossing the junction with Carisbrooke Road and into Harlech Street. At the end of Harlech Street you will reach the main County Road (A59). Cross over County Road at the traffic lights and then proceed down Andrew Street. At the top of Andrew Street you can see St Luke's Church sat in the corner of the ground.

The main railway station in Liverpool is Lime Street which is over three miles from the ground and is really too far to walk (although it is mostly downhill on the way back to the station), so either head for Kirkdale station or jump in a taxi (about £6). Otherwise you can catch various buses from the bus station which is seven minutes walk away from Lime Street and is well signposted. Either the 19, 19a, 20, 21 or 311 will drop you right outside the ground at a cost of about a £1. The buses are run by Arriva and the journey takes about 15 to 25 minutes dependent on traffic.

Thanks to Geoff Barnes for providing the directions from Kirkdale station.

■ Local Rivals

Liverpool.

Everton

Admission Prices

Home Fans:

Main Stand -
Adults* £33,
Over 65's £23
Under 16's £19

Main Stand Top Balcony
Adults* £31,
Under 16's £17

Family Enclosure
Adults*£31,
Under 16's £17

Bullens Stand (Upper Tier)
Adults* £33,
Under 16's £19

Bullens Stand (Lower Tier)
Adults* £28,
Over 65's £21,
Under 16's £17

Bullens Stand (Lower Tier Paddock At Front)
Adults* £31,
Under 16's £17

Gwladys Street (Upper Tier)
Adults* £31,
Juniors £17

Gwladys Street (Lower Tier)
Adults* £28
Over 65's £21,
Juniors £17

Park Stand
Adults* £34,
Juniors £19

Away Fans:

Bullens Stand (Upper Tier)
Adults* £33,
Under 16's £19

Bullens Stand (Lower Tier)
Adults* £28,
Over 65's £21,
Under 16's £17

Bullens Stand (Lower Tier Paddock At Front)
Adults* £31,
Under 16's £17

* For fixtures against Liverpool and Manchester United, the ticket price quoted above is increased by £4. For fixtures against Arsenal and Chelsea, the ticket price quoted above is increased by £2. Over 65's & Under 16's prices remain unchanged.

Programme & Fanzines

Official Programme: £3
Satis Fanzine: £1
Speke From The Harbour: £1

Record Attendance

78,299 v Liverpool,
Division One, September 18th, 1948.

Modern All Seated Attendance Record:
40,552 v Liverpool
Premier League, December 11th, 2004.

Average Attendance

2006-2007: 36,738 (Premier League)

Stadium Tours

Tours of the ground are available at a cost of; Adults £8.50, Concessions £5, or there is a family ticket available (2 adults + 2 children) at £20. Tours take place daily except Saturdays and some matchday Sundays. Call the Club on 0151-330-2305 to book.

Did You Know?

That the club takes its name from the nearby Everton district of Liverpool.

Fulham

Craven Cottage

Ground Name:	Craven Cottage
Capacity:	24,600 (all seated)
Address:	Stevenage Road, London, SW6 6HH
Main Telephone No:	0870-442-1222
Fax No:	0207-384-4715
Ticket Office:	0870-442-1234
Ticket Office Fax No:	0207-384-4810
Team Nickname:	The Cottagers
Ground Opened:	1894
Home Kit Colours:	Black & White

Official Website:
www.fulhamfc.com

Unofficial Websites:
Fulham Web - www.fulhamweb.com
Fulham Supporters Club - www.fulhamsc.com
The Green Pole - www.thegreenpole.pwp.blueyonder.co.uk
Independent Message Board - www.voy.com/13865/
There's Only One F In Fulham - http://fulham.rivals.net/default.asp?sid=906 (Rivals Network),
Fulham Supporters Trust - www.backtothecottage.co.uk

■ What's The Ground Like?

On one side of the ground is the Stevenage Road Stand, which has recently been renamed the Johnny Haynes Stand after the former Fulham great. It previously had terracing at the front, but this has now been made all seated. The stand was originally designed by Archibald Leitch (who designed a number of football grounds and stands in the early part of the 20th century) and was opened in 1905. Considering its age, it can be forgiven for having a number of supporting pillars and old wooden seating in its upper tier. It does though have a fine classic looking gable on its roof, labelled Fulham Football Club.

Opposite is the aptly named Riverside Stand. which sits on the banks of the River Thames. This all-seated, covered stand was opened in 1972. It is slightly raised above pitch level and has small sets of steps at the front of the stand by which spectators can access it. It also has a row of executive boxes running across the back of it and also houses a television gantry. There are a couple of small windshields to either side, plus it has a couple of supporting pillars. Overlooking the ground from one corner, between the Johnny Haynes Stand and Putney End, is the unique Pavilion building, which many fans refer to as 'the Cottage' (although this is technically incorrect as the original cottage after which the ground is named, was demolished many years ago). This looks somewhat misplaced, being more reminiscent of a small cricket pavilion rather than something found at a football ground, but it does add to the overall character.

Both ends which were previously terraced have now been replaced by two new large all-seated, covered stands that look fairly similar in design. They both, however, have some supporting pillars, which is disappointing. The Hammersmith End has one large pillar towards the front and middle of the stand, whilst opposite the Putney End has a row of pillars running across the stand, about a third of the way down it. Attached to these stands in three corners of the ground are some three-storey structures that are used to house corporate executive boxes. An unusual feature is that the teams enter the field from one corner of the ground, by the Cottage and then make their way up onto the pitch as it is raised. The only disappointment is that the fabulous old floodlights that the ground previously had have been removed and replaced by a nondescript modern set.

■ Future Ground Developments

Kevin Freeman informs me; 'The club have gained planning permission to build a new 30,000 seater stadium on the present Craven Cottage site. However the problem with this scheme is the cost - heading up towards £100 million at the last count. It is therefore likely that the Club will further re-develop the ground in stages, presumably by infilling the corners and enlarging/replacing existing stands, until an economically viable capacity is reached. The club will only seek to relocate elsewhere if this cannot be achieved (i.e. if the necessary amended planning consents aren't forthcoming)'.

■ What Is It Like For Visiting Supporters?

Away fans are housed to one side of the new Putney End Stand, on the river side of the ground. The stand will be shared with home supporters, with away fans being allocated around 3,000 seats, which is just under half of the overall capacity of this stand. One huge benefit that the new Putney End stand has over the old terrace, is that it has a roof. There are a couple of supporting pillars that could impede your view, but this only applies to certain seats in Row DD and above. The legroom is ample and as the rows of stands seem to have been constructed from metal and plywood, rather than concrete, fans can't resist making some noise by stamping up and down on it. A number of burger vans provide the usual fare of hot dogs (£2.50), cheeseburgers (£2.80) and bacon rolls (£2.60). Alcohol is also available from stalls at the back of the stand, with bottles of Fosters priced at £3 per bottle. Please note that smoking is not allowed in the stands or at your seat.

I have been previously to Craven Cottage on a number of occasions and on a nice summer day, this is one of my favourite grounds. From the walk from the tube station through a park, to having a pint overlooking the River Thames, this can be quite an enjoyable experience and I have never had any problems there. The walk down Stevenage Road to the away entrance, gives you the chance to admire the quaint red brick facade of the Johnny Haynes Stand, whilst inside you can enjoy modern facilities, and apart from the game, you can still catch glimpses of rowers making their away along the Thames.

I have to say the recent redevelopments have made a great ground even better and there is now a superb blend of the new and the old, giving the ground great individuality and character. My only grumble has been sometimes the rather large police presence outside the ground (including mounted police and dog handlers), before and after the games that I have attended. One would have thought they were expecting a riot. On one of my visits the Birmingham fans were chanting to the Fulham fans, "you only sing when you're rowing!"

One other item of interest is that Fulham is the only Club that I know of that has a designated area of the ground reserved for 'neutral supporters'. This is located on one side of the Putney End, adjacent to the away fans section. I guess that the original idea was to attract tourists to London to a game. However, for each game there seems to be a good mix of home, away and neutral fans in this area.

■ Where To Drink?

David Frear adds; 'The Crabtree on Rainville Road (10 minutes from the ground) welcomes all away supporters and as a Fulham season ticket holder I can tell you that as long as you don't watch your football at Loftus Road you can be assured of a warm welcome'. To find this pub go along Stevenage Road away from the Cottage and the away end. On reaching the home end of the ground, turn left along an alley which runs behind the stand. When you reach the River Thames turn right and walk along the riverside path. You will reach the Crabtree on your right. Andrew Johnson recommends; 'the Zulu Bar (formerly the Kings Head), on Fulham High Street, is one of the nearest to the ground and is always popular with away fans'. Otherwise near to the tube station is the Eight Bells and just further along Fulham High Street is The Larrik and O'Neills.

Some of the other pubs near to the ground have been designated home supporters only, so alternatively some away fans use the pubs south of the river (across Putney Bridge). The Dukes Head is recommended, which has nice views overlooking the River Thames towards the ground and does good food. It is a Youngs pub with a cosmopolitan atmosphere as it is located next to a number of rowing clubs. Allow twenty minutes to walk from the pub to the ground.

■ How To Get There & Where To Park?

From the North M1:

Thanks to Robert Donaldson, a visiting Stockport County fan, for providing the following directions; 'At the end of the M1, turn right (west) onto the A406 (North Circular) and follow it towards Harrow for nearly 4.5 miles. Turn left (east) onto the A40 heading into London (passing

close to Loftus Road and after a little over 4 miles turn right (west) onto the A402 for just about 350 yards. Here you turn left (south) along the A219 for a little over half a mile. This brings you into Hammersmith where you turn right onto the A315 and then after just 130 yards or so turn left (south) back onto the A219. Follow this road for a little over a mile, and the ground is down the side streets off to your right.'

From The North M40 & West M25:
Leave the M25 at Junction 15 and take the M4, which then becomes the A4, towards Central London. After around two miles branch off left into Hammersmith Broadway (before the flyover). Go around the ring road around central Hammersmith, keeping to the right. Then take the A219 Fulham Palace Road. Keep straight on this road, passing Charing Cross Hospital on your left. After about another half a mile turn right into Crabtree Lane for the ground.

From the South M25:
Leave the M25 at Junction 10 and take the A3 towards Central London. After around eight miles, leave the A3 at the turn off for the A219. Take the A219 towards Putney. Continue straight on this road, down Putney High Street and across Putney Bridge. You will see the ground on your left.

Parking is possible in the streets around the ground but they are controlled by council parking meters, so make sure you bring some change, (£1.60 per hour) and early arrival is advised. Parking, however, is free in these areas in the evenings and on Sundays.

■ By Tube
The nearest station is Putney Bridge, which is on the District Line. The ground is about a fifteen minute walk. Turn left out of the station and then just follow the other supporters. You get a nice pleasant walk through Bishops Park along the riverbank to the ground (note that the park is closed after evening games).

■ Local Rivals
Chelsea, QPR and Brentford.

■ Admission Prices
Fulham operate a four category system of ticket pricing (A+, A, B, C) whereby the most popular matches will cost more to watch than the least popular ones. The highest category (A+) ticket prices are shown below, with the lowest category (C) ticket prices shown in brackets.

Home Fans:

Riverside Stand:
Adults £45 (£30),
Over 65's/Students £30 (£15),
Juniors £20 (£5)

Johnny Haynes Stand (Centre & Wings):
Adults £45 (£30),
Over 65's/Students £30 (£15),
Juniors £20 (£5)

Johnny Haynes Stand (Outer Wings):
Adults £40 (£25),
Over 65's/Students £30 (£15),
Juniors £20 (£5)

Hammersmith & Putney Ends:
Adults £40 (£25),
Over 65's/Students £30 (£15),
Juniors £20 (£5)

Away Fans:

Adults £40 (£25), Over 65's/Students £30 (£15),
Juniors £20 (£5)

■ Programme & Fanzine
Official Programme: £3.
One F In Fulham Fanzine: £2.

■ Record Attendance
49,335 v Millwall,
Division Two, October 8th, 1938.

Modern All-Seated Attendance Record:
24,554 v Liverpool
Premier League, May 5th, 2007.

■ Average Attendance
2006-2007: 22,608 (Premier League)

■ Stadium Tours
The Club offer tours of the ground on the last Thursday and Saturday of the month (except matchdays). The cost of the tour is Adults £9.95, Children (under 12) £5.95. Tours should be booked in advance by calling 0207-384-4777.

■ Did You Know?
The Club was originally formed in 1879 as 'Fulham St Andrews' Cricket & Football Club. The 'St Andrews' was dropped from its name in 1888.

Liverpool

Anfield

Ground Name:	Anfield
Capacity:	45,362 (all seated)
Address:	Anfield Road, Liverpool, L4 0TH
Main Telephone No:	0151-263-2361
Main Fax No:	0151-260-8813
Ticket Office:	0870-220-2345
Ticket Office Fax:	0151-261-1416
Ground Tours:	0151-260-6677
Pitch Size:	110 x 75 yards
Club Nickname:	The Reds
Year Ground Opened:	1884
Home Kit Colour:	All Red

Official Website:
www.liverpoolfc.tv

Unofficial Websites:
Kop Talk - www.koptalk.com
Liverpool Mad - www.liverpool-mad.co.uk
(Footy Mad Network)
This Is Anfield - www.thisisanfield.com
Red & White Kop - www.redandwhitekop.net

What's The Ground Like?

Walking up to the ground alongside Stanley Park, I have to say, that from a distance, Anfield is not particularly impressive. Inside though, the ground is wonderful and only the most critical of visitors would find fault with it. The famous Kop Terrace at one end of the ground, has been replaced by a huge stand designed to emulate the old Kop, hence its odd shape (kind of semi-circular) and single large tier. The other end, the Anfield Road Stand, part of which is given to away supporters, is the most recent addition to the ground. It has boosted not only the overall capacity of the stadium, but has given Anfield a more balanced and enclosed feel as all corners are now filled. On one side of the stadium is the large, two-tiered Centenary Stand, where the front tier leg room is the tightest I have ever known. Opposite is the Main Stand, the oldest in the ground and looking its age with a number of supporting pillars. This stand has a TV gantry suspended beneath its roof. In the corner between the Kop & Centenary stands is an electric scoreboard, which, surprise, surprise, shows the match score in bright red letters.

Around the outside of the ground, there are the Bill Shankly Gates on Anfield Road. These wrought-iron gates have the legendary Liverpool phrase 'You'll Never Walk Alone' displayed above them. There is also a statue of the great man, Bill Shankly, near the Club shop. Also along Anfield Road, there is the moving memorial to the victims of the Hillsborough disaster, which always has flowers adorning it.

Future Ground Developments

The Club have received planning permission to build a new 60,000 all-seated stadium, to be located in nearby Stanley Park. Preliminary work will commence on building the new stadium during 2007 and it is planned that it will be open for the start of the 2010/11 season. The stadium will feature a 17,000-capacity, single-tier Kop stand.

What Is It Like For Visiting Supporters?

Away fans are located in the Anfield Road Stand at one end of the ground, where just under 2,000 seats are available, although this can be increased for cup games. This stand is also shared with home supporters, some of whom will be sitting in the small seated tier above the away fans. Malcolm Dawson, a travelling Sunderland supporter adds; 'Try to avoid getting tickets sold as restricted view, for the rear rows of the Anfield Road Stand as it can be difficult to see the goals with people standing up in front of you'.

Kimberly Hill adds; 'Restricted view doesn't even begin to describe what it was like. The Wolves fans insisted on standing so it was like trying to watch the game through a letterbox!' The facilities within the stand are not bad. There is a Ladbrokes betting outlet and the refreshment kiosks sell a wide variety of burgers, hot dogs and pies, including a 'Scouse Pie' at £1.80.

I have always found it to be a good day out at Anfield, getting the feeling that you are visiting one of the legendary venues in world football. This is enhanced with the teams coming out to 'You'll Never Walk Alone' reverberating around the ground, with the red and white scarves and flags of the fans displayed across the Kop, at the beginning of the match. The atmosphere is normally great, so sit back and enjoy the experience.

■ Where To Drink?

The Arkles pub near to the ground (see directions by car), is known as the away fans pub, but as can be expected it can get extremely crowded. Mark Parsons, a visiting Aston Villa fan adds; 'We arrived at the Arkles at about 1.15pm and already found it packed out, with fans queuing outside to get in. We asked a very helpful WPC for any other away-friendly pubs and were told to go to the Flat Iron which was a five-minute walk away. Although the pub was mostly full of Liverpool fans, the bars were mixed and all were very friendly. There is also a good chippy located on the other side of the road. To find this pub, turn left at the junction where Arkles is (with the ground over to your right down Anfield Road). Head away from ther ground and the pub is down on the right-hand side.'

Brian Mcllwrick informs me; 'I got to the ground at around 1.30pm and decided to enter the away end early, only to find that they don't serve alcohol to away fans. Be warned!'

■ How To Get There & Where To Park?

Follow the M62 until you reach the end of the motorway (beware of a 50mph speed camera about a quarter of a mile from the end of the motorway). Then follow the A5058 towards Liverpool. After three miles turn left at the traffic lights into Utting Avenue (there is a McDonalds on the corner of this junction). Proceed for one mile and then turn right at the Arkles pub for the ground. If you arrive early (around 1pm) then there is street parking to be found. Otherwise it is an idea to park in the streets around Goodison and walk across Stanley Park to Anfield, or you can park in a secure parking area at Goodison itself which costs £6.

By Train

Kirkdale station is the closest to the ground (just under a mile away). However, it may be more advisable to go to Sandhills station as this has the benefit of a bus service to the ground, which runs for a couple of hours before and a couple of hours after a game and drops you within easy walking distance of the ground. Gary Beaumont adds; 'The best route for away fans from the city centre if they want to use public transport is definitely the Merseyrail Northern Line to Sandhills where they alight and catch the special Soccerbuses; trains can be caught from Liverpool Central and Moorfields. If fans are buying their train tickets in Liverpool, ask for a return to Anfield as opposed to Sandhills even though that's where you're getting off. The advantage of doing this is that the train ticket is valid also for the Soccerbus and the additional fare is only £1 return as opposed to £1 each way that you'd have to pay on the bus if you only bought your ticket to Sandhills. If fans want to get a taxi from Lime Street, they're about £6'. Both Sandhills & Kirkdale stations can be reached by first getting a train from Liverpool Lime Street to Liverpool Central and then changing there for Kirkdale.

The main railway station in Liverpool is Lime Street which is over three miles from the ground and is really too far to walk (although it is mostly downhill on the way back to the station), so either head for Sandhills or Kirkdale stations or jump in a taxi. Craig Hochkins adds; 'You can catch various buses from the bus station, which is seven minutes walk away from the train station and is well signposted. Either the 17a, 17b, 17c or the 26 will drop you right outside the ground at a cost of about £1. The buses are run by Arriva and the journey takes about 15 to 25 minutes depending on traffic'.

Walking Directions From Kirkdale Station:

On exiting from Kirkdale Station turn right and then cross the railway bridge, you will see a pub opposite called the 'Melrose Abbey', (which has been recommended). Walk up Westminster Road, alongside the pub and continue along it, passing the Elm Tree pub. Follow the road around the right hand bend and then turn left into Bradwell Street. At the end of Bradwell Street you will come to the busy County Road (A59). Cross over this road at the traffic lights and then go down the road to the left of the Aldi superstore. At the end of this road you will reach the A580 Walton Lane. You should be able to see Goodison Park over on your left and Stanley Park in front of you. Cross Walton Lane and either enter Stanley Park following the footpath through the park (keeping to the right), which will exit into Anfield Road and the away end. Or bear right down Walton Lane and then turn left down the road at the end of Stanley Park for the ground. Thanks to Jon Roche for providing these directions.

■ Local Rivals

Everton & Manchester United.

■ Admission Prices

The Club operate a category system, so that ticket prices vary with the opposition being played. The categories A & B are shown in brackets:

Home Fans:

Main Stand:
Adults (A) £34, (B) £32

Centenary Stand:
Adults (A) £34, (B) £32

The Kop:
Adults (A) £32, (B) £30

The Kop Family Ticket:
1 Adult (A) £32, (B) £30, + up to 2 Children (each child charged at half adult price ticket)

Anfield Road Stand:
Adults (A) £34, (B) £32

Anfield Road Family Ticket:
1 Adult (A) £34, (B) £32 + up to 2 Children (each child charged at half adult price ticket)
OAP's All Stands - (A) £24, (B) £22.50

Away Fans:

Anfield Road Stand:
Adults (A) £34, (B) £32
OAP's (A) £24, (B) £22.50
Juniors (A) £17, (B) £16

Programme & Fanzines

Official Programme: £3
The Liverpool Way Fanzine: £2
Red All Over The Land Fanzine: £1.50

Record Attendance

61,905 v Wolverhampton Wanderers
FA Cup 4th Round, February 2nd, 1952.

Modern All Seated Attendance Record:
44,983 v Tottenham Hotspur
Premier League, January 14th, 2006.

Average Attendance

2006-2007: 43,561 (Premier League)

Stadium Tours & Museum

The Club offer tours of the ground, which operate on a daily basis, except Bank Holidays and matchdays. There is also a museum at the ground and the Club offer combined tour & museum tickets as well as individual museum entrance. The costs are:

Ground Tour & Museum:
Adults: £10, Children & OAP's £6

Museum Only:
Adults: £5, Children & OAP's £3

For details of family tickets and for making tour bookings call: 0151-260-6677.

The Club also offer combined tour, museum and lunch packages, with lunch being taken in one of the executive boxes in the Centenary Stand. The cost of this is Adults £28.95, Under 14's £18.95, Under 8's £12.95, Under 5's £7.95.

Did You Know?

The Centenary Stand was officially opened in 1992, and was called so to celebrate 100 years of the Club being in existence. Prior to this that side of the ground was known as the Kemlyn Road Stand.

Manchester City

City of Manchester Stadium

Ground Name:	City Of Manchester Stadium
Capacity:	48,000 (all seated)
Address:	Sportcity, Rowsley St, Manchester, M11 3FF
Main Telephone No:	0870-062-1894
Main Fax No:	0161-438-7999
Ticket Office:	0870-062-1894
Ticket Office Fax:	0161-438-7810
Team Nicknames:	The Blues or Citizens
Year Ground Opened:	2002
Pitch Size:	116.5 x 78 yards
Home Kit Colours:	Sky Blue & White

Official Website:
www.mcfc.co.uk

Unofficial Websites:
Unofficial Man City - www.uit.no/mancity/
MCFC Stats - www.mcfcstats.com
Blueview - http://manchestercity.rivals.net/default.asp?sid=914 (Rivals Network)
Centenary Supporters Association - www.reddishblues.com/CSAWebsite/CSA.htm

What's The Ground Like?

After playing at Maine Road for 80 years, the Club moved to the new City Of Manchester Stadium in August 2003. The stadium was originally built for the Commonwealth Games, held in 2002. After that event it was agreed Manchester City would become the new tenants, thus incurring the envy of clubs who would also relish the chance to gain such a wonderful stadium. The club have spent £20m in refitting costs, so that it is now more of a football ground rather than an athletics stadium. The running track has been removed and the stands extended further downwards (adding a further 10,000 seats to the capacity) so that the spectator areas are closer to the playing action.

The stadium has a bowl design and is totally enclosed. Both stands on either side of the pitch are virtually identical, being semi circular in shape, three-tiered, with a row of executive boxes running across the stands between the second and third tiers. The ends are smaller in size, being two tiers high, again with a row of executive boxes, but this time running across the back just below the roof. Both these ends are of the more traditional rectangular design. The second tier around the stadium slightly overhangs the lower. The roof runs continuously around the stadium stretching up over the stands and down to the ends, creating a spectacular effect. There is a perspex strip just below the roof and the spectator areas, allowing light to reach the pitch. The upper tiers are steeper than the lower, ensuring that spectators are kept close to the playing action. Iain Macintosh adds; 'An interesting feature of the new stadium is the openable louvres in each of the four corners. These are located at either end of the level three seating in the East and Colin Bell stands. These are closed when in use, however, when the stadium is unoccupied, they are opened to allow the wind to blow through the enclosed bowl, helping keep the grass pristine'. There is also a small basic electric scoreboard in one corner of the stadium, in between the East & Key 103 stands, adjacent to the upper tier of the away fans section'.

Peter Llewellyn adds; 'Many City fans still call their new home Eastlands, used when it didn't have an official name. Some have suggested The Blue Camp, others New Maine Road but officially it's The City of Manchester Stadium. Unlike many other stadiums and stands, there are no letters across the seats, so there is nothing like MCFC spelt out across them'.

Man City get my vote for the weirdest-looking mascots in the league. Whilst most clubs have elected to re-create some furry creature, Man City have as their mascots a pair of aliens called 'Moonchester' and 'Moonbeam'.

What Is It Like For Visiting Supporters?

The stadium is certainly less intimidating for away fans than Maine Road ground and from the outside it looks simply spectacular. However, I think because it looks so good from the outside the expectations are raised somewhat; when you actually enter, you are a little disappointed as the inside does not match the exterior, looking somewhat bland in comparison.

Away fans are located in one side of the Key 103 (South) Stand at one end of the ground, in both the upper and lower tiers, where up to 3,000 fans can be accommodated (4,500 for cup games). The view of the action is pretty impressive although the leg room is a little tight. The facilities are also pretty good with spacious concourses, large flat plasma television screens showing the game and a good selection of food on offer, including chips and the delicious 'Football's Famous Chicken Balti Pie' (£2.20). On offer is also a 'pie and a pint' for £4.

Atmosphere within the new ground is sadly lacking compared to Maine Road, but I'm sure this will develop in time. I did hear though on my visit one good rendition of the Man City fans anthem 'Blue Moon'. My only real complaint was the lack of distance between the home and away supporters. Only a few seats and a row of stewards stood in-between the two sets of fans, which led to a lot of unpleasant baiting between the two. And of course it was always the away fans who were adjudged to be causing the problems by the stewards (although I'm sure that if I visited on another occasion I probably would have seen the same Man City fans baiting in the same manner) and this led a number of away fans on my visit being escorted out of the stadium. After the game has finished fans are kept apart immediately outside via a large fence which is erected by the Police, which seems to lead to a lot of exchanges of unpleasant abuse. Some away fans have suggested that it may be best to keep colours covered on making your way back to your transport. Please note that smoking is not permitted within the stadium.

Gaining entry to the stadium is rather different than most other grounds. Rather than give your ticket to a turnstile operator, you swipe your ticket across a sensor which then allows entry. Stewards are on hand if you have any problems. Peter Llewellyn adds; 'If you are an adult trying to get into the stadium using a concession ticket (OAP or child) the stewards will know and you'll be ejected.

Where To Drink?

There are not a great deal of pubs around the stadium, and the few available are predominantly for home support. However, The Stanley (aka Sports Bar) pub does let in away fans in small numbers. It is about a ten-minute walk away from the stadium, just set back from the main A6010 (Pottery Lane), going towards Ashburys train station. The easiest way to find it is to locate the large Asda store behind one side of the stadium (there is also a McDonalds outlet next door to the store, plus there is a cafe located inside it) and on facing the superstore turn right and proceed down the main road, you will come to the pub on the left. It does cost £1 for adults to enter the pub, (they even stamp your hand as if you were entering a nightclub) but children are at least admitted free. Inside there is a large screen showing SKY Sports, good service and a good mix of home and away support. Keith Bradley, a visiting Newcastle United fan informs me; 'About ten minutes walk from the ground is the Bradford Inn on Bradford Road. Although looking a bit run down from the outside, it was full of away fans, fairly friendly and the bar staff tried to be as efficient as they could in serving the large numbers. Otherwise alcohol is available inside the stadium (lager £2.40, cider £2.40, John Smiths bitter £2.30).'

Dave Clinton adds; 'If you want a pint beforehand then it is probably best to drink in the city centre. My tip, as we do, would be to head to the Printworks in Manchester, near Victoria station. There is a connecting tram service from Piccadilly. There are loads of pubs at the Printworks, with plenty of choice of food. It's a 20-minute walk away from the stadium or a five minute cab ride, (about £3). The pubs around Piccadilly itself are not too clever; Deansgate would be a good place to head for if you are taking in the City centre, this is about 30 minutes walk, with a load of bars down the bottom end going towards Victoria station. The alternative cheaper pubs near the ground are Mary Ds, or The Crossroads on Grey Mare Lane. Mary Ds does restrict entrance to Blues only on derby days, however, it's a fantastic football atmosphere and there has been no trouble in there to date'. Mary Ds is located on Grey Mare Lane, across the road from the away entrance behind the huge new sculpture, that looks like it was inspired by a game of Kerplunk! Chris Fogarty adds; 'Away fans should avoid the Queen Victoria pub at the bottom of Grey Mare Lane'.

How To Get There & Where To Park?

The stadium is located in the North East of Manchester.

From the South M6:
Leave the M6 at Junction 19 and follow the A556 towards Stockport and then join the M56 going towards Stockport. Continue onto the M60 passing Stockport and heading on towards Ashton Under Lyne. Leave the M60 at Junction 23 and take the A635 towards Manchester. Branch off onto the A662 (Ashton New Road) towards Droylsden/Manchester. Stay on the A662 for around three miles and you will reach the Stadium on your right.

From The M62:
Leave the M62 at Junction 18 and then join the M60 Ashton Under Lyne. Leave the M60 at Junction 23 and take the A635 towards Manchester. Branch off onto the A662 (Ashton New Road) towards Droylsden/Manchester. Stay on the A662 for around three miles and you will reach the Stadium on your right.

Iain Macintosh informs me; 'I find this an easier route to the ground; Leave the M60 at Junction 24 and take the A57 (Hyde Road) towards Manchester. Turn right onto the A6010 (Pottery Lane). There are quite a number of unofficial car parks on both sides of Pottery Lane, costing around £5 per car. Pottery Lane becomes the Alan Turing Way and goes right past the stadium on your left'.

Car Parking:

There is some parking available at the stadium itself which costs £5 per car. The East Car Park is nearest to the away entrance. Please be aware that there is a residents only parking scheme in place in the streets near to the ground, which extends about a mile out from the stadium. So if you want to street park, it means parking further away and then walking to the stadium. Some unofficial car parks have sprung up mostly charging around £5 per car. Peter Llewellyn adds; 'The road links are busy even on non-match days so make sure you allow plenty of time. The stadium is part of Sportcity so car users should follow the brown Sportcity signs until near the stadium'.

By Train

The closest train station is Ashburys which is a short five minute train ride away from Manchester Piccadilly Station. The stadium is about a ten-minute walk away from Ashburys station. As you come out of the station turn left and after proceeding up the road you will come to the stadium on your left.

Otherwise if you have time on your hands then you can embark on the 20/25 minute walk from Piccadilly Station to the stadium. At the bottom of the main station approach turn right into Ducie Street. At the end of the road turn right onto Great Ancoats Street. Cross over the road, then the canal and turn left into Pollard Street - this is well marked as a walking route to "Sportcity". Continue straight along Pollard Street which leads onto the A662 Ashton New Road and you will come to the stadium on your left.

A shorter route from the station is to use the new exit to Fairfield Street (the taxi rank). As you come off the platforms, it's in the left hand corner of the main concourse. Lifts or escalators down. (There's also an exit from the little concourse off the bridge near platforms 13/14.) At the street exit head toward the railway over bridge, under that, then left again under the railway (Travis Street continuing into Adair Street), left at the end and right into Pollard Street (then as above).

Alternatively you can get a taxi from Piccadilly Station (around £4.50) or a bus from Piccadilly Gardens - Go down the main approach from the station, then along London Road to Piccadilly Gardens; normal service and special matchday buses leave from the right hand side of the square (between Lever Street and Oldham Street) - £1 each way. 216 and 217 the main service buses, but 185, 186, 230, 231, 232, 233, 234, 235, 236, 237, X36 and X37 also go from the city centre to the stadium (and 53 and 54 from the city's ring road). On the return, the special buses leave from Ashton New Road just across from the away end.

Thanks to Steve Parish for providing the above directions and bus information.

Local Rivals

Manchester United.

Admission Prices

Like a number of clubs, Manchester City operate a category system (A, B & C) for matches, whereby the most popular matches cost more to watch.

Home Fans*:

Colin Bell Stand (level 2 middle tier):
Adults £38 (A) £34 (B) £30 (C), No Concessions.

Colin Bell Stand (levels 1 & 3):
Adults £36 (A) £32 (B) £28 (C),
Concessions £21 (A), £20 (B), £19 (C)

East Stand;
Adults £36 (A) £32 (B) £28 (A),
Concessions £21 (A) £20 (B) £19 (C)

North Stand;
Adults £30 (A) £27 (B) £23 (C),
Concessions £16 (A) £14 (B) £13 (C)

Key 103 (South) **Stand**;
Adults £30 (A) £27 (B) £23 (C),
Concessions £16 (A) £14 (B) £13 (C)

Away Fans*:

Key 103 (South) **Stand;**
Adults £30 (A) £27 (B) £23 (C),
Concessions £16 (A) £14 (B) £13 (C)

*A discount of £1 is available on these ticket prices, if purchased prior to matchday. Please note that tickets have to be purchased in advance and are not on sale on the day of the game.

Programme & Fanzines

Official Programme: £3 (on sale inside the ground).
King Of The Kippax Fanzine: £2.
City Till I Cry Fanzine: £1.50.

Record Attendance

At The City Of Manchester Stadium:
47,304 v Chelsea,
Premier League, February 28th, 2004.

At Maine Road:
84,569 v Stoke City,
FA Cup 6th Round, March 3rd, 1934.

Average Attendance

2006-2007: 39,872 (Premier League)

Stadium Tours

The club offer daily tours of the stadium. The tours cost; Adults £8.75 & £4.75 for concessions. The tour also includes a visit to the Club Museum & the City Sports Bar. Tours should be booked in advance by calling: 0870 062 1894.

Did You Know?

In 1957-58 Manchester City scored 104 goals in Division One and conceded 100, the only instance in football league history of a club scoring and conceding a century of goals.

Manchester United

Old Trafford

Ground Name: Old Trafford
Capacity: 76,100 (all seated)
Address: Sir Matt Busby Way, Manchester, M16 0RA
Main Telephone No: 0870-442-1994
Fax No: 0161-868-8804
Ticket Office (Sales): 0870-442-1999
Ticket Office (Enquiries): 0870-442-1994
Stadium Tours: 0870-442-1994
Club Nickname: The Red Devils
Year Ground Opened: 1910
Pitch Size: 116 x 76 yards
Home Kit Colours: Red, White & Black.

Official Website:
www.manutd.com

Unofficial Websites:
Red11.Org - www.red11.org
M-U-F-C - www.m-u-f-c.co.uk
Red Issue - www.redissue.co.uk (Footy Mad Network)
United We Stand - http://manchesterunited.rivals.net/ (Rivals Network)
Red News Fanzine - www.rednews.co.uk
Shareholders United - www.shareholdersunited.org
Independent Supporters Association - www.imusa.org
Stretford End - www.stretfordend.co.uk
Munich 58 - www.munich58.co.uk

■ What's The Ground Like?

With the completion of an additional tier of seating in the North East & North West corners, costing some £45m, Old Trafford, then the largest league ground in Britain, has got even bigger. Whether the Club continue with the expansion of Old Trafford by replacing the old Main (South) Stand, remains to be seen. The proximity of a railway line directly behind this stand has prevented redevelopment in the past, but I would not be surprised if this eventually happens as the Club have nowhere else left in the stadium that they can expand upon.

Old Trafford has always been a special place as it was one of the few grounds where the stands envelop the corners. Although more grounds are now also totally enclosed, Old Trafford's sheer size still makes it a bewildering sight. Both ends, which look almost identical, are large two-tiered stands. Each are steep, with a large lower tier and smaller upper tier. The three-tiered North Stand, at one side of the ground, is the largest capacity stand of any League Ground in England. The corners each side of the North Stand are also filled with seating and extend around to meet both ends. These redeveloped stands dwarf the older Main (South) Stand on the opposite side. This stand is single-tiered, with a television gantry suspended below its roof. All the stands have a row of executive boxes at the back of the lower tier.

The ground looks a little imbalanced with the smaller older Main (South) Stand looking somewhat out of place with its larger, newer neighbours. However, in my opinion the best views of the ground are from the front of this stand and from the away section, as you look out upon the three newer, larger sides. Still, if this Main Stand was to be redeveloped in the same manner as the others, then the ground would possibly be the envy of Europe.

Unusual aspects of the ground include the raised pitch, and that the teams enter the field from the corner of the Main Stand. Outside the ground is the Sir Matt Busby Statue fronting the impressive green-glassed East Stand facade. There is also a clock and plaque in remembrance of the Munich disaster.

What Is It Like For Visiting Supporters?

Away fans are located in one corner of the ground, taking up part of the East and South stands. The view from the away sections are excellent and up to 3,000 away supporters can be accommodated. Fans are normally searched on the way into the ground by the stewards and once inside there are a number of refreshment kiosks. These sell a range of Shire Foods pies at £2 (but alas no balti pies) and other refreshments. The away fans section is set back from the pitch as there is a disabled area to its front. The leg room between rows is a little tight, as well as the space between the seats themselves, but the good thing is that the away fans can really make some noise from this part of the stadium.

As you probably know Old Trafford is billed as the 'Theatre Of Dreams' and is certainly one of the best grounds in the country. However, if you have never been there before, be prepared to be a little disappointed, as the reality will probably not meet your pre-conceived expectations. Getting tickets for Man Utd home games is pretty difficult even if you are a member of the club, so make sure you have tickets before you travel.

Where To Drink?

The three pubs nearest the ground (The Trafford, Sam Platts and The Bishops Blaize) generally won't let you in if you wear away colours. The best bet is probably the city centre or along one of the stops on the Metrolink. On my last couple of visits I have drunk at the Quadrant pub which had a mixture of home and away fans and a couple of handy Chinese/Chippies nearby. The pub is about a 10-15 minute walk away from Old Trafford, in the direction of the Cricket Ground (see tip for parking below for more info). Andy Syborn adds 'Away fans are okay to drink in the Bridge at Sale. It is two stops from Old Trafford on the Metro (about eight minutes journey time)'. Alternatively alcohol is normally served within the ground, although for some high profile games the Club opt not to sell any.

How To Get There & Where To Park?

From the South:
Leave the M6 at Junction 19 and follow the A556 towards Altrincham. This will lead you onto the A56 towards Manchester. Keep on the A56 for six miles and then you will come to see Sir Matt Busby Way on your left. The ground is half a mile down this road on your left, although on matchdays this road may well be closed to traffic.

From the North:
Leave the M6 at Junction 30 and take the M61 towards Bolton. At the end of the M61, join the M60. Leave the M60 at Junction 9 and follow the A5081 towards Manchester. After about two miles you will reach Sir Matt Busby Way on your right for the ground.

From The West:
Follow M56 until its end and then take the M60 (W&N) as for Trafford Centre. At Junction 7 leave M60 and take the A56 towards Stretford. Stay on the A56 for 2.1 miles then you will come to see Sir Matt Busby Way on your left. The ground is half a mile down this road on your left, although on matchdays this road may be closed to traffic. Thanks to Brian Griffiths for providing these directions.

Parking:

There are lots of small private car parks near to the ground, otherwise it is street parking. Peter Bennett suggests parking at Old Trafford Cricket Ground (cost £5). Try to arrive early (before 1pm) as if you arrive later, it takes ages leaving the car park after the game. Gareth Hawker adds; 'I parked at the Salford Quays Lowry Mall, a ten-minute walk away from the stadium, the cost of which was £3. There was virtually no traffic on leaving, and the road takes you straight onto the M601 which joins up with the M62/M6. This avoids the congestion of the traffic heading South'.

Alternatively:
Park in Altrincham town centre and take the Metrolink to the ground (20 minutes). Some pubs such as the Bricklayers Arms in Altrincham town centre, will allow parking for the afternoon, as long as you enjoy a pre-match drink (they also do good food). Kevin Dixon-Jackson adds; 'You can get the Metrolink to Old Trafford from Ladywell Halt, in Eccles, where there is also free secure parking. You can reach Eccles from the M60 (take the Carrington spur J8 A6144(M)) or M602 Motorway (leave at the first junction for Eccles, turn right, and right again at the lights, onto Eccles New Road. Secure parking is immediately on your right. You are only 200 yards away from the Drinking Capital which is Eccles town centre!'

My Tip For Parking & Getting Away After The Game:
Going along the A56, as the stadium emerges in front of you, follow the signs for Old Trafford Cricket Ground, which means that you will bear off the A56 to the right. At the end of the park on your left and before you reach the Cricket Ground, turn right into Great Stone Road. Just over the hill you will see a pub called the Quadrant, which is next door to a chip shop. There is plenty of street parking in this area, up to around 1.15-1.30pm. You are only a ten minute walk away from the ground. The Quadrant pub itself, I found okay to have a drink in. After the game, head away from Old Trafford (keeping the Quadrant pub on your left) along the side streets. You will reach the A5145 (Edge Lane). Turn right down here and you will eventually join up again with the motorway and avoid all those traffic jams on the A56. This worked brilliantly for me after an England game and I was back in Birmingham shortly after 6.45pm.

By Train/Metrolink

Probably the best way to get to the stadium is by Metrolink or train from Manchester Piccadilly mainline station, as Old Trafford has both its own railway station next to the ground and a Metrolink station which is located next to Lancashire County Cricket Club on Warwick Road, which leads up to Sir Matt Busby Way.

Chris Kilcourse adds; 'The Metrolink also has another branch line going to Eccles from Manchester Centre. There are two stops to leave the tram – Pomona and Exchange

Quay. These are on the opposite (Salford) side of the ground – probably a quieter line on Matchdays. Pomona is the closest to the ground, only a short walk away and closer than Lancashire CC. Exchange Quay is the one to use for return journeys as the trams get full and may not stop at Pomona going back'.

Amit Basu informs me; 'If using the Metrolink, away fans are better off taking the Altrincham-Bury route and getting off at Old Trafford station, by the cricket ground – just follow the crowds for the football. While the nearest stations to the ground are probably Pomona or Exchange Quays on the Eccles line, they are not that convenient for getting to or from the away end. However, when leaving, if you have a train to catch after the game, avoid Old Trafford Metrolink at all costs! The best bet is to get the train from Old Trafford station to Piccadilly – the entrance to the station is immediately outside the away end'.

Local Rivals
Manchester City, Liverpool and from a little further afield Leeds United.

Admission Prices
Please note that home section tickets are normally made only available to members of the club, which are then normally allocated by a ballot system (unless you want to buy a corporate hospitality ticket). Tickets rarely make general sale, although it does sometimes happen (especially in the early rounds of domestic and European Cup competitions), so it is worth checking. There always seems to be a number of ticket touts operating around the ground, but I dread thinking how much they would be asking for a ticket.

Home Fans:

North Stand (Lower Tier Level 1 Upper Centre):
Adults £42, Concessions £21

South Stand (Centre):
Adults £42, Concessions £21

North Stand (Lower Wings):
Adults £40, Concessions £20

South Stand (Lower Wings):
Adults £40, Concessions £20

North Stand (Lower Outer Wings):
Adults £38, Concessions £19

South Stand (Lower Outer Wings):
Adults £38, Concessions £19

North Stand (Middle Tier Level 2):
Adults £38, Concessions £19

North East and West Quadrants Stand (Level 2):
Adults £38, Concessions £19

North East and West Quadrants Stand (Level 1):
Adults £34, Concessions £17

North Stand (Top Tier Level 3):
Adults £30, Concessions £15

East/West Stand (Upper & Middle Tiers):
Adults £30, Concessions £15

East/West Stand (Lower Tier):
Adults £25, Concessions £12.50

Family Area:
Adults £31, Concessions £15.50

Away Fans:

South Stand:
Adults £38, Concessions £19

South East Corner:
Adults £34, Concessions £17

* Under 16's are admitted to all parts of the stadium for just £10. Disabled supporters are admitted free, however places need to be pre-booked with the Club.

Programme & Fanzines
Official Programme: £3.
Red Issue Fanzine £1.50.
Red News Fanzine £2.

Record Attendance
Record Attendance (For Old Trafford):
76,962 - Wolves v Grimsby, FA Cup Semi Final, March 25th, 1939.

Modern All Seated & Manchester United Attendance Record:
76,098 v Blackburn Rovers (Highest at a UK all-seated Club ground)
Premier League, March 31st, 2007.

Average Attendance
2006-2007: 75,826 (Premier League)

Stadium Tours
The club offer tours of the stadium, which are available daily (except matchdays and the day before a European game). The tour also includes a visit to the Club Museum and costs; Adults £10 & Under 16's & over 65's £7. There are family tickets available which offer a discount on these prices. To book your tour call the club on 0870-442-1994 (Option 3).

Did You Know?
That due to extensive damage to the stadium caused by German bombing during the Second World War, the Club had to play its home games for eight years at Manchester City's Maine Road ground.

Middlesbrough

Riverside Stadium

Ground Name: Riverside Stadium
Capacity: 35,100 (all seated)
Address: Middlesbrough, Cleveland, TS3 6RS
Telephone No: 0844-499-6789
Main Fax No: 01642-757-690
Ticket Office: 0844-499-1234
Ticket Office Fax: 01642-757-693
Stadium Tours: 0844-499-6789
Club Nickname: Boro
Year Ground Opened: 1995
Pitch Size: 115 x 75 yards
Home Kit Colours: All Red

Official Website:
www.mfc.co.uk

Unofficial Websites:
Fly Me To The Moon - http://middlesbrough.rivals.net/default.asp?sid=892 (Rivals Network)
SmogChat - www.smogchat.com
Southern Supporters Club - http://mss.org.uk

What's The Ground Like?

The stadium was opened in August 1995 after the Club left its former home of Ayresome Park where it had played since 1903. The new stadium has further been improved with the 'filling in' of the corners on either side of the West Stand, adding another 5,000 seats to the overall capacity. These extensions mean that the Riverside is now totally enclosed, vastly improving its overall feel. The West Stand is slightly larger than the other three sides, which makes the appearance somewhat imbalanced. Although it looks great from the outside (especially so at night, when illuminated and visible from miles around), inside it is somewhat bland. It seems to lack character, but I'm sure this will develop in time. There is an electric scoreboard at each end of the stadium, whilst outside the main entrance you will find a pair of statues dedicated to two former Boro greats, George Hardwick & Wilf Mannion. In between the statues are the old entrance gates to Ayresome Park, which is a nice link with the Club's history.

What Is It Like For Visiting Supporters?

Away supporters are housed in the South Stand at one end of the stadium, which is shared with home supporters (with the obligatory 'no-man's land in between). Up to 3,450 fans can be accommodated in this area. I was quite impressed with the facilities inside the ground and the view from the away section is excellent. One thing to point out is that there is very little in the way of pubs or eating establishments nearby, so you will need to head into the town centre for these (see recommendations below). Please also note that the whole stadium has now been made a no-smoking one; this includes the concourses as well as the seating areas. Normally a friendly day out.

Where To Drink?

Chris Taylor recommends Doctor Browns, a ten minute walk away from the ground at the bottom of Corporation Road, in the town centre. This pub serves real ale, has Sky TV and on my last visit had a good mix of home and away fans, both inside and outside of the pub. On the corner opposite the pub, is also a sandwich bar, which was doing a brisk trade in, amongst other things, trays of roast potatoes and gravy. To find this pub; If you were standing outside the stadium with the main entrance behind you, head over to your left and turn right down the road, going under a bridge. A little way down this road on your left, there is an underpass (there are usually some programme & fanzine sellers standing by its entrance). Go down through the underpass and as you emerge on the other side turn right and go down the road and through another underpass. You will emerge in a small retail park (there is a McDonalds over on your right), which you walk through unto you come to a main road. Turn right along this road and you will see the Doctor Browns pub over on your left. Otherwise, there is a bar at the back of the away stand within the ground (£2.50 per pint).

How To Get There & Where To Park?

It is quite easy to find. Just follow the A66 (signposted Teesside from the A1) past Darlington's new ground and on into Middlesbrough. Carry on up the A66, through the centre of Middlesbrough and you will pick up signs for the Riverside Stadium. Although there is no parking available directly at the stadium itself, there are a number of private parks (mostly on waste land) nearby.

Jerry Hill adds; 'I would suggest that away fans should follow the route marked "away coaches" from the A66, as this passes many private car parks along the river, all priced at £4'. Bear in mind though that if you do park at one of these car parks, then it may take 45 minutes or so after the game, before you can exit them. Otherwise, as the stadium is about one mile from the town centre you could also consider parking in a long stay car park in the town centre (about a 15-20 minute walk away from the ground).

By Train

The ground is walkable from Middlesbrough train station which is on Albert Road. Although there is a direct train service from the North West, fans travelling from other parts of the country, will most likely find themselves changing at Darlington, for Middlesbrough.

If you come out of the main entrance, turn left onto Zetland Road. Then left again into Albert Road and proceed under the railway bridge. Turn immediately right into Bridge Street East, going past the Bridge pub (not recommended for away fans) and then take the next right into Wynward Way. The stadium is down this road. If you come out of the rear station entrance, turn right onto Bridge Street East. Go straight past the Bridge pub and then take the next right into Wynward Way for the ground.

Thanks to Glenn Brunskill for providing the directions.

By Air

The nearest airport is Teesside which is located just under 13 miles away, just outside Darlington. Bus service number 20 runs between the Airport and Middlesbrough, but the service is infrequent. It may be an idea instead to head into Darlington and take a train to Middlesbrough, or to get a taxi from the airport to Middlesbrough which would cost around £17.

Local Rivals

Sunderland, Newcastle United.

Admission Prices

Like a number of other clubs a category scheme for ticket prices is in operation (Premium & Normal), whereby the most popular games cost more to watch. Normal category match prices are shown in brackets below:

Home Fans

West Stand Upper Tier:
Adults £40 (£31), Concessions £25 (£22)

West Stand Lower Tier:
Adults £35 (£26), Concessions £18 (£15)

East Stand Upper Tier:
Adults £38 (£30), Concessions £22 (£19)

East Stand Lower Tier:
Adults £35 (£27), Concessions £18 (£15)

North Stand:
Adults £31 (£24), Concessions £18 (£15)

South Stand:
Adults £31 (£24), Concessions £18 (£15)

Away Fans:

South Stand:
Adults £31 (£24), Concessions £18 (£15)

Concessions apply to Over 65's and Under 16's.

Programme & Fanzines
Official Programme: £3.
Fly Me To The Moon Fanzine: £1

Record Attendance
For The Riverside Stadium:
35,000 England v Slovakia
Euro 2004 Qualifier, June 11th, 2003.

For A Middlesbrough Game At the Riverside
34,814 v Newcastle United,
Premier League, March 5th, 2003.

For A Middlesbrough Game At Ayresome Park:
53,536 v Newcastle United,
Division One, December 27th, 1949.

Average Attendance
2006-2007: 27,729 (Premier League)

Stadium Tours
The Club conduct tours of the stadium on weekdays plus Sundays. The tours cost £5 for adults and £2 for senior citizens and children. Tours must be booked in advance on 0844-499-6789.

Did You Know?
When the Riverside Stadium opened in 1995, it was the largest new football ground to have been built in England since the 2nd World War.

Newcastle United

St James' Park

Ground Name:	St. James' Park
Capacity:	52,327 (all seated)
Address:	St. James' Park, Newcastle-upon-Tyne NE1 4ST
Main Telephone No:	0191-201-8400
Fax No:	0191-201-8600
Ticket Office:	0191-261-1571
Pitch Size:	110 x 73 yards
Club Nickname:	The Magpies or The Toon
Year Ground Opened:	1892*
Home Kit Colours:	Black & White

Official Website:
www.nufc.co.uk

Unofficial Websites:
NUFC.com - www.nufc.com
Tyne Talk - www.tyne-talk.tk (Sports Network)
Talk Of The Tyne - www.talkofthetyne.com (Rivals Network)
True Faith - www.true-faith.co.uk

■ What's The Ground Like?

The ground has largely been rebuilt in recent years and is unrecognisable from the St James' Park of old. On approaching the ground, it looks absolutely huge, as it appears to have been built on raised ground. I particularly liked St James' Park as it is totally enclosed and has a great atmosphere. With the completion of the additional tier to the Milburn & Leazes (Sir John Hall) Stands, the capacity has been increased to over 52,000. These stands have a huge lower tier, with a row of executive boxes and a smaller tier above. This development has created the largest cantilever structure in Europe and has a spectacular-looking roof, which allows natural light to penetrate through it (and hence is good for the pitch). However the ground now looks somewhat imbalanced with one half of the ground being significantly larger than the other two sides.

■ Future Ground Developments

The Club have announced plans to redevelop the Gallowgate End of the stadium. The plans, which also inclue the construction of a new conference c entre, hotel and residential apartments, would see the overall capacity of the ground increase to around 60,000. The plans are subject to local authority approval and as of yet no formal timescales as to when this might take place have been announced.

■ What Is It Like For Visiting Supporters?

Away fans are housed in the Sir John Hall Stand in the North West corner of the ground, in the very top tier of the stand . Up to 3,000 fans can be accommodated in this section for Premiership games and a larger allocation is available for cup games. Be warned though that it is a climb of 14 flights of stairs up to the away section and that you are situated quite far away from the pitch. So if you are scared of heights or have poor eyesight then this may not be for you. On the plus side you do get a wonderful view of the whole stadium, plus the Newcastle skyline and countryside in the distance. Also the legroom and height between rows are the best that I have come across and the facilities on offer are pretty good. The concourse is spacious and there are a fair selection of pies on offer including the delicious 'Football's Famous Chicken Balti Pie' plus the usual burgers and hot dogs, all served in Newcastle United branded packaging (which made me wonder if their sales were affected when playing Sunderland!). There are also televisions on the concourse, showing live the game being played, with separate refreshment areas which serve alcohol, again in Newcastle United branded plastic glasses. Beware that most games are sold out in advance and trying to get tickets can be extremely difficult. So don't travel unless you have one.

Jeremy Gold, a visiting Leyton Orient supporter adds; 'The visitors section is on level seven at the top of the stand. The view is a long way from the pitch, although it is still good. If you suffer from vertigo, don't go! The stewarding at the game I went to was fairly strict. However people were being warned against gesturing before they were thrown out. Unfortunately some people didn't take the hint and about five or six made the long trip back down the fourteen flights of stairs!'

The atmosphere in St James' Park can be electric and it is certainly one of the best footballing stadiums in the country. I personally found the Geordies friendly and helpful and a trip to Newcastle can be one of the better away trips in the Premier League.

■ Where To Drink?

The ground is one of the few in the country that is literally right in the centre of the city. You are only a few minutes walk from the main shopping areas of Newcastle. There are plenty of bars to choose from in the city centre, but most away fans tend to favour the pubs opposite and around Newcastle Railway Station. A Head Of Steam, The Lounge and O'Neills are all recommended, but some of these bars will only admit fans if colours are covered and none of them admitted children. Alternatively there is Idols which has strippers and is popular with both home and away fans. Alcohol is also served within the ground.

Jackie Milburn statue.

■ How To Get There & Where To Park?

At the end of the A1(M) continue on the A1 and then the A184 towards Newcastle. Continue along this road, bearing left onto the A189. Continue over the River Tyne on the Redheugh Bridge, from which the ground can be clearly seen. Carry on straight up the dual carriageway (St James Boulevard). This leads directly to the Gallowgate end of the ground. As the ground is so central there are a number of pay and display car parks in the vicinity.

Jason Adderley, a visiting West Brom fan, adds; 'An easier way into the City is to stay on the A1 until the exit for Westerhope. Leave the A1 go straight over two roundabouts and then follow the signs for the Royal Victoria Infirmary (Queen Victoria Road) - parking here is in a multi storey and allows a reasonably quick getaway after the game'.

Peter Luckett informs me; 'The traffic in the city centre can be a nightmare and so is parking. My recommendation for fans travelling from the South is to head for Heworth, which is near Gateshead adjacent to the A184. It has a Metro Station and a long term car park where you can leave your car for a cost of £1.10. You can then catch the metro direct to the stadium at a cost of £2.40 return.

■ By Train

Newcastle Central Railway Station is half a mile from the ground and takes 10-15 minutes to walk.

Thanks to Ian Kavanagh for providing these directions; 'Come out of the station, across the two zebra crossings and head right onto Grainger Street. Follow this road up to the second set of traffic lights (at Pizza Hut). This will see you at the top of the Bigg Market - Drinker's Paradise! You should have met a throng of black and white shirts by now, but failing that, bear left onto Newgate Street and follow the road all the way around to the roundabout with Gallowgate. Following this road all the way round will lead you straight to St James' Park and the away fans' section'.

Andrew Saffrey adds; 'If you're feeling lazy, you can get buses 36, 36B, 71, 87 or 88 from Berwick Street (across the road from station), up to the ground. The fare should be about 50p'. Whilst Claire Stewart informs me; 'You can also get the metro from inside the train station up to the ground, which has its own "St. James' Park" stop. Go on the metro from the railway station to Monument Metro Station where you need to change trains to go to St James' Park. You can also walk up to the ground from Monument Station. It's pretty easy to find, and if you do happen to get lost, then just follow the black and white crowd!

■ By Air

Newcastle Airport is located seven miles away from the City Centre. The easiest way to get into Newcastle is to go by the Metro transit system. The airport has its own Metro station which is situated next to the passenger terminal. There are frequent departures to the City Centre and the journey time is 23 minutes. This costs £2 for a single ticket or £3 return (£3.80 at peak periods). You can also purchase a 'day saver' ticket for £3.50 which allows you unlimited travel on the Metro System for one day. Change at Monument Metro Station for a Metro to St James Park Station.

■ Local Rivals
Sunderland, Middlesbrough.

■ Admission Prices
Due to the large number of season ticket holders, there are only around 2,500 tickets available to home fans for each game (more if the away team do not take up their full allocation). These tickets are normally put on sale, at 9am on the Monday, two weeks before a particular home game (but check out the official website for full details). There are also a number of 'Executive Seats' available for each game, but obviously they are priced accordingly.

Home Fans:

Milburn Stand: (Platinum Club):
Adults £53, Senior Citizens £44,
No further concessions.

Milburn Stand: (Bar 1892):
Adults £51 (Row A £44),
Senior Citizens £44 (Row A £38),
No further concessions.

Milburn Stand: (Sovereign Club):
Adults £49, Senior Citizens £42,
No further concessions.

Milburn Stand: (Black & White Club):
Adults £49, Senior Citizens £42,
No further concessions.

Milburn Stand (Level 7):
Adults £39 (Row F £33),
Senior Citizens £32 (Row F £26),
Juniors £20 (Row F £17).
Milburn Stand (Paddock):
Adults £38, Senior Citizens £32, Juniors £19.

East Stand & Paddock:
Adults £38, Senior Citizens £32, Juniors £19.

Sir John Hall Stand (Sports Bar):
Adults £47, Senior Citizens £40,
No further concessions.

Sir John Hall Stand (including corners):
Adults £32, Senior Citizens £26, Juniors £17.

Sir John Hall Stand (Level 7):
Adults £28 (Row F £23),
Senior Citizens £24 (Row F £21),
Juniors £16 (Row F £14).

Newcastle Brown Stand (Gallowgate End):
Adults £32, Senior Citizens £26, Juniors £17.

Family Enclosure:
Adults £22, Senior Citizens £19, Juniors £7.

Away Fans:

Sir John Hall Stand:
Adults: £32, Senior Citizens £26, Juniors £17.

■ Programme & Fanzines
Official Programme: £2.50.
The Mag Fanzine: £2.
True Faith Fanzine: £1.50.

■ Record Attendance
68,386 v Chelsea,
Division One, September 3rd, 1930.

Modern All Seated Attendance Record:
52,327 v Manchester United
Premier League, August 28th, 2005.

■ Average Attendance
2006-2007: 50,686 (Premier League)

■ Stadium Tours
The Club offer daily tours of the ground on non-matchdays at 11am & 1.30pm. The cost of the tour is Adults £10, Concessions £7, or a family ticket (2 adults + 3 children) costs £34. Tours must be pre-booked by calling 0870-850-8074. As part of the tour a visit to the Club Museum is also included.

■ Did You Know?
The Gallowgate End gets its name from the former location of the town gallows where in times gone by, public executions took place.

* Although the Club didn't move in until 1892, the land had been used for football since 1880.

Portsmouth

Fratton Park

Ground Name: Fratton Park
Capacity: 20,288 (all seated)
Address: Frogmore Road, Portsmouth, PO4 8RA
Main Telephone No: 02392-731204
Main Fax No: 02392-734129
Ticket Office: 0871-230-1898
Ticket Office Fax: 0871-230-1899
Team Nickname: Pompey
Year Ground Opened: 1898
Pitch Size: 115 x 73 yards
Home Kit Colours: Blue, White & Red

Official Website:
www.pompeyfc.co.uk

Unofficial Websites:
Pompey Till I Die - www.pompeytillidie.com
Pompey Online - www.pompeyonline.com

What's The Ground Like?

A few seasons back a new covered home end was completed, bringing a vast improvement on the previous open terrace. It is a good sized single-tiered stand and is called the Fratton End and is the tallest stand at the ground. The opposite end, the Inter-cash Milton End is uncovered and open to the elements. It is all seated and this end is given to away fans. There is a small moat in front of this area. Both side stands are two-tiered and originally had terracing at the front, which has now been replaced with seating. The South Stand dates back to 1925, and is starting to show its age. However, it still has some character with an old fashioned-looking media gantry perched on its roof and raised team dugouts at its front. Opposite the North Stand looks somewhat plain and functional. Both the North & South Stands are two-tiered and have a number of supporting pillars. The ground is completed by a superb-looking set of tall floodlights that were first used in 1962.

If you get the chance to wander around the outside of the ground beforehand then make sure to go down to the home end to look at the mock-Tudor facade in Frogmore Road that is now partly used as a club shop, but still overlooks the entrance to the Fratton End.

Future Ground Developments

The Club have recently announced ambitious plans to move to a new state-of-the-art stadium, to be built at the city's dockyard. The £600m development will see the construction of a spectacular-looking 36,000-capacity all-seated stadium on the waterfront, plus a number of residential apartments and retail units. The joint venture between the Club and Sellar Property Group, will also see the redevelopment of Fratton Park. The new stadium is being designed by Swiss based architects Herzog & DeMeuron, who are responsible for the 2008 Olympic Stadium in Beijing. Planning permission has yet to be granted for the scheme, but if things go to plan, then Pompey could be playing at their new stadium in 2010. In the meantime the Club have applied for planning permission to cover the Milton Road End with a temporary roof. This would be good news for away fans and could be in place sometime during the 2007/08 season.

What Is It Like For Visiting Supporters?

With the Inter-cash Milton End being uncovered and being one of those former terraces that have been converted to all seating, it is not one of the better stands in which to view a game. The facilities are not particularly great and the leg room tight. The sight of portaloos as you go through the turnstiles does little to raise enthusiasm and it has to be said that it is probably the worst away stand in the Premiership. However, once you put all that to one side (if you can) then at least Fratton Park is a proper-looking football ground, with a great atmosphere (which is aided by a drummer and bell ringer in the home end). So sit back and enjoy it as such grounds now are becoming few and far between with the advent of new stadia being built.

The Inter-cash Milton End can accommodate just over 3,000 supporters but this is divided between home and away support, with the normal allocation for away supporters being around 2,000. On my last visit the end was split between home and away fans, but praise to the home support who got behind their team but in a non-intimidatory way towards the away fans. Fans were literally separated by a netted area only three seats wide, but there were no problems whatsoever. The delicious 'Football's Famous Chicken Balti Pie' (£2.20) is available inside the ground. Please note that the Club no longer allow smoking in the seated areas of the ground.

Chris Saunders, a visiting Middlesbrough fan, adds; 'In terms of facilities the ground is light years away from Premiership standard, but the atmosphere is electric with the legendary 'Play Up Pompey' echoing around the ground. The Portsmouth fans are a great bunch and made me most welcome. If you are feeling hungry then there is a McDonalds and KFC across the road from the ground. As mentioned the Inter-cash Stand doesn't have a roof, so if you are going, take a coat just in case it rains and some sunglasses if it is sunny, and if it's really sunny some sunblock!'

■ Where To Drink?

On my last visit I went to the Good Companion pub, which is on the main A2030 about a five minute walk away from the ground. It is a large pub serving Gale real ales and had a good mix of home and away support. I also noticed that it was doing a brisk business in food. Martin Hewitt recommends the Harvester, but advises away fans to avoid the Milton Arms, Shepherds Crook and the Newcome Arms, whilst Ian Pratt suggests the Brewers Arms which is 'always popular with away fans'.

Graham Fewster an exiled Pompey fan Down Under, adds; 'a pub I would recommend is the Connaught Arms. Popular with home and away fans, they serve a good selection of draught beers as well as some great pasties. The pub is located at the junction of Penhale and Guildford Road, which is roughly 200 yards away from Fratton Road but the walk is somewhat longer. But it is worth it, take it from me!'.

Otherwise drink in Portsmouth city centre or down at Southsea before the game. Remember Portsmouth is still a major naval port and hence some of the pubs can get quite rowdy at weekends.

■ How To Get There & Where To Park?

Go along the M27 (ignoring the M275 turn off for Portsmouth town centre) and continue on to the A27. At the junction with the A2030 turn right towards Southsea/Fratton and just continue straight along the A2030 and eventually you will see the ground in front of you, just slightly to your left. There is a large car park behind the TY Europe Stand, but this is for home supporters only. So it is mostly street parking for away fans. This is best found on the right hand side of the A2030 before you reach the Good Companion pub.

■ By Train

The nearest local train station is Fratton, which is a ten-minute walk away. Portsmouth train station is at least a 25-minute walk away.

On arrival at Fratton by train you pass the ground on the left. Fratton station has a footbridge as the only way out. At the top of the stairs from the platform turn left onto the footbridge (from which you can see the floodlights of Fratton Park) and exit into Goldsmith Avenue. (Note that if the gate on the footbridge is closed you need to turn right on the footbridge and exit via Platform 1, turn left as you exit the station, walk 30 metres and go back over the footbridge to Goldsmith Avenue.) Turn left along Goldsmith Avenue and walk about half a mile passing straight around a small roundabout (by the Pompey Centre). Then turn left into Frogmore Road and the entrance to the Ty and South stands is 100m ahead. For the Milton End stay on Goldsmith Avenue for another 100m and turn left into Apsley Road. The entrances to the Milton End are 100m ahead.

Thanks to Peter Coulthard for providing the directions.

■ Local Rivals

Southampton.

■ Admission Prices

Home Fans:

South Stand (Upper Centre):
Adults £37, Over-60s £28, Under-16s £23

South Stand (Upper Wings):
Adults £35, Over-60s £26, Under-16s £22

South Stand (Lower Family Enclosure):
Adults £29, Over-60s £20, Under-16s £15

South Stand (Lower Milton Enclosure):
Adults £29, Over-60s £22, Under-16s £15

North Stand (Upper Centre):
Adults £37, Over-60s £28, Under-16s £23

North Stand (Upper Wings):
Adults £35, Over-60s £26, Under-16s £22

North Stand (Lower Tier):
Adults £35, Over-60s £26, Under-16s £22

Fratton End (West Stand):
Adults £35, Over-60s £26, Under-16s £22

Milton End:
Adults £28, Over-60s £20, Under-16s £15

Away Fans:

Milton End:
Adults £28, Over-60s £20, Under-16s £15

Programme & Fanzine
Official Programme £3
True Blue Fanzine £1.50
Park Life Fanzine £1.50

Record Attendance
51,385 v Derby County
FA Cup 6th Round, February 26th, 1949.

Modern All-Seated Attendance Record:
20,240 v Liverpool, May 7th, 2006.
Premier League, October 15th, 2005.

Average Attendance
2006-2007: 19,862 (Premier League)

Other Places Of Interest
Southsea adjoining Portsmouth houses the naval base and includes historic ships such as HMS Victory. You can get a short boat trip around the harbour showing which warships are in dock. Southsea itself is quite pleasant with a small beach and funfair. In fact, when I went to the game I met a strange lady who travelled down to Portsmouth for each game by herself from Wolverhampton! When asked why, she replied that she had been taken to Southsea as a child and therefore liked to visit it before each game. So there you go; it wasn't the football that was the attraction!

Simon Eddy adds; 'there is a new development called the Gunwharf Quays, which has opened adjacent to the historic ships' dockyard. There are a number of bars, restaurants, plus a bowling alley, cinema and shopping factory outlet. For more details visit their website at www.gunwharf-quays.com'. The quays incorporate the spectacular Spinnaker Tower, which is well worth a visit for some stunning views from over 300 feet up. Anyone intending to visit the City Centre, Gunwharf Quays or the Old Portsmouth area before the game would be better off entering the city on the M275 rather than the A2030.

Did You Know?
That the first football league match to be played under floodlights took place at Fratton Park on 22 February 1956, when Portsmouth played Newcastle in a Division One fixture.

Reading

Madejski Stadium

Ground Name: Madejski Stadium
Capacity: 24,200 (all seated)
Address: Bennett Road, Reading, RG2 0FL
Main Telephone No: 0118-968-1100
Fax No: 0118-968-1101
Ticket Office: 0870-999-1871
Ticket Office Fax: 0870-999-1001
Team Nickname: The Royals
Pitch Size: 102 x 70 metres
Year Ground Opened: 1998
Home Kit Colours: Royal Blue & White

Official Websites:
www.readingfc.co.uk
www.backtheboys.com

Unofficial Websites:
Hob Nob Anyone? - www.royals.cx
Off At Eleven - www.offateleven.com (Rivals Network)
Vital Reading - www.reading.vitalfootball.co.uk/index.asp (Vital Football Network)

What's The Ground Like?

This stadium opened in 1998 is light years away from the old Elm Park, the Club's former home for over a century. It is purpose built on the very outskirts of Reading, close to the M4, and the complex even boasts a hotel attached to the back of the West Stand. So if you have plenty of money and don't fancy the journey home, or if miraculously you have pulled inside the ground....

The stadium is of a fair size and is totally enclosed, with all four corners being occupied. Three sides are single-tiered, whilst on one side the West Stand is two-tiered, including a row of executive boxes. The ground has been designed with the supporter in mind as the supporters are very close to the pitch and the acoustics are good. The stadium also has a video screen in the South East corner.

The stadium, named after Reading's multi-millionaire chairman, is shared with London Irish Rugby Club and was recently voted as having the best facilities for disabled supporters in the League. Often at football matches you can still make out the white lines used for the previous rugby match.

Future Ground Developments

The Club have received planning permission to increase the capacity of the stadium to 38,000. This would involve further extending three sides of the stadium (the West Stand would remain as it is) and replacing the roof. Work will commence in the Summer of 2008 and will take a couple of years to complete.

What Is It Like For Visiting Supporters?

Away fans are located in one end of the stadium, in the Fosters Lager South Stand, where up to 4,300 can be accommodated (although the normal allocation is 2,100). The facilities in this stand are good with plenty of leg room and the views of the pitch are superb, as there is good height between rows. Away fans can really make some noise in this stand, so make the most of it. Entrance to the stadium is by ticket only and if tickets are still available for away supporters then they can purchase them on the day at the South Stand ticket office located between gates 9 & 10. You actually get into the stadium by not actually handing your ticket to a turnstile operator, but instead inserting it into a ticket reader which scans the bar code on the ticket. This always confuses visiting fans. Near to the stadium are outlets of McDonalds, KFC & Pizza Hut.

I first visited this stadium shortly after it opened and again recently. When I first went in 1998 I truly believed that it was a fantastic stadium. Subsequently after going back and with a number of other new stadiums being built during that time, the Madejski seems just like another nice functional ground. Considering that as it also lacks character and that essential 'wow' factor and coupled with the fact that there are few facilities around the stadium such as pubs for away fans, then there is not a lot to 'write home about'. Add on that you can experience long delays in trying to leave the official car parks and that the security staff outside the entrance to the stadium seemed to view someone in possession of a camera as almost a common criminal, then all in all the Madejski, in my opinion, is not one of the better days out in the League.

Where To Eat & Drink?

Apart from a Harvester on the road towards Reading, there are no pubs as such near to the ground. I however did locate a Holiday Inn which was around a 15-minute walk away. The hotel had a small bar inside it, but then attached had a larger Irish themed separate bar area, called Callaghans. This bar had Sky Television, but as you would expect was very crowded with away fans and served drinks at what I can only term as 'hotel prices'. Across the road from the hotel is a Harry Ramsden's fish & chip shop (take-away only). To find this hotel, leave the M4 at Junction 11 and take the A33 towards Reading, turn right at the first roundabout into Imperial Way. Go down this road and you will come to the hotel on your left. There is also street parking to be found in this area.

Alcohol is available inside the stadium, where Courage Bitter & Fosters Lager (£2.80 per pint) are on offer, plus the delicious 'Football's Famous Chicken Balti Pie', steak and kidney pies and pasties (all at £2.40) . James Days adds; 'I would recommend heading to Friar Street in the town centre where there are about 10-15 different bars and pubs to choose from, all pretty friendly' However, I have been informed that not many of these town centre pubs allow fans in wearing colours. Next to the ground on a Retail Park are the following food outlets; McDonalds, KFC & Pizza Hut. Otherwise it may be an idea, especially if you are making the journey by train, to drink in the centre of Reading before the game.

Dave McKerchar adds; 'The Three Guineas on the station approach has been designated as an away fans pub. It offers a range of eight real ales and is listed in the CAMRA good beer guide. It has a big screen Sky TV and it also does food'.

How To Get There & Where To Park?

If you are travelling along the M4 from the west you can see the stadium on your left. Leave the M4 at Junction 11, bear left on to the A33 relief road which leads you directly to the stadium. The Madejski Complex is well signposted from Junction 11.

Kevin Gray informs me; 'Please note that as a recent visitor to Reading it is worth advising away fans that getting off the M4 at Junction 11 westbound can be a bit of a pain. On match days a long tail back can start on the motorway as far as one mile away from this junction. This should be approached with caution and patience. As kick-off approaches it can take 40 minutes to complete the journey from the back of the Junction 11 queue to the designated parking sites. So allow extra time for your journey'.

Car Parking

There is a car park at the ground and at the nearby speedway/greyhound track, both of which cost £7. They hold about 2,500 cars between them. However if you do not arrive in good time before the game you may find that they are already full.

Mark Sugar adds; 'Don't park in the nearby Business Park, unless there is an individual unit charging for matchday parking. You may find yourself with a parking ticket if you do, or even clamped. The Club, in the interests of crowd safety, now prevent traffic from leaving the car parks until ten minutes after the final whistle'.

If you arrive early enough then there is street parking to be had along Imperial Way. To find this hotel, leave the M4 at Junction 11 and take the A33 towards Reading. After you come off M4 and head towards the stadium on the A33, turn right at the first roundabout into Imperial Way. There is also some parking at the Old Depot by the Courage Brewery on the A33/Imperial Way roundabout at a cost of £7 per car.

Alternatively the Club operate a 'Park & Ride' scheme at Foster Wheeler at Shinfield Park. This costs for the return shuttle bus; Adults £3, Children £1.50. From Junction 11 of the M4, take the B3270 towards Earley and then follow the signs to 'Football Car Park C'. The car park opens at 1pm for Saturday afternoon games with the first bus departing at 1:30pm.

By Train

Get the train to Reading station and then the No 79 'Football Special' bus. The buses leave just down from the station, commencing at 1pm for Saturday afternoon games. Once you come out of the main station entrance turn right and they are about 200 yards down the road on the opposite side - there is normally one waiting. Dave Stuttard, a visiting Leicester City fan informs me; 'I would recommend getting in the bus queue no later than 45 mins before kick off as all football traffic goes down the same dual carriageway to the stadium'. The fare is £3 return for adults and £1.50 for children and normally takes about fifteen minutes to get to the ground.

Paul Willems, a visiting Bristol City supporter adds; 'The bus from the station is good, provided that away fans do not cause any trouble. If you do then the buses (quite rightly, editor) refuse to pick you up after the game. I have bitter experience of this, when the slowest police escort in history by Thames Valley Police got me back to the station at 7.30 pm!'

Nicholas Small provides the following walking directions from the railway station to the ground:'I would estimate that the ground is about three miles away from Reading Station, and that unless you walk quite quickly, the journey could take over an hour: Leaving the station, head straight up the road in front of you, crossing over Friar Street onto Queen Victoria Street and heading towards the town centre. Upon reaching Broad Street, you will find yourself opposite the John Lewis store. Cross and head down a narrow passageway (Chain Street) which runs down the right hand side of John Lewis. Soon, you reach a churchyard, which you can cross, bearing right, to the corner of Gun Street and Bridge Street. Cross to the other side of Bridge Street and continue down, turning right into Fobney Street. At the end here, you will soon encounter a couple of blue footpath/cyclepath signs, which point the way to the Madejski Stadium. These will lead you down the left hand footpath alongside the busy A329, which becomes the A33 after about 1200 yards. Keep following this road and eventually you will come to a roundabout. Take the road ahead and continue walking along the roadside. You will briefly walk along a dirt track by the roadside as the A33 crosses a waterway, before walking down the bank to the towpath. The towpath now continues straight ahead towards the stadium, still following the blue cycle path signs. You can't miss it from here, but it is still at least a further 15 minutes walk away'.

Local Rivals
Swindon Town, Oxford United, Wycombe Wanderers.

Admission Prices
The Club operate a match category policy (Platinum, Gold & Silver) whereby the more popular matches cost more to watch. The lowest band 'Silver' prices are shown below in brackets.

Upper West Stand*
Adults £41 (£34),
Over 65's & Under 21's £33 (£24),
Under 16's £26 (£17),
Under 12's £21 (£11)

All other areas of the stadium*
Adults £39 (£32),
Over 65's & Under 21's £31 (£22),
Under 16's £25 (£16),
Under 12's £20 (£10)

* Reading Club Members qualify for a discount on the above prices (can be up to £4 per ticket).

Programme
Official Matchday programme - £3.

Record Attendance
At The Madejski Stadium:
24,122 v Aston Villa
Premier League, February 10th, 2007.

At Elm Park:
33,042 v Brentford,
FA Cup 5th Round, February 19th, 1927.

Average Attendance
2006-2007: 23,856 (Championship)

Did You Know?
That the stadium was built on the site of an old rubbish tip. A number of metallic vents can be seen in the vicinity of the stadium. They are there to prevent the build-up of methane gas coming from the buried rubbish underground.

Sunderland

Stadium of Light

Ground Name: Stadium Of Light
Capacity: 49,000 (all seated)
Address: Stadium Of Light, Sunderland, SR5 1SU
Main Telephone Number: 0191-551-5000
Main Fax No: 0191-551-5123
Ticket Office: 0845-671-1973
Ticket Office Fax No: 0191-551-5150
Stadium Tours: 0191-551-5055
Team Nickname: The Black Cats
Pitch Size: 105 x 68 metres
Year Ground Opened: 1997
Home Kit Colours: Red & White

Official Website:
www.safc.com

Unofficial Websites:
Ready To Go - www.readytogo.net
Supporters Club (Heart Of England Branch) - http://safcsahoe.co.uk
RedandWhiteBarmy - http://sunderland.rivals.net (Rivals Network)
One Sunderland - www.onesunderland.com
SAFC Chat Banter (Sport Network) - www.SAFCbanter.co.uk

What's The Ground Like?

The stadium was opened in 1997, after the Club left their former home of Roker Park where they had played for 99 years. The stadium is totally enclosed and is truly magnificent. I would say that it is one of the best stadiums in England. It is composed of two three-tiered stands (at one end and one side of the pitch), whilst the others are two-tiered. Unfortunately, sitting at the back of the highest tiers means a limited view of the majority of the stadium, hence the feeling of being a bit cut off. The West Stand also has a row of executive boxes (which you can sit outside if you wish). There is a large electronic scoreboard at either end. You really have to experience not only the stadium but also the occasion that is Sunderland to believe it. Away fans are housed at one end of the stadium, in the two-tiered Metro FM (South) Stand.

Currently, with half the stadium being larger than the other, it looks a little imbalanced from the away end. However, looking at the larger stands, one feels that if the Club added a tier to the remaining sides an even more remarkable stadium would emerge.

Outside the stadium there are some reminders of the former Monkwearmouth Colliery, on the site of which the stadium was built. Behind the West Stand there is a large red wheel, an emblem of the lifts that used to take the miners down to the mines. Also outside one corner of the stadium is a large miners lamp. If you feel a little mischievous, then ask the nearest Sunderland fan whether it is a Geordie Lamp. Don't worry, you won't get any physical abuse, just a long lecture that the lamp is in fact a Davy lamp!

The stadium was voted as the 'Best Away Ground' in the Football League Awards in 2007.

Future Ground Developments

Kevin Davis informs me; 'The club have secured planning permission to add another 7,200 to the Metro FM (South) Stand, which would take the capacity to 55,000. The club have not yet confirmed when (if ever) they will go ahead with this. If the club then proceed after this to add another tier to the McEwans Stand the final capacity would be around 64,000'.

What Is It Like For Visiting Supporters?

If you can only get to one stadium this season, then go to this one. I found the stadium almost overwhelming, the PA system deafening (especially when the classical piece 'Dance Of The Knights' from Prokofiev's 'Romeo & Juliet' is played before the players come on to the pitch at the start of the game and U2's 'Elevation', as the teams come out of the tunnel) and the Sunderland supporters exceptionally friendly (I was even given a Sunderland shirt by one supporter!). But bear in mind you are not allowed to smoke or swear inside the stadium. If you persist with either you may find yourself being ejected from the ground! Away fans are located in the South Stand at one end of the stadium, where around 3,000 fans can be housed. The facilities and views of the playing action from this stand are excellent. On the food front, the delicious 'Football's Famous Chicken Balti Pie' (£2.10) is available inside the stadium, along with pasties (£2.10), sausage rolls (£1.60), cheese burgers (£2.60), chicken burgers (£2.70) and hot dogs (£2.50). Alcohol is also available at £2.60.

Where To Drink?

There are bars inside the ground, however they get really crowded. I would recommend the William Jameson (Wetherspoons pub) in the centre of town for a drink before or after the game, as it has a great atmosphere. Graham Dutton recommends the new Yates's bar opposite Wetherspoons. Whilst Maurice Perry informs me; 'Try Idols on High Street West, in the city centre, which has good beer and scantily clad barmaids and dancers. The beer is not bad too! Away fans are welcome'. Whilst Jason Adderley a visiting West Brom fan adds; ''The Albion pub, on Victor Street, off Roker Avenue, is a five minute walk from the ground, with some parking nearby. I've used this pub the last three times I've visited Sunderland with West Brom. Always friendly and the landlord even puts on complimentary snacks after the game. Otherwise there is a chippy a couple of doors away. An all round top boozer'. Stephen Lundell informs me; There are also another couple of bars worth mentioning, both a five minute walk away form the stadium, on the road approaching the Wearmouth bridge on the North (Stadium Side) of the river. There are two social clubs - The Sunderland Companions club, and the Democratic Club, which both get very busy, and will offer a warm welcome to away supporters, and serve cheap beer'.

If you have a bit of time of your hands, then you may like to try the Harbour View on the sea front, which is around a 15-20 minute walk away. Simply go along Roker Avenue (opposite the main entrance to the stadium) until you reach the seafront. Turn left along the front and you will see the pub up on the left. The pub which has previously been listed in the CAMRA Good Beer Guide, serves good beer, reasonably priced food (with its own matchday menu) and has a large screen television. As the name of the pub suggests you get some good views along the coast from its location.

How To Get There & Where To Park?

Exit the A1 at Junction 62, the Durham/Sunderland exit and take the A690 towards Sunderland. After about eight miles, you will reach a roundabout, at which turn left onto the A19, signposted for the Tyne Tunnel. Stay in the left hand lane and take the second slip road towards Sunderland (signposted Stadium Of Light, A1231 Sunderland). This takes you onto a bridge crossing over the River Wear. Turn right onto the A1231 following the signs for Sunderland. Go straight over four roundabouts into Sunderland.

Then go through two sets of traffic lights (keeping in the left hand lane at the second set, going straight on towards Roker rather than the city centre) and you will see the Stadium car park on your right, about a mile after the traffic lights. However there is only limited parking at the ground, so alternatively, you can park in the city centre and walk to the ground (about 10-15 minutes). The traffic for a couple of miles around the ground was solid when I went so allow plenty of time for your journey.

There is also a 'Park & Ride' scheme in operation on matchdays, free for both home and away supporters. This is situated at Sunderland Enterprise Park, which is well signposted just off the A1231. Buses run every five minutes, for 90 minutes before kick off and continue after the game until everyone has gone.

By Train/Metro

Chris Rutter informs me; "Sunderland train station in the city centre is walkable from the stadium (around 15 minutes). From the train station, exit between W.H.Smith and the bakery. Turn left and walk down "High St West" and then turn left again and walk up Fawcett St to the Wear Bridge. From here you can see the stadium as it is on raised ground. Simply cross the bridge, and turn left into Millennium Way, opposite the Wheatsheaf pub (home fans only). The away turnstiles are located on the side of the ground which is straight ahead".

Ashley Smith adds; "The Metro stations called the 'Stadium of Light' and 'St. Peters' both serve the stadium. The metro provides regular and rapid transport from both Newcastle and the South of Sunderland. Both stations are only a few minutes walk from the stadium, although away supporters should alight at St Peters Station as that is closer to their entrance. This provides an alternative to the regular rail services. Please note though that after the game the Stadium of Light metro station only operates Northbound (i.e. towards Newcastle) and St Peters metro station only operates Southbound (i.e. towards Sunderland centre).

By Air

The nearest airport is Newcastle which is located 24 miles away. However the journey is pretty straightforward as both the Stadium Of Light and Newcastle Airport are both served by the Metro transit system. There are frequent departures to Sunderland and the journey time is just under an hour.

Sunderland

■ Local Rivals
Newcastle United, Middlesbrough.

■ Admission Prices
At the time of going to press the matchday prices for the 2007/08 season had yet to be announced. Last season's prices are shown below.

Sunderland operate a two category system of ticket pricing (A & B) whereby the most popular matches will cost more to watch than the least popular ones. Category (B) ticket prices are shown in brackets.

All Areas Of The Stadium:
Adults - £30 (£20)
Concessions - £25 (£20)
Juniors - £10 (£8)

■ Programme & Fanzines
Red & White Review Official Programme £3
A Love Supreme Fanzine £2
Sex & Chocolate Fanzine £1.50
The Wearside Roar Fanzine (TWR) £2

■ Record Attendance
At The Stadium Of Light:
48,353 v Liverpool,
Premier League, April 13th, 2002.

At Roker Park;
75,118 v Derby County,
FA Cup 6th Round Replay, March 8th, 1933.

■ Average Attendance
2006-2007: 29,246 (Championship)

■ Did You Know?
That the Stadium is built on the site of the former Monkwearmouth Colliery. At the top of the former colliery lift a sign read 'Into the Light'. The stadium name was chosen to reflect the mining heritage of the area.

Tottenham Hotspur

White Hart Lane

Ground Name: White Hart Lane
Capacity: 36,214 (all seated)
Address: Bill Nicholson Way, 748 High Rd, Tottenham, London, N17 0AP
Main Telephone No: 0870-420-5000
Main Fax No: 020-8365-5005
Ticket Office: 0870-420-5000
Ticket Office Fax: 0870-420-5001
Team Nickname: Spurs
Pitch Size: 110 x 73 yards
Home Kit Colours: White & Navy Blue

Official Website:
www.tottenhamhotspur.com

Unofficial Websites:
The Spur - www.thequake.com/thespur.html
Northern Spurs - www.northernspurs.co.uk
Top Spurs - www.topspurs.com
The Spurs Web - www.thespursweb.com (Rivals Network)
My Eyes Have Seen The Glory - www.mehstg.com
Unofficial Spurs - www.web-teams.co.uk/Home.asp?team=tottenhamhotspurfc

■ What's The Ground Like?

I have always been a great fan of White Hart Lane, ever since my first visit way back in 1987. It has always been one of my favourite grounds in London to visit.
In recent years the ground has virtually been rebuilt, making it one of the best in the country. It is totally enclosed which really adds to the overall look of the ground and can make for a great atmosphere.
Both ends have huge 'Jumbotron' video screens, built into the roof, which are a unique feature. All the stands are two-tiered with a row of executive boxes/concourse and are of roughly the same height giving the ground a well-balanced look. Only the East Stand on one side has a couple of large supporting pillars, otherwise there are no obstructions to your view. A TV gantry is also suspended from beneath the roof of this stand, whilst on top a gold coloured Cockerel sits proudly. Another unusual feature of the stadium is the Police Control Box suspended underneath the roof in the South West corner, looking like some kind of UFO!

■ Future Ground Developments

Steve Edwards informs me; 'Haringey Council have now approved plans for the redevelopment of the East Stand at White Hart Lane. When completed this will increase the capacity of White Hart Lane to 50,000. However, the Club will not go ahead with the redevelopment until the Government improve transport links around the stadium. The Club have even mooted that if the transport situation is not adequately resolved, they would leave the Lane and possibly move to the new Wembley Stadium or the future London Olympic Stadium'.

■ What Is It Like For Visiting Supporters?

Away fans are housed in one corner of the ground in between the South & West Stands, where up to 2,900 supporters (if demand requires it) can be accommodated, in the lower and upper tiers. If you have a ticket for the upper tier then prepare yourself for quite a climb to reach the away area. You are, however, rewarded with a great view of the action from this section and the legroom is ample. The facilities in this newish stand are above average. On the down side, there is little space between the away and home fans. As you would expect, there is plenty of banter between the two, but the stewards tend to take a tougher line on the away support. On my last visit a number of fans were ejected from the ground, plus there were repeated warnings to away fans to remain seated. One strange aspect of sitting in the upper tier is having the Police Control Box directly above you, where a number of uniformed faces can be seen peering down on the away fans. The delicious 'Football's Famous Chicken Balti Pie' (£2.20) is available inside the ground. I have always quite enjoyed my trips to Tottenham. White Hart Lane is excellent and the atmosphere generally good, however it is wise to exercise caution around the ground and you may consider keeping colours covered.

■ Where To Drink?

Dave Thomas, a visiting Birmingham City fan informs me; 'We found a nice little boozer up a side road, called the Antwerp. Popular with both home and away fans, it is highly recommended. To find it, take a right turn when you come out of White Hart Lane Station, and then right onto the main High Road. You pass the ground on your left and then go right into Church Road. Walk down the road under a bridge and the pub is on the right opposite Bruce Castle Park. There are bouncers on the door but there's no problem getting in. Richard Crouch recommends The Park right by Northumberland Park station. This is a small comfortable pub about ten minutes walk along Park Lane from the away end. Also the Bricklayers Arms (no away colours) is recommended. Carsie, a Spurs fan from Belfast adds; 'I would recommend the Three Compasses which is situated in Queen Street (behind Middlesex University), which is a five-minute walk from White Hart Lane Station'.

There is also a Wetherspoons outlet called the Gilpins Bell, which is a ten-minute walk away from the stadium. A fair-sized pub, it also has a good sized beer garden, which on my last visit on a hot day in August was crammed with fans, including some away supporters. Coming out of White Hart Lane railway station turn right and then left along the High Road. You will pass the Bricklayers and Coach & Horse pubs. The Gilpins Bell is located a little further down on the right-hand side.

Inside the ground alcohol is served in the refreshment areas. This is in the form of plastic bottles of Carlsberg at £2.50 per 500ml bottle. But please note that alcohol is not served in the away section at half time.

■ How To Get There & Where To Park?

Leave the M25 at Junction 25 and take the A10 towards Enfield. Continue on the A10 through Enfield and at the roundabout with the North Circular (A406), turn left onto the A406 (Sterling Way). Turn right into Fore Road (the A1010) which becomes the High Road and you will come to the ground on your left. Sharon Genge adds 'if you arrive around midday, you can park at the local schools which are very easy to find. For £5 you can park until 6pm which is ample time to get back to the car after an afternoon match'.

The editor of My Eyes Have Seen The Glory fanzine adds: 'There is another way to get to the ground avoiding the A10 and A406. When you come off the M25, take the A10 turning and then turn left at the first set of lights into Bullsmoor Lane. Follow the road until a busy crossroads with traffic lights. Go straight over and you are on Meridian Way (A1055). This road takes you straight down to Tottenham. Just keep going straight (over roundabouts and traffic lights and past the site at Picketts Lock) until you pass Tesco's on the left hand side. After going through the traffic lights here, go through the next set and turn right at the lights after those (Sedge Road). If you park around this area you will be able to get away fairly quickly and will be close to Northumberland Park station and conveniently located for The Park Pub which is right next to the station. There are also a lot of towaway zones directly around the ground, so check the parking restrictions before you leave your car or you might face a trip to Wood Green (not recommended at the best of times) and a £100 bill to get your car back!'

■ By Tube/Train

The nearest tube station is Seven Sisters on the Victoria Line. The ground is about 20 minutes walk away, but there are plenty of buses running up Tottenham High Road to the ground. You can also get a train from Seven Sisters to White Hart Lane station, which is nearest to the stadium, being only a few minutes walk away. This is served by trains from Liverpool Street, where there is a handy Wetherspoons pub and Cornish pasties outlet opposite. Richard Crouch adds 'The best station to get to White Hart Lane from is Northumberland Park. Come out of the station and cross the road and you are in Park Lane. It is a ten-minute stroll to the ground'.

■ Local Rivals

Arsenal.

■ Admission Prices

Common with most Clubs, Tottenham operate a category system (A,B & C) for matches whereby tickets cost more for the most popular matches (category A). Concessions are also normally only available in the North Stand to Club Members, apart from some matches which are deemed by the Club to be 'family matches' where Senior Citizens and Under-15s can purchase tickets at half the adult price, in the South Stand.

Home Fans:

West Stand Upper Tier:
Adults £71 (A), £52 (B), £42 (C)

West Stand Lower Tier:
Adults £61 (A), £48 (B), £39 (C)

East Stand Upper Tier:
Adults £61 (A), £48 (B), £39 (C)

East Stand Upper Tier (Restricted View):
Adults £50 (A), £42 (B), £34 (C)

East Stand Lower Tier:
Adults £51 (A), £40 (B), £35 (C)

East Stand Lower Tier (Restricted View):
Adults £40 (A), £34 (B), £30 (C)

South Stand Upper Tier:
Adults £44 (A), £36 (B), £32 (C)

South Stand Lower Tier:
Adults £39 (A), £32 (B), £28 (C)

North Stand Upper Tier:
Adults £44 (A), £36 (B), £32 (C)
Over 65/Junior Member £22 (A), £18 (B), £16 (C)

North Stand Lower Tier:
Adults £39 (A), £32 (B), £27 (C)
Senior/Junior Member £19 (A), £16 (B), £14 (C)
Disabled: £39 (A), £32 (B), £27 (C)

Away Fans:

South Stand Upper Tier:
Adults £44 (A), £36 (B), £32 (C)

South Stand Lower Tier:
Adults £39 (A), £32 (B), £27 (C)

Normally no concessions are made available to away fans, but check with your own Club first.

■ Programme & Fanzines

Official Programme £3
One Flew Over Seaman's Head Fanzine £2
Cock A Doodle Do Fanzine £2
My Eyes Have Seen The Glory Fanzine £2

■ Record Attendance

75,038 v Sunderland,
FA Cup 6th Round, March 5th, 1938.

Modern All Seated Attendance Record:
36,247 v Everton
Premier League, October 15th, 2005.

■ Average Attendance

2006-2007: 35,739 (Premier League)

■ Did You Know?

The Club were originally formed in 1882 as Hotspur FC. They chose the Hotspur name after the Shakespeare character Harry Hotspur.

West Ham United

Boleyn Ground

Ground Name:	Boleyn Ground (but still known by a lot of fans as Upton Park)
Capacity:	35,146 (all seated)
Address:	Green Street, Upton Park, London, E13 9AZ
Main Telephone No:	020-8548-2748
Fax No:	020-8548-2758
Ticket Office:	0870-112-2700
Pitch Size:	110 x 70 yards
Club Nickname:	The Hammers or Irons
Year Ground Opened:	1904
Home Kit Colours:	Claret & Blue

Official Website:
www.whufc.com

Unofficial Websites:
Knees Up Mother Brown - www.kumb.com
West Ham Online - www.westhamonline.net
Hammers Mad - www.westhamutd-mad.co.uk
(Footy Mad Network)

■ What's The Ground Like?

On one side of the ground is the impressive-looking Dr Martens Stand that was opened in 2001. This large two-tiered stand (which is reputedly the largest league ground stand in London), has a capacity of 15,000. Its most striking feature can only be seen externally, where an elaborate facade comprising two castle turrets has been built around the reception area entrance. The turrets have been modelled on those appearing on the club crest. It is nice to see a club actually trying to instil some character into a new stand. Opposite is the smaller two-tiered East Stand, which was opened in 1969. Both ends are large, smart, two-tiered stands. In the North East and South West corners there are video screens installed as well as an electronic score board in the South West corner. There is also a Digital Clock above The Bobby Moore Stand.

Just outside the ground near the Boleyn Pub is the handsome statue of England captain Bobby Moore, holding aloft the World Cup Trophy which England won in 1966. The statue shows Moore being hoisted aloft by fellow West Ham players Geoff Hurst and Martin Peters with Everton defender Ray Wilson.

■ Future Ground Developments

The building of a new East Stand plus extensions to the existing Bobby Moore & Centenary Stands, have been postponed by the Club. The developments would have taken the capacity of Upton Park to 40,500, but have now been put on 'ice' pending financial backing for them.

■ What Is It Like For Visiting Supporters?

Away fans are housed in one end, in the lower tier of the relatively new North Stand (also known as the Centenary Stand). The usual allocation for away supporters is 2,200, but if demand requires, away fans can be allocated the whole of the lower tier of the North Stand, where up to 3,600 supporters can be accommodated. The ground is compact, with the fans seated close to the pitch.
This, coupled with the passionate support of the West Ham faithful, can make for a vibrant atmosphere. However, this can be intimidating for away supporters, so exercise caution around the ground. I personally enjoyed my visit and it is certainly not as bad as it was a few years ago and the West Ham fans can still give a rendition of their club anthem 'I'm forever blowing bubbles....'. Inside the ground the delicious 'Football's Famous Chicken Balti Pie' (£2.20) is available.

■ Where To Drink?

I have been advised by a number of supporters that most

of the pubs around the ground are quite partisan, and are for home supporters only. The Boleyn Pub on the corner near to the ground, plus Queens, The Greengate, Wine Bar, Village and 'The Central' pubs on Barking Road should all be given a wide berth by away fans. Kevin Hosking adds; 'Probably the best option for away fans is the Wetherspoons outlet called Millers Well which is opposite East Ham Town Hall. It is about a twenty-minute walk away along Barking Road (although it may be an idea to travel to East Ham tube station before the game, go to the pub and then walk to the ground). Another good option is the Denmark Arms also on the Barking Road near the East Ham Town Hall; this is a large pub which shows all live football games'. Lou Pearman adds; 'Away fans may also be able to drink in the Duke Of Edinburgh near to Upton Park Tube Station. Turn left out of the tube station and walk to the mini roundabout and it's on your right. There are also a few pie 'n' mash shops nearby (a traditional East End favourite). Turn right out of the tube station and just opposite is Duncans Pie n Mash. Don't be put off by the queue, because they don't hang about and serve you very quickly'.

■ How To Get There & Where To Park?

Directions from the M25:
Travel to M25 Junction 27, and go on to the M11 southbound. Follow the M11 south until it divides to join the A406 (North Circular Road). Take the left hand fork signposted A406 South. Do not follow the signs for the City.

The end of the motorway joins the A406 from the left, creating a 4 lane road for a short distance. You need to be in one of the outside 2 lanes (this can be tricky if traffic is heavy). Proceed south (dual carriageway with slip roads) passing the junctions for Redbridge, and Ilford.

Leave the A406 at the Barking junction. At the roundabout at the bottom of the slip road, turn right, taking the 3rd exit towards East Ham (Barking Road). Proceed West along Barking Road through several sets of traffic lights until you have passed the lights at East Ham Town Hall (big red Victorian building on the left just before the lights). 3/4 mile further, you pass the ground on your right (behind a parade of shops, including the Hammers Shop). At the next lights (Boleyn Arms Pub on the right hand corner), turn right into Green Street. The main entrance to the ground is 200 yards on your right. Thanks to Gareth Howell for providing the directions.

On Saturday matchdays, parking is very restricted with little or no off-road parking. The best areas to look for spaces are roads left of Barking Road, once you are past the lights at East Ham Town Hall. Andy Wright suggests; 'You can park at Newham General Hospital, where there is a pay and display car park, which costs £1.50 for four hours, or £3.50 for six. To find the hospital; From Barking Road, passing the ground on your right, after a few traffic lights turn left into Prince Regent Lane (Newham General is signposted at the lights), the hospital is just up this road and is about a 15 minute stroll away from the ground'.

Rob Wells adds; 'As a season ticket holder who travels to home games from Nottingham I can offer an alternative route from the M11 to avoid the nightmare of Barking Road on a Saturday. After leaving the M11 on the A406 take the exit for A12 signposted Stratford. Stay on this road taking the underpass to the Green Man roundabout, which is a major junction. Then take the A11, again signposted Stratford. After about three miles turn left onto the A112 signposted East Ham, through Plaistow. Carry on over the junction with Barking Road (A124). Third left after this junction is Glen Road, which takes you to the aforementioned Newham Hospital for parking. I find this journey a lot easier, although not recommended for midweek matches as the traffic gets too heavy'.

Alex Stewart suggests an alternative route; 'Come off the M25 at J29 and take the A127 to Upminster. Park at Upminster tube station (£1 for the day) and for £3.50 you can get a return ticket to Upton Park which will get you there in less than 25 minutes'.

Chris Ackrill agrees; 'I've experimented over several years with various routes to the stadium, and my conclusion is that it saves time and frustration by parking well in the suburbs and getting a tube. Getting anywhere near the ground by road can easily add on an hour, and it'll be the hardest hour's drive you've ever had. Things are no better on Sundays either'.

■ By Train/Tube

The nearest tube station is Upton Park which is on the District, plus the Hammersmith & City Lines. The station is a short walk from the ground. Please note that West Ham tube station is nowhere near the ground. Steve Cook adds; 'the queue at Upton Park tube station after the game can be horrendous. You are better off going for a couple of pints and letting the queues die down. There are plenty of pubs along Plaistow High Road which are only a 5-10 minute walk from the stadium and as long as visitors are 'well behaved' they are more than made welcome'. Adam Long, a visiting Reading fan, informs me;

'After the game you are probably best to walk up to East Ham, which will at least mean you will get a seat, before everyone else gets on at Upton Park'. Craig Belcher, a visiting West Brom fan, adds; 'Rather than face the long queues at Upton Park, we walked down to the next station on the line, Plaistow, which is only a ten-minute walk away from Upton Park. We managed to get on a tube okay, as apparently according to station staff the tubes are not filled to full capacity on leaving Upton Park". Just turn left after Upton Park station, into Harold Road. Walk down to the end of this road (it becomes Terrace Road) and then bear left into Pelly Road/Clegg St. At the bottom of Clegg Street is a T-junction with Plaistow High Street. Turn right into the High Street and Plaistow station is further down on the left.

Andrew Saffrey suggests; 'Forest Gate station is about 25 minutes walk from Upton Park, and it's much less busy than Upton Park Station after the final whistle. It is served by local Great Eastern trains from Liverpool Street. Turn right out of the station, then left at the corner next to the pizza shop into Hampton Road. Walking down Hampton Road, turn first right into Richmond Road, a small street with traffic calming and lots of roundabouts. Go straight down this road and this eventually becomes Green Street. Then for the long walk down Green Street which has lots of shops and takeaways, before arriving at Upton Park'.

■ Local Rivals
Chelsea, Millwall, Tottenham, Charlton.

■ Admission Prices
In common with most clubs, West Ham operate a category system (A & B) for matches whereby tickets cost more for the most popular matches (category A).

Home Fans

Dr Martens & East Stands (Upper & Lower Centre):
Adults £61 (£49), Senior Citizen/Juniors* £33.50 (£27)

Dr Martens & East Stands (Upper & Lower Wings):
Adults £55 (£45),
Senior Citizen/Juniors* £30.50 (£26)

Dr Martens (Upper Corners):
Adults £49 (£43),
Senior Citizen/Juniors* £27.50 (£23)

Dr Martens (Lower Corners):
Adults £43 (£34),
Senior Citizen/Juniors* £24.50 (£20)

Bobby Moore Stand (Upper):
Adults £49 (£43),
Senior Citizen/Juniors* £27.50 (£23)

Bobby Moore Stand (Lower):
Adults £43 (£34),
Senior Citizen/Juniors* £24.50 (£20)

Centenary Stand (Upper & Lower Tiers):
Adults £43 (£34),
Senior Citizen/Juniors* £24.50 (£20)

Away Fans

Centenary Stand (Lower Tier):
Adults £43 (£34),
Senior Citizen/Juniors £24.50 (£20)

* Senior Citizens and Juniors who are also Club members can gain a further discount on this matchday price.

■ Programme & Fanzines
Official Programme: £3.50
On The Terrace Fanzine: £2
Over Land And Sea: £2.50

■ Record Attendance
42,322 v Tottenham Hotspur
Division One, October 17th, 1970.

Modern All Seated Attendance Record:
35,050 v Manchester City
Premier League, September 21st, 2002.

■ Average Attendance
2006-2007: 34,719 (Premier League)

■ Did You Know?
The Boleyn Ground takes its name from a house which once stood in Green Street, next to the ground. The house had two prominent castle-like turrets and became referred to by the locals as the Boleyn Castle. The house has long since been demolished. Upton Park is the name of the area that the ground is located in.

Wigan Athletic

JJB Stadium

Ground Name: JJB Stadium
Capacity: 25,000 (all seated)
Address: Robin Park, Newtown, Wigan, WN5 0UZ
Main Telephone No: 01942-774-000
Fax No: 01942-770-477
Ticket Office: 0871-663-3552
Pitch Size: 110 x 60 metres
Team Nickname: Latics
Year Ground Opened: 1999
Home Kit Colours: Blue with White & Green

Official Website:
www.wiganlatics.co.uk

Unofficial Websites:
The Cockney Latic - www.cockneylatic.co.uk (Rivals Network)
Ye Olde Tree & Crown - www.yeoldetreeandcrown.34sp.com
Little Wigan - www.littlewigan.com
Ultimate Wigan - www.ultimatewigan.co.uk

What's The Ground Like?

The JJB Stadium was opened in 1999 after the Club moved from its former home of Springfield Park, where it had been in residence since the Club's formation in 1932. Saying that the new JJB is superb, would be an understatement; it is truly magnificent. It is similar in design to Huddersfield's McAlpine Stadium, having both been built by the same company. However the JJB stadium is different in that the stands are rectangular (compared to the semi-circular ones at Huddersfield) and both ends have the supporting steel girders suspended from beneath the roof, rather sitting above the stand itself. The four stands are of roughly the same height and there is an electric scoreboard above the Adidas Stand, on one side of the stadium. The stadium is not totally enclosed, all corners being open. There is plenty of leg room between the rows of seats and the views of the pitch were excellent. The stands seem to rise up quite steeply and do sit back a fair distance from the pitch. Apparently the pitch utilises some sort of new type of grass - on my visit the pitch was immaculate. The stadium is shared with Wigan Warriors Rugby League club.

What Is It Like For Visiting Supporters?

Away fans are located in the North Stand at one end of the stadium. Up to 5,400 visiting supporters can be accommodated in this area. I was thoroughly impressed with the stadium and found the Wigan supporters to be genuinely hospitable and knowledgeable about their football. The stadium has been designed so that even a few supporters can really make some noise, which makes for a good atmosphere. My only criticism was that the ground seemed a bit short on catering facilities, which led to long queues and with no queuing system, resulting in a free-for-all scrum at the counter! Scott Carpenter, a visiting Newcastle fan, adds; 'the concourses seemed too small for the large amount of away fans attending on my visit, which led to it being rather uncomfortably crowded at half time'.

Of interest outside the ground is Robins Park, where Wigan play their reserve games and athletics meetings are held. There is quite a sizeable stand on one side of the Park, which was better than a lot that I have seen at other grounds around the country. A thoroughly pleasant day out and I would say that it is likely to be one of your better away trips this season.

Where To Drink?

The traditional pub for away fans visiting the JJB Stadium

is the Red Robin, which is only a few minutes walk away from the ground opposite the Cinema Complex. At the stadium itself is the Marquee Bar which is specifically for away supporters to use and also welcomes families.

John Heeley from Wigan adds; 'I can happily recommend paying a visit to The Orwell at Wigan Pier before going to the stadium. It is an award winning pub with a good selection of traditional ales and regular guest beers. The food is also good. The pub is situated on the canal side and a short walk from the pub along the canal will take you to the ground. It is also only 5 minutes walk from both the train stations'. Having visited the Orwell myself, I can certainly echo the above comments. If you follow the A49 into Wigan from the motorway, you will pass the pub on your right.

The Swan & Railway pub in the town centre, opposite the entrance to Wigan North Western Railway Station is best avoided by away supporters.

How To Get There & Where To Park?

From The South:
Leave the M6 at Junction 25 then take the A49 to Wigan. After around two miles you should pass an Aldi store on your left, before reaching a large roundabout that is traffic light controlled. Turn left at this roundabout into Robin Park Road and continue into Scot Lane. The ground is down Scot Lane on your right.

From The North:
Leave the M6 at Junction 26 and follow the signs for Wigan town centre (this road meets the A49) then turn left into Robin Park and continue into Scot Lane.
The ground is down Scot Lane on your right.

Car Parking:

There is a large free car park at the stadium, behind the away end. This costs £4. As you may expect though, there is sometimes quite a delay in getting out of this car park after the game, especially if there has been a larger than normal crowd in attendance. Make sure though that you avoid parking on the nearby Retail Park, as parking there is restricted to two hours and I have been informed of a number of fans who have ended up getting parking tickets (£50) because of this.

Thanks to Steve Booth for providing the directions above.

By Train

Wigan's central railway stations (Wigan North Western & Wallgate stations) are a good 20 minute walk from the ground. So either take a taxi, or break up the journey with a few pub stops on the way! On exiting from either station head under the railway bridge and keep to the right. Follow the road (A49), making sure you stick to the right for around 10 minutes. You should pass the Seven Stars Hotel and then pass under a second railway bridge. The Robin Park complex and the JJB Stadium should then be visible. Turn down Robin Park Road and you are there.

Local Rivals

Manchester City, Preston North End, Bolton Wanderers & Burnley.

Admission Prices

In common with most clubs, Wigan operate a category system (A, B C) for matches whereby tickets cost more for the most popular matches (category A). Category C prices are shown below in brackets.

Home Fans:

West Stand
Adults £35 (£25),
Concessions £30 (£20)

East Stand (Centre)
Adults £35 (£25),
Concessions £30 (£20),
Junior Members £12 (£12)

East Stand (Wings)
Adults £32 (£22),
Concessions £27 (£18),
Junior Members £12 (£12)

South Stand
Adults £35 (£25),
Concessions £30 (£20),
Under 16's £10 (£10),
Under 11's £5 (£5)

Away Fans:

North Stand
Adults £35 (£25),
Concessions £30 (£20)

Programme & Fanzine

Matchday Programme - £3
Cockney Latic Fanzine - £1

Record Attendance

At JJB Stadium:
25,016 v Liverpool
Premier League, February 11th, 2006.

At Springfield Park:
27,526 v Hereford United
FA Cup 2nd Round, December 12th, 1951.

Average Attendance

2006-2007: 18,158 (Premier League)

Did You Know?

That Wigan played their first ever game in the Football League on August 19th, 1978.

Barnsley

Oakwell

Ground Name:	Oakwell
Capacity:	23,009 (all seated)
Address:	Grove Street, Barnsley, S71 1ET
Main Telephone No:	01226-211-211
Fax No:	01226-211-444
Ticket Office No:	0871-226-6777
Team Nickname:	The Tykes
Year Ground Opened:	1888
Pitch Size:	110 x 75 yards
Home Kit Colours:	Red & White

Official Website:
www.barnsleyfc.co.uk

Unofficial Websites:
Barnsleyfc.net - www.barnsleyfc.net
Supporters Trust - www.bfcst.org.uk
Tykes Mad - www.barnsley-mad.co.uk
(Footy Mad Network)
Total Tykes - www.totaltykes.com (Rivals Network)

What's The Ground Like?

Approximately three sides of the ground were re-developed in the 1990's. On one side is the particularly attractive two-tiered covered East Stand running along one side of the pitch. Opened in March 1993, this stand has a capacity of 7,500. Opposite is the older West Stand, part of which dates back to 1904. It was made all seated in the mid-1990s, but is only covered at the rear. On its roof is perched an ugly-looking television gantry which obscures a probably more attractive gable. At the Pontefract Road End (now named the Enterprise plc Stand) of the ground is an all seated, covered stand for home supporters, which has a capacity of 4,500. The other end, the North Stand, was previously an open terrace, but is now a relatively new single-tier, covered stand, housing 6,000 supporters. This is the most recent addition to the ground being opened in 1999 and has greatly enhanced the overall look of Oakwell. The North Stand is shared between home and away supporters. The amount of seats given to away supporters varies according to demand. An unusual feature of the ground is a purpose-built stand for disabled supporters. This is a three-floor structure that sits at the corner between the East & South Stands. There is also a new electric scoreboard at one corner of the North Stand, on top of a newly-constructed security control room.

Future Ground Developments

Scott Kilner informs me; 'The club are looking to replace the old West Stand. It is anticipated that the new development will be more or less identical to the existing two-tiered East Stand. However no firm timescales have been set as to when this might happen'.

What Is It Like For Visiting Supporters?

Away fans are housed in the new North Stand, where the facilities are good. The normal allocation for away supporters is 2,000 tickets although, if demand requires

it, then the whole of this stand can be allocated (6,000). This club I found to be particularly friendly from the car park attendant to the programme seller. Even the P.A. announcer had a sense of humour (although a little optimistic), when he announced that perhaps the visiting fans would like to come up again to see the next Barnsley home game, so that we could see a decent game of football! However, I have reports of fans getting hassle at Barnsley (especially in the town centre) and stewards acting a little heavy-handed, although I've never personally had any problems. It is advisable to keep colours covered especially around the town centre.
The delicious 'Football's Famous Chicken Balti Pie' (£2.30) is available inside the ground, along with cheeseburgers (£2.80), hot dogs (£2.70), sausage rolls (£2) and chips (£1.70).

Where To Drink?
Paul Sammon, a lifelong Tyke, recommends the Outpost on Sheffield Road. The pub is a ten-minute walk from the ground. Ricardo Marconi, a visiting Birmingham City fan recommends; 'The Holleywell Inn, on the Oakwell Road near to the old Barnsley Brewery. A friendly boozer with a good mix of home and away fans'. Gary Holding, a visiting Blackburn supporter adds; 'There was no alcohol on sale inside the ground for the away fans, but a few minutes walk from the away end is the Metro Dome - an all-in-one leisure centre, which has a bar inside which serves good food and ale'. Drinking in the town centre is generally not recommended, especially near the Bus & Train Stations, although on my last visit I had a hassle-free pint (or two) in the Wetherpoons in the centre of town, but I should point out that I wasn't wearing colours.

How To Get There & Where To Park?
Leave the M1 at Junction 37 and take the A628 towards Barnsley. Stay on this road (the ground is well signposted) and you will eventually see the ground on your right. There is a fair-sized car park located at the ground.

By Train
Barnsley railway station is about a ten-minute walk away. This station is served by trains running between Sheffield & Leeds.

From the train station turn left away from the town centre and head towards the bridge that the dual carriageway runs over. Go under the bridge and turn left up the slip road and then take the first road on the right and head towards the Metro Dome leisure complex at the top of the hill. Oakwell is now clearly visible. Thanks to Ian Ambler & Bryn Williams for providing the directions.

Local Rivals
Sheffield United, Sheffield Wednesday, Rotherham United.

Admission Prices
Like a number of Clubs, Barnsley have introduced a category system for ticket prices (A & B), whereby the most popular matches cost more to watch.

Home Fans:

East & West Stands (Upper Tier):
Adults £22,
OAP/Juvenile £13
Under-11s £7

East & West Stands (Lower Tier):
Adults £21,
OAP/Juvenile £12,
Under-11s £6

Barnsley Chronicle Family Area:
Adults £22,
OAP/Juvenile £13,
Under-11s £7

Enterprise plc Stand (Pontefract Road):
Adults £20,
OAP/Juvenile £12,
Under-11s £6

Away Fans:

North Stand:
Adults £20
OAP/Juvenile £12
Under-11s £6

Programme
Official Programme £2.50.

Record Attendance
40,255 v Stoke City,
FA Cup 5th Round, February 15th, 1936.

Modern All Seated Attendance Record:
22,650 v Manchester City
Division One, March 11th, 2000.

Average Attendance
2006-2007: 11,231 (Championship)

Did You Know?
That in 1897 the Reverend Tiverton Preedy originally formed the Club as Barnsley St Peters.

Blackpool

Bloomfield Road

Ground Name: Bloomfield Road
Capacity: 9,491 (all seated)
Address: Seasiders Way, Blackpool, Lancashire, FY1 6JJ
Main Telephone No: 0870-443-1953
Fax No: 01253-405-011
Pitch Size: 112 x 74 yards
Team Nickname: Seasiders
Year Ground Opened: 1899
Home Kit Colours: Tangerine & White

Official Website:
www.blackpoolfc.co.uk

Unofficial Websites:
www.blackpool.vitalfootball.co.uk
(Vital Football Network)
AVFTT - http://blackpool.rivals.net/default.asp?sid=912
(Rivals Network)

What's The Ground Like?

The Club announced in 2000 their intention to totally redevelop Bloomfield Road into a new 16,000-capacity all-seated stadium. Phase one of the project was completed in February 2002, with the opening of the new North & West Stands. Phase two, the rebuilding of the South & East Stands, is yet to start.

The single-tiered West & North Stands are located at one side and at one end of the ground. They are impressive-looking and the North West corner between them has also been filled with seating, so that this area of the ground is enclosed. At the back of the West Stand is a row of executive boxes. A personal gripe is that while understanding the Club's need for revenue, naming the West Stand, 'The Pricebusters Matthews Stand' rather than just 'The Sir Stanley Matthews Stand', seems somewhat crass. Both the other sides of the ground have now been demolished. On the East side of the ground an open temporary 'golf style' seated stand has been erected to house away supporters, whilst at the South end of the ground still awaits a new stand to be constructed. Outside the North Stand of the ground is a statue of the former Blackpool legend Stan Mortensen.

Future Ground Developments

After demolishing the old South Stand in 2003, the Club have yet to embark upon the building of its replacement. However, with the Club gaining promotion to the Championship, Chairman Karl Oyston has pledged that a new South Stand will be in place for the 2007/08 season. However, the Club are still considering whether to erect a 'temporary stand' or build something more permanent. Either way, it is unlikely that there will be a roof on this new area. Erecting such a stand would increase the capacity of Bloomfield Road to just under 13,000.

What Is It Like For Visiting Supporters?

With delays to the building of the new South Stand, away fans will once again for this season find themselves being housed in a temporary stand on the Eastern side of the ground. The stand is more reminiscent of the type found at the 18th hole of the British Open Golf Championships, rather than at a football ground and has a capacity of 1,700. The facilities are basic and the stand has no roof, leaving fans exposed to the elements.

Dave Croston, a visiting Tranmere fan adds; 'it was raining on our visit and the walkway in front of the the away stand soon became a grey-coloured quagmire, with large pools of water forming on it. I would suggest that heavy footwear is recommended on rainy days. Add to this the inadequate small portakabin toilets, the food facilities that were housed in a tiny wooden building with one narrow opening from which to gain your food or beverage, with only one person at a time being served, then it all added up to not a very pleasant experience'. However the leg room is adequate and you do get a good view of the playing action being housed close to the pitch. Remember to wrap up well in winter as the wind that comes off the Irish Sea can go right through you! On the whole, though I found the ground to be a welcoming one, I just hope they build that new South Stand soon!

Where To Drink?

Nigel Richardson, a visiting Hull City fan recommends the 'No 1 Bar, which is a Working Mens Club that is adjacent to the away supporters entrance to the ground on Bloomfield Road. It was very welcoming and admits away fans for a small fee'. Steve Gardner, a visiting Gillingham fan informs me; 'A good family pub close to the ground is the Waterloo in Waterloo Road - genuinely family-friendly except in the games area. Clean, comfortable and friendly; Sky TV on large screens and reasonable, inexpensive food'.

There are plenty of pubs in Blackpool town centre to choose from. Mike Latham recommends the Dunes pub on Lytham Road (Airport End). In his words; 'it serves the best pint of Boddies in the world!'. Steve Lumb adds; 'Another good pub is the Wetherspoons pub called the Auctioneer on Lytham Road, near Blackpool South Station. It's about 10 minutes walk to the ground and serves cheap beer and brilliant grub.'

How To Get There & Where To Park?

Leave the M6 at Junction 32. Follow the M55 into the outskirts of Blackpool and continue straight along this road until you see the ground on your right. The ground is located about half way between the Pleasure Beach and the Tower and is about a quarter of a mile inland from the south shore. Large pay and display car parks are located just across the road from the ground (£1). Damian Feeney adds; 'It's worth bearing in mind that the car parking does increase during the holiday season to £3.20 for the required period. It runs from the Spring Bank Holiday until the end of the Illuminations. The canny can find on-street parking instead.' Matthew Stimpson, a visiting Halifax Town fan informs me; 'Please note that unlike most towns and cities in England the pay and display car parks near to the ground still charge after 6pm. Some visiting fans on my visit assumed that they would be free after 6pm and ended up with a parking ticket'.

By Train

The closest railway station to the ground is Blackpool South and is around a ten-minute walk away. However fewer trains stop at this station with most calling at Blackpool North. Blackpool North station is around two miles away and therefore you may wish to jump in a cab to the ground.

Mark Gillatt adds; 'For anyone arriving by train at Blackpool North a cheaper alternative than a taxi may be the number 11 bus from the bus station across the road. Buses to Lytham St Annes pass the end of Bloomfield Road and run every eight minutes. Fans should alight at the Bridge House pub (okay for a pint) and walk down Lonsdale Road to the ground'.

Local Rivals

Preston North End & Burnley.

Admission Prices

Home Fans*:

Pricebusters Matthews (Centre):
Adults £21.50,
OAPs £17,
Under-19s £14
Under-16s £12.50

Pricebusters Matthews Stand (Wings):
Adults £19,
OAPs £15,
Under-19s £12.50
Under-16s £11

Pricebusters Matthews Stand (Outer Wings):
Adults £18,
OAPs £14,
Under-19s £11
Under-16s £9.50

Brands Scaffolding North West Stand:
Adults £18,
OAPs £13,
Under-19s £9,
Under-16s £7.50,
Under-11s £6

All In Property Services Family Area:
Adults £18,
OAPs £13,
Under-19s £9,
Under-16s £7.50,
Under-11s £6

North Stand:
Adults £18,
OAPs £14,
Under-19s £11
Under-16s £9.50

Away Fans*:

Adults £18,
OAPs £13,
Under-19s £9
Under-16s £7.50

* A 50p discount on these prices per ticket is available if the ticket is purchased prior to matchday.

Programme & Fanzines

Official Programme: £2.50.

Record Attendance

38,098 v Wolverhampton Wanderers,
Division One, September 19th, 1955.

Modern All Seated Attendance Record:
9,491 v Norwich City
FA Cup 3rd Round, January 27th, 2007.

Average Attendance

2006-2007: 5,952 (League One)

Did You Know?

At the end of the nineteenth century, the ground was the home of South Shore FC and was called Gamble's Field. When South Shore amalgamated with Blackpool FC it was renamed Bloomfield Road.

Bristol City

Ashton Gate

Ground Name: Ashton Gate
Capacity: 21,479 (all seated)
Address: Ashton Road,
Bristol, BS3 2EJ
Main Telephone No: 0117-963-0630
Fax No: 0117-963-0700
Ticket Office: 0870-112-1897
Team Nickname: The Robins
Year Ground Opened: 1904
Home Kit Colours: Red & White

Official Website:
www.bcfc.co.uk

Unofficial Websites:
The Incider - www.theincider.com
BristolCityNet - www.bristolcitynet.co.uk
(Rivals Network)
One Teram In Bristol Forum - www.otib.co.uk
Bristol City Band -
http://members.freezone.co.uk/bcfcband/

What's The Ground Like?

The Atyeo stand at one end of the ground is a handsome, covered all seated single-tiered stand. It was opened in 1994, replacing a former open terrace and made a great difference to the overall look of the ground. At the other end is the smaller, covered Wedlock Blackthorn Stand housing the away supporters. On one side, is the two-tiered GWR Dolman Stand, with the lower tier used as a family area. Opposite, the Brunel Ford Williams Stand is an older-looking single-tiered stand, with several supporting pillars. A small band resides in one corner of the Atyeo Stand which on occasion helps to boost the atmosphere.

Future Ground Developments

The Club have ambitious plans to transform Ashton Gate into a modern 30,000 capacity stadium. The first phase of this will be the building of a new Wedlock Stand, which will once again become the traditional home end at Ashton Gate. The stand will also include 16 corporate hospitality boxes and will cost in the region of £7m to build. The Club then have future plans to redevelop both the Williams & Dolman Stands. However, due to financial pressures the Club have yet to embark on the redevelopment and no firm timescales as to when it might begin have been announced.

What Is It Like For Visiting Supporters?

Away supporters are housed at one end in the Wedlock Blackthorn Stand, where the normal allocation is 2,800. If required, this can be increased to 5,500. The acoustics are excellent, so even a small number of away fans can generate some noise. The facilities are pretty standard, plus there are a number of supporting pillars running across the front, which could impede your view. The delicious 'Football's Famous Chicken Balti Pie' (£2.20) is available inside the ground. A day out at Bristol City, in line with the general improvement in football, is now far more enjoyable for away fans than it once was.

Where To Drink?

Alex Webber recommends the Pumphouse and the Nova Scotia for away supporters by the waterfront, but adds that pubs nearer to the ground such as the Hen & Chicken and The Rising Sun should be given a wide berth. The Robins pub, which is situated a few minutes walk from the away end and was a favourite for away fans has now, alas, become a pub for 'home supporters' only. Please note that alcohol is not available to away fans inside the ground.

Bristol City

How To Get There & Where To Park?

Leave the M5 at Junction 18, travel along the Portway (A4) following signs for Bristol Airport/Taunton (A38). Over the swing bridge (Brunel Way), branching left into Winterstoke Road, and you will see the ground on your left. Parking at the ground is for permit holders only, so it is a case of finding some street parking.

By Train

The nearest railway station is Parson Street which is around a ten-minute walk away from the ground. However few trains stop at this station so you are more likely to end up at Bristol Temple Meads mainline station instead. This station is at least two miles from the ground and hence too far to walk, so best to jump in a taxi (around £6). Neil Le Milliere, a visiting Exeter City supporter adds 'don't try and walk it from the station unless you really have to and then allow at least three-quarters of an hour for the journey'. Chris Davis says; 'there are buses which leave from behind the Atyeo Stand at the end of the game which go to the centre of Bristol and Temple Meads Station at a cost of £1. Although predominantly for home fans, away fans could also use them'.

Local Rivals

Bristol Rovers, Cardiff City & some fans consider Swindon Town to be local rivals.

Admission Prices

The Club operate a category system (B & C) whereby different ticket prices are charged according to the opposition being played. Category B is the highest ticket price and category C prices are the lowest and are shown in brackets.

Home Fans*:

Dolman Stand (Centre):
Adults £28
Over 65's £22
Students & Under 16's £19

Atyeo Stand:
Adults £23
Over 65's £18
Students £13
Under 16's £13 (£7 in Block B)

Dolman Stand (Upper Wings & Lower Tier):
Adults £26
Over 65's £20
Students £16
Under 16's £16 (£7 in the Lower Tier)

Williams Stand: (except Block L)
Adults £26
Over 65's £20
Students £16
Under 16's £16

Williams Stand: (Block L)
Adults £23
Over 65's £18
Students £13
Under 16's £13

Away Fans*:

Wedlock Stand:
Adults £23
Over 65's £18,
Students & Under 16's £13

* The prices quoted above are for tickets purchased in advance of the game (up to 11am for Saturday kick-offs and 5.30pm for evening kick-offs. Tickets purchased later on matchdays normally cost £2 more, although Under 16's tickets in Atyeo Block B and Lower Dolman can cost up to £5 extra.

Programme & Fanzines

Official Programme - £2.50
One Team In Bristol Fanzine £1.20.
Cider'ed Fanzine £1.

Record Attendance

43,335 v Preston North End,
FA Cup 5th Round, 1935.

Modern All Seated Attendance Record:
20,007 v Bristol Rovers
Division Two, January 16th, 1996.

Average Attendance

2006-2007: 10,986 (League One)

Did You Know?

That the Dolman Stand was opened in 1970 and was named after a former Club Chairman, Harry Dolman.

Burnley

Turf Moor

Ground Name:	Turf Moor
Capacity:	22,546 (all seated)
Address:	Harry Potts Way, Burnley, BB10 4BX
Main Telephone No:	0870-443-1882
Fax No:	01282-700-014
Ticket Office:	0870-443-1914
Pitch Size:	115 x 73 yards
Nickname:	The Clarets
Year Ground Opened:	1883
Home Kit Colours:	Claret & Blue

Official Website:
www.burnleyfootballclub.com

Unofficial Websites:
London Clarets - www.londonclarets.com
Clarets Mad - www.clarets-mad.co.uk (Footy Mad Network)
Claret Flag - www.claretflag.com (Rivals Network)
The Longside - www.thelongside.co.uk (Sport Network)

■ What's The Ground Like?

Burnley have played continually at Turf Moor since 1883, which is one of the longest continual occupations of ground by one club in the Football League. Half the ground was redeveloped in the mid-1990s with two smart-looking new stands being opened. The first of these, the James Hargreaves Stand, was opened in early 1996. It has two large tiers, with a row of executive boxes housed between them. This stand replaced the famous Longside Terrace, which was a big, steep covered terrace. Later in 1996 the Jimmy McIlroy Stand was opened at one end of the ground. This is a similar-looking stand to the James Hargreaves Stand, which gives half the ground a uniform look. The other two sides of the ground are much older and look out of place next to their shiny new neighbours. The Bob Lord Stand at one side of the pitch was opened in 1974. It is a small all-seated single-tiered stand, with windshields to either side. The David Fishwick Stand (formerly known as the Cricket Field Stand) at one end of the ground was opened in 1969. Again it is a simple-looking single-tiered stand that has some supporting pillars.

■ Future Ground Developments

The club are looking to purchase the adjacent Cricket Club, which would allow the redevelopment of the Cricket Field Stand. It is proposed to build a two-tiered stand with a capacity of 7,000. However this is dependent on finding a suitable site for the Cricket Club to relocate to. The old recreation ground in Fulledge had been a possibility, but plans were scrapped due to local opposition. Therefore the re-development of the Stand has been put 'on hold'. If the Cricket Club are unable to relocate, then Turf Moor's capacity may be increased by adding a second tier to the Bob Lord Stand, or the Club may even consider moving to a new stadium. Thanks to Dave Watson for providing the information.

■ What Is It Like For Visiting Supporters?

Away fans are housed in the covered David Fishwick Stand (formerly the Cricket Field Stand, named because there is a cricket field behind it) at one end of the ground. This stand accommodates 4,125 supporters. Burnley are generally a well-supported club and there is normally a good atmosphere; however, this can sometimes become quite intimidating for the away supporter, so exercise discretion.

Neil Iwanicki, a visiting Aston Villa fan adds; 'The away stand has two pillars which can affect your view and has old, wooden seats instead of plastic ones. The concourses below the stand are not for the faint-hearted if your team has a large away following, as it is like a rugby scrum to get a drink. There are some Burnley fans in the James Hargreaves Stand who do their best to get the atmosphere going, but they never really succeeded on my visit. If you travel by official club coaches, then you'll get a police escort from the M65 to the ground'.

■ Where To Drink?

Tony Moore recommends the 110 Club on Yorkshire Street near the ground. This private club allows away supporters in for a nominal admission fee (20p). The club serves good reasonably priced food and children are also welcomed. They also offer a 'Claret & Blue' bitter at only £1.10 per pint. Matthew Harrison informs me; 'the Bridge pub', which is around ten minutes walk away from the ground, serves good beer and food and is fine for away supporters'. Whilst Mike Dean, a visiting Norwich City supporter adds; 'We enjoyed the Talbot pub (opposite the Sparrow Hawk) for pre match drinks. It is a good sized pub with a large screen tv and plenty of sensible home fans, plus well kept real ale on tap'.

Paul Hanson adds 'Another place I could recommend is the Queen Victoria Public House. The away fans are always directed/encouraged to park in one location, by the side of the Burnley fire station; Pass there, away from the football ground and proceed for about 100 yards where you will find the entrance to the Queen Victoria (Brewers Fayre establishment). The ground is no more than 10 minutes walk away. Away fans visit regularly wearing their colours'. Pete Mitton also recommends the Cricket Club; 'the clubhouse at the Cricket Club (you can also park there) is open on matchdays and visitors are always made welcome (wearing colours), which is ideal as it is right next door to the ground'. Andrew Woodhall sent in this comment about the Cricket Club bar that he overheard from a visiting Gillingham fan; "Two pints of Theakstons, a bowl of pie and peas and a cigar....and still change from a fiver!" Mark Elliott informs me'; 'The Woodman Inn on Todmorden Road (about a half a mile up the road from the ground) is a small & friendly enough place for away supporters, providing they are sensible and don't mind a bit of banter, plus the pub has a large screen which shows Sky Sports'.

Ian Pilkington advises 'The Turf Hotel on Yorkshire Street and pubs in the town centre are best avoided. Colours are best covered up in and around the centre of town'.

How To Get There & Where To Park?

Leave the M6 at Junction 29 and onto the M65. Leave the M65 at Junction 10 and follow signs for Towneley Hall. This road eventually goes past the ground. There is a car park available at the cricket ground, by Turf Moor, which costs £3. Otherwise, street parking.

By Train

There are two train stations in walking distance of Turf Moor, Burnley Central and Burnley Manchester Road. Central station is around a 20-minute walk away from the ground and is mostly served by local trains. Manchester Road is a 15-minute walk away and is served by the faster express service. Walking directions from both are as follows:

Manchester Road

Upon leaving the station cross the main road towards the cinema. The ground should be clearly visible in the distance straight ahead. Turn left down Centenary Way, an unmissable dual carriageway (A682) going downhill towards the ground. A few minutes walk will bring you to a roundabout. Turn right under the canal bridge into Yorkshire Street (A671), down which you will reach Turf Moor on your left, with the away stand the first to be reached. Thanks to Rob Quinn for providing this information.

Central Station

Walk out of the station and across the road down towards a small retail area including Fads and Halfords Cycles. You will reach the inner ring road (A679), where you turn left and after about 200 yards you will reach a set of traffic lights. Turn right at the lights into Church Street (A682). Continue down Church Street until you reach a large roundabout at which you turn left under the canal bridge into Yorkshire Street (A671). Continue down this road and you will reach Turf Moor on your left, with the away stand the first to be reached. Thanks to Paul Hanson for providing the directions.

Local Rivals

Blackburn Rovers, Preston North End, Bolton Wanderers, Blackpool.

Admission Prices

Home Fans:

Bob Lord Stand
Adults: £22, Over 60's £14, Under 18's/Students £20, Under 16's £11

James Hargreaves (Upper)
Adults: £22, Over 60's £14, Under 18's/Students £20, Under 16's £11

James Hargreaves (Lower)
Adults: £20, Over 60's £13, Under 18's/Students £16, Under 16's £10

Jimmy McIlroy (Upper)
Adults: £19, Over 60's £12, Under 18's/Students £17, Under 16's £9

Jimmy McIlroy (Lower)
Adults: £18, Over 60's £12, Under 18's/Students £16, Under 16's £9

Away Fans:

David Fishwick Stand:
Adults: £19, Concessions £12, Juniors £9

Programme & Fanzine

Official Programme £2.50.
Bob Lord's Sausage Fanzine: £1.

Record Attendance

54,775 v Huddersfield Town,
FA Cup 3rd Round, February 23rd, 1924.

Modern All Seated Attendance Record:
22,310 v Preston North End
Division One, March 4th, 2000.

Average Attendance

2006-2007: 12,459 (Championship)

Did You Know?

That when the David Fishwick Stand was first opened in 1969, it incorporated underfloor heating for the comfort of supporters. After two seasons the Club were forced to switch it off, due to its high running costs.

Cardiff City

Ninian Park

Ground Name: Ninian Park
Capacity: 20,376
Address: Sloper Road,
Cardiff, CF11 8SX
Main Telephone No: 02920-221-001
Fax No: 02920-341-148
Ticket Office: 0845-345-1400
Pitch Size: 110 x 70 yards
Team Nickname: The Bluebirds
Year Ground Opened: 1910
Home Kit Colours: All Blue With White Trim

Official Website:
www.cardiffcityfc.co.uk

Unofficial Websites:
Valley Rams - www.valleyrams.com
A Sleeping Giant - www.ccfcsleepinggiant.com
(Rivals Network)
Vital Bluebirds - www.cardiff.vitalfootball.co.uk
(Vital Football Network)
Cardiff City Mad - www.cardiffcity-mad.co.uk
(Footy Mad Network)

What's The Ground Like?

Ninian Park is what I can only describe as a 'proper traditional' football ground. As Cardiff are looking to move to a new stadium, then I suggest you visit this gem before its too late and it is gone forever...

The John Smiths Grange End is a large formerly open terrace that now has a roof installed. This end is shared between home and away supporters. Opposite is the Spar Family Stand. This small, covered, all-seated stand has a number of supporting pillars running across the front. The overall appearance of this stand has changed recently, with the roof repainted with a large advert for the Clubs sponsors Redrow. On one side of the ground is the Popular Bank Stand. This has a raised seating area to its rear and terracing at its front. There are a couple of supporting pillars in the seated area, whilst the roof does not cover the front terrace. Painted onto the roof is a huge advert for a local bread maker. On the other side of the ground is the Grandstand. This two-tiered stand is covered and all seated and again has some supporting pillars. The ground also benefits from having some striking floodlight pylons at each corner of the ground.

Future Ground Developments

The Club have received planning permission to build a new 30,000 capacity stadium, on the present site of the Leckwith Athletics Stadium, opposite Ninian Park. Preliminary work has already begun on the site, the first phase of which is to build a new athletics stadium nearby. The scheme will also see the building of a retail park and Ninian Park. once vacated would be sold for residential housing. The stadium will cost £38m to construct and will be built in such away that it could be subsequently expanded to 60,000 if required. It is hoped that the Club will take up residence in their new stadium by Christmas 2008.

What Is It Like For Visiting Supporters?

Away fans are housed on one side of the John Smiths Grange Terrace at one end of the ground. Around 1,000 away fans can be accommodated in this covered area, but this can be increased if demand requires it (maximum 2,000). Strangely, this area has a mix of seating to the front and terrace to the rear. This end is also shared with home supporters with the obligatory 'no-mans' land in-between. Food is available in the form of a range of pies (£1.90), pasties (£1.60), hot dogs (£2.50), bacon rolls (£2.50), cheese burgers (£2.60), and chips £1 and the intriguely-named 'Welsh burger' (£2.50). I personally did not experience any problems when I went, but it is worth bearing in mind that the Cardiff fans are passionate about their club and this can make for an intimidating atmosphere. I would recommend that colours are kept covered up around the ground and in the adjacent car parks.

Scott Chapman, a visiting Plymouth Argyle supporter adds; 'I found Cardiff to be particularly intimidating. There were a large amount of police on duty and away fans had to receive a police escort out of the ground after the game had ended; not the most pleasant of away trips last season.'

Where To Drink?

Most of the pubs near to the ground can be intimidating for away supporters and are not recommended. However there is the Cornwall Hotel, 5-10mins walking distance from the ground in Cornwall Street (Taxi £2.50 from Central station). As Mike Dibble says; 'I use the Cornwall pre-match and have never witnessed any trouble over the last five or so years I have frequented it, Away fans are left to enjoy a trouble-free pint. It has the usual variety of beers on tap including Brains and has a useful Chinese/chippy directly opposite for a munch.'

How To Get There & Where To Park?

To avoid driving through the centre of Cardiff, leave the M4 at junction 33 and take the A4232 towards Cardiff/Barry. Keep on the A4232 towards Cardiff and then leave the dual carriageway at the B4267 exit, signposted 'Cardiff (Leckwith) Athletics Stadium'. After about half a mile you will see Ninian Park over on your right. There is a huge car park across the road from the ground and at the nearby Athletics Stadium.

By Train

The nearest train station is Ninian Park Halt, on a local line served by trains from Cardiff Central. Alternatively, as Barry Hodges informs me; 'Grangetown station is around a 10-15-minute walk away from Ninian Park and is served by fairly frequent trains from Cardiff Central that continue onto Penarth or Barry Island. On leaving Grangetown station turn left, cross the main road and then turn right into Sloper Road for the ground'.

Local Rivals

Swansea City and from a little further away, Bristol City.

Admission Prices

Home Fans:

Grandstand Upper Centre:
Adults £30*, OAP's/Under 16's £22

Grandstand Upper Wings:
Adults £25*, OAP's/Under 16's £15

Grandstand Lower:
Adults £24*, OAP's/Under 16's £15

Popular Bank Seating Centre:
Adults £25*, OAP's/Under 16's £15

Popular Bank Seating Wings:
Adults £24*, OAP's/Under 16's £15

Popular Bank Terrace:
Adults £16, OAP's/Under 16's £10

John Smiths Grange End Terrace:
Adults £20, No Concessions

Spar Family Stand:
Adults £18, OAP's £10, Under 16's £5

Away Fans:

John Smiths Grange End (Seating):
Adults £25*, OAP's/Under 16's £15

John Smiths Grange End (Terrace):
Adults £22, OAP's/Under 16's £15

* A discount of £2 is available on these ticket prices, if purchased prior to matchday.

Programme & Fanzines

Official Programme £3
The Thin Blue Line Fanzine £1
Barmy Army Fanzine 70p
Ramzine Fanzine £1

Record Attendance

For Ninian Park:
61,556 Wales v England, October 14th, 1961.

For A Cardiff Match:
57,893 v Arsenal
Division One, April 22nd, 1953.

Average Attendance

2006-2007: 16,594 (Championship)

Other Places of Interest

A popular destination with visiting supporters is the Millennium Stadium. Although no longer hosting the domestic football cup finals, it is still one of the best stadiums in Britain. The stadium offers regular tours on most days throughout the year and is only a couple of minutes walk from Cardiff Central railway station.
The tour itself costs:

Adults: £5.50
Children 5-16 years: £3
Children Under 5's: Free
Concessions (OAP's, Students, Unemployed): £3.50
Family Ticket: 2 Adults + 3 Children £17

I have been on the tour myself and would definitely recommend it. It lasts around 45 minutes and is full of interesting facts, coupled with a sense of humour. You can book your tours on: 02920-822-228.

Did You Know?

Before moving to Ninian Park in 1910, the Club played at a number of other venues, including Sophia Gardens, the present home of Glamorgan Cricket Club.

Charlton Athletic

The Valley

Ground Name:	The Valley
Capacity:	27,111 (all seated)
Address:	Floyd Road, Charlton, London, SE7 8BL
Main Telephone No:	020-8333-4000
Main Fax No:	020-8333-4001
Ticket Office:	0871-226-1905
Ticket Office Fax:	020-8333-4011
Pitch Size:	112 x 73 yards
Team Nickname:	The Addicks
Ground Opened:	1919
Home Kit Colours:	Red & White

Official Website:
www.cafc.co.uk

Unofficial Websites:
Net Addicks - www.netaddicks.com (Rivals Network)
CAFC-Fans - www.cafc-fans.co.uk

What's The Ground Like?

The construction of the North Stand has transformed the ground. What was a separate single-tier stand is now a large two-tiered affair, extending and completely enclosing the North East & North West corners.
The redevelopment of this area of the ground was completed in 2002 and in total houses 9,000 fans.
Both sides have also been redeveloped in the mid-1990s and anyone who saw the derelict Valley a few years back now wouldn't believe their eyes. The West Stand on one side is a good-sized two-tiered stand, whilst opposite is the smaller, single-tiered East Stand, where the vast open terrace, reputedly the country's biggest, was located until demolished in the 1990s. There is a row of executive boxes that run across the back of this stand and it has a television gantry suspended beneath its roof. The older South Stand, behind the goal, is given to away supporters and now looks out of place in its smart surroundings.
On one side of this is a police control box. The stadium doesn't have any floodlight pylons as such, but has rows of small floodlights running across the tops of the stands. The stadium is overlooked by a block of flats beyond the South Stand and it is not uncommon to see fans out on their balconies watching most of the game for nothing.
In one corner of the stadium between the Jimmy Seed (South) & East Stands, there is a large video screen.
Outside the ground there is a statue of Charlton's legendary former goalkeeper Sam Bartram.

Future Ground Developments

Mike Keeler informs me; 'The Club have now got planning permission from Greenwich Council to increase the capacity of the Valley to 31,000. This will involve adding a second tier to the East Stand as well as the 'filling in' of the South East corner of the stadium. Formal time scales have yet to be announced as to when this will take place, but it is believed that work will start within the next two years'.

George Packman adds; 'The Club intend to increase the capacity of the Valley to over 40,000. Following on from the first phase of the scheme, which would see an additional tier added to the East Stand, the Club then intend to redevelop the Jimmy Seed (South) Stand.
This would be replaced with a similar-looking structure to the existing North Stand. This would result in the Valley becoming totally enclosed and boosting capacity to 37,000. Lastly a third tier could be added to the new

South Stand at a later stage, meaning that the Valley would have a final capacity of 40,600'.

What Is It Like For Visiting Supporters?

Away fans are housed in the Jimmy Seed (South) Stand at one end of the ground, which is slightly raised above pitch level, making for a generally good view. Up to 3,000 away fans can be accommodated in this end. However, if the visiting team are unlikely to sell their full allocation of 3,000 tickets, then this end may be shared with home fans. This stand, being older than the rest of the ground, looks somewhat tired and those used to other modern Premiership grounds may find it somewhat of a shock.

Peter Inwood, a visiting Leeds fan adds; 'There is one solitary supporting column in the entire ground and guess where it is? Right in the middle, behind the goal, in the away supporters end. Very annoying it is as well. However, I would commend the stewards, who took a relaxed attitude to the away supporters who stood throughout the match, although expect to be searched on the way in'. Otherwise the height between rows is good and the stand quite steep, keeping you fairly close to the playing action. It is worth noting that if your team is allocated the whole stand, that there are refreshment areas on either side of the stand. As to be expected, those located by the entrance turnstiles tend to be busiest, whilst those on the other side of the stand are normally less congested. The refreshment kiosks serve the usual array of hot dogs, pasties and burgers. These outlets are supplemented by separate hot dog stalls. There is also a Ladbrokes betting kiosk inside the ground.

I was quite impressed with the atmosphere at the Valley and I can see why many away fans see it as one of their favourite away days to the capital. The Charlton fans are clearly passionate about their team, but in a non-intimidating way. I had a pleasant day out and would go again. I was particularly impressed with the loud P.A. system that played some great music before the game commenced and it was no surprise when just before the teams came out onto the pitch that 'Into The Valley....' rocked around the stadium. It is worth noting that you can only gain entrance to the ground by ticket, which you have to buy from a ticket booth beforehand.

Where To Drink?

Simon Phillips informs me that 'The Antigallican, a big pub near Charlton station, seems to be the favourite haunt of away supporters'. However, it can get very busy and this is not helped by the local police not allowing fans to drink outside. It is a rather basic pub but has real ale available (albeit a lone handpump) and also offers a selection of filled rolls and pork pies. Colin Gilham recommends the 'Rose of Denmark' on Woolwich Road. The pub not only allows in away supporters but absolutely welcomes them. They have a photo display on the wall of fans from visiting clubs that have frequented the pub this season and it also has Sky television'. Please note that this is a home supporters-only pub after the game. To find these pubs, come out of Charlton station and turn left into Charlton Church Lane and the Antigallican pub is down on the right hand corner. If you continue down to the T-junction with the Woolwich Road and turn left you will reach the Rose of Denmark further down on the left.

There is also the Charlton Liberal Club, to which away fans are welcome on payment of an entry fee of £1. This is more spacious, less busy, has a large-screen television and families are welcome. The club can be found by turning right out of Charlton station and walking 300 yards up the hill on the left hand side of the road, past the row of shops. The club is a five-minute walk from the away end, but like the Rose Of Denmark, it becomes a home supporters-only venue after the game. Alternatively alcohol is available in the away end before kick off, but strangely not at half time.

How To Get There & Where To Park?

Leave the M25 at Junction 2 and follow the A2 towards London. When the A2 becomes the A102(M), take the A206 towards Woolwich and you will come to the ground on your right. If you cross over the Thames or reach Blackheath, then you have gone too far. There is street parking, but due to a local residents parking scheme, not in close vicinity to the ground or Charlton railway station. However as you come off the A2 onto the A206, there is some street parking to be had on your right, in a couple of streets, before you reach the Rose of Denmark pub. Colan Hyde informs me that you can also park at the Thames Barrier visitor centre (cost £5). Colin Gilham adds; 'There is some street parking to be had around the industrial estates in the area, in Westmoor Street, Eastmoor Street (the very road where the club was apparently formed 100 years ago!), Warspite Road and Ruston Road. If you are coming up the Woolwich Road from the the Blackwall Tunnel, then as you go past the ground, the industrial estates are on the left-hand side.

By Train/Tube

The ground is in walking distance of Charlton railway station, which is served by Charing Cross and London Bridge mainline stations. On Saturdays there are also services from Cannon Street station.

Colin Gilham informs me; 'Come out of Charlton station into Charlton Church Lane (all exits lead onto this road). and turn right and cross over to the other side. Take the next left into Floyd Road and then right into Valley Grove for the away section entrance'.

Darryl Chamberlain adds; 'Although Charlton station is very close to the Valley, many people will find it easier to take the (far more reliable) tube. Using the Jubilee Line to get to North Greenwich station and then take a short ride on buses 161, 472 or 486 to get to the ground'.

Local Rivals

Crystal Palace, Millwall & West Ham.

Admission Prices

Home Fans:

Adults £20-£35
OAP's/Under 18's £20-£25
Under16's: £15-£20

Away Fans:

Adults: £25-£35
OAP's/Under 18's: £15-£25
Under 16's: £5-£20

Programme & Fanzines
Official Programme £3.
Valley View Fanzine £1.

Record Attendance
75,031 v Aston Villa
FA Cup 5th Round, February 12th, 1938.

Modern All Seated Attendance Record:
27,111 v Chelsea
Premier League, September 17th, 2005.
(This record has subsequently been equalled).

Average Attendance
2006-2007: 26,050 (Premier League)

Other Places Of Interest
The ground is in walking distance of the River Thames and the Thames Barrier, which is worth a visit, if only to admire the views of Canary Wharf and the Millennium Dome.

Did You Know?
In the 1970s Charlton boasted the largest ground in the League, with a capacity of some 66,000 fans.

Colchester United

Layer Road

Ground Name: Layer Road
Capacity: 6,200
Address: Layer Road, Colchester, Essex, CO2 7JJ
Main Telephone No: 0871-226-2161
Fax No: 01206-715-327
Team Nickname: The U's
Year Ground Opened: 1937*
Pitch Size: 110 x 70 yards
Home Kit Colours: Blue & White

Official Website:
www.cu-fc.com

Unofficial Websites:
ColUOnline - www.coluonline.com (Rivals Network)
Swedish Supporters Club - www.barside.com

What's The Ground Like?

The ground is the smallest in the league and is really showing its age. With the Club pursuing its aim of moving to a new stadium then (perhaps understandably) there has been little noticeable recent investment in Layer Road.

At one end is the small, covered Layer Road End terrace, which is given to away fans. Reaching only nine terraced steps in height, it is rather on the compact side. Opposite, the Clock End is a small, newish, covered all-seater stand. It is a strange affair, having more rows of seats on one side of the stand than the other. It also has a number of supporting pillars that run across the front of it and is situated very close to the playing action. Again it is on the small side, having only five rows of seating at its lowest point. As its name suggests it does have a clock at the back of it, which I noticed was well protected in the event of a stray shot being aimed in its direction.

The Main Stand on one side is again covered and is seated in the middle with covered terrace to either side. I noted that the roof supports in this stand were particularly rusty and that the stand had wooden seating to its rear, the latter probably there since the stand was opened in 1933. The terrace located on the side of the Main Stand towards the Layer Road End looks a different structure to the rest of the Main Stand and therefore I can only assume that this was added to it at some stage. On the roof of the Main Stand rests a small covered platform for television cameras. The other side is a mostly covered terrace and is known as the Barside Popular Terrace. It runs about two-thirds of the length of the pitch, with the covered area straddling the half way line, with a portion of open terracing located towards the Clock End. This stand has supporting pillars which may obstruct your view. The ground is completed with a modern set of floodlights.

An unusual feature of the ground is that the Club have a flag pole located next to the Club Offices, where a Club Flag is proudly displayed on matchdays (on my last visit I witnessed a few stewards pretending to salute the flag as it was hoisted up.

Future Ground Developments

The Club have received planning permission to build a new 10,000 capacity stadium at the Cuckoo Farm site just off the A12 in Colchester. The new ground will have four covered sides with approximately 30 hospitality boxes, parking facilities and a direct link road from the A12.
It has the same designers as the McAlpine Stadium in Huddersfield. If all goes to plan then the Club should be kicking off in their new stadium for the start of the 2008/09 season.

What Is It Like For Visiting Supporters?

Visitors are housed in the small Layer Road End, where at least there is cover and you are close to the playing action. However there are a number of supporting pillars running along the front of this stand which could be annoying whilst trying to watch the game. Up to 650 supporters can be accommodated in this area. A small number of seats (196) are also made available to away supporters, but unusually they are at the opposite end to the away terrace in the Clock End.

The acoustics of the Layer Road Terrace are particularly good and away supporters can really make some noise from this end. With the main singing contingent of Colchester fans located to the right of this terrace in the Popular Side, then this makes for a good atmosphere.
A small refreshment hut offers pies, sausage rolls (£1.80) and burgers (£2.70).

Where To Drink?

The nearest pub to Layer Road is the Drury at the top of Layer Road, which is generally okay for away fans, unless it is a high profile match. A better bet may be to head towards the town centre where you will pass the Dragoon pub. Jonathan Hull adds; 'for a drink near the ground try the Dragoon in Butt Road which is on the way to the ground, almost opposite the police station. It is in the Campaign For Real Ale guide, serves good ales and does a mean chilli on match days. It is full of Col U fans but of the friendly real ale drinker variety'. To find this pub, with the Club's ticket and administrative offices behind you turn left and go down Layer Road. You will pass the Drury pub on your left and then at the T-junction turn right into Butt Road. Continue down this road passing Colchester Barracks on the right and just further down is the Dragoon Pub which serves a range of Adnams beers. If you carry on down Butt Road, passing the Police Station on your left, proceed through the underpass towards the main shopping area. Turn right into St Johns Street and on the right is another CAMRA listed pub, the Fox & Fiddle, which serves a number of real ales. Almost next door is the Playhouse, which is a Wetherspoons outlet. This former theatre is a spectacular setting for a bar, and is well worth a visit. It is about a 15-minute walk from the ground into the town centre. However it will probably take about 20 minutes to walk back as it is mostly uphill.

Peter Mansell adds; 'A great pub for visiting fans who like quality real ale is called The Odd One Out, situated at the bottom part of Mersea Road 15 minutes walk away from the ground. It has won the best real ale pub in Essex award on more than one occasion'.

How To Get There & Where To Park?

The ground is situated one mile south of the town centre. Thanks to Richard Lay for providing the directions below:

From The North:
Leave the A14 and then join the M11. Come off the M11 at J8 (Stansted Airport/A120) and follow the A120 towards Braintree & Colchester. The A120 joins the A12 and you then come off at the next junction (26) and take the A1124 towards Colchester West/Halstead. At the top of the slip road turn left at the roundabout and continue along Essex Yeomanry Way and the London Road towards the town centre. Proceed to traffic lights (MFI store on your right). Turn right and follow this road to its end where a pub (Leather Bottle) is on left. Turn left and follow until traffic lights at Boadicea Way, where you turn right. Go to its end and then turn left; this is Layer Rd and the ground is about 1/4 mile further down on the left.

From The South:
Leave the M25 at junction 28 and head east. Leave the A12 before you reach Colchester at the Halstead/ Cambridge turn off. Turn right at top of slip road and continue along Essex Yeomanry Way, left at roundabout into London Road. Then as above.

Richard also informs me; 'Parking is easiest in Boadicea Way or in one of the side roads to the right and this will leave about a 5-7 min walk to the ground'. On the car parking front David Battson adds; 'there is a small unofficial car park about 200 yards from the ground. There is also a Park and Ride scheme which is well signposted (situated at Sobroan barracks). Cost for the unofficial car park is £2.50 per car, and holds between 50 to 100 cars. The Matchday Park and Ride is slightly larger and is £2 per car. However, the buses can be every 20 minutes or so'.

By Train

The nearest station to the ground is Colchester Town which is around a ten-minute walk away and is a seven-minute journey time away from Colchester mainline station where most fans are likely to end up at. The main Colchester station is really too far from the ground to walk, so either get another train to Colchester Town station or jump in a taxi, which should cost about £5. If you arrive early at Colchester mainline station and decide to walk to the ground (crossing through the town centre) then it should take about 40 minutes.

Local Rivals

Ipswich Town, Southend United and Wycombe.

Admission Prices

Home Fans:

Main Stand (Seating)
Adults £23, Concessions £15

Clock End (Seating)
Adults £20, Concessions £14

Barside Terrace
Adults £19, Concessions £12

Family Area
Adults + 1 Child Under 12 £20, Additional Adult £20, Additional Under 12 £5

Away Fans:

Clock End Seating
Adults £20, Concessions £14

Layer Road End Terrace
Adults £19, Concessions £12

Programme

Official Programme £3

Record Attendance

19,072 v Reading
FA Cup 1st Round, November 27th, 1948.

Average Attendance

2006-2007: 5,270 (Championship)

Did You Know?

That prior to the building of the Clock End, that end of the ground was once called the Spion Kop, as it previously was an open bank of terracing.

Coventry City

Ricoh Arena

Ground Name: Ricoh Arena
Capacity: 32,500 (all seated)
Address: Phoenix Way, Foleshill, Coventry, CV6 6GE
Main Telephone No: 0870-421-1987
Fax No: 024-7623-4099
Club Nickname: The Sky Blues
Year Ground Opened: 2005
Pitch Size: 105 x 68m
Home Kit Colours: Sky Blue & White

Official Website:
www.ccfc.co.uk
Ricoh Arena Coventry - www.ricoharena.com

Unofficial Websites:
Lets All Sing Together - www.letsallsingtogether.com
Gary Mabbutt's Knee – http://coventrycity.rivals.net/default.asp?sid=885 (Rivals Network)
CovCityFC - www.covcityfc.com

What's The Ground Like?

Like many grounds built in this country in the last ten years, the new Coventry stadium is functional and fairly conservative in its design. Three sides of the stadium, which are large single-tiered stands are fairly bland affairs. Happily, the complex has an exhibition centre attached to its West side, resulting in a unique-looking stand that gives more of a continental feel. Known as the Telent West Stand, it has a small tier of seats overhanging the larger lower tier, with a row of corporate hospitality boxes running along the back of the lower section. Along the top of the stand is a large area of white panelling (adorned with the logo of the stadium sponsors) that runs along the length of the stand and around the corners of either side of it. In one of these corners is located a Police Control box. Below the white panelling is a large-windowed corporate hospitality area.

The stadium is fully enclosed with all corners of the stadium being filled with spectator seating and all the stands are of the same height, giving it a symmetrical look. There a number of clear perspex panels located in the roof at the South end of the stadium, plus a large strip of perspex that runs around the stadium just below the roof at the back of three sides. These measures allow more natural light to enter the stadium, which helps the growth of the grass pitch. There is also a large video screen type scoreboard located in one corner of the stadium between the Jewson South and Tesco East Stands.

Outside the stadium on the back of the East Stand, fans can admire the 'Sky Blues Wall Of Fame'. This consists of six large panels, each dedicated to a former Coventry City great such as John Sillett, Jimmy Hill etc... The panels contain bricks that have been purchased by fans, which have their choice of inscriptions on. These type of schemes are popular around the country at a number of other grounds. I did send my cheque off to the Club with my choice of inscription which was; 'Coventry Are Rubbish' but for some reason I'm still waiting for my brick to appear!

The stadium was built by Laing O'Rourke, the same company who built the Millennium Stadium in Cardiff. It is owned by Coventry City Council, with the Football Club having a lease agreement to use the stadium. The stadium was opened in August 2005. Coventry City previously played at Highfield Road, their home since 1899.

What Is It Like For Visiting Supporters?

The location of away fans for the 2007/08 season is to be changed. Instead of being behind the goal in the Jewson South Stand, away supporters will be accommodated to one side of the Jewson South Stand (Blocks 6 & 7) towards the corner with the Telent West Stand. Around 3,000 supporters can be seated in this area. The angle of the stand is quite steep, meaning a fair bit of effort to climb to the top. Normally a steep stand means that fans are close to the playing action, but not here. Not only is there a sizeable red-coloured track surrounding the playing area, but this in turn is a considerable distance from the pitch itself. This does lead to some viewing problems, especially when the action is taking place at the other end. The leg room is adequate for most and the stadium does have good acoustics, which should help boost the atmosphere. Behind the stands there are spacious concourses and a number of food and drink outlets serving amongst other things the delicious 'Football's Famous Chicken Balti Pie' (£2.20), as well as steak & kidney pies, pasties, hot dogs and burgers (£2.50). Alcohol is also available in the form of Carling Lager & Worthington Bitter (both £2.60 a pint). The Club also offer a 'pie and a pint' for £4.60. The concourses also have a number of televisions which show the game being played inside.

Matt Walters, a visiting Reading fan adds; 'The Ricoh, as the tannoy announcer puts it, is one of the more interesting-looking new grounds when compared to others such as the Walkers Stadium! The acoustics are superb which creates a great atmosphere. However I found the seats to be quite uncomfortable, which is disappointing bearing in mind that this is a brand new stadium'. I have also received reports of supporters being regularly ejected from the stadium for persistent standing, so be on your best behaviour.

Where To Drink?

Robert Nunn, a visiting Reading fan informs me; 'Myself and a friend parked in Longford, about a ten-minute walk away from the stadium, and found a host of pubs situated along Longford Road. Whilst most looked quite partisan and only had Sky Blue shirts in, the "JK English Pub" was most welcoming. This Indian/Pub had a pub feel (pool table, jukebox, etc) but was also an Indian restaurant. On Saturday's it also does a £5 all you can eat lunchtime buffet'. To find this pub, coming away from the North Stand at the Ricoh, follow the towpath over the canal for about 400 yards passing the Tesco Extra on your right (which also has a cafe). When you come on to Longford Road, head right, towards Coventry city centre and the pub is around 200 yards on your right-hand side. Jamie Greenway adds; 'The Black Horse Pub, in between Longford and Exhall, has been attracting a fair amount of away supporters for most games. If you go to the top of Longford Road and around the roundabout towards Exhall, its on the right and normally has a burger van outside'. Paul Hunt, a visiting Norwich City supporter recommends 'the Coach and Horses on the Longford Road. Not the greatest-looking pub from the outside, but a very friendly welcome, with Sky sports television and tasty rolls on offer. The only drawback was the lone real ale pump, that alas was not on. We also parked there while we went to the match'.

If you are looking for food then the Simply Scrumptious sandwich bar is worth a mention as it does a wide range of freshly filled sandwiches and baguettes and also hot Shire Pies & Pasties (including Chicken Balti Pie) at very reasonable prices. To find it again go up to the roundabout and turn left into Winding House Lane and then left again into Hen Lane. The sandwich bar is down by the junction with Holbrook Lane'.

How To Get There & Where To Park?

Leave the M6 at Junction 3. Take the A444 towards the city centre and after one mile you will reach the stadium on your left.

Parking at the stadium is for permit holders only and fans are being encouraged to use the Park & Ride facilities plus a number of satellite car parks in operation on matchdays. There is a good-sized retail park located next to the stadium, but I guess restrictions will be put in place on matchdays. In addition a 'residents only' parking scheme has been put in place for all residential streets within a mile of the ground. The Club are utilising a number of car parks within walking distance of the stadium, in such places as factory units and local schools. The cost per car for these official car parks is £5. Colin Peel informs me; 'When you park up at one of the official 'park & walk' car parks, then you don't actually pay the £5 charge at the car park itself, but instead you are given a form by one of the car park attendants, which you have to get stamped at the stadium after you have paid. When I said that this seemed a bit cumbersome, the attendant pointed out the potential risk to them, at these car parks if they were handling hundreds of pounds in cash, so the arrangement was for their protection. However, the "parking paypoint" at the stadium was makeshift in the extreme - not a kiosk but an ordinary window which opened just far enough for you to slide your fiver under'.

Park & Ride Scheme

The Cub will have a Park & Ride scheme available on matchdays, which cost £7 per car (including return bus travel to the stadium for all the car's occupants). This is located at the Jaguar Research & Development in Whitley, Coventry and is located primarily for supporters coming up from the South and going to the stadium via the M1 junction 17 and then the A45 to Coventry. Continue on the A45 towards Coventry and at the large roundabout that is the junction with the A46 continue on the A45. At the next roundabout follow the signs for the 'Jaguar/Racquet Centre' to take you to the parking facility. The Club are asking fans to pre-book their Park & Ride space by calling 0247-623-6986.

Dominic Byrne, a visiting QPR supporter adds; 'I took the A444 from Junction 3 of the M6. Shortly before the roundabout that is right next to the stadium, there is a slip road on the left. There was parking in the slip road and in the light industrial estate by Makro. I chose the latter and parked easily on the street. This resulted in a quick getaway after the game'.

There is also a private car park run by Leisure Ireland, located a few minutes drive away from Junction 3 of the M6. It has 200 spaces and is then a 15-minute walk away from the stadium. It advertises as secure parking and apparently getting back to the motorway after the match is very easy. The cost to park there is £5 per car. To find the car park, follow the 'pink arrow' signs from Junction 3 of the M6. Fans are encouraged to pre-book their places online at their website: www.walktrot.com.

By Train

Coventry train station is about three and half miles away from the stadium and really is too far to walk. There is a shuttle bus that operates from the bus station to the Tesco/Arena stadium complex. It departs every 10 minutes and costs £3 return (for adults), otherwise jump in a taxi.

Lori Kilpatrick adds; 'there is a bus stop directly outside the train station, from which most passing buses go to the Pool Meadow Bus Station. On checking that the bus indeed goes to the Bus Station ask for a "match day ticket" which will cost you £3 and will cover all journeys on that day in Coventry (note no change is given on Coventry buses so have the exact cash ready). Get off at Pool Meadow and look for the stand from which the Football Special Service operates (there will probably be a number of other fans in the vicinity). The service number is 101 and runs every 10 minutes from two hours prior to kick off and then returns every five minutes, for one hour after the game has ended. Buses depart after the match from outside the Jewson South Stand'. Tim Sansom, a visiting Ipswich Town fan adds; 'After the match there was a massive queue for the six football special buses going back to the city centre. We decided not to wait and walked up to the roundabout (signposted Holbrooks) by the stadium and caught the number 13 service back into the city'.

Local Rivals

Aston Villa, Leicester City, Birmingham City, West Bromwich Albion, Wolverhampton Wanderers.

Admission Prices

Home Fans:

Telent West Stand (Centre):
Adults £23, Concessions £11.50, Under 18's £11.50, Under 16's £10.50*, Under 12's £9.50*, Under 7's £8.50*

Tesco East Stand (Centre):
Adults £23, Concessions £11.50, Under 18's £11.50, Under 16's £10.50*, Under 12's £9.50*, Under 7's £8.50*

Telent West Stand (South Wing):
Adults £22, Concessions £11, Under 18's £11, Under 16's £10*, Under 12's £9*, Under 7's £8*

Tesco East Stand (Wings):
Adults £22, Concessions £11, Under 18's £11, Under 16's £10*, Under 12's £9*, Under 7's £8*

Jewson South Stand (Wings):
Adults £22, Concessions £11, Under 18's £11, Under 16's £10*, Under 12's £9*, Under 7's £8*

Coventry Evening Telegraph North Stand:
Adults £22, Concessions £11, Under 18's £11, Under 16's £10*, Under 12's £9*, Under 7's £8*

North East Corner:
Adults £21, Concessions £10, Under 18's £10, Under 16's £9*, Under 12's £8*, Under 7's £7*

North West Corner:
Adults £20, Concessions £10, Under 18's £10, Under 16's £9*, Under 12's £8*, Under 7's £7*

Away Fans:

Jewson South Stand:
Adults: £22 Senior Citizen: £11, Junior £10.

* A further discount on this ticket price is available for Junior Sky Blue Members. In some areas of the stadium Under 7's who are Junior Sky Blue Members and accompanied by an adult are admitted free.

Programme & Fanzines

Official Programme £3
Twist & Shout Fanzine £1

Record Attendance

At Highfield Road:
51,455 v Wolverhampton Wanderers
Division 2, April 29th, 1967.

At the Ricoh Arena:
28,120 v Middlesbrough
FA Cup 4th Round, January 28th, 2006.

Average Attendance

2006-2007: 20,541 (Championship)

Did You Know?

That the sky blue club colour was introduced in 1889. The city used to be a major producer of coloured materials, especially sky blue. There is an old expression 'As true as Coventry Blue'.

Crystal Palace

Selhurst Park

Ground Name: Selhurst Park
Capacity: 26,309 (all seated)
Address: Selhurst Park, London, SE25 6PU
Main Telephone No: 0208-768-6000
Fax No: 0208-771-5311
Ticket Office Enquiries: 0871-2000-071
Club Nickname: The Eagles
Year Ground Opened: 1924
Pitch Size: 110 x 74 yards
Home Kit Colours: Red & Blue

Official Website:
www.cpfc.co.uk

Unofficial Website:
Holmesdale Online - http://holmesdale.cjb.net

■ What's The Ground Like?

Both ends of the ground have had new stands constructed in recent years, much improving the overall look of the ground. The two-tiered Holmesdale Road Stand is at one end, and is where the bulk of home supporters congregate. This stand has a large lower tier, with a smaller upper tier that overhangs it. The stand looks impressive and has a large curved roof, as well as windshields on either side of the upper tier. Opposite is the Whitehorse Lane Stand. This is unusual in having a single tier of seating, with a double row of executive boxes above them. A video screen perches on the roof, which somehow doesn't look as if it was meant originally to be fitted there. This stand has now been renamed the 'Croydon Advertiser Family Stand'. One side is the large, covered, single-tiered Arthur Wait stand, while on the other side the Main Stand is also single-tiered. Both stands are now beginning to show their age; for example both have wooden seating and the Main Stand has a row of small floodlights perched on its roof and both have a number of supporting pillars. The Arthur Wait Stand has a TV gantry suspended beneath its roof. Michael Clement adds; 'To add a bit of razzmatazz to the beginning of games, the club now play a programme of loud music, as the teams emerge onto the pitch'. This includes playing 'Glad All Over' by the Dave Clarke Five, which is enthusiastically joined in to by the Palace fans.

■ What Is It Like For Visiting Supporters?

On the whole Crystal Palace is a fairly relaxed ground to visit and you are unlikely to encounter any problems, except perhaps getting stuck in the traffic on the way to the game! Away fans are located in one side of the Arthur Wait Stand near to the Holmesdale Road End, where just over 2,000 away supporters can be accommodated. Nikita, a visiting Gillingham fan adds; 'If you are seated towards the rear of the stand then you will find that you are sitting on old wooden seats and there is very little leg room'. Plus the views of the playing action are not particularly great from the back of the stand, due to the overhang of the roof. And if that is not enough then there is the odd supporting pillar to contend with too!

On my last visit there was a particularly good atmosphere within the ground, especially from the home fans in the Holmesdale Road End, which is situated to the left of the away section. I was impressed with the Palace fans, who clearly were passionate about their Club, but in a non-intimidatory manner, towards away fans. In fact there was plenty of good banter going on between the two sets of supporters. Within the Arthur Wait Stand, there are plenty of refreshments available, including burgers (£2) and chips (£1). However, if there is a sizeable away support, then getting food and drink could be a problem, as there is only one small refreshment area to cater for the whole away support. Plus as there is no formal queuing system, then joining the scrum that inevitably ensues at the counter is not for the faint-hearted so you may consider getting something outside the ground before the game starts .... Also if you do happen to visit the Gents, watch out for the small downward flight of steps to the toilets. I almost went flying!

■ Where To Drink?

Opposite Thornton Heath Railway Station there is a Wetherspoons pub, popular with both home and away supporters. It is about a 15-minute walk from here to the ground (as you come out of the pub turn right and follow the other fans). There are plenty of Kebab & Chip shops available on the route to the ground.

Phil Moore recommends the following pubs around Selhurst Park, where on the whole, away fans are tolerated:

As Phil says; 'Good news for real ale lovers is that Palace is surrounded by more CAMRA listed pubs than ever, I think there are 4-5 in the CAMRA Good Beer Guide. Not to mention the two new Wetherspoon outfits'

Around Selhurst Railway Station:

Two Brewers - Gloucester Road
From the station cross the road using the zebra crossing and turn right (heading away from ground). Gloucester Road is third on the left. Comfortable cottage type pub. Small public bar, Shepherd Neame ales on sale -rare outside Kent.

Clifton Arms - Clifton Road
Turn left out of the station and take the 3rd road on the left. This is the nearest pub to Stadium. A big Victorian corner pub well known for high quality of ales. Selection changes weekly. 3 or 4 bitters always on. Drawback: due to popularity away fans will only be admitted if they turn up early. After One thirty it's Palace season ticket holders only past the doorman.

Around Thornton Heath Railway Station:

The Railway Telegraph - Brigstock Road
From the station cross the road (zebra) and turn right. Pub is 100 yards down this road. A spacious Youngs house. Firm favourite with away fans. Also there's a Wetherspoons pub directly opposite the station.

Around Norwood Junction Railway Station:

The Alliance - Station Road (by clock tower)
A gem. Usually two real ales. Narrow shape of bar does means it can get crowded when waiting for service. Bar staff are friendly.

Wetherspoons - South Norwood High Street
A few doors down from the Alliance. Standard Wetherspoons fare.

The Ship - South Norwood High St
From Station turn right at Clock Tower into the High Street. Continue down to cross roads with Portland Road. Cross with care and carry on for another 100 metres. The Ship is a free house with 3-4 real ales and ciders. Has wooden floor, juke box, Sky TV. Very noisy.

The Portmanor - Portland Road
From Station Turn right at Clock Tower into the High St. Continue down to crossroads with Portland Road. At crossroads turn right heading downhill under railway bridge You can't miss the pub. Do not be put off by garish disco decor; this place serves great beers. Usually 3 real ales. Banks of TVs behind the bar are continuously screening football.

Alternatively alcohol is served inside the ground.

■ How To Get There & Where To Park?

Leave the M25 at Junction 7 and follow the signs for the A23 to Croydon. At Purley bear left onto the A23 at its junction with the A 235 (to Croydon). You will pass roundabouts and junctions with the A232 and A236 as you pass Croydon, after which the A23 bears left at Thornton Heath (at the Horseshoe pub roundabout). Here you must go straight over, into Brigstock Road (B266), passing Thornton Heath Station on your left and bearing right on to the High Street. At the next mini roundabout, (Whitehorse Road/Grange Road) go left into Whitehorse Lane. The ground is on your right.

Richard Down informs me; 'An alternative route for fans coming from the North, is to leave the M25 at Junction 10 and follow the A3 towards London. After about ten miles you will reach the Tolworth roundabout at which you turn right onto the A240 towards Epsom. After about three miles turn onto the A232 towards Sutton. Follow the A232 through Sutton and Carshalton and just before reaching Croydon, turn left onto the A23 north towards Thornton Heath'. Where the A23 bears left at Thornton Heath (at the Horsehoe pub roundabout). Here you must go straight over, into Brigstock Road (B266), passing Thornton Heath Station on your left and bearing right on to the High Street. At the next mini roundabout, (Whitehorse Road/Grange Road) go left into Whitehorse Lane. The ground is on your right.

There is plenty of street parking in the area. Please note that the traffic can be pretty bad on Saturdays even without football traffic, so make sure you allow yourself some extra time to make the journey.

■ By Train

The nearest railway stations are Selhurst or Thornton Heath which are served by London Victoria main line station, Clapham Junction, London Bridge (every 30 mins) and East Croydon (every 15 mins). You can also use Norwood Junction station which is also served by Victoria, but is a little further away. It is then a 10-15-minute walk to ground. Please note that Crystal Palace station is nowhere near the ground.

If you are coming from outside London, it may be an idea to purchase a 'Travelcard' at the first tube station you encounter (or some train operators also allow you to add this onto your train ticket) and tell the clerk that you want a 'Travelcard' that will cover you as far as Selhurst or Thornton Heath. The card then allows you unlimited travel on the tube and trains within the London travel zone and avoids having to buy a ticket for each leg of the journey.

■ Local Rivals
Charlton Athletic, Millwall (and a little further away) Brighton & Hove Albion.

■ Admission Prices
Common with most Clubs, Crystal Palace operate a category system (A, B & C) for matches whereby tickets cost more for the most popular matches (category A).

Executive Area/Directors Box:
Adults £50 (B £45) (C £40),
Concessions £33 (B £30) (C £27)

Main Stand:
Adults: £40 (B £35) (C £30),
Concessions £23 (B £20) (C £17)

Croydon Advertiser Family (Whitehorse Lane) **Stand:**
Adults: £30 (B £25) (C £20),
Concessions £18 (B £15) (C £12)
Under 16's £13 (B £10) (C £7)

Holmesdale Stand (Gallery):
Adults: £37 (B £32) (C £27),
No Concessions

Holmesdale Stand (Upper):
Adults: £35 (B £30) (C £25),
Concessions £18 (B £15) (C £12)

Holmesdale Stand (Lower):
Adults: £30 (B £25) (C £20),
Concessions £18 (B £15) (C £12)

Arthur Wait Stand (Including Away Fans):
Adults: £30 (B £25) (C £20),
Concessions £18 (B £15) (C £12)

■ Programme
Official Programme: £3

■ Record Attendance
51,482 v Burnley
Division Two, May 11th, 1979.

Modern All Seated Attendance Record:
26,193 v Arsenal
Premier League, November 6th, 2004.

■ Average Attendance
2006-2007: 17,474 (Championship)

■ Did You Know?
Palace, wearing blue and white at the time, were a working men's team, founded by employees at the Crystal Palace in 1861.

Hull City

Kingston Communications Stadium

Ground Name:	Kingston Communications Stadium
Capacity:	25,504 (all seated)
Address:	The Circle, Walton St, Hull, HU3 6HU
Main Telephone No:	0870-837-0003
Fax No:	01482-304-882
Ticket Office:	0870-837-0004
Ticket Office Fax:	01482-304-923
Team Nickname:	The Tigers
Year Stadium Opened:	2002
Pitch Size:	114 x 78 yards
Home Kit Colours:	Amber & Black

Official Website:
www.hullcityafc.net

Unofficial Websites:
Amber Nectar - www.ambernectar.com
Hull City Online - www.hullcity.com (Footy Mad)
Southern Supporters - www.hcss.org.uk

What's The Ground Like?

The Kingston Communications Stadium (commonly referred to as the KC Stadium) was opened in December 2002. It cost almost £44m to build, by Birse Construction and is home to both Hull Football & Rugby League Clubs. I'm not a fan of most of the bland new grounds, but the KC Stadium is an exception to this rule. Built in a parkland setting, the stadium can be seen for some distance around and will undoubtedly win awards for its impressive design.

The stadium is totally enclosed, with the West Stand being around twice the size of the other three sides. The roof rises up and curves around the West Stand, giving the stadium an interesting look. Inside the curves continue as each of the stands slightly bow around the playing area, drawing the eye to sweep panoramically around them. Each stand is single-tiered, apart from the two-tiered West Stand. This stand also has a row of executive boxes running across its middle. There is an electric scoreboard at the North End of the stadium, where the Police Control Box is also situated. The pitch looked in excellent condition on my visit in January, plus it has had under-soil heating installed. The P.A. system within the stadium is also excellent. All told this is a stadium that would not look out of place in the Premiership.

Future Ground Developments

Craig Harper informs me; 'The Club have plans to add an additional tier to both the East & South Stands, which will increase the capacity of the KC Stadium to around 34,000'. However, no firm timescales have been announced as to when this may take place.

What Is It Like For Visiting Supporters?

Away fans are located in the North Stand End of the ground, where up to 4,000 supporters can be housed, although the normal allocation is half that number. As you would expect a visit to the KC Stadium is far pleasanter than it was to the old Boothferry Park. The facilities available are good, plus there is not a bad view of the playing action to be found anywhere (although you are a little set back from the pitch). On the concourse alcohol is available, plus burgers, pies etc.. including the delicious 'Football's Famous Chicken Balti Pie' (£2.20). I found the atmosphere to be good within the stadium, but unfortunately there is an element of Hull support that feels the need to berate away supporters throughout the game. This, coupled with the fact that there are no pubs nearby that welcome away fans, means that although it is a truly magnificent stadium it is still not the greatest of days out.

Please note that the stadium has been designated a no-smoking and a no-standing area. The latter decree does seem a little ridiculous. This has led to some unpleasant confrontations between away fans and stewards, so you have been warned. You can, however, smoke on the concourses but not at your seat.

Where To Drink?

There are a number of pubs within a few minutes walk of the stadium, but these are all designated as being for home supporters only. Most local fans still seem to be heading for pubs situated around Boothferry Park. These are best avoided by away fans particularly the Silver Cod and 'Admiral of the Humber' pubs. Otherwise you can head for the nearby City Centre, where there are plenty of pubs to be found. David Jenkin, a visiting Exeter fan recommends; 'the Sandringham pub, near to Hull main station, in the City Centre. On my visit the pub was both friendly and welcoming'.

Robert Walker adds; 'If you are walking to the stadium from the City Centre there are several pubs on Spring Bank, including the Editorial and the Tap and Spile.
Or there is the Admiral of the Humber (a Wetherspoons outlet) on Anlaby Road near Hull Paragon Railway Station'.
Whilst Keith Brown informs me, 'behind Paragon station is another pub called the Yorkshireman, which was okay'.
Otherwise alcohol, Carling & Tetleys are served within the stadium at £2.50 per pint. However for some high profile matches, the club do not provide alcohol to away supporters.

How To Get There & Where To Park?

The stadium is fairly close to the old Boothferry Park ground, but slightly nearer to the town centre, which is 3/4 of a mile away. If you used to approach the old ground down Anlaby Road, pass the ground on your right, go under the railway bridge, and at the second set of traffic lights, turn left into Walton Street and you're there.

From The West:

Leave the M62 at Junction 38 and join the A63, towards Hull. Stay on the A63 and the stadium is clearly signposted (KC Stadium) as you approach Hull.
About one mile from the centre of Hull leave the A63 (also signposted for the Hull Royal Infirmary) and take the 2nd exit at the roundabout. Turn left at the lights and then over the flyover, right at the next lights and the ground is down on the right.

From The North:

Leave the A164 at the Humber Bridge Roundabout and take the first exit into Boothferry Road. The stadium is 3 miles down this road on the left.

Car Parking

Jo Johnson informs me; 'the stadium has its own massive car park right next to the stadium, with access from Walton Street. It is floodlit, with a covered surface (that is, not a mud bath) and open to home and away supporters alike. If you get there early and want to go into the City centre, there is a park and ride bus to and from the car park. The cost of parking for the game is £3. It's easier to park at Hull than at any ground I know of - but there is one drawback, namely, getting away again at the end of the game. It can take up to half an hour if you park a long way from the exits. Also, visitors need to be aware that there are two exits onto Walton Street after a game, the one to the right as you face Walton Street allows right turns only, and the one to the left allows left turns only. Visitors will want the left one to get straight back onto Anlaby Road'.

Alternatively there is a Park & Ride facility signposted off the A63 (shared with home supporters). Many fans opt to park in one of the many town centre car parks and then walk out to the stadium. Chris Bax adds; 'It is perhaps easiest to park at the Infirmary (clearly signposted from the A63) where parking is only £2 for 4 hours (£3 for 8). It's a 10-15-minute walk to the ground from there'.

Whilst Robert Walker adds; 'The most convenient car park in the city centre is the Pryme Street multi-storey car park, which is open to 7.30pm. Leave the A63 at the Myton Street exit and head North towards the city centre. You will pass Paragon station on your left. At the next traffic lights turn right into Spencer Street and then immediately left into Prospect Street and follow road round to the right into Pryme Street. Car park entrance is on right. There is also an NCP car park at the end of Pryme Street and Council surface car parks off Freetown Way.
To walk to Stadium cross over Ferensway and walk along Spring Bank. Turn left onto Derringham Street by Polar Bear pub and right onto the walkway to the stadium'.

Please note that some residential areas near to the stadium have been made residents only parking zones, so don't park there as you may well end up with a parking fine. John Womersley adds; 'There is some street parking less than five minutes walk away. Leave the A63 at the Humber Bridge Roundabout and take the first exit into Boothferry Road. Pass Boothferry Park and forward onto Anlaby Road towards the Hull Royal Infirmary, You will pass the KC stadium on your left. Go over the flyover and turn right at The Eagle pub into Coltman Street, then take the 2nd right into Cholmley St then 4th right into the Boulevard. There are many side streets without parking restrictions. To get to the ground simply walk to the top of the Boulevard and go up the pedestrian walkway to the stadium. To get home simply go the other way down the Boulevard, then left into Hessle Rd, after 1/4 mile you'll come to a roundabout which takes you onto the A63 (Clive Sullivan Way) and M62.

By Train

The stadium is 15 minutes walk from Hull Paragon station. Visiting fans should leave the railway station on the south side and turn right onto Anlaby Road. Go straight ahead along this road for the stadium. Thanks to Robert Walker for providing the train information.

Local Rivals

Grimsby Town, Scunthorpe United and from a little further afield Doncaster Rovers and Leeds United.

Hull City

Admission Prices

Home Fans:

De Vries West Stand (Lower Tier):
Adults £23
Concessions £14

De Vries West Stand (Upper Tier):
Adults £22
Concessions £12

De Vries West Stand Family Section (Lower Tier):
Adults £18
OAP's £14
Juniors £10

De Vries West Stand Family Section (Upper Tier):
Adults £18
OAP's £12
Juniors £9

Ideal Standard East Stand:
Adults £21
Concessions £12

Ideal Standard East Stand Family Section:
Adults £17
OAP's £12
Juniors £9

MKM South Stand:
Adults £23
Concessions £12

MKM South Stand Family Section:
Adults £17
OAP's £12
Juniors £9

Away Fans:

Smith & Nephew North Stand:
Adults £23
Concessions £12

Programme

Official Programme: £2.50.

Record Attendance

At The Kingston Communications Stadium:
25,280 England U21's v Holland U21's
February 24th, 2004

For a Hull game:
24,311 v Leeds United,
Championship, January 30th, 2007.

At Boothferry Park:
55,019 v Manchester United,
FA Cup 6th Round, February 26th, 1949.

Average Attendance

2006-2007: 18,114 (Championship)

Did You Know?

That Hull City are the only league team with two previous grounds, The Boulevard and Boothferry Park, still in existence.

Ipswich Town

Portman Road

Ground Name: Portman Road
Capacity: 30,300 (all seated)
Address: Portman Road, Ipswich, IP1 2DA
Main Telephone No: 01473-400-500
Fax No: 01473-400-040
Ticket Office: 0870-111-0555
Pitch Size: 112 x 70 yards
Team Nickname: Blues or Tractor Boys
Year Ground Opened: 1888
Home Kit Colours: Blue & White

Official Website:
www.itfc.co.uk

Unofficial Websites:
Those Were The Days - www.twtd.co.uk (Rivals Network)
Ipswich Town MAD - www.ipswichtown-mad.co.uk (Footy Mad Network)
Tractor Boys - www.tractor-boys.com
Singing The Blues - www.stb-online.co.uk (Sport Network)

What's The Ground Like?

The overall look of the ground has greatly improved, with the re-development of both ends in recent years. Both these ends, the Greene King (South) Stand and the North Stand, are similar in appearance and size, and dwarf the smaller older stands, located on each side of the ground. Unusually, both ends have a larger upper tier which overhangs slightly the smaller lower tier. Both have windshields to either side of the upper tier and they are complete, with some spectacular floodlights perched on their roofs. Both sides are much older stands and now look quite tired in comparison. On one side, the fair-sized Britannia Stand is a three-tiered covered stand, with a row of executive boxes running across its middle. Opposite is the smaller Cobbold Stand. Again it is two-tiered and has a row of executive boxes. However it is only partly covered, with the small lower tier of seating being open to the elements. Outside are two statues of two former Ipswich and England managers. One is of World Cup winner Sir Alf Ramsey and is located on the corner between the Cobbold and North Stand, while Sir Bobby Robson's statue is placed behind the Cobbold stand in Portman Road.

What Is It Like For Visiting Supporters?

Away fans are placed in one corner in the upper tier of the Cobbold Stand at one side of the pitch. Up to 1,700 away supporters can be accommodated (or according to some - crammed in). An additional 400 seats are also made available in the Family Section of the Cobbold Stand, where further concessions are available. Although the views from this area are not too bad, the legroom is a little cramped and, as with the rest of the stand, the facilities are beginning to show their age. On the plus side, away fans can really make some noise from this stand, contributing to a real great atmosphere.

Chris Watkins, a visiting Coventry City fan adds; 'I felt on my visits to Portman Road that the stewarding was a little over the top with fans being persistently asked to sit down. There was also a sizeable Police presence, for what really is a low profile fixture'.

I have always found this to be a friendly place and pleasurable day out, even though I've never seen my team win there! I even on one occasion got accosted by some

Ipswich fans, whilst coming out of the railway station and ended up accompanying them on a pub crawl before the game. Overall Portman Road is a good day out although it does seem to take an eternity to get there!

■ Where To Drink?

Alas, the main away supporters' pub for many a year, the 'Drum & Monkey' has now closed down. So at the moment there is really only the Station Hotel, near to the ground. This is located just outside the railway station and has been a traditional meeting place for away fans. Other pubs in the area such as the Victoria, the Hare & Hounds and the Swan, are very much home pubs and are best avoided by away fans.

■ How To Get There & Where To Park?

Follow the A14 around Ipswich, until you see the turning for Ipswich (A137). Stay on this road and you will eventually see the ground on your left. Bill Leggate adds 'there is extremely limited on-street car parking around the ground. There are, however, three pay-and-display parks in Portman Road with a total of about 800 spaces. It costs £3.50 to park your car there for the Saturday afternoon. Early arrival is recommended to ensure a space close to the ground. There are several town centre car parks within 10 minutes walk, all of which are well signposted,' plus there there is a multi-storey car park located next to the railway station, which costs £5 on a Saturday afternoon and £3 weekday evenings.

■ By Train

The ground is only a quarter of a mile away from Ipswich train station. You will see the ground as you come into the station. Ipswich is served by trains from London Liverpool Street and Peterborough.

■ Local Rivals

Norwich City, Colchester United.

■ Admission Prices

The prices quoted below are for those tickets purchased prior to matchday. Tickets purchased on matchday can cost up to £2.50 more per ticket.

Home Fans:

Cobbold Stand (Upper Premium Seats):
Adults £46, OAP's £34.50, Under 16's £23

Cobbold Stand (Upper Centre):
Adults £31.50, OAP's £20.50, Under 16's £9.50

Cobbold Stand (Upper Wings):
Adults £26.50, OAP's £18.50, Under 16's £9.50

Cobbold Stand (Family Area Lower Tier):
Adults £22.50, OAP's £15.50, Under 16's £6.50

Britannia Stand (Upper Premium Seats):
Adults £35.50, OAP's £20.50, Under 16's £9.50

Britannia Stand (Upper Centre):
Adults £31.50, OAP's £20.50, Under 16's £9.50

Britannia Stand (Upper Wings):
Adults £27.50, OAP's £19.50, Under 16's £9.50

Britannia Stand (Upper Outer Wings):
Adults £26.50, OAP's £18.50, Under 16's £9.50

Britannia Stand (Family Area Upper Tier):
Adults £26.50, OAP's £18.50, Under 16's £6.50

Britannia Stand (Family Area Lower Tier):
Adults £22.50, OAP's £15.50, Under 16's £6.50

Greene King South Stand (Premium Seats):
Adults £38.50, OAP's £28.50, Under 16's £19

Greene King South Stand (Upper Tier):
Adults £27.50, OAP's £19.50, Under 16's £9.50

Greene King South Stand (Lower Tier):
Adults £22.50, OAP's £15.50, Under 16's £9.50

North Stand (Upper Tier):
Adults £27.50, OAP's £19.50, Under 16's £9.50

North Stand (Lower Tier):
Adults £22.50, No Concessions

Away Fans:

Cobbold Stand (Upper Wing):
Adults: £26.50, Over 65's: £18.50, Under 16's: £9.50

If the size of the away support requires it then additional seating can be made available in the lower tier at a reduced ticket price compared to the Upper Tier.

■ Programme

Official Programme: £3

■ Record Attendance

38,010 v Leeds United,
FA Cup 6th Round, March 8th, 1975.

Modern All Seated Attendance Record:
30,152 v Norwich City
Division One, December 21st, 2003.

■ Average Attendance

2006-2007: 21,975 (Championship)

■ Did You Know?

That Ipswich claim to have been one of the first clubs to use goal nets in 1890.

Leicester City

Walkers Stadium

Ground Name: Walkers Stadium
Capacity: 32,500 (all seated)
Address: Filbert Way,
Leicester, LE2 7FL
Main Telephone Number: 0870-040-6000
Main Fax No: 0116-247-0585
Ticket Office: 0870-040-6000
Ticket Office Fax No: 0116-229-4404
Club Nickname: The Foxes
Pitch Size: 110 x 76 yards
Home Kit Colours: Blue & White

Official Website:
www.lcfc.co.uk

Unofficial Websites:
For Fox Sake - www.forfoxsake.com
The Fox Fanzine - www.foxfanzine.com (Rivals Network)
FilbertStreet.Net - www.filbertstreet.net
The Cunning Fox – www.norfox.net
South Coast Foxes - www.southcoastfox.netfirms.com
Foxes Talk Forum - www.foxestalk.co.uk/forums/
The Blue Army - www.thebluearmy.co.uk
Supporters Club Hinckley Branch - www.lcschinckley.co.uk

What's The Ground Like?

IIn August 2002 the club moved into its new home, only a stone's throw away from their old Filbert Street ground. The stadium was built by Birse Construction at a cost of £35m, is completely enclosed with all corners being filled with seating. The sides are of a good size, built in the same style and height. Running around three sides of the stadium, just below the roof, is a transparent perspex strip, which allows more light and facilitates pitch growth. On the remaining side is a row of executive boxes. Completely encircling the stadium and hanging from the roof itself is a collage of player images, along with adverts for the sponsors of the stadium, Walkers. There are also some basic looking (red LCD display) electric scoreboards at either end.

Like most new stadiums, this is functional but lacks character. I don't know whether I'm starting to suffer from 'new stadium fatigue' having visited so many in the last few years, but to me it seemed somewhat bland-looking both inside and out. Unusually the public address system is also broadcast on the speakers around the outside of the stadium. The Walkers Stadium does have one redeeming feature - atmosphere. The acoustics are very good and both sets of supporters can really make some noise, making for an enjoyable visit. The stadium is also used periodically for other sports such as rugby.

Future Ground Developments

The stadium has been built in such a way, that if required, an additional tier could be built onto the East Stand. This would increase the capacity to just under 40,000.

What Is It Like For Visiting Supporters?

Away supporters are housed in the North East corner of the stadium, where just over 3,000 fans can be accommodated. The view of the playing action is good (although you are set well back from the pitch) as well as the facilities available. The concourse is comfortable and there is your normal range of hot dogs, burgers and pies available (including the Pukka Balti Chicken pie £2.50, served in a tray with a fork). There are television screens on the concourse showing the game going on within the stadium. My only slight grumble was that the gents toilets are poorly designed. They have a narrow 'zig zag corridor' of an entrance which hindered people coming in or out and didn't help the major traffic flow at half time! On the positive side though, the atmosphere within the stadium was good, with the home fans singing on both sides of the away section. The atmosphere is further boosted by a huge bare-chested drummer, who is located at the back of the home section, immediately to the left of the away fans. The stewarding was also pretty relaxed. The teams come out to the Post Horn Gallop tune, reminiscent of horse riding and even fox hunting! (Leicester are nicknamed the Foxes).

Paul Groombridge, a visiting Gillingham fan adds; 'From the far upper seats of the away section, the view was pretty good, though from there, you'd probably complain of being too far away from the action (I thought it was okay). One good thing about being at the top of the away section - you can use the plastic transparent panels as pretty good drums when singing!'

I have received a number of reports of away fans being treated somewhat heavily handed by the local constabulary around the stadium and of some even being 'frog marched' from the railway station to the ground. Although these measures may be deemed necessary, in order to prevent violent disorder, doesn't do much for the overall away day experience at Leicester. Stuart Bible informs me; 'Just to confirm that the Police presence at Leicester Station is completely over the top. As a visiting QPR fan recently we were 'guided' to the Hind Pub & promptly asked to drink up at 2pm. All 25 of us were then escorted by 38 Police (I counted them) a Dog & 3 Police vans. Of the 25 were 3 children under 10! They should save their heavy-handedness for the day that there might be a real threat of trouble'.

Where To Drink?

The ground is walkable from the city centre (15-20 minutes), where there are plenty of pubs to be found. Most of the pubs near to the stadium are home fans only. In particular 'The Victory' and 'The F Bar' pubs should be avoided by visiting supporters. Plus the 'Half Time Orange' pub located just over the road from the away end, is a members-only Leicester City bar.

Andy Jobson, a visiting Southampton fan informs me; 'Probably the best bet for away fans is the Counting House pub on Freemens Common Road. It has a good mix of both sets of supporters, with all the normal facilities on offer'. Beaumont Fox adds; 'This pub is located just off the Aylestone Road, past the Local Hero pub (home fans only) and the Mecca Bingo Hall. It does though exclude away supporters when the game is deemed to be a 'high profile' one'.

Andrew Whitefield, a visiting Ipswich supporter also recommends 'The Leicester Gateway, on Gateway Street, near to the hospital. This is quite a big pub, busy but not overcrowded, with a mixture of home and away fans. It offers a wide selection of beers, including real ales and has a simple match day menu for food of burgers, sausage baps, chips etc... which were enjoyable and good value'. This pub is listed in the CAMRA Good Beer Guide and is around a 15 minute walk away from the away entrance. With the away entrance at your back, turn left and go along the back of the stand. When you reach the Leicester City Club Shop, bear right and cross over the road. Follow this road down to the junction with Upperton Road. Turn right at the T-junction and then you need to cross over the road to the opposite side and then continue right to you reach Jarrom Street. Go along Jarrom Street and take the fourth left into Gateway Street. The pub is a short distance along this road on the right.

For those arriving by train 'The Hind' pub across the road from the station serves a selection of real ales. Otherwise alcohol is available inside the stadium.

How To Get There & Where To Park?

Leave the M1 at Junction 21, or if coming from the Midlands, follow the M69 until the end of the motorway (which meets the M1 at Junction 21). Take the A5460 towards Leicester city centre. Continue on this road, until you go under a railway bridge. Carry on for another 200 yards and turn right at the traffic lights into Upperton Road (sign posted Royal Infirmary) and then right again into Filbert Street. The new stadium is visible just behind the old Filbert Street ground.

Allow yourself a little extra time to get to the ground as traffic does tend to get quite congested near the stadium. Plenty of street parking to be found (especially around the Upperton Road area), although as Greg Barclay warns; 'don't double park as the traffic wardens tend to have a field day at every match'. Alternatively you can park at Leicester Rugby Club (£3) which is a ten-minute walk away from the stadium.

By Train

The train station in the city centre is walkable from the ground and should take you around 20-25 minutes. There is normally a heavy police presence around the station.

Thanks to Philip Draycott for providing the following directions from the station to the ground;

'Come out of the station, cross the road in front of the station and proceed to the left. Follow this round to the right and now you are walking with the main Central Ring Road (Waterloo Way) on your left. Keep this to your left as the pavement becomes a separate path and the road sinks down into a dip down to your left. A quick left and right to stay on the pathway as it crosses New Walk and you go down the left hand side of New Walk Museum. The pathway rejoins the main road as pavement again and you see a small recreation ground (Nelson Mandela Park) on your right. Turn right into Lancaster Rd and then cross the park to the crossings over the main road by the public lavatories. Head for the Victory pub opposite (not recommended for away fans), turn left across the front of the Leicester Royal infirmary. First right into Walnut St and you can see the stadium behind the old Filbert Street ground'.

Local Rivals
Derby County, Nottingham Forest, Coventry City.

Admission Prices
Leicester operate a three tier category system (A+, A, & B) whereby admission prices are higher for the most popular games. Discounts on these prices are available to members of the Club (including Fox Cubs).

Sample 'B' prices are shown below

Home Fans:

West Stand (Blocks A2, B1, B2, B3, C1)
Adults £29
Senior Citizens (60 years+) £20
Young Adults (Under 22) £20
Under 16's £12
Under 12's £5

West Stand (Blocks A1, C2)
Adults £22
Senior Citizens (60 years+) £20
Young Adults (Under 22) £20
Under 16's £12
Under 12's £5

Alliance & Leicester Stand (Block G2, H1, K1, L):
Adults £25
Senior Citizens (60 years+) £20
Young Adults (Under 22) £20
Under 16's £12
Under 12's £5

Alliance & Leicester Stand (Block G1)
Adults £22
Senior Citizens (60 years+) £20
Young Adults (Under 22) £20
Under 16's £12
Under 12's £5

Alliance & Leicester Stand (Block J1, J2, J3)
Adults £27
Senior Citizens (60 years+) £20
Young Adults (Under 22) £20
Under 16's £12
Under 12's £5

North Stand
Adults £22
Senior Citizens (60 years+) £20
Young Adults (Under 22) £20
Under 16's £12
Under 12's £5

South Stand (Block G1)
Adults £22
Senior Citizens (60 years+) £20
Young Adults (Under 22) £20
Under 16's £12
Under 12's £5

Away Fans:

Adults £22
Senior Citizens (60 years+) £20
Young Adults (Under 22) £20
Juveniles: £17

In addition to these prices there may also this season be what the Club call 'fans fixtures'. These will be typically say League Cup games against lower opposition. Prices for these fixtures (all areas of the ground) are: Adults £15, Concessions £10, Juveniles £8.

Programme & Fanzines
Official Programme: £3.
The Fox Fanzine: £1.
When You're Smiling Fanzine: £1.

Stadium Tours
The Club run tours on a daily basis (except matchdays). The cost is: Adults £5 & Under 16's £2. However there is a minimum charge of £20 per tour, so unless there are sufficient numbers in your group paying the individual prices that add up to £20 or more, then the minimum charge will apply. The club also have a charity and school rate of £2 per person (maximum 30 people). Call the Club on 0116 229 4532 to book.

Record Attendance
At Walkers Stadium
32,148 v Newcastle United
Premier League, December 26th, 2003.

At Filbert Street
47,298 v Tottenham Hotspur,
FA Cup 5th Round, February 18th, 1928.

Average Attendance
2006-2007: 22,267 (Championship)

Did You Know?
The Club used to be called Leicester Fosse but changed their name to Leicester City after the original club folded in 1919.

Norwich City

Carrow Road

Ground Name: Carrow Road
Capacity: 26,034 (all seated)
Address: Carrow Road, Norwich, NR1 1JE
Main Telephone No: 01603-760-760
Ticket Office: 0870-444-1902
Fax No: 01603-613-886
Team Nickname: The Canaries
Year Ground Opened: 1935
Undersoil Heating: Yes
Pitch Size: 114 x 74 yards
Home Kit Colours: Yellow & Green

Official Website:
www.canaries.co.uk

Unofficial Websites:
German Canaries - www.german-canaries.de
Wrath Of The Barclay - www.wrathofthebarclay.co.uk
Forces2Canaries - www.forces2canaries.co.uk
On The Ball City - www.norwichcity-mad.co.uk (Footy Mad Network)
From The Terrace - www.fromtheterrace.co.uk/norwich
Yellow Army - www.yellowarmy.co.uk
NCFC Fans - www.ncfc-fans.co.uk
Stella Canaries - www.stellacanaries.com
Capital Canaries - www.capitalcanaries.com
Yarmouth Yellows - www.yarmouthyellows.co.uk

What's The Ground Like?

Carrow Road has been virtually rebuilt since the early 1980's, with all four sides of the ground having new stands. The newest of these is the Jarrold South Stand at one side of the pitch which was opened in 2004. It is an impressive-looking cantilever, single-tier, all-seated stand, that can house up to 8,000 supporters. It is unusual in having not one, but three separate television gantries suspended beneath its largely perspex roof. This stand was further extended in 2005 and now surrounds the corner of the ground where it joins the Norwich & Peterborough Stand, 'filling in' that area. The rest of the ground is also all seated and all stands are covered. Both ends look particularly smart, being large two-tiered affairs, complete with a row of executive boxes. They also have a pair of large floodlight pylons protruding from their roof. On the remaining side is the Geoffrey Watling City Stand. This single-tiered stand is smaller than both ends and houses amongst other things the Directors Box and Press Area. This stand extends around to meet the ends at both corners, giving the ground an enclosed look on that side.

Future Ground Developments

Oliver Napthine informs me; 'The new South Stand has been built in such a way that an additional tier can be added at a later stage if required. This development would increase the capacity to around 30,000'. Jon Springall adds; 'An additional tier could also at some stage (the foundations are already in place) be added to the Geoffrey Watling Stand, which would further raise the capacity to around 35,000'.

What Is It Like For Visiting Supporters?

Away fans are housed on one side of the new South Stand, on one side of the ground. As you would expect from a new stand the facilities and view of the playing action are good. The normal allocation in this area is 2,500 fans although this can be increased further for cup games. If you are located at the very back of this stand then you can enjoy some fine views across the city, including Norwich Cathedral. The Club I found to be particularly friendly and relaxed. I certainly would rate it as one of the better away days, even though it seems an eternity to get there. As Delia Smith is on the board of Norwich City, the food available within the ground has been spruced up a fair bit and is very good. The Club even bake their own pies which not only include the usual array such as steak & kidney, chicken & mushroom, but also a number of 'matchday specials' (which change from game to game) such as beef in red wine gravy & cheese, mushroom and garlic. Please note that smoking is not allowed anywhere in the ground.

Tom Jameson, a visiting Sheffield United fan informs me; 'I recently visited Carrow Road and found it to be a pleasant, relaxing atmosphere which made for a very enjoyable day out. We were the first away supporters to sit in the new South Stand, towards the right hand side of the stand, towards the Barclay End. The stand is very modern, and offers a decent view of the action with plenty of leg room. One problem I did encounter was the tendency of the stewards to order away supporters to keep seated throughout the game. This led to our fans singing 'Sit down, if you hate Wednesday' instead of the usual 'Stand up, if you hate Wednesday' and 'Sit down, stand up', which did not go down too well with the stewards who in my mind very harshly ejected one supporter from the stadium. So it is advisable to comply with the steward requests, although I did find it all rather annoying'. Allan Pearcey, a visiting Birmingham City supporter adds; 'Our fans stood throughout the game, with no interference from the stewards or Police. I thought too that the food at the ground was somewhat overrated'.

Where To Drink?

I found that the number of good pubs situated between the train station and the ground were plentiful and friendly. In fact it almost ended up being a pub crawl before the match had begun! The traditional haunt of away fans for many years was the Clarence Harbour, but this alas is now making way for a housing development. Most fans now seem to be heading instead for the 'Compleat Angler', which is by the river opposite the railway station (around 5-10 minutes walk from the ground)'. This pub seems to have now taken over the mantle of the 'away fans pub'.

Rob Emery informs me; 'Not far away from the ground and towards the City Centre a new leisure complex called the Riverside has opened. This has a number of drinking and eating establishments, including a Wetherspoons outlet. But it is predominantly an area for home supporters and most of the bars there will not admit or serve fans in away colours.' Paul Palmer adds; 'The Wetherspoons outlet which is a Lloyds No.1, admits away supporters as long as colours are covered'. Nicholas Mead suggests; 'the Coach and Horses on Thorpe Road brews its own beer and is around a 10-minute walk away from the ground'.

How To Get There & Where To Park?

The ground is well signposted from the A11 and A47. From the southern bypass (A47) take the A146 into the city. At the traffic lights turn right and follow the outer ring road: Left at the roundabout. Right at the next lights. Follow the inner ring road round to the right, over the river and the ground is on your right. If in doubt follow signs for the the railway station until you get to the river (where the rail station is off to the left and ground on your right).

David Clarke informs me that 'The best car park for away fans is Norfolk County Hall, which is well sign posted on the left of the A146, as you follow signs towards the ground from the Southern Bypass. It is currently £3 and can hold about 2000 cars, and does usually fill up by 2pm for games where the away team bring loads of fans'. Martyn Swan adds; 'It's advisable to get to the car park before 1pm if you want a decent spot, otherwise you may get stuck in spaces at the back, and it can then take ages at the end of the game to exit'.

By Train
The ground is walkable from Norwich train station. If you ignore all those wonderful pubs it should take you around 5-10mins to walk to the ground. From the station turn left and head for the Morrisons supermarket and you should see the ground behind that.

Local Rivals
Ipswich Town

Admission Prices
The Club operate a match category policy (A & B, Saver, Super Saver, Saver Special) whereby the more popular matches cost more to watch. Saver prices are shown below in brackets. For certain games such as Carling Cup games, these ticket prices may be further reduced.

Away Fans:

Adults: £26 (£19),
Concessions & Under 16's £19 (£13),
Under 12's £12 (£7)

Concessions apply to senior citizens over 60 years of age and students in full time education.

Programme & Fanzine
Official Programme; £3
Y'Army Fanzine £1

Record Attendance
Record Attendance:
43,984 v Leicester City
FA Cup 6th Round, March 30th, 1963.

Modern All Seated Attendance Record:
25,552 v Manchester United
Premier League, April 9th, 2005.

Average Attendance
2006-2007: 24,646 (Championship)

Did You Know?
That the Club's former ground until 1935 was called 'The Nest'. An apt name for a team called the Canaries.

Plymouth Argyle

Home Park

Ground Name: Home Park
Capacity: 19,500 (all seated)
Address: Plymouth, PL2 3DQ
Main Telephone No: 01752-562-561
Fax No: 01752-606-167
Ticket Office: 0845-338-7232
Team Nickname: The Pilgrims
Shirt Sponsors: Ginsters
Home Kit Colours: Green & White

Official Website:
www.pafc.co.uk

Unofficial Websites:
Greens On Screen - www.greensonscreen.co.uk
London Supporters Club - www.pasalb.co.uk
Rub Of The Greens - www.rubofthegreens.com
(Rivals Network)

What's The Ground Like?

During 2001 Home Park was transformed, with three sides of the ground being completely rebuilt. Both the ends and one side of the ground have been replaced by single-tiered, covered all seated stands. Most impressively, the corners between these stands have been filled so that the ground is totally enclosed on those sides. This just leaves the Grandstand at one side of the pitch, as the only remnant of the old Home Park. This classic-looking stand dates back to the late 1940s and is partly covered to the rear. For the 2007/08 season the original terrace at the front of the stand has been made all-seated to comply with government and league regulations. Home Park is the most westerly and southerly league ground in England.

Future Ground Developments

The Club intend at some point to 'finish the ground' by redeveloping the old Grandstand. It is intended to build a multi-tiered stand with a capacity of 6,000 seats. However at present the Club do not have the necessary finances to pursue this project.

What Is It Like For Visiting Supporters?

Away fans are housed in the Barn Park End, which is now all seated and covered. As you would expect from a new stand the facilities and views of the playing action are both good. The normal allocation for this end is 1,300 seats, although this can be increased to 2,022 if demand requires it. The atmosphere is normally good and even though I have received a number of reports of the stewarding being somewhat over-zealous in the away end, on my last visit it was fine. No problems were encountered outside the ground and on the whole it was a good day out. The only down side was that the concourse was a bit cramped and with a sell-out away end it was rather crowded. The delicious 'Football's Famous Chicken Balti Pie' (£2.30), is available inside the ground, along with pasties (£2.30) and Cheeseburgers (£2.80).

Where To Drink?

Probably the best bet is the Britannia which is a sizeable Wetherspoons outlet and around a 10-minute walk away from the ground (from the car park outside the football ground, turn left and the pub is down the road on the right hand corner). For most matches the pub, which is busy normally, has a queue of fans waiting to get in outside, but this is controlled by the security staff so you don't normally have to wait too long to gain entrance. Although away fan-friendly, the pub doesn't tolerate away supporters singing their club's songs and any who do are quickly ejected from the premises, so you have been warned. Near to the pub is normally a van selling pasties, which looked to be doing a roaring trade on my last visit.

Plymouth Argyle

Opposite the Britannia is the Embassy Club which is best avoided by away fans. Terry from Plymouth also recommends the Pennycomequick (great name!) if you are walking to the ground from the railway station, as does Bob Rees, a visiting West Ham United fan, who also commented on their home-made pasties. Otherwise alcohol is available within the ground.

How To Get There & Where To Park?

Take the M5 to the South West and at the end of the motorway continue onto the A38 (The ground is well signposted from the outskirts of Plymouth on the A38). On entering Plymouth, turn left onto the A386. When this road splits into two, keep on the left hand side (signposted Plymouth) and after about a mile you will see the ground on your left. The ground is well signposted 'Plymouth Argyle Home Park' on the way into Plymouth.

There is quite a large car park at the ground, which is free. It is operated on a 'first in before the game, first out after the game basis'. If you are last in, then on average it takes around half an hour to clear. The car park is normally full by 2.30pm on matchdays. There is some street parking if you drive past the ground, heading away from the city centre.

By Train

Plymouth railway station is about one and a half miles away, so either grab a cab (£3) or embark on the 20-minute walk. As you come out of the station turn right and down the hill and under the railway bridge. Just keep walking straight along this road and you will soon see the floodlights of the ground in the distance.

Local Rivals

Exeter City & Torquay United. And from a little further afield, Bristol City.

Admission Prices

All Fans*

* Home fans wanting to sit in the Grandstand Lower Tier will be charged £18 for an adult ticket wherever purchased.

Tickets purchased prior to matchday:
Adults £21, Concessions £14, Children £5

Matchday Prices:
Adults £23, Concessions £16, Children £5

Programme & Fanzine

Official Programme: £2.50
Rub Of The Greens Fanzine £1

Record Attendance

43,596 v Aston Villa,
Division Two, October 10th, 1936.

Average Attendance

2006-2007: 13,543 (Championship)

Other Places Of Interest

Considering you will have probably spent hours getting there, I suggest you make a weekend of it in Devon. If you go into the centre of Plymouth, make sure you walk down the front to the 'Hoe' (where Drake was playing bowls when he heard about the arrival of the Spanish Armada). The views of Plymouth Sound from here are superb.

Did You Know?

That the Club nickname, the Pilgrims, is named after the Pilgrim Fathers who set sail for the New World from Plymouth, on board the Mayflower in 1620.

Preston North End

Deepdale

Ground Name:	Deepdale
Capacity:	22,225
Address:	Sir Tom Finney Way, Preston, PR1 6RU
Main Telephone No:	0870-442-1964
Main Fax No:	01772-693-366
Ticket Office:	0870-442-1966
Ticket Office Fax No:	01772-693-365
Team Nickname:	The Lilywhites
Pitch Size:	110 x 77 yards
Home Kit Colours:	White & Navy

Official Website:
www.pnefc.net

Unofficial Websites:
Lilywhite Magic - www.lilywhites.net
Irish Supporters Club - http://homepage.eircom.net/~pne/
Who's That Jumping Off The Pier? - http://prestonnorthend.rivals.net/default.asp?sid=941 (Rivals Network)
Supporters Football Team - www.pnembt.co.uk
PNEFans.net - www.pnefans.net

■ What's The Ground Like?

Three-quarters of the ground has now been redeveloped in recent years, with three new stands being put in place. Work has now begun in redeveloping the final stand, the Pavilion side. This new stand will have a capacity of 5,000 (increasing the overall capacity of Deepdale to 24,000) and it is hoped that the new stand will be open in early 2008. The new stand will really boost the overall look and feel of the stadium and will be a welcome addition.

The three existing stands are excellent-looking all seater stands, complete with some spectacular-looking floodlights. They are of the same height and style and are all large, covered, single-tiered stands. Each has a likeness of a past player outlined on the seats and is named after that player. Tom Finney, Bill Shankly and goalkeeping legend Alan Kelly are all honoured and this makes a welcome change from the boring letters outlined on most new stands. I wonder which past player will feature with the new stand? Outside the stadium near to the entrance to the National Museum of Football is a statue of former Preston legend Tom Finney.

■ What Is It Like For Visiting Supporters?

Away fans are housed in the modern Bill Shankly Stand at one end of the pitch. Normally the allocation for away fans is approximately half of this stand (3,000 seats) and it is shared with home supporters. However, for teams with a large away support, then the whole end can be allocated, raising the allocation to 6,000.

The views of the playing action and facilities within this stand are excellent. The stand is particularly steep, meaning that fans are kept relatively close to the pitch. On the concourse there are TV's by the refreshment serving areas showing the game live and with the bars being open during the game, this is too much of a temptation for some. There is a wide range of food available including bacon rolls, roll over hot dogs, burgers and even vegetarian 'butter' pies. I particularly enjoyed my last visit as the fans, stewards and even police all seemed to be fairly friendly and there was a good atmosphere being generated within the ground.

■ Where To Drink?

The favoured pub for away fans, the 'Toy Soldier' on the nearby Deepdale retail park, has now been closed for some time. The closest pubs to the ground are 'Sumners' and 'The Garrison' both up Tom Finney Way (used to be called Deepdale Road) from the ground. The pubs sit opposite one another and are both okay for away fans, although the Garrison seems to be the preferred choice with away supporters.

The atmosphere in Sumners is friendly, with both home and away supporters mixing freely (although note that away fans are not admitted when there is a local derby). There is a good sized beer garden & car park at the pub. Sometimes the pub does charge for parking but this can be redeemed against a purchase at the bar. Good food is available and children are allowed in. James Pritchett adds to get to the Sumners; 'Make sure you go towards Sainsburys and away from the Town Centre and it should take five minutes. As you go past Sainsburys turn right at the lights and it is half way up the hill, opposite another pub called the Garrison. It should be full, but friendly. The Garrison is on the opposite side of the road and has recently been refurbished. The pub welcome a mix of away and home support and are friendly towards families. It serves Theakstons on draught.'

Paul Billington adds; 'In all honesty visiting fans should avoid town centre pubs simply because the police will move you on quickly if they see you and most pubs will refuse to serve away fans. If you arrive by train I would recommend the Vic and Station not for the decor but simply convenience. Another pub worth considering is The White Hart on Watling Road (approx. 500 yards east of Sumner's and the Garrison, up past Fulwood Barracks). It is another Scottish & Newcastle pub with "Sizzling Platters" and other such delights of an inexpensive and good quality menu. A good alternative if the others prove too busy. Ample car parking and children welcome'. Otherwise alcohol is served within the ground.

■ How To Get There & Where To Park?

Leave M6 at Junction 31 and follow signs Left for Preston. Go up a steep hill (often a police speed trap on the hill, so stick to 30) and follow the road down to a mini roundabout (speed camera by the BP garage on the left). At the roundabout with the Hesketh Arms turn right into Blackpool Road. Go straight on over three sets of lights and just before a fourth set the ground appears, set slightly back on the left. Parking is mainly in the streets surrounding the ground.

Mike Holroyd adds; 'as you turn right at the Hesketh Arms roundabout into Blackpool Road and then pass a park on the left there is now another speed camera to watch out for. The Police also sometimes set up another mobile speed trap on the forecourt of the fire station on the left, so watch your speed. Plus as you near the ground don't be tempted to park up on the grass verges, you are likely to find after the game that you have been given a ticket for it!' Steve Thornley informs me; 'Parking for cars is available for £3 a car at Moorfields Special School. The car park is manned by volunteers from the school and all proceeds go into school funds. Just follow the directions above and at the last set of traffic lights continue straight on for about 200 yards, and you will see the school on the left near Moor Park'.

Kate Abbatt suggests; 'If you want to avoid the pre and post-match traffic, here's a handy tip to avoid it. Instead of leaving the M6 at Junction 31, carry on to Junction 31a signposted, Preston East and Longridge. (This is a limited junction as you can only leave northbound and join southbound.) Keep in the right hand lane and go across the roundabout signposted Preston east, football ground and museum. Across the next roundabout (Anderton Arms on your right) and then left at the next one. At the next lights, go right onto Watling Street. You will go past the White Hart and a row of shops. At next lights by Fulwood Barracks, keep in the left hand lane. You can either park in Sumners, (turn left straight after the lights) or follow the road up to the big junction at Blackpool Road and the ground is on your left and take your chances with on-street parking. Sumners is better as you are the right side of the ground to get away quick after the game. Blackpool Road gets badly snarled up after games and the lights don't help it'.

■ By Train

Preston station is around a mile and a half from the ground and takes around twenty five minutes to walk, although you will pass some good pubs on the way. Leave the Preston railway station via the main entrance, and head right at the top of the drive. This is the main High Street. Continue along the High Street, passing all the regular big name shops. Some good pubs and eateries can be found down side streets off the High Street, so if you have time, take a look. Try the Old Black Bull, and Academy, the later being about the last place on the High Street that will allow away supporters before you get to Deepdale. Colours are not recommended around town. The High Street (or Church Street/Fishergate as it's known) is about a mile long, and you will pass a church and a bike shop as you come to its end. Simply carry on walking along this street, and when you reach the ring road, you head straight over the large traffic lights, heading towards a pub called the County Arms opposite the prison. Turn left along the road here passing the County Arms (which is not recommended for away supporters) and continue along Deepdale road. On the left is Tom Finney sports bar, a home fans only pub, but if you have no colours you may get in. The ground is now another half mile in a straight line along this road. Thanks to Kevin Wrenn for supplying the directions and general information.

■ Local Rivals

Blackpool, Burnley & Blackburn Rovers.

■ Admission Prices

Home Fans*:

Sir Tom Finney Stand (Premium Area):
Adults £25, No Concessions

Sir Tom Finney Stand:
Adults £23, Students/OAP's £14, Under 16's £8

Sir Tom Finney Stand (Family Area):
Adults £23, OAP's £14, Under 16's £6

Alan Kelly Town End:
Adults £22, OAP's £14, Under 16's £8

Bill Shankly Stand:
Adults £22, OAP's £14, Under 16's £8

Pavillion Stand:
Adults £23, Students/OAP's £14, Under 16's £8

Away Fans*:

Bill Shankly Stand:
Adults £22, OAP's £14, Under 16's £8

* The prices shown are the matchday admission prices. Discounts of up to £2 are available on these prices if the ticket is purchased prior to matchday.

■ Programme
Official Programme £2.50.

■ Record Attendance
42,684 v Arsenal,
Division One, April 23rd, 1938.

Modern Attendance Record:
20,383 v Leeds United
Championship Play-Off Semi-Final,
May 8th, 2006.

■ Average Attendance
2006-2007: 13,931 (Championship)

■ National Museum Of Football
John Messner informs me; 'The Museum is located within the two new stands of Deepdale. The exhibits include a gallery on the history and development of the game in England, along with how it has played a role in the social history of the nation over the years. This gallery runs the length of the Tom Finney Stand. The Museum also features an interactive gallery, where visitors can explore elements of the game, including tactics, rules, equipment, and grounds. There is an Special Exhibitions Gallery, whose first exhibition will be on Wembley Stadium. A gallery charting the history of Deepdale, and a gallery to feature art and other visual items from the Museum's vast collection'.

For visiting supporters attending a match, then please note that the Museum will be open until 2.30pm on Saturday matchdays and 7.30pm on evening matchdays. The museum is free to enter. To check out other opening times and gain more information about the museum, please visit their website at www.nationalfootballmuseum.com.

Richard Johnson, a visiting Sheffield Wednesday fan adds; 'Just to say that we visited the National Football Museum and it is brilliant! An excellent assortment of the history of the game, shirts, trophies, match balls, video clips, interactive displays, how football was/is portrayed in the media, etc etc. Well worth a visit by all football fans, young and old - and, it's free!'

■ Did You Know?
That Preston won the inaugural Football League in 1888-89 and they also won the FA Cup that year. In recognition of this achievement they were bestowed the privilege of not having to change into away colours, if their kit clashed with the home opposition.

Queens Park Rangers

Loftus Road Stadium

Ground Name: Loftus Road Stadium
Capacity: 19,100 (all seated)
Address: South Africa Road, London, W12 7PA
Main Telephone No: 020-8743-0262
Ticket Office: 0870-112-1967
Fax No: 020-749-0994
Pitch Size: 112 x 72 yards
Team Nickname: The Superhoops
Year Ground Opened: 1917
Home Kit Colours: Blue & White

Official Website:
www.qpr.co.uk

Unofficial Websites:
QPR Mad - www.qpr-mad.co.uk (Footy Mad Network)
qprnet.com - www.qprnet.com (Rivals Network)
Dave's QPR Website - www.queensparkrangersfc.com
Loyal Supporters Association - www.qpr-lsa.co.uk

What's The Ground Like?

Loftus Road has a compact feel, as the ground is totally enclosed, with supporters being close to the pitch. An unusual aspect is that all four stands are roughly the same height, their roofs meeting at all four corners with no gaps. The South Africa Road Stand on one side of the ground, has a larger upper tier, compared to the lower tier, with a row of executive boxes running across the middle. There are a couple of supporting pillars in this stand. The other side, the Ellerslie Road Stand, is single-tiered, with a television gantry suspended below its roof. Both ends are similar-looking two-tiered stands. There is a small electric scoreboard at the away end of the ground, dividing the two tiers. The ground oozes character and there is nothing similar in the league. However, Loftus Road is starting to look tired, having had little recent investment.

What Is It Like For Visiting Supporters?

Away fans are situated in the upper tier of the School End, where around 1,200 fans can be accommodated. If demand requires it then the lower tier can also be allocated, increasing the number of places available to about 2,500. If the away club only takes the upper tier allocation, then the lower tier is allocated to home supporters. However, unlike most other grounds the upper tier of the School End doesn't necessarily mean a better view as James Brooks, a visiting Derby fan, informs me; 'Unless you sit right at the front of the upper tier, you can't see all the goal at the near end or indeed the last couple of yards of the pitch'.

I must say that on my three visits, I have found the stadium lacking a little in atmosphere. Also the leg room between rows of seats was a little tight. There is normally quite a large police and steward presence, and you should expect to be searched before you enter the away end. However on the plus side I have never experienced any problems there, as it is generally relaxed and friendly. Dan Markham, a QPR fan disagrees with me; 'It is virtually impossible to have such a small compact enclosed stadium, and not have a tremendous atmosphere. You are close to the pitch, close to the visiting fans and most importantly close to the action'. Another plus point was that the food that was served within the ground was quite good and the service prompt. Please note that smoking is not allowed anywhere in the ground.

Richard Wilson, a visiting Birmingham City supporter adds; 'A word of advice for away fans. They are often very slow at the turnstiles at Loftus Road. I would seriously suggest arriving half an hour before kick off, or risk missing the start of the game'.

Where To Eat & Drink?

Grant Donnohoe recommends the Springbok right by the ground (near the ticket office). Come out of White City Underground station, go down the road right in front of the station; the Springbok is down on the left. Around Shepherds Bush Green is O'Neills and Walkabout which are both okay for away fans. To find Shepherds Bush Green; exit Shepherds Bush Underground (the Hammersmith & City Line station), turn left out of the station and the green is a short way down the road on the right. Diagonally across Shepherds Bush Green opposite the Central line entrance to Shepherds Bush Underground Station, is a retail complex called Vue, which upstairs includes a Wetherspoons outlet. Please note that alcohol is not available in the away end.

On the eating front David Frodsham adds; 'On my travels to many football grounds, I have yet to find a wider selection of food available than on the Uxbridge Road. The cosmopolitan inner city nature means that you can almost eat your way around the world. From the normal range of cafes, burger bars, fried chicken outlets and chippies, there are Indian, Chinese, Thai and Jamaican outlets. There are Lebanese and Indian kebab shops, the latter selling "doner" kebabs made with Indian spices! Inside the ground there is a range of Shire Foods pasties, sausage rolls and pies available, including the delicious 'Football's Famous Chicken Balti Pie.'

How To Get There & Where To Park?

From The North/West:
At the end of the M40, take the A40 towards Central London. At the point where the A40 becomes the A40(M), turn off onto the A40 towards White City/Shepherds Bush and turn right into Wood Lane, turn right into South Africa Road for the ground.

Daniel Sleigh, a visiting Nottingham Forest fan informs me; 'There is a car park on the Ariel Way industrial opposite the BBC Television Centre. The car park located at the end of Silver Road (near the Royal Mail unit) costs £7 and is open 12:00-19:00 for afternoon games and 16:30 -23:00 for evening games'. Matt Garside from Southampton adds; 'It's probably cheaper to just park on the road in this area as it costs £4.80 for three hours parking'.

By Train/Tube

I tend to use Shepherds Bush tube station, simply because there seems to be more pubs around this area. There are in fact two Shepherds Bush tube stations, one on the Central Line and the other on the Hammersmith & City line. The latter is nearer to the ground, which is about a ten-minute walk. Leaving the tube station turn right and the ground will come into view further down on the right. Michael Howard, a visiting Reading supporter recommends; 'White City Tube on Wood Lane (opposite the BBC Television Centre). It's nearer the ground and less people seem to use it on match day'. Please note that Queens Park tube station is nowhere near the ground!.

Jonathan Burt adds; 'the nearest train station to the ground is Kensington Olympia which can be accessed via Watford or Clapham Junction. It is normally much quicker to get to the ground this way rather than using the tube line, it really cuts down the journey time. Olympia station is about 20 to 25 minutes walk away from the ground, or about 10 to 15 minutes walk away from Shepherds Bush Green.

Local Rivals

Brentford, Fulham, Chelsea.

Admission Prices

Home Fans*:

South Africa Road
Adults £25, OAP's/Under 21's £15, Under 16's £8

Ellerslie Road Stand
Adults £23, OAP's/Under 21's £14, Under 16's £8

Loftus Road Stand
Adults £22, OAP's/Under 21's £13, Under 16's £8

East & West Paddocks
Adults £20, OAP's /Under 21's £12, Under 16's £8

Away Fans*:

School End Stand
Adults £22, OAP's/Under 21's £13,
Under 16's £8 8

* Please note that under 8's can be admitted free to the ground, as long as they are accompanied by an adult and a ticket has been issued prior to matchday. Maximum of two children per adult.

Programme & Fanzine

Official Programme £3
A Kick Up The R's Fanzine £2.50

Record Attendance

35,353 v Leeds United,
Division One, April 27th, 1974.

Modern All Seated Attendance Record:
19,002 v Manchester City
Division One, November 6th, 1999.

Average Attendance

2006-2007: 12,405 (Championship)

Did You Know?

That Queen's Park Rangers became the first league club to install an artificial pitch, which was first used in the 1981-82 season.

Scunthorpe United

Glanford Park

Ground Name:	Glanford Park
Capacity:	9,183
Address:	Doncaster Rd, Scunthorpe, DN15 8TD
Main Telephone No:	0871-221-1899
Fax No:	01724-857-986
Pitch Size:	111 x 73 yards
Team Nickname:	The Iron
Year Ground Opened:	1988
Kit Manufacturers:	Carlotti
Home Kit Colours:	Claret & Blue

Official Website:
www.scunthorpe-united.co.uk
Claret And Blue Army - www.claretandbluearmy.tk

Unofficial Website:
Iron-Bru Net - http://iron-bru.net/ (Footy Mad Network)

What's The Ground Like?

The club left the Old Show Ground and moved to the new Glanford Park in August 1988. It is somewhat box-like in appearance with all four stands being an equal height. The ground is totally enclosed with all four corners having been filled (with advertising hoardings). The home end is terracing, whilst the other three sides of the ground are all seated. The main downside is the many supporting pillars to impede your view. The Club seem to have gone a bit over the top, with each stand having a named sponsor. Gone are East, West, North & South Stands. In are; Grove Wharf, Scunthorpe Telegraph, Study United & AMS Stands!

What Is It Like For Visiting Supporters?

Away fans are housed in the AMS Stand (aka the South Stand) at one end. This is all seated and can house 1,650 supporters. If demand requires it, then extra seats can be made available in the south corner of the West Stand. I had somewhat of an uneventful day out at Scunthorpe, with no problems incurred. However I do have to say that the ground lacked atmosphere, possibly because there were few away supporters on my visit.

James Broadbent adds; 'the ground is very easy to find on the edge of town. Scunthorpe is generally a friendly place to visit, where you can have decent banter and a good day out. To help boost the atmosphere the club allow drums and musical instruments to be brought into the ground'.

On my last visit to the ground I witnessed an amusing incident, when in the League Cup tie against Birmingham City, the stewards tried to insist that away fans sat down rather than standing up. Of course this met with chants of; 'Stand up, if you love the Blues!' to which the stewards looked somewhat dismayed at, with many Birmingham fans continuing to stand up. One poor steward was dispatched to sort this 'problem' out. I have to say he used a unique and an effective approach, during a lull moment in the away fans' singing, a voice from the back of the stand, was heard singing; 'Sit down and watch the game! Sit down and watch the game!'. You guessed it, it was the lonely steward singing! Still it had the desired effect! Well, for a while anyhow...

Where To Drink?

There is one pub right at the entrance to the ground called 'The Old Farmhouse', which as Bryan Woods informs me 'This pub welcomes all fans but no colours are allowed'. There is another pub near the ground called the Berkeley, a favourite haunt for away supporters. To find this Sam Smiths pub go past the ground (or park there first) and follow the main road towards Scunthorpe and it is on the left hand corner of the first roundabout you reach.

If coming by train, then the Honest Lawyer on Oswald Road is well worth a visit. Although a modern pub inside, it has been listed in the CAMRA Good Beer Guide and has a number of beers on offer. Also on Oswald Road is the Blue Bell which is a Wetherspoons outlet.

Across the road from the ground there is a Retail Park with a number of eating outlets such as a Tesco's Cafe, KFC & McDonalds.

Scunthorpe United

■ How To Get There & Where To Park?
The ground is on the outskirts of Scunthorpe, making it easy to find from the motorway. Leave the M180 at Junction 3 and take the M181 for Scunthorpe. At the end of this motorway, you will see the ground on your right. Turn right at the first roundabout onto the A18 and right again into the large car park at the ground.

■ By Train
Scunthorpe station is over two miles away from the ground. Therefore a taxi is probably the easiest way to reach the stadium. However, if you have time on your hands and are feeling fit..... Turn left out of the station and head towards the crossroads (facing a church) and turn right into Oswald Road, going past a set of traffic lights and the Honest Lawyer and Blue Bell pubs. At the next traffic lights turn left into Doncaster Road (where there are a number of fast food outlets). Then just go straight down this road and you will eventually reach Glanford Park on your left. Otherwise catch the number 7 or 8 `Yellow Line' bus from the bottom of Doncaster Road (outside the Atlantis Chippy) down to the ground (fare £1).

■ Local Rivals
Hull City, Grimsby Town, Lincoln City, Doncaster Rovers.

■ Admission Prices
The Club operate a category system (A & B), whereby the most popular games cost more to watch. Category B prices are shown in brackets.

Home Fans*:

Scunthorpe Telegraph West Stand (Exec Area):
Adults £28 (£27),
OAP's £21 (£20),
Under 17's £16 (£15)

Scunthorpe Telegraph West Stand:
Adults £19 (£18),
Concessions £12 (£11)

Grove Wharf East Stand:
Adults £17 (£16),
Concessions £11 (£10)

Study United North Stand:
Adults £15 (£14),
OAP's/Students £10 (£9),
Child £6 (£5)

Away Fans:

AMS Stand (Away)
Adults £19 (£18)
Concessions £12 (£11)

* Home fans can qualify for a £1 discount on these tickets if they are club members.

■ Programme
Official Programme: £2.50

■ Record Attendance
At Glanford Park:
8,906 v Nottingham Forest,
League One, March 10th, 2007.

At The Old Showground:
23,935 v Portsmouth,
FA Cup 4th Round, January 30th, 1954.

■ Average Attendance
2006-2007: 4,043 (League One)

■ Did You Know?
That the 'Lindsey' from Scunthorpe and Lindsey United was dropped from the club's title in the mid 50's.

Sheffield United

Bramall Lane

Ground Name:	Bramall Lane
Capacity:	32,609 (all seated)
Address:	Bramall Lane, Sheffield, S2 4SU
Main Telephone No:	0870-787-1960
Fax No:	0870-787-3345
Ticket Office:	0870-787-1799
Club Nickname:	The Blades
Year Ground Opened:	1862*
Pitch Size:	112 x 72 yards
Home Kit Colours:	Red, White & Black

Official Website:
www.sufc.co.uk

Unofficial Websites:
Bladesmen - www.bladesmen.co.uk
Greasy Chip Buttie - www.greasychipbuttie.co.uk
Supporters Club - www.suscwb.co.uk
The Blades Online - www.thebladesonline.com (Rivals Network)
Unitedite.co.uk - www.unitedite.co.uk
Red & White Wizards - www.redandwhite-wizards.co.uk
Swinton Blades - www.swintonblades.com
Sheff-Utd.co.uk - www.sheff-utd.co.uk
Gallon Of Magnet - www.gallonofmagnet.co.uk

■ What's The Ground Like?

Bramall Lane has to me been one of the most underrated grounds in the country. The construction of three large modern-looking stands, plus the filling in of three corners (albeit one corner is filled with administrative offices), makes it a great ground and one that has character. Both sides of the ground are large single tiered stands. Whilst the Global Windows Stand is a fairly plain-looking stand, the Capital One Stand, which sits opposite, is probably the smartest-looking stand at Bramall Lane. This stand has the corners filled in, by offices on one side and a family seated area on the other, called the Streetwise Corner, in a corporate sponsorship deal. At the back of the stand are a row of executive boxes and on its roof is a small gable, reminiscent of when many older grounds featured them. At one end is the Kop Stand, which is slightly disappointing as it has two large supporting pillars. Opposite is the Gordon Lamb (Bramall Lane) Stand, the oldest present and where the away fans are housed. This stand is two-tiered and looks odd as it has two large supporting pillars in the upper tier. It also has an electric scoreboard, perched between the two tiers. The corner between this stand and the Capital One Stand at one side of the pitch was filled in with seating during 2006 and has further enhanced the overall look of the stadium. The stadium is balanced, with all four stands being of the same height.

Dave Croft adds; 'a lot of Blades fans sentimentally call the ground "Beautiful downtown Bramall Lane", as a match day announcer used to welcome the away fans with this description'.

■ Future Ground Developments

The Club have announced their medium term intention to replace the Hallam FM Kop End with a new two-tiered stand. This will boost the capacity by a further 4,000 seats. Joel Beighton informs me; 'In addition the Club have announced plans to build a leisure complex at the back of the Global Windows (South) Stand. This will include a large casino, a new club shop, club museum and a health club'. However the Club are yet to announce when these works will commence, but once completed the overall capacity of Bramall Lane will rise to 36,000.

■ What Is It Like For Visiting Supporters?

Away fans are housed in the two-tiered Gordon Lamb (aka the Bramall Lane) Stand at one end of the ground, where up to 5,200 supporters can be accommodated. However the normal allocation is 2,700 as only the upper tier is normally open. If demand requires it then the lower tier can be allocated as well. Please note that the front of the lower tier of this stand is uncovered, so if your team has a large away following hope it doesn't rain! Chris Bax adds; 'Any tickets still available for the away end can be purchased from two dedicated away ticket windows just up from the turnstile entrances'. The delicious 'Football's Famous Chicken Balti Pie' (£2.20) is available inside the ground.

The United fans are particularly passionate and vocal about their club. This makes for a great atmosphere at games, but also can make it somewhat intimidating for the away supporter. It was one of those grounds that by just listening to the crowd you could tell what was happening on the pitch. I found it quite amusing as having to go for a leak just before half time, I could hear the home crowd shout Goo-on as a Sheffield attack began. Then this got louder & louder as the United team got closer to the goal, Goo-on, Goo-on, Goo-On! and then the air turned blue as whoever it was missed the chance!

■ Where To Drink?

The favoured pub for away fans is the 'Royal Standard' on St Marys Road (A61), near to McDonalds (although the pub do some good bar snacks themselves). Nick Turrell, a visiting Brighton fan adds; 'About a ten minute walk away on Queens Road is 'The Earl', which on our visit was okay for away fans to drink in'. Otherwise somewhat further along the road from the away end (about 3/4's of a mile past the B&Q on the left) is the Bridge pub which also has been recommended to me.

Paul Webb, a visiting Birmingham City fan adds; 'On a number of occasions we have visited the Norfolk Arms pub in the centre of Sheffield. It is by the Ibis Hotel and not far from the train station. A friendly, traditional pub with regulars that make you welcome. It's walkable to the ground, or the bar staff can order a taxi while you leave your car there'. Also near to the station is the Globe, which as Simon Lorch, a visiting Chelsea fan says: 'I found that the Globe pub around a five-minute walk from the station and a 15 minute walk from the ground welcomed home and away fans as long as there was no singing. The majority of fans there were Chelsea and the doors where policed 2 hours before the game but it was a nice friendly pub serving good ale'. Also near to the station is 'The Howard' that is frequented by away fans and recommended by Tyler Tedesco, a visiting West Ham United fan.

The pubs near to the ground such as the 'Sheaf House', 'Railway Hotel', the 'Golden Lion' and on Bramall Lane; 'The Railway' & 'Cricketers' are for home fans only. Otherwise alcohol is available inside the ground.

■ How To Get There & Where To Park?

From The North:
Leave the M1 at Junction 36 and follow the A61 into Sheffield. Follow the A61 into Sheffield passing Hillsborough Stadium on your right. Continue along the A61, which becomes the ring road around the western side of the city centre. You will eventually reach a roundabout at the junction with the A621. At the roundabout turn right onto the A621 Bramall Lane. The ground is a short way down on the left.

From The South:
Leave M1 at Junction 33 and take the A630 into Sheffield City Centre. On reaching the inner ring road follow signs for A621 Bakewell, the ground is about a quarter of a mile the other side of the city centre. It is located on the A621 (Bramall Lane). Street Parking.

Alternatively, if you want to avoid Sheffield City Centre, then you may find it easier to park at Meadowhall Shopping Centre (unless of course it is in the run up to Christmas or the January sales, when the centre is very busy), just by Junction 34 of the M1, where you can park for free. You can then take a yellow tram to the City Centre and then walk to the ground. The tram journey time is around 20 minutes and costs less than £2 return.

Mark Needham adds; 'it's worth noting that if you are coming up from the south, that you can leave the M1 at Junction 29 (Chesterfield) and follow signs for Sheffield A61. This is particularly useful if the M1 is slow around J30, as it often is!'

■ By Train

The ground is walkable from Sheffield mainline train station, (10-15mins). As you come out of the station take the right fork which is Shoreham Street and continue down this street to the ground.

■ Local Rivals

Sheffield Wednesday, Barnsley, Rotherham United & Leeds United.

■ Admission Prices

The Club operate a four-tiered system (A+, A, B & C) of matchday ticket prices, whereby the most popular games cost more to watch. Category A+ prices are shown below with Category C prices shown in brackets.

Home Fans:

Global Windows (South) Stand:
Adults £34 (£15),
Concessions £24 (£10)

Capital One Stand:
Adults £32 (£15),
Concessions £22 (£10)

Sheffield United

Streetwise Corner:
Adults £32 (£15),
Concessions £22 (£10)

Hallam FM Kop:
Adults £30 (£22),
Concessions £15 (£10)

Junior Blades Under 16's & Under 10's
All home areas of the stadium:
Under 16's £12 (£10), Under 10's £5 (£5)

Away Fans:

Gordon Lamb (Bramall Lane) **Stand:**
Adults £30 (£22),
Concessions £15 (£10)

Programme
Official Programme £3

Record Attendance
68,287 v Leeds United,
FA Cup 5th Round, February 15th, 1936.

Modern All Seated Attendance Record:
32,604 v Wigan Athletic
Premier League, May 13th, 2007.

Average Attendance
2006-2007: 30,834 (Championship)

Did You Know?
Bramall Lane is the oldest major football ground in the world. The first game of football was played there in 1862. Although fellow Sheffield side Hallam FC's Sandygate ground is officially the oldest football ground in the world, Bramall Lane is the oldest venue to still be hosting professional matches.

* The ground originally opened as a cricket ground in 1855, but the first football match was not played there until December 1862, when Sheffield FC (who are the oldest club in the world, being formed in 1857) played Hallam.

Sheffield Wednesday

Hillsborough

Ground Name: Hillsborough
Capacity: 39,814 (all seated)
Address: Hillsborough, Sheffield, S6 1SW
Main Telephone No: 0870-999-1867
Main Fax No: 0114-221-2122
Ticket Office: 0870-999-1867 (option 2)
Ticket Office Fax: 0114-221-2401
Club Nickname: The Owls
Year Ground Opened: 1899
Pitch Size: 115 x 75 yards
Home Kit Colours: Blue & White

Official Website:
www.swfc.co.uk

Unofficial Websites:
London Owls - www.londonowls.co.uk
Owls Zone - www.owlszone.co.uk
AnzOwls - www.anzowls.com
Owls Online - www.owlsonline.com (Rivals Network)
Owlstalk - www.owlstalk.co.uk
Vital Sheffield Wednesday - www.sheffwed.vitalfootball.co.uk (Vital Football Network)

What's The Ground Like?

Although the ground has not had the level of new investment some other clubs have recently received, it is still a beautiful ground oozing character. It has four large separate stands, all of which are covered and are roughly the same height, giving a uniform feel to the stadium. On one side is the North Stand. This large single-tiered stand, opened in 1961, was hailed as an architectural marvel, as at the time it was the largest cantilever stand ever built in Britain and only the second such type of stand to have been constructed (the first was at the Old Showground in Scunthorpe). The two-tiered South Stand is the largest of the stands and is superb-looking. Considering that it was opened in 1914 and was designed by the famous football ground architect Archibald Leitch, it is a testimony after so much time that we still marvel at it. Plus it still outshines many new stands that have been built even in recent years. On its roof is the trademark of a Leitch main stand, the gable. This triangular structure on the roof, contains a clock and is adorned with a copper football. The stand has a large lower tier with a small upper tier above. At the back of the lower tier is a row of executive boxes. The team dugouts and Directors Box are located on this side.

At one end is the Spion Kop. This was previously a huge open bank of terrace that was at one time the largest in Britain. It gained a roof in 1986 and was made all-seated in 1993. Opposite is the West Stand or Leppings Lane End. This two-tiered stand was opened in 1966, in time for the Club to host some World Cup games played that year. Like the Kop, it has a number of large supporting pillars. One corner of the ground is filled with seating between the North & West Stand, this area is uncovered. On the other side of the West Stand is an electric scoreboard, under which is tucked a Police Control Box. Unusually for such an old ground, it doesn't have a set of floodlight pylons. Instead the stadium is illuminated by lights running across the front of the stand roofs.

Outside the ground near the main entrance is a memorial to the 96 fans who died at Hillsborough in 1989, at the FA Cup Semi Final between Liverpool & Nottingham Forest. The memorial is normally covered in flowers left by those who wished to pay their respects.

What Is It Like For Visiting Supporters?

Away fans are normally placed in the upper tier of the West Stand (the Leppings Lane) end of the ground, where up to 3,700 away supporters can be accommodated. If there is a particularly large following (or for an FA Cup Tie) then the corner described above may also be made available, plus the lower tier of the West Stand. This can take the allocation up to 8,000. There are a number of supporting pillars in the West Stand, which could impede your view. Inside there is a range of Shire Foods pies available including the Chicken Balti Pie (£2.40). The refreshments, though, are served from behind a metal mesh, which gives the area a prison-like feel.

I had an enjoyable day out at Hillsborough, where I found the atmosphere around the ground to be relaxed.

I thought the ground was certainly one of the best in the League, if not the country, in terms of setting and attractiveness. Lee Hicklin adds; 'About a hundred yards down Leppings Lane there is a programme and football memorabilia shop, which is worth a visit'.

Where To Drink?

The 'Horse & Jockey' pub is the designated pub by the police for away fans. It is located on Wadsley Lane, about a 5-10-minute walk away from the away end. Go down to the bottom of Leppings Lane, cross Catch Bar Lane and then left into Middlewood Road. Then turn right into Wadsley Lane, passing the Park Hotel and the pub is about 300 yards further up on the right hand side of the road. However I will warn you that this pub is a fair jaunt (20 minutes or so from the ground) and that the walk is a challenging uphill one!

Terry Potts recommends the 'Wadsley Jack' on Rural Lane. It's about a twenty-minute walk (uphill), going away from Sheffield centre. Dave Reid informs me 'if you continue up the road there is the Rose & Crown pub which also welcomes away supporters'. Derek Hall, a visiting Hartlepool fan adds; 'Another cracking pub is The Beehive, near the Wadsley Jack', Also I did pass a couple of pubs (the Norfolk Arms & The Red Lion) on the way into Sheffield on the A61 from the M1, where away fans were drinking. Bill Harris, a visiting Millwall fan adds; 'I found an excellent pub called The New Barrack Inn on the A61 just before McDonalds on the way to the ground. Forget the exterior, inside the pub has some excellent decor and no juke boxes or fruit machines. Although on my own I was made to feel very welcome and spent a good couple of hours talking football to the locals'.

Please note that alcohol is not available to visiting supporters in the away section of the ground.

How To Get There & Where To Park?

Leave the M1 at Junction 36 and follow the A61 into Sheffield, continuing for about eight miles. You will see Hillsborough Stadium on your right. This is not the shortest route to the ground, but definitely the easiest and avoids Sheffield city centre. There is some street parking to be had if you arrive early, otherwise there are some unofficial car parks along the A61 that charge in the region of £3. Gary Rickett-Ambrose adds; 'There is a car park directly behind the Kop and the Wednesday Club shop. It is called the wednesdayite car park and is open to fans of both teams. It costs £5 for visitors'.

Matthew Nicholls, a visiting Gillingham supporter adds; 'I find it easier to park at Meadowhall Shopping Centre (unless of course it is in the run up to Christmas or the January sales, when the centre is very busy), just by Junction 34, of the M1, where you can park for free. I then take a yellow tram to Leppings Lane, which costs less than £2 return and takes about 35 minutes'.

By Train

Sheffield railway station is situated in the town centre, two miles from the ground. Either get a taxi up to the ground or the bus station is a one-minute walk from the railway station. Cross over at the pedestrian crossing, and follow the signs. Head for the far side of the terminus. Bus no 53 to Ecclesfield runs regularly to the ground (every ten minutes), as well as numbers 77 & 80 (every 15 minutes), the journey time is about 30 minutes. Jeremy Dawson informs me; 'if arriving by train, by far the easiest way to get to the ground is by tram, which runs every ten minutes during the day. Leaving the station on a blue tram, you can either change to a yellow one in the city centre, which takes you to Leppings Lane (right by the ground), or stay on the blue one to Hillsborough, which is 10 minutes walk to the ground'. The journey time of the tram is around 20 minutes. Matt Wilcock adds; 'on matchdays regular shuttle buses run from the road at the far side of the bus station. They are marked 'Football'.

Local Rivals

Sheffield United, Leeds United, Rotherham United, Barnsley, Chesterfield & Doncaster Rovers.

Admission Prices

Home Fans:

Windsor Foodservice South Stand:
Adults £27*, Concessions £16*

Sheffield Assay Office North Stand:
Adults £25*, Concessions £15*

Hallam FM Kop:
Adults £22*, Concessions £12

Family Enclosure:
Adults £22*, Concessions £11

Away Fans:

West Stand (Leppings Lane End):
Adults £21*, Concessions £12

Concessions apply to over 60's, under 16's and student members of the Club.

* Please note that a £1 discount is available on this price if the ticket is purchased prior to matchday.

Programme

Official Programme - £2.50.

Record Attendance

72,841 v Manchester City,
FA Cup 5th Round, February 17th, 1934.

Average Attendance

2006-2007: 23,222 (Championship)

Did You Know?

That the ground was known as Owlerton Stadium, until being renamed Hillsborough in 1914.

Southampton

St Mary's Stadium

Ground Name:	St Mary's Stadium
Capacity:	32,689 (all seated)
Address:	Britannia Rd, Southampton, SO14 5FP
Main Telephone No:	0845-688-9448
Main Fax No:	02380-727-727
Ticket Office Enquiries:	0845-688-9288
Ticket Office Sales:	0800-280-0050
Stadium Tours:	0845-688-9288
Club Nickname:	The Saints
Year Ground Opened:	2001
Pitch Size:	112 x 74 yards
Home Kit Colours:	Red & White

Official Website:
www.saintsfc.co.uk

Unofficial Website:
Saints Forever - www.saintsforever.com

What's The Ground Like?

The Club moved from The Dell to the new St Mary's Stadium in 2001. In some ways this saw the Club returning to its roots as it was originally founded as 'Southampton St Marys', hence the club nickname 'The Saints'. To be truthful the stadium looks, quite simply, superb. Although comparisons have been made with the Riverside in Middlesbrough, St Mary's is better as all sides are built in the same style and are of the same height. The stadium is completely enclosed, with all corners being filled with seating. There are also two great-looking screens sitting on the roofs at each end. Running around three sides of the stadium, just below the roof, is a transparent perspex strip that allows more light and facilitates pitch growth. On the remaining side there is a row of executive boxes. The crowd are set well back from the playing action, as firstly there is a cinder track surrounding the playing surface and secondly the pitch itself must be the largest in the League (although the playing area does not use all of it).

What Is It Like For Visiting Supporters?

Away fans are located in the Northam Stand at one end of the stadium, where normally up to 3,200 fans can sit. For cup games this allocation can be increased to 4,750. The view of the playing action and the facilities within this stand are excellent. Leg room is good, although the width of the seating seemed to be a bit narrower than other grounds (either that, or I am putting on weight!).
The concourse behind the stand features a Ladbrokes, has TVs which show the game as it is played and a number of eating and drinking outlets. There are plenty of staff and the queues never seemed to get particularly long, which was a pleasant surprise. A range of Hollands Pies (£2) are on offer (to me, apart from the Shire Foods Balti Pie, these are the best range you can get), plus burgers (£2.50) and hot dogs (£2.50). There is also a 'Pie & Pint' outlet, that as the name suggests, only serves beer (£2.50 per pint) and pies. Perhaps they should rename it as 'Heaven'! Please note that smoking is not allowed anywhere in the stadium.

I thoroughly enjoyed my visit to St Mary's and would happily return. The stadium has (contrary to other reports) a great atmosphere and the facilities are first class.
I particularly commend the Club for the friendliness of their staff, from the stewards to the catering staff.
Even as I left the stadium, a steward wished me an enjoyable journey home! Considering that away

supporters are almost treated with contempt at some other clubs, this was a refreshing change. Coupled with the relaxed attitude of the home supporters and the excellent facilities, this to me makes a visit to St Mary's one of the best days out in the League.

Phil Jones adds; 'There was an excellent view from all around the ground and the atmosphere was good. I was impressed by their having toilet facilities around the perimeter of the ground which are accessible prior to the turnstiles opening. Well done Southampton, it's the little touches like these, for the fans' comfort and enjoyment of the day, which make all the difference'.

Colin Peel informs me; 'there is quite a good football memorabilia shop near the stadium on Old Northam Road called "The Football Shop". It is worth a visit'.

■ Where To Drink?

As most fans seem to end up in the city centre before the game, there are plenty of pubs to choose from. Daren Wheeler recommends the following pubs; The Prince of Wales, The Bevois Castle and The Station as good friendly pubs for away fans. Whilst The Eagle and The Anchor (next to the East Street indoor shopping centre) have also been recommended to me. Ocean Village also has a lot of friendly drinking holes'. I found a good mix of home and away fans in a Wetherspoons pub, The Standing Order in the city centre. Remember though, that the stadium is a good twenty-minute walk away.

I did discover a small pub called the Chapel Arms (formerly the Le Tissier Arms), which was only five minutes walk away from the stadium. Although a predominantly 'home' pub you seem to be able to get served okay if you arrive fairly early or have colours covered (for some reason they started to refuse serving away fans nearer kick off time). To find this pub, simply go to the corner of the stadium that has the Saints Superstore on it (between the Itchen & Chapel Stands) and then walk towards the city centre along the road, that runs beside the river and you will come to the pub on your right. Chris Hayward recommends 'the Coopers Arms on Belvedere Road (5-10mins walk away from the ground). Good for both home and away supporters and is amongst the closest to the away coaches dropping off point in Britannia Road through the local industrial estate'.

Graeme Miles, a visiting Norwich supporter, adds; 'The Bevois Castle does a fantastic full English breakfast for £2 on Saturday matchdays. It is well worth a visit as it is very welcoming towards away supporters. If travelling by train, I would also recommend alighting at St Denys Station, as this is slightly closer to the ground (about a 25-minute walk away), and there are three pubs within a two minute walk (Bevois Castle is about 5/10 mins from here) The Dolphin, The Junction and also The South Western, which is in the CAMRA Good Beer Guide. Their selection of Real Ales is fantastic! Around the St Denys area, there is also plenty of street parking'.

Paul Squire, a visiting Plymouth fan recommends the Junction, on Priory Road in St Denys, where he and his friends were made welcome as visiting fans. Otherwise alcohol is served within the ground.

■ How To Get There & Where To Park?

From the M3 take the A33 into Southampton. Continue on the A33 until you reach the junction with the A3024 Northam Road and turn left onto this road towards Northam. Then turn right onto the B3038, Britannia Road for the stadium.

There is hardly any parking available at the stadium for away fans (for home fans you can pay £5 for a car parking ticket in advance and park across the road from the stadium) and there are parking restrictions in force for the local area. Most fans seem to be just heading for the city centre car parks and then embarking on the 15-20-minute walk to the stadium. I did this and parked in an NCP car park, which cost £5. I should point out though, that after the game the roads around the city centre become almost gridlocked. It took me over an hour to get away afterwards.

Alternatively, on my last visit I noticed a number of fans parking around the Marina area and then taking the ten minute walk to the ground. Parking in this area has the advantage that at the end of the game, you can avoid the city centre gridlock, by heading along the coast on the A3024 and then onto the M271/M27. Barry Sear suggests 'I parked in Woolston (on the other side of the Itchen Toll Bridge) where there is plenty of street parking, and made the 15-20 minute walk from there to the ground over the Itchen toll Bridge. To get there, you leave the M27 at Junction 8 and follow the A3025 to Woolston. I was back on the M27 within 10 minutes of getting back to the car'. Colin Peel informs me 'I parked at the NCP car park called "Bargate" at the junction of Palmerston Road and Houndwell Place. The cost was a mere £2 for 4 hours and it was only a 10-minute stroll to the ground'.

Gavin Ellis, a visiting Arsenal supporter informs me; 'There is a free park and ride scheme in operation specifically for away supporters. This is situated just off junction 8 of the M27. The traffic in Southampton really made London look provincial, and I'd definitely not recommend people driving into the centre'. John Josephs, a visiting Newcastle supporter adds; 'After leaving the motorway at Junction 8 and heading towards Southampton, there are clear AA signs for the Visitors Park and Ride car park which is opposite a big Tesco superstore. Although it says pass holders only, this doesn't apply any more. They were checking match tickets at the entrance. I got there at about six which was two hours before kick-off. There were six buses waiting but hardly any supporters. Once there were enough people to fill half a bus it left. 15 minutes later and we were at the stadium. Afterwards the buses were waiting and although the police stop all cars after the match in a fairly wide area the buses can still leave. Ten minutes later we were back at the car park and within 5 minutes I was on the M27 heading home. The car park is well organised with really friendly stewards and bus supervisors. I can recommend this to anyone.' Other fans have also recommended the park & ride to me, so on my last visit on a Saturday, I thought I would give it a try. I arrived at the Park & Ride at 11.45am to be informed that it didn't run until 1pm and then 'only if we have enough fans to fill the bus'. I didn't fancy hanging around so I left the car park and drove to St Marys instead. However other fans that I spoke to arriving later found the service okay.

By Train

The stadium is located around one and a half miles away from Southampton station (where there is also quite a large car park), which should take about 30 minutes to walk. There is also a shuttle bus in operation taking fans from the station to the ground. This operates from the Blechynden Terrace bus stop outside the station.

Turn left out of the station's southern entrance and walk up Western Esplanade, which becomes Civic Centre Road. Remain on the Civic Centre Road and walk between the Civic Centre and the Marlands Shopping Centre. Eventually a crossroads is reached with the Nationwide Building Society on one corner and Lloyds Bank on another. Cross into New Road and follow this road across a park and past a college. Eventually you will reach a complex road junction with a number of traffic lights. Cross Kings Way into Northam Road and follow this road for a quarter of a mile until you reach the ground on your right. There are signs provided by the local council, which direct fans from the station to the ground.

Thanks to Scott Lydon, Jeff Manning & David Furnell for providing the directions.

You can also walk to the ground from St Denys station, which is about a 25-minute walk away. Kay Wilkinson provides the following directions: 'Leave the station on the platform 4 (South Western Arms Pub side) and proceed past the pub, which is on your right hand side and continue on down this road, past the Junction Inn and over the Horseshoe Bridge (this goes over the railway.) Take the next left, Dukes Road and follow this for about 3/4 of a mile past various industrial units and round past Mount Pleasant School, which is on your right. At this T-junction turn left into Mount Pleasant Road and walk over the railway (tip, if the train gates are down use the footbridge - you can sometimes wait here for 20 minutes). You then continue along this road, which changes into Radcliffe Road, past the mosque on your right and this road will take you all the way down to the underpass to the Stadium. This is the most direct route. If you want to visit the Dolphin Pub mentioned above you exit the station on Platform One side using the bridge across the road and the Dolphin is directly in front of you. To visit the Bevois Castle pub follow the directions into Dukes Road and half way down this road is a right turn, this will take you out into Bevois Valley, turn left and the pub is about 3 minutes walk away on a road junction on the right hand side.
To get to St Marys from here you can either walk up the hill following the road continuously, past the hospital and the fire station on your left, when you reach the main road, Northam Road, cross and pass through the bridge to the ground. Alternatively you can walk down the hill and take the first right, Mount Pleasant Road and follow the directions as from St Denys Station above'.

Local Rivals

Portsmouth.

Admission Prices

The Club operate a category system (gold & silver) whereby tickets for the most popular games cost more. Silver prices are quoted below in brackets.

Home Fans*:

Kingsland & Itchen Stands (Centre):
Adults £28 (£25),
No Concessions.

Kingsland & Itchen Stands (Wings):
Adults £26 (£22),
OAP's & Teenagers £19 (£17),
Juniors £13 (£10).

Northam & Chapel Stands:
Adults £26 (£22),
OAP's & Teenagers £19 (£17),
Juniors £13 (£10).

Away Fans:

Northam Stand:
Adults £26 (£22)
OAP's & Teenagers £19 (£17)
Juniors £13 (£10)

* Members of the Club can qualify for a discount on these ticket prices, for the family sections of the stadium.

Programme & Fanzine

Official Programme: £3
Beautiful South Fanzine: £1

Record Attendance

32,151 v Arsenal
Premier League, December 29th, 2003

Average Attendance

2006-2007: 22,720 (Championship)

Stadium Tours

The Club offer tours of the stadium at a cost of: Adults £9, Children (Under 13) £4.50, Senior Citizens £3. Family Tickets are also available at £22.50 (2 adults and 2 children). Tours need to be booked in advance on 0845-688-9288.

Did You Know?

That the Club's first ever ground was called the Antelope Ground.

Stoke City

Britannia Stadium

Ground Name: Britannia Stadium
Capacity: 28,383 (all seated)
Address: Stanley Matthews Way, Stoke On Trent, ST4 4EG
Main Telephone No: 01782-592-222
Main Fax No: 01782-592-221
Ticket Office: 0871-663-2007
Ticket Office Fax: 01782-592-201
Pitch Size: 115 x 75 yards
Team Nickname: The Potters
Year Ground Opened: 1997
Home Kit Colours: Red & White

Official Website:
www.stokecityfc.com

Unofficial Websites:
Oatcake Fanzine - www.oatcake.co.uk (Rivals Network)
Wheels In Motion - www.scwim.org.uk

What's The Ground Like?

The stadium, opened in 1997, looks imposing from afar as it is perched on a hill with hardly any buildings around it. It does look good, though, especially when lit up at night. It is a vast improvement on the old Victoria Ground which has now sadly been demolished. It is a fair-sized stadium comprising three separate stands. One of these, the Boothen End and Sentinel East Stand, extends around one corner of the ground, enclosing the stadium in that area. On the other side of the ground is the John Smith's Stand, which is the tallest at the Britannia. This imposing stand has a large lower tier of seating with a smaller tier above. Situated between the tiers is a row of executive boxes. There are quite large open areas to each side of this stand, which detract from the overall look of the stadium. If these could be filled at some point, then the ground would benefit greatly. The Big AM South Stand at one end of the stadium is allocated to away supporters. This simple-looking stand is like the rest of the stadium, all seated and covered, with windshields to either side. It is, however, quite steep, meaning that fans are kept close to the playing action. Unusually the teams come onto the pitch from one corner of the ground, between the Big AM South Stand and the John Smith's Stand. In the corner on the other side of the Big AM South Stand is a large electric scoreboard.

Tim Green adds; 'Behind the Boothen End there are three statues of the legendary former player Sir Stanley Matthews, which were unveiled by Kevin Keegan'. The club also have a couple of unusual looking mascots, with a blue coloured hippo called 'Pottermus' and his white girlfriend 'Pottermiss', obviously this is what happens to hippos when they visit the Potteries!

Future Ground Developments

Stephen Armstrong informs me; 'If Stoke City gain promotion to the Premier League, then the ground capacity would probably be increased by filling in the gap between the Boothen End and the John Smiths Stand. This would take the capacity to over 30,000'.

What Is It Like For Visiting Supporters?

Away fans are housed in the separate Big AM South Stand at one end of the ground, where up to 4,800 supporters can be accommodated. At first I was quite perturbed by a large sign advising fans that persistent standing would result in ejection from the ground;

however the facilities and view of the action from this stand are good. The concourse is adequate and there is a large choice of refreshments available such as Wrights pies at £2 each, sausage rolls (£1.50), cheeseburgers (£2.40), rollover hot dogs (£2.60) and chips (£1.30). Alcohol is also available in the form of Carlsberg lager (bottles £3), Bitter (pint £2.50), Strongbow cider (can £2.50) and Smirnoff Ice (bottle £2.60).

The stadium is quite high up in an exposed position and the open corners can mean that a cold wind can whip through the stadium, so bear this in mind, especially in the winter months. I thought the inside of the stadium was quite disappointing being rather bland and lacking character, although I'm sure that this can be developed in time. Listen out though for the Stoke anthem 'Delilah' being sung by the home fans, they can still give a great rendition of that Tom Jones classic song. It is worth bearing mind though that the Stoke fans are passionate about their club and this can make for an intimidating atmosphere, so it is best to keep colours covered around the ground. Outside at the back of the away stand there is an enclosed fenced off area, to keep away and home supporters apart, especially after the game has finished.

Where To Drink?

There is a distinct lack of pubs near to the ground as it is built away from other buildings. Therefore I would recommend that you grab a drink on the way into Stoke. James Diamond informs me 'There is a Holiday Inn and Harvester Pub next to the ground. Car parking in the Harvester car park costs £3'. Also close to the stadium is a Power League complex that also has a bar, which also allows in away fans, shows SKY television and you can even park in their car park for £4.50. Otherwise alcohol is available at the back of the away end, but queues can be lengthy, especially if there is a big support.

Kevin McPadden, the landlord of the Potters Bar adds; 'We are prepared to offer our hospitality to all visiting teams en route to the Britannia Stadium. We have a full menu of food and drinks available all day, children are welcome in a designated area, coaches welcome by appointment. The pub in Meir Park is approximately six minutes drive from the Britannia Stadium and is located on the A50 Uttoxeter/Stoke road. For further details please telephone 01782 395649 and ask for Kevin or Pat'.

How To Get There & Where To Park?

Leave the M6 at Junction 15 and then go straight across the roundabout onto the A500 towards Stoke. As you see the stadium over on your right and some wasteland over on your left (where the old Victoria Ground used to be) turn right onto the A50 towards Uttoxeter. You will then pass the stadium on your right and then at the next island go around and come back on yourself for the stadium entrance. Roger Davis informs me 'Visitors can purchase car park tickets for the stadium car parks from their own club at a cost of £4 per car'. Please note though that these tickets must be purchased in advance.

Matt Goldstraw adds; 'If you have a ticket for the official south car park, then after going onto the A500 towards Stoke from junction 15 of the M6, leave the A500 at the first junction and turn right at the large roundabout onto the A34 towards Stafford. Go past a red petrol station and the Staffordshire Knot pub and after about a mile you will reach a small roundabout that on the right has the entrance to Trentham Awakes (previously known as Trentham Gardens). Turn left and then continue straight on for about three miles. You will pass a golf club, a Toby Carvery, go over a railway bridge, over the canal and past an Esso garage. Then at a set of traffic lights where there is an obvious industrial estate to the right, turn left on to Stanley Matthews Way for the stadium'.

Alternatively there are still some parking spaces at various commercial sites between the old Michelin car park and the site of the old Victoria Ground. Bear in mind though that if you do park by the Victoria ground, allow a good 20 minutes to walk (mostly uphill) to the stadium. If you are intending parking in this area then from Junction 15 proceed along the A500, passing the junction with the A34. The stadium will appear over on the right and the open site of the demolished Victoria ground will appear on your left. Leave the A500 at the next junction and turn left to go down to this area.

Andy Fenwick, a visiting Sunderland fan, adds; 'Don't be tempted to park on wasteland around the stadium, you may well end up as I did with a parking ticket waiting for you on your return'.

By Train

Stoke station is just under three miles from the stadium and really is too far to walk, so it is probably best to hire a taxi. Tim Rigby, a visiting Wolves fan adds 'there are some shuttle buses than run from Glebe Street in Stoke up to the Britannia Stadium, which depart every 15 minutes before kick off. There are return buses after the game back to Glebe Street from behind the Sentinel (East) Stand'. Björn Sandström adds; 'To catch this bus, turn right from the station and head down Station Road.
At the bottom of Station Road at the traffic lights by the Roebuck Hotel, turn right to go along Leek Road (A52). Then go across the A500 dual carriageway and into Glebe Street which is straight across in front of you.
You should then see the line of buses that will take you to the stadium. It is only about a five-minute walk from the station'. The shuttle bus costs for a return ticket £3 Adults, £2 Children and £1.50 OAP's.

Local Rivals

Port Vale & Crewe Alexandra.

Admission Prices

Home Fans*:

John Smith's Stand (Upper Tier)
Members: Adults £21, Under 17/OAP £13, Under 11 £9
Non Members add £4 membership fee to price stated above.

Stoke City

John Smith's Stand (Lower Tier):
Adults £20, Under 17/OAP £12, Under 11 £9

Genesis Boothen End:
Adults £19, Concessions £12

Sentinel (East) Stand:
Adults £19, Under 17/OAP £12, Under 11 £9

Family Area:
Adults £17, OAP's £12, Under 17 £10, Under 11 £5.

Away Fans*:

Big AM Stand:
Adults £19, Concessions £12.

* An additional £2 supplement on these ticket prices will be charged where the Club deem the game to be a 'Premium Fixture'.

Programme & Fanzines

Official Programme: £3.
The Oatcake Fanzine: £1.20.

Record Attendance

At the Britannia Stadium:
28,218 v Everton,
FA Cup 3rd Round, January 5th, 2002.

At the Victoria Ground:
51,380 v Arsenal
Division 1, March 29th, 1937.

Average Attendance

2006-2007: 15,863 (Championship)

Did You Know?

That the ashes of the late great Sir Stanley Matthews are interred in a place somewhere below the Britannia Stadium pitch.

Watford

Vicarage Road

Ground Name: Vicarage Road
Capacity: 19,900 (all-seated)
Address: Vicarage Road, Watford, WD18 0ER
Main Telephone No: 0870-111-1881
Fax No: 01923-496-001
Ticket Office: 0870-111-1881
Team Nickname: The Hornets
Year Ground Opened: 1922
Pitch Size: 115 x 75 yards
Home Kit Colours: Yellow & Red

Official Website:
www.watfordfc.com

Unofficial Websites:
Independent Supporters Association - www.geocities.com/wfcwisa
Blind, Stupid & Desperate - www.bsad.org
Glory Horns - www.gloryhorns.co.uk
Vital Watford - www.watford.vitalfootball.co.uk (Vital Football Network)

What's The Ground Like?

The ground has had both ends redeveloped during the 1990's along with the front of the Rous stand. Both ends are large single-tiered stands, with some strange-looking floodlights perched on the roof. There is just one side that lets the ground down. The East Stand is a mish mash of a couple of old stands and an open seated area in one corner. Otherwise there is a vast improvement from the Vicarage Road of old. Away supporters used to have a long walk to the away end as you had to walk around some allotments. However this is no longer the case, as away fans are now housed in the Vicarage Road Stand, previously the home end, at the opposite end of the ground. There is a large video screen in the corner between the Rous & Vicarage Road Stands. Vicarage Road is shared with Saracens rugby club.

Future Ground Developments

Steve Beattie informs me: 'The Club have finally started the long-awaited development of Vicarage Road. Initially the developments will not be noticeable to the majority of fans, as the works are mainly upgrades of home and corporate areas and are to be carried out as phased developments over a three-year period culminating in the redevelopment of the old East Stand.

'Firstly the Rookery will see a new sports bar and catering areas and an improved wider concourse and will be completed for the start of the 2007/08 season. The dressing rooms and players' tunnel will be relocated to a new building replacing the temporary executive boxes in the Rookery/Rous corners (affectionately known as 'Celebrity squares!'), with seating above. Other works to the Rous will see various hospitality suites bolted on to the back of the stand. This work goes on to the close season. It is planned to infill all corners of the ground eventually which, when the East Stand is finally rebuilt, should create a good atmosphere.

'To help finance these developments the club has leased 'fresh air' space above the entrances and behind the Rookery stand to housing developers who will build key worker accommodation that will 'wrap around' the stadium. When all the works are complete in 2009 the stadium capacity will be increased to around 23,000'.

Richard Bailey adds; 'The current away area (the Vicarage Road Stand) is not included in the redevelopment plans, although it has been stated by the Club that away fans will probably be moved to the new south east corner of the stadium when it is completed'.

What Is It Like For Visiting Supporters?

Away fans are housed in the Vicarage Road Stand at one end of the ground. This stand is normally shared with home supporters (with the obligatory 'no-man's land' in between) or if demand requires it the whole of this stand (capacity 4,500) can be given to away fans. I've always found this club friendly on my four visits and have never had any hassle, although at times there can be a heavy police presence around the ground and in the town centre. Inside the ground, the delicious 'Football's Famous Chicken Balti Pie' (£2.50) is available. On the first occasion that I visited Vicarage Road, I met a Watford supporter in a pub who gave me a free ticket to that night's game against Luton. I was also impressed with this chap as at the time he had visited 91 League grounds with Watford. Perhaps he was in some part my inspiration for doing the '92'.

Where To Drink?

Christopher Harrison, a visiting Middlesbrough fan recommends 'Macs Bar' in Fearnley Street. 'It is only a couple of hundred yards from the ground and they even had a barbecue in the beer garden'. The bar is situated off Cassio Road and is clearly visible when taking the route to Vicarage Road from the town centre via Market Street. The pub is only a few minutes walk away from the away turnstiles. Otherwise the ground is in walking distance of the town centre, where along the High St you will find a few pubs including a large Wetherspoons outlet called the Moon Under Water. Rob Sterry adds, 'Away fans should avoid the Red Lion, outside the ground'. Please note that alcohol is not sold in the away section.

How To Get There & Where To Park?

There are some private matchday car parks available at some industrial units near the ground.

By Train/Tube

The nearest station is Watford High Street, a ten-minute walk away from the ground. However you are likely to come into Watford Junction train station, which is about a 20 minute walk. Thanks to Albert Fuller for providing the directions from Watford Junction to the ground;

Leave the station & take the main road straight opposite (Clarendon Road) all the way (over Ring Road at lights) up to the High Street. Turn left and go past Wetherspoons (Moon Under Water) on your right and then take the first right after 100 yards into Market Street. Continue along again crossing Ring Road to T-junction & then left at an excellent chip shop. Vicarage Road is the next right turn. Should take around 15-20 minutes to walk.

Watford also has its own London Underground tube station, which is on the Metropolitan Line and is situated just under one mile from Vicarage Road. However overland trains from London normally have a shorter journey time.

Local Rivals

Luton Town.

Admission Prices

At the time of going to press the Club were yet to announce their admission prices for the 2007/08 season. Prices for last season are shown below:

All areas of the ground
Category A matches:
£35 adults, £15 concessions

Category B matches:
£25 adults, £15 concessions

Category C matches:
£20 adults, £15 concessions

Concessions apply to Over 65's, Young Adult 16-19yrs, Student under 25 and Under 16's

Programme
Official Programme £3

Record Attendance
34,099 v Manchester United,
FA Cup 4th Round Replay, February 3rd, 1969.

Modern All Seated Attendance Record:
21,590 v Sunderland
Division One, November 27th, 1999.

Average Attendance
2006-2007: 18,682 (Premier League)

Did You Know?
That the Rookery End originally got its name from the Rookery Silk Mill that used to be situated behind the ground at that end.

West Bromwich Albion

The Hawthorns

Ground Name: The Hawthorns
Capacity: 28,003 (all seated)
Address: Halfords Lane, West Bromwich, West Midlands, B71 4LF
Main Telephone No: 0871-271-1100
Main Fax No: 0871-271-9861
Ticket Office: 0871-271-9780
Ticket Office Fax No: 0871-271-9781
Team Nickname: The Baggies
Year Ground Opened: 1900
Pitch Size: 115 x 74 yards
Home Kit Colours: Navy & White

Official Website:
www.wba.co.uk

Unofficial Websites:
Baggies.Com - www.baggies.com
Unofficial West Brom - www.westbrom.com
WBA Unofficial - http://westbromwichalbion.rivals.net (Rivals Network)
Disabled Supporters Club – www.wba-dsc.co.uk
Albion Till We Die - www.albiontillwedie.co.uk
Jon Want Fans Site - www.jonwant.com

■ What's The Ground Like?

With the completion of the East Stand in 2001, the Club had achieved its objective in completely rebuilding the Hawthorns to make it a modern stadium. Not only has the ground received a much needed face lift, but it is now totally enclosed and all seated. The East Stand is an impressive, large single-tiered stand, which has been well integrated with the rest of the ground. It has a row of executive boxes running along the back, and to each side of the stand the previous open corners have been filled with corrugated sheeting. There is a thin supporting pillar on each side of the stand to support the corner structures. This stand, along with all other areas of the ground, has been designated a no smoking area. On the other side is the relatively new but smaller, Halfords Lane Stand, stretching around two corners of the ground. The home end, the Birmingham Road Stand is large, covered, and quite steep. At the other end away fans are housed in the Smethwick end, which is also a relatively new stand. Two new video screens have been installed in opposite corners of the ground, one at the Smethwick End side of the East Stand and the other in the opposite corner of the Halfords Lane Stand.

An interesting feature of the ground is that in one corner of the ground (between the East Stand & Birmingham Road End) you will notice perched up on a wall, a large Throstle standing on a football. This has been kept over from the previous stand (it used to sit above the clock on the half time scoreboard) and maintains the links with tradition. Outside the ground on the same corner are the 'Jeff Astle Memorial Gates' erected in tribute to the legendary striker.

■ Future Ground Developments

Jordan Muckley informs me; 'Following the purchase and demolition of the Woodman Pub, which sat outside one corner of the ground, between the Birmingham and

West Bromwich Albion

East Stands, the Club have applied for planning permission to redevelop this part of the stadium, so that ground capacity can be raised to over 30,000. This will see the corner being 'filled' to the same height as the East Stand. The Club also have plans at some point to redevelop the Halfords Lane Stand'.

■ What Is It Like For Visiting Supporters?

Away fans are housed on one side of the Smethwick End, where the normal allocation is 3,000 seats. This means that this stand is shared with home supporters. For cup games, the whole of this stand can be allocated to away fans, raising this figure to 5,200. The facilities and the view of the pitch in the Smethwick end are okay, although the leg room is a little cramped. I have been to the Hawthorns on a number of occasions and have always found it to be a fairly friendly place. The only thing against a visit in terms of a day out is a nearby pub for away fans, meaning that most elect to drink inside the ground instead. Considering that the concourse at the back of the Smethwick End is pretty small in comparison to its overall capacity, then it has an uncomfortable feel, especially when there is a large away support. One tip on finding your seat in this stand, is to remember that although your ticket is marked with the letter of the row, say Row B Or Row LL, the plates indicating the row in the stand read B1 or LL1. As you would expect a number of fans get confused by the addition of the number 1 and start to wander around the stand looking for their seat. So you have been warned. Also in first gaining entry to the stand, the Club operate automatic turnstiles, where you have to put your ticket (which has a bar code on it) into a slot reader, which allows the turnstiles to admit you. There are stewards on hand if you get a problem and on my last visit fans were also being searched before entering the ground. Strangely I noticed that fans were not allowed to bring in takeaway food from the nearby McDonalds.

Look out for the West Brom mascot called 'Baggie Bird', who does a good job of entertaining the away fans before the game. This even involves going in goal and challenging players to take a shot!

■ Where To Drink?

Huw Morris, a West Brom fan, recommends The Vine which is about a 20-minute walk from the ground. From Junction 1 of the M5 turn left towards West Bromwich town centre (opposite direction to the ground). Take the first left into Roebuck Street. The Vine is down on the left. You can also street park in this area and walk to the ground. If you continue towards West Bromwich going over a small mini roundabout, then on the right just before the lights is the Desi Junction pub. This Asian run pub does an excellent 'Balti Buffet'. For £4.95 per adult, you can each as much as you like and I found the food to be pretty good. The buffet is available all day on a Saturday and you can wash it down with a pint of Cobra beer. Alcohol is also available within the ground (on my last visit £2.30 for a can of Carling or Worthington), along with the delicious 'Football's Famous Chicken Balti Pie' (£2.20).

Sean Mowat, a visiting Sheffield United supporter adds; 'As you pass the ground on the right on the main Birmingham Road, carry on about another half a mile and there is a pub on the right set back off the road called the Royal Oak. We've been in the last two times we've visited WBA. The beer is okay and they also serve Asian food (try the chicken kebabs!). We found it to have a friendly atmosphere'.

■ How To Get There & Where To Park?

The ground is located on the A41 (Birmingham-West Bromwich Road). If approaching from outside the area the ground is about half a mile from Junction 1 of the M5. On leaving the M5 take the A41 towards Birmingham; the ground is on your right. Beware though of speed cameras on this stretch of the A41. Street parking, or alternatively, there are a few private matchday car parks at some local industrial units near the ground, or at Hawthorns station which costs £4.

■ By Train/Metro

The closest railway stations are The Hawthorns which is about five minutes walk from the ground and Smethwick Rolfe Street, which is about a 15-minute walk from the ground. The Hawthorns is served by a Metro service from Birmingham Snow Hill station, whilst Smethwick Rolfe Street is served by local trains from Birmingham New Street. The Metro service takes eight minutes to The Hawthorns from Birmingham Snow Hill and trains run every 15 minutes. Please note though that train tickets are not valid on the Metro and that you have to buy a separate ticket for it (ask for a £1.50 matchday special adult return). C Price adds; 'On Halford Lane just below the train/Metro stop is a chip shop called the Hawthrones (which, yes, is spelt incorrectly). Fish and chips cost under £2 and are of good quality and it also serves pies and kebabs'.

■ Local Rivals

Wolverhampton Wanderers, Birmingham City, Aston Villa.

■ Admission Prices

Common with most clubs, West Brom operate a category system (A,B & C) for matches whereby tickets cost more for the most popular matches (category A).

Home Fans:

East Stand (Upper Tier)
Adults £28
Over 60's/Under 18's £27
Under 16's £25

East (Lower Tier) **& Halfords Lane Stands**
Adults £26
Over 60's/Under 18's £15
Under 16's £18 (A) £13

Birmingham Road & Smethwick Ends
Adults £23
Over 60's/Under 18's £14
Under 16's £11

Away Fans:

Smethwick End
Adults £23
Over 60's/Under 18's £14
Under 16's £11

Programme & Fanzine
Official Programme £3
Baggies Newspaper Fanzine - £1.50

■ Record Attendance

64,815 v Arsenal
FA Cup 6th Round, March 6th, 1937.

Modern All Seated Attendance Record:
27,751 v Portsmouth
Premier League, May 15th, 2005.

■ Average Attendance

2006-2007: 20,311 (Championship)

■ Did You Know?

That the Club were once called the West Bromwich Strollers. The Club changed their name to Albion in 1880.

Wolverhampton Wanderers

Molineux

Ground Name: Molineux
Capacity: 28,500 (all seated)
Address: Waterloo Road, Wolverhampton, WV1 4QR
Main Telephone No: 0870-442-0123
Main Fax No: 01902-687-006
Ticket Office: 0870-442-0123
Ticket Office Fax No: 01902-687-003
Team Nickname: Wolves
Year Ground Opened: 1889
Undersoil Heating: Yes
Pitch Size: 116 x 74 yards
Home Kit Colours: Gold & Black

Official Website:
www.wolves.co.uk

Unofficial Websites:
The Wolves Site - www.wolvesfansite.co.uk
Berlin Wolves - www.geocities.com/berlinwolves/
Wolf Message Board - www.the-wolf.co.uk

What's The Ground Like?

Molineux has been completely rebuilt in recent years, with the oldest stand, then called the John Ireland Stand (since renamed the Steve Bull Stand) being opened in 1979. Three other stands were then built in the early 1990s with the Jack Harris Stand the last to be completed in December 1993. The stadium itself is superb and is made up of four separate stands, complete with a couple of posh video screens in two corners, which show the game as it is being played. Both ends are large single-tiered stands (one of which the Stan Cullis Stand has a small clock perched on its roof), whilst both sides are two-tiered with a row of executive boxes along the middle. Both the side stands are unusual in being oval in shape, meaning that those sitting on the halfway line are furthest away from the playing action. It is a pity that the stands do not go all the way around the ground (the corners of the ground are largely open) as this would make it a truly wonderful stadium. Martyn Wells adds; 'the clock on the Stan Cullis Stand is the original timepiece that sat atop the old Molineux Street Stand since the 1930s. It was moved when the stands were redeveloped'.

What particularly impresses me about Molineux is that quality shows, getting the feeling that little expense has been spared in its construction. This is perhaps best summed up by the two statues that sit outside the ground. The impressive statue of Billy Wright is probably the finest football statue located at any ground in Britain. It sits outside the main entrance to the club offices. In 2003 the same designer, James Butler produced another statue, this time of former player and manager Stan Cullis, that is located by the entrance to the ticket office at the back of the stand bearing the man's name.

Future Ground Developments

Phil Painter informs me; 'plans have been drawn up to increase Molineux's capacity to 43,000, by adding an additional tier to both ends of the ground, plus completely rebuilding the Steve Bull Stand'. The Club have purchased the necessary land to do this, but have also confirmed that the expansion will not begin until Wolves have established themselves in the Premier League'.

What Is It Like For Visiting Supporters?

Away fans are normally housed on one side of the Jack Harris stand at one end of the ground, where around 2,000 fans can be accommodated. For games where there is a larger away following, then the away supporters are not given an 'end' as such, but are instead housed in the lower tier of the Steve Bull Stand along the side of the pitch. Up to 3,200 away supporters can be housed in this area. Fans are sat quite far back from the playing area, which gives the illusion that the pitch is larger than at most other grounds. Musical delights at the ground include just before kick off, 'Hi, Ho, Silver Lining' with the crowd singing 'Hi, Ho, Wolverhampton!' The catering facilities within the ground are pretty good, serving a good range of pies, hot dogs and burgers (£2.20).

On one visit I got talking to a couple of Wolves fans on the train up to Wolverhampton and they suggested going for a drink in the city centre before the game. I had an enjoyable time and they even took me right up to the away supporters entrance, shook my hand and wished me luck! Very hospitable. I personally did not experience any problems on my visits, but I have received a number of reports of others that have not been so lucky. It is strongly advised that colours are kept covered around the ground and city centre (and that goes for your cars too). I have also heard of objects and other unmentionables being thrown down on away supporters from the upper tier of the Steve Bull Stand. The Club are trying to stamp this out, but it may be an idea to wear that 'lucky' cap if your team's fans are to be housed in this area!

Where To Drink?

There are a number of pubs dotted around the ground, but they tend to be 'members only' for home fans. The Great Western, behind Wolverhampton train station has been recommended to me and I have enjoyed a good pint of real ale (Holdens & Bathams) there myself. However the pub is only really suitable for small numbers of away fans, who are not wearing colours. Tim Rigby adds; 'To find it, turn right out of the station entrance, and go down through the underpass. Turn right, and walk out of the old Low Level Station and it's in front of you on the opposite side of the road'. The Prince Albert, also nearby to the train station should be avoided by away supporters.

The ground is also in walking distance of the city centre, where there are plenty of pubs. However, some of them can be quite partisan so use your discretion. Cath Rosedon adds; 'If you are coming down the A449 from the M6, then approximately four miles from the city centre there is a pub called the Moreton Arms which serves good meals at reasonable prices'.

How To Get There & Where To Park?

From The South:
Leave the M6 at Junction 10 and take the A454 right into Wolverhampton (be wary of speed cameras on the A454). On reaching the traffic island that intersects with the ring road, turn right. As you approach the 2nd set of lights look for the signs for football parking. The ground is over the 2nd set of lights on the right. Alternatively if you turn left into the city centre you may find a space in one of the many council-run 'pay & display' car parks. The Civic Hall car park normally remains open for night matches.

From The North:

Leave the M6 at Junction 12 and take the A5 towards Telford and then turn onto the A449 towards Wolverhampton. On reaching the traffic island that intersects with the ring road, turn right. Then as South.

Thanks to Paul Judd, an exiled Wolves fan in Milton Keynes, for providing the directions.

By Train

The ground is walkable from the train station in the centre of city (15 minutes). Leave the station and proceed straight on towards the town centre and as you reach the inner ring road turn right. Just follow the ring road as it continues in a circular pattern around to the left. Eventually you will see the Molineux on the right.

Local Rivals

West Bromwich Albion, Birmingham City & Aston Villa.

Admission Prices

Home Fans:

Billy Wright Stand:
Adults £29, Concessions £17,

Billy Wright (Family Enclosure):
1 Adult + 1 Under 17: £32,
Additional Adult £27, Additional Senior Citizen £14,
Additional Junior £9

Steve Bull Stand:
Adults £27, Concessions £14,

Stan Cullis Stand:
Adults £23, Concessions £13

Jack Harris Stand:
Adults £23, Concessions £13

South West Corner:
Adults £23, Concessions £13

Away Fans:

Jack Harris Stand:
Adults £23, Concessions £13

Steve Bull Stand:
Adults £27, Concessions £14.

Concessions apply to over 65's and under 17's.

Programme & Fanzines

Official Programme: £3
Load Of Bull Fanzine: £1.50

Record Attendance

61,305 v Liverpool
FA Cup 5th Round, February 11th, 1939.

Modern All Seated Attendance Record:
29,396 v Manchester United
Premier League, January 16th, 2004.

Average Attendance

2006-2007: 20,094 (Championship)

Did You Know?

On February 17th, 1973, Kenny Hibbitt scored in a match for Wolves against Newcastle United. His brother Terry equalised for Newcastle.

Bournemouth

Fitness First Stadium

Ground Name: Fitness First Stadium
Capacity: 10,700 (all seated)
Address: Dean Court, Kings Park, Bournemouth, Dorset, BH7 7AF
Main Telephone No: 01202-726-300
Fax No: 01202-726-301
Ticket Office: 08700-340380
Pitch Size: 105 x 78 metres
Team Nickname: The Cherries
Year Ground Opened: 1910 (pitch rotated 90° in 2001)
Home Kit Colours: Red & Black

Official Website:
www.afcb.co.uk

Unofficial Websites:
RednBlack - www.rednblack.net (Rivals Network)
Norwegian Supporters Club - http://home.no.net/afcbnb

■ What's The Ground Like?

Anyone who visited the old Dean Court will not recognise the completely redeveloped ground. In a matter of months the old ground was completely demolished and a new stadium built. This currently comprises three new permanent stands and a temporary stand at the South End of the ground. The three permanent stands are of roughly the same design and height and are quite smart-looking, with the Main Stand having a row of executive boxes to its rear. Each is a covered single-tiered stand, with good views of the playing action, with perspex wind shields at each side. The stand roofs have perspex panels, helping get more light to the pitch. They sit at each side of the pitch and at one end. During the 2005/06 season the Club installed a 1,100 capacity seated stand at what was previously the open South End of the stadium, giving the ground a better overall look. The corners of the ground are also open and these are home to some unusual-looking floodlights. The pitch has been rotated 90 degrees from its old position and if you ever visited the old ground, try figuring out where the old Brighton Beach End was located!

■ Future Ground Developments

The Club still intend at some point to build a permanent fourth stand at the South end of the stadium.
If completed the overall capacity would rise to around 12,000, but no firm timescales have been announced as to when this is likely to take place.

■ What Is It Like For Visiting Supporters?

Away fans are located on one side of the East Stand, at one side of the pitch. The normal allocation for this area is 1,500, but this can be increased to 2,000 if required. The stand is shared with home supporters, offers a good view of the playing action and generates a good atmosphere. The facilities are okay and beer is served on the concourse as well as such delights as 'Football's Famous Chicken Balti Pie' (£2.20). For larger games the temporary South Stand at one end of the ground may be allocated to away supporters. Although I have yet to view a game from this particular stand, my experience of others at other grounds around the country has not been that good with the temporary facilities being less than desirable. If you add to this the fact that the new stand does not have a roof and is open to the elements, then you could end up having a wet, miserable afternoon.

Please also note that the stadium is a no smoking one, which met with cries of 'get your fags out for the lads' from the away support. (But note the stewards may throw you out if you are caught smoking in the seated areas). Bournemouth is a nice seaside town, with good nightlife, so why not make a weekend of it?

Where To Drink?

There is a bar behind the Main Stand, called the Cherry Tree, which welcomes away supporters to its downstairs bar. There is one pub by the dual carriageway, called the Queens Park, that is popular with both home and away fans. The pub shows Sky Sports and serves Ringwood real ale. On my visits it has been pretty relaxed, with home fans tending to congregate in the bar and the away fans in the lounge. To find this pub, simply walk away from the ground, on the road going from the main entrance to the stadium. At the end of the road turn left and the pub is a little way up on the left.

How To Get There & Where To Park?

Follow the A338 towards Bournemouth. The ground is situated on the left of the A338 in the outskirts of Bournemouth. If you keep looking up to the left as you go into Bournemouth you will eventually see the tops of the ground floodlights. At this point take the next exit off the A338 and turn left towards the ground. There is a large car park located at the ground. Alternatively, there is a council run car park, on the opposite side of the dual carriageway, which is handy for getting away quickly after the game.

By Train

The nearest train station is Pokesdown, which is roughly a mile from the ground and is around a 15-minute walk away. However, most trains arrive at Bournemouth Central, which is around a half-hour walk to the ground. Either try to get a train to Pokesdown or grab a cab (£7-£8). If you do arrive at Pokesdown station (which is served by trains from London Waterloo), then exit the station (there is only one exit) and turn right down the main Christchurch Road (A35). Proceed for about 400 metres and then turn right into Gloucester Road. Dean Court is located down the bottom of this road. Thanks to Andy Young for providing the directions from Pokesdown station.

If you arrive at Bournemouth Central, then leave the station by the South exit, thereby facing an Asda Supermarket. Turn left and walk down to the main Holdenhurst Road. Turn left (going away from the town centre) and then keep straight on along Holdenhurst Road for around 25 minutes, reaching the Queens Park pub (recommended by this Guide). Continue straight on past the pub until you reach a roundabout at which you turn right into Kings Park Drive. The ground is down the bottom of this road on the left. Alternatively you can catch a Yellow number 2 bus to the ground, normally a half hourly service. Come out of the station again by the South exit, facing Asda and turn left until you get to a Texaco garage. There is a bus stop with shelter on the same side of the road. Ask the driver to let you off near Kings Park Drive. Please note that if you decide to use the same service coming back, take a yellow number 2 bus as this is a circular service'. Thanks to Richard Barnes for supplying the directions from Bournemouth Central.

Local Rivals

Southampton, Brighton, Portsmouth and from further afield Reading & Leeds.

Admission Prices

Home Fans*:

Main Stand Executive (Pullman) Area:
Adults £28, Concessions £17, Junior Cherries £15

Main Stand (Outer Centre): Adults £23.50,
Over 65's/Under 16's £16, Junior Cherries £14

Main Stand (Wings). Adults £20, Over 65's/Students £13.50, Under 16's £12.50, Junior Cherries £10.50

Main Stand (Family Area); Adults £16, Over 65's/Students £8.50, Under 16's £6.50, Junior Cherries £4.50

North Stand: Adults £17, Over 65's/Students £8.50, Under 16's £7.50, Junior Cherries £5.50

East Stand (Centre): Adults £21, Over 65's/Students £13, Under 16's £11.50, Junior Cherries £9.50

East Stand (Wings): Adults £18, Over 65's/Students £9.50, Under 16's £7.50, Junior Cherries £5.50

Away Fans:

East Stand: Adults £18, Over 65's £9.50,
Under 16's £7.50

South Stand: Adults £17, Over 65's £8.50,
Under 16's £7.50

* Concessions apply to over 65's, under 16's and students (upon proof of student status).

Programme & Fanzine

Official Programme: £3
View from the tree Fanzine: £1

Record Attendance

10,375 England v Poland
Under 19 Friendly, February 6th, 2007

For a Bournemouth match:
9,359 v Brentford,
League One, May 6th, 2006.

Before the ground was redeveloped:
28,799 v Manchester United
FA Cup 6th Round, March 2nd, 1957.

Average Attendance

2006-2007: 5,335 (League One)

Did You Know?

That the Club was originally formed in 1899 as Boscombe FC. For a number of years the Club played in Kings Park, which is next to the site of the current stadium.

Brighton and Hove Albion

Withdean Stadium

Ground Name: Withdean Stadium
Capacity: 8,850 (all seated)
Club Contact Address: 8th Floor, Tower Point, 44 North Road, Brighton, BN1 1YR
Stadium Address: Tongdean Lane, Brighton, BN1 5JD
Main Telephone No: 01273-695-400
Fax No: 01273-648-179
Ticket Office: 01273-776-992
Team Nickname: The Seagulls
Year Stadium Opened: 1936
Pitch Size: 110 x 75 yards
Home Kit Colours: Blue & White

Official Website:
www.seagulls.co.uk

Unofficial Websites:
North Stand Chat - www.northstandchat.com
Brighton Fans - www.brightonfans.com
This Is The Albion - www.thisisthealbion.co.uk
BHAFC.Net - www.bhafc.net (Rivals Network)

What's The Ground Like?

Brighton's original Goldstone Ground was closed in 1997 after being the Club's home since 1902. The Club then spent two seasons in exile, ground sharing at Gillingham before returning to the South Coast in 1999 to take up temporary residence at the Withdean Athletics Stadium, whilst also looking for a suitable site to build a new stadium. After a long-drawn-out battle the Club have finally received planning permission to go ahead with the building of a new ground on the outskirts of Brighton and so, hopefully in the next few years the Club will say farewell to the Withdean.

The initial impression of the stadium is of its picturesque surroundings, set into a hillside and mostly surrounded by woodland, giving it somewhat of a rural look. On three sides of the stadium are a number of basic 'temporary stands' which are uncovered and hence open to the elements. Only the North Stand on one side of the ground can be described as permanent, as this was in existence prior to the football club taking up residence (and will no doubt remain when the Club eventually leave). This is the only stand that has some roof cover, albeit only partially to the rear and has a large Pavilion type building located behind it, which looks quite out of place at a football ground. The pitch is surrounded by an athletics running track, hence the supporters are set well back from the field of play. Although the temporary stands are generally on the small side, this cannot be said of the South Stand. This stand was designed by McAlpine and has a capacity of 4,500.

Future Ground Developments

After four years of wrangling and red tape, the Club were given permission by Central Government to build a new 22,000 capacity stadium at Falmer on the outskirts of Brighton. However, the saga continues as it has been revealed that some errors have subsequently been found in the planning application and the final decision has now been passed back to the Government for review. It is hoped that a positive decision will be made soon. If the Club receives the green light, it is hoped that construction of the new ground could be started in 2008 with the Club kicking off in its new home for the start of the 2010/11 season.

What Is It Like For Visiting Supporters?

Away fans are housed in the West Stand at one end of the stadium, in a small 'temporary' stand, more reminiscent of the structures at golf's British Open than a football ground. This seated stand is uncovered and has a capacity of 900 seats. On occasion this may also be shared with Brighton supporters, if the away Club elects to take a smaller allocation. Fans are set very well back from the pitch as there is a semi-oval grassed area behind the goal and then a running track in between that and the stand itself.

You would expect from such an open stadium that the atmosphere would be fairly flat. However, the Brighton supporters really try hard to get behind their team and this made for a good atmosphere. The fans also make the most of the temporary nature of the stands, by making quite a large din by stamping their feet on the metal floor. The open nature of Withdean makes a visit daunting on a cold, wet day.

Malcolm Townrow, a visiting Plymouth Argyle fan informs me; 'I had heard previously that the Brighton ground was a bit bleak, but I can honestly say it was one of the most if not the most friendly places I've visited as a visiting supporter anywhere. The stewards were first class and being able to mix with home fans in the Sportsman's directly next to the pitch was a joy. Parking the car was no problem and even the stewards out there and the bus drivers gave excellent service. Even though we won 2-0 which I suppose colours my view of things, all in all the experience was superb. No being shoved around by police with no humanity and they showed every courtesy and consideration for all fans. I'm glad it didn't rain though!'

Neil Cullen, a visiting Southampton fan, adds, 'I went with the attitude that the Withdean would be a poor ground, with poor facilities. But after a great day out there I left with the thought that it was a nice place to visit. The Sportsman pub was friendly and there was a good crack with the home supporters who were welcoming. The stewards and ground staff were friendly and helpful, more than you can say about a lot of places you visit. Okay the pitch was a long way off, and luckily we had sunshine, but all in all a good day out'.

I had a fairly enjoyable day out at the stadium. This was my last ground visited of the current 92 and the club were most accommodating in allowing me to have my photo taken on the pitch before the game. Special thanks to Club Secretary, Derek Allan for his hospitality.

Where To Drink?

Mark Collins informs me 'the Sportsman at the rear of the North Stand is now open on matchdays, though expect it to be crowded'. Otherwise Peter Hodd suggests 'the Preston Brewery Tap, located one mile south of the stadium, on the main A23 and is football friendly, but very crowded. Outside Brighton main line station there are a number of excellent pubs'. Phil Kramer recommends the Evening Star, on Surrey Street. It is away fan friendly and only two minutes walk away from the station. It is in the CAMRA good beer guide and serves real Sussex ale and cider'. Please note that alcohol is not served within the stadium.

How To Get There & Where To Park?

The stadium is located two miles away from the town centre and is just off the London Road (A23). There is no parking allowed within a mile of the ground, due to matchday restrictions in place around the stadium (one of the conditions that was agreed for allowing Brighton to play there). Kevin Ditch informs me that 'there is an excellent park and ride scheme which is available about one mile north of the ground, at Mill Road. Given that 90% of away fans come from the north and travel down the M23/A23, this is the ideal site, as it is right next to the main road'. Colin Peel adds 'I found the Park & Ride scheme to be brilliant; I got back in my car after the game, for the start of Sports Report!'. Remember that your match ticket includes a park and ride ticket for either the train or bus.

By Train

The nearest railway station is Preston Park which is about a 10-15-minute walk from the ground. The station is served by trains from London Victoria, Kings Cross & London Bridge (it is cheaper to travel from the latter two). On coming out of the station and walking down to the bottom of the hill, turn left along the A23 for the stadium or right for the Preston Brewery Tap pub. After the game there is a football special waiting which takes you back along the short journey to Brighton. I chose to do this by parking in the city centre and then getting the train (it only takes five minutes) to Preston Park. This way you get the chance to sample the pubs around the station!

Local Rivals

With a lack of other league clubs in the area, Brighton fans have focused on Crystal Palace.

Admission Prices

Home Fans:

North Stand (Centre): Adults £26,
Senior Citizens £18, Under 16's £16.50

North Stand (Wings): Adults £24.50,
Senior Citizens £17.50, Under 16's £16

South Stand (Centre): Adults £23.50,
Senior Citizens £16, Under 16's £14.50,

All Other Areas Of The Stadium:
Adults £22.50, Senior Citizens £15, Under 16's £13.50

Away Fans:

West Stand:
Adults £22.50, Senior Citizens £15, Under 16's £13.50

Please note that as part of the restrictions imposed on the Club when playing at Withdean, no match tickets will be on sale on the day of the game. All match tickets must be bought in advance and contain vouchers to use local transport to and from the stadium. This voucher is also valid for the train journey between Brighton & Preston Park.

Programme & Fanzine

Official Programme £3.
One F In Falmer £1.

Record Attendance

At The Withdean Stadium:
7,999 v Southampton, Championship, April 8th, 2006.

At the Goldstone Ground:
36,747 v Fulham, Division Two, December 27th, 1958.

Average Attendance

2006-2007: 6,239 (League One)

Did You Know?

That the Withdean Stadium is the only Football League ground that has an athletics track surrounding the playing area.

Bristol Rovers

Memorial Stadium

Ground Name: Memorial Stadium
Capacity: 11,916
Address: Filton Avenue, Horfield, Bristol BS7 0BF
Main Telephone No: 0117-909-6648
Fax No: 0117-907-4312
Team Nickname: Pirates
Year Ground Opened: 1921
Shirt Sponsors: Cowlin Construction
Home Kit Colours: Blue & White Quarters

Official Website:
www.bristolrovers.co.uk

Unofficial Websites:
BRFC 1883 - www.gashead.dial.pipex.com
Black Arab - www.blackarab.org
Supporters Club - www.bristolroverssc.co.uk

What's The Ground Like?

The club moved to the ground in 1996 and two years later bought the ground from the then owners Bristol Rugby Club. Although the Memorial Ground has seen some changes since the Football Club took up residence, it still has the feel of a rugby ground about it. On one side is the DAS Stand, which with its pavilion looks more like a cricket stand. It has a row of hospitality boxes across the top, with a few rows of seats in front. Below is an area of terrace. Just under this stand's roof is a television gantry and a small electric scoreboard. The stand runs for about half the length of the pitch and straddles the half way line. On one side of it, towards the Bass End is a small covered terrace, used as a family area, whilst the other side has a small covered area of temporary seating. Opposite is the Mead Civil Engineering (MCE) Stand, taller than the DAS Stand, but similar in length. This stand has covered seating to its rear and terracing at the front. It has open terracing to either side, one of which is given to away supporters. The team dugouts are located in front of this stand, although the dressing rooms are located behind the DAS Stand. This leads to quite a procession of players and officials at half time and full time. At one end is the Bass End, which is a covered terrace. Opposite is the unusual-looking (South) Stand. This was originally erected as a temporary stand, to fill the previously empty end. It has now been opened for a few seasons, although it still looks, with its green seats and bright white roof, more suitable for an outdoor showjumping competition than a football ground. The stand only runs for just over half the width of the pitch, has several supporting pillars running across the front and has been nicknamed 'the tent' by Rovers fans. The ground is shared with Bristol Shoguns Rugby Club.

Future Ground Developments

The Club have received planning permission to re-develop the Memorial Ground, into a 18,500 capacity stadium. The scheme will involve completely re-building the ground, moving the pitch in an eastward direction and incorporating residential accommodation around the outside of the stadium. Tony Hughes adds; 'Work will commence on the building of the new stadium in December 2007. The extent of the works will mean that the Club will ground share with Cheltenham Town for around 18 months, before returning to the new Memorial Stadium for the start of the 2009/10 season.

What Is It Like For Visiting Supporters?

Up to 1,100 away supporters are mostly housed in an open terrace on one side of the Mead Civil Engineering (MCE) Stand. This area is open to the elements so you might get wet if it rains. The open terrace makes it difficult for away fans to really generate some noise. If the weather is poor then it may be a better bet to head for one of the seats that are made available to away fans in the XXXX South Stand at one end of the ground. I must recommend the huge Cornish pasties (£2) that are sold at the ground, huge and tasty, plus they even do vegetarian ones which makes a change. Also on offer are a range of pies including the delicious 'Football's Famous Chicken Balti Pie'. I did not experience any problems on my visits, however I noted that the Rovers fans seemed to tolerate away fans rather than being over friendly. They can still do a good rendition of their club anthem 'Goodnight Irene', when the occasion stirs.

I found it quite amusing that the Rovers fans are nicknamed Gasheads. Nick Wootten of Bristol informed me that this term comes from where the old Eastville stadium in Bristol was sited, next to a (sometimes smelly) gas works! In fact it was rumoured that if Rovers were losing at half time, the gas would be turned up, to put off the opposition!

■ Where To Drink?

Pete Stump recommends; 'The Victoria pub on the Gloucester Road (five minutes walk from the ground) which usually has a comfortable mix of home and away fans - unfortunately it's not that big and does get busy'. Rhys Gwynllyw, a visiting Wrexham supporter recommends the Annexe Inn, which is 'friendly and has previously been listed in the Good Beer Guide. Last time I was there it had seven real ales on tap. I had no hassle at all in my Wrexham top'. Steve Pugh adds; 'The Annexe Inn is in Nevil Road, which is about ten minutes walk from the ground. You can find it by following the signs for the County Cricket Ground'. Otherwise there is a bar behind the clubhouse terrace that allows away supporters in. I have been informed that 'away fans should avoid the John Cabot pub'.

■ How To Get There & Where To Park?

Exit M5 at junction 16 (signposted Filton) and join the A38 (South) towards Bristol city centre. The ground is about five miles down the A38. You will pass the large British Aerospace works and further on, you will pass on your left the Royal George and Duke Of York pubs. At the next traffic lights, the Memorial Ground is signposted to the left and is about 100 yards down this road. If you go over the lights you will see the Wellington pub on your right. There is a fair amount of street parking around the sides and back of the pub.

■ By Train

The nearest railway station is Filton Abbey Wood, which as Peter Moody informs me; 'is approximately 1.5 miles or 20-25 minutes walk away from the ground'. More likely though you will end up at Bristol Parkway which is about two miles away from the ground and is really too far to walk from, so you are probably best to jump in a taxi or buses 73 & 74 run from the station past the stadium.

■ Local Rivals

Bristol City, Swindon Town, Cheltenham Town & Cardiff City.

■ Admission Prices

Home Fans*

DAS Stand (Centre Seating):
Adults £20, Concessions £16.50

DAS Stand (Wings Seating):
Adults £17.50, Concessions £9.50

DAS Stand (Terrace):
Adults £14.50, Concessions £7.50

Mead Civil Engineering (MCE) Stand (Seating):
Adults £18, Concessions £10

Mead Civil Engineering (MCE) Stand (Terrace):
Adults £12.50, Concessions £6.50

Family Terrace:
Adults £12.50, Concessions £5.50

(South Stand):
Adults £15, Concessions £8

Bass Terrace End:
Adults £12.50, Concessions £6.50

Away Fans*

Mead Civil Engineering (MCE) Stand (Terrace):
Adults £12.50, Concessions £6.50

South Stand (Seated):
Adults £15, Concessions £8

* The above prices quoted are for tickets purchased prior to matchday. Tickets purchased on matchday cost £2 more per ticket.

■ Programme

Official Programme: £2.50.

■ Record Attendance

At The Memorial Stadium:
11,433 v Sunderland,
Worthington Cup 3rd Round, October 31st, 2000.

At Eastville;
38,472 v Preston North End,
FA Cup 4th Round, January 30th, 1960.

■ Average Attendance

2006-2007: 5,126 (League Two)

■ Did You Know?

The stadium, when opened in 1921, was called the Memorial Ground, in memory of those Bristol Rugby players who served their country in the First World War.

Please note that due to the rebuilding of the Memorial Ground, from December 2007 the Club will be playing their home games at Cheltenham Town's Whaddon Ground. Please see page 132 for details.

Carlisle United

Brunton Park

Ground Name: Brunton Park
Capacity: 16,981
Address: Warwick Road,
Carlisle, CA1 1LL
Main Telephone No: 01228-526-237
Fax No: 01228-554-141
Pitch Size: 117 x 72 yards
Year Ground Opened: 1909
Team Nickname: The Cumbrians
Home Kit Colours: Blue & White

Official Website:
www.carlisleunited.co.uk

Unofficial Websites:
Reeves Is Offside Again! - www.kynson.org.uk
Vital Carlisle - www.carlisle.vitalfootball.co.uk
(Vital Football Network)
CUFC Online - www.cufconline.org.uk
(Footy Mad Network)

■ What's The Ground Like?

The Cumberland Building Society Stand on one side of the pitch is a relatively new covered, all seated stand, which looks quite smart. The other side is an old partly covered (to the rear) Main Stand, which has seating at the back and a terraced paddock to the front. The central part of this stand was built in 1954 with the wings added at a later stage. The Warwick Road End is a covered terrace that has a peculiar-looking roof. The other end, the Petterill End (aka The Waterworks End), is a small open terrace, which after refurbishment has now been re-opened after being closed for a number of years. There is also an electric scoreboard at this end, which is also known as the Waterworks End. The ground also has some strange-looking floodlights.

Another unusual aspect of the ground is that the central point of the East Stand, is located just off the half way line. This means that one side of the stand extends past the one goal line, whilst the other side falls short of this. This was due to the fact that the Club were intending to rebuild the whole ground and move the pitch a few yards further north, but alas the development funds ran dry.....

■ What Is It Like For Visiting Supporters?

Away fans are normally located in the Petterill End terrace at one end of the ground. This area houses around 1,700 fans and is open to the elements, so be prepared to get wet. If demand requires it, then part of the Cumberland Building Society (East) Stand (towards the Petterill End) on one side of the pitch, can also be allocated. The facilities and the view of the playing area from the East Stand are good. Steve Barrie adds; 'If away supporters are allocated part of the East Stand, then they will find that they are only separated from home fans by a piece of fabric spread across the seats and a bit of plastic ribbon. It tends to create a lively atmosphere between the two sets of fans and can also be a little intimidating'. I personally found the Carlisle fans to be friendly and helpful and had a pleasant afternoon there.

■ Where To Drink?

There is one pub near the ground, 'The Beehive' which is on the main A69 (Warwick Road). The pub allows away supporters in and serves a good pint of Theakstons. Further down the road towards the town centre is the White House, which is more spacious, but won't allow away fans in wearing colours. Otherwise there is the Carlisle Rugby Club next to Brunton Park on the Warwick Road that has a club bar, allows in away supporters and is family-friendly. Barrie Mossop recommends another Theakstons House, the Howard Arms, which is on Lowther Street. This is just off Warwick Road, towards the Town Centre, down from the White House. Simon Tunstall adds; 'At the back of the main car park there is the Stoneyholme Golf Club, which has a bar, serves food and welcomes fans on matchdays'. Paul Sawyers adds; 'I would recommend the Lakeland Gate for a drink on match days, which is a family-friendly pub'.

■ How To Get There & Where To Park?

The ground is easy to find. Leave the M6 at junction 43 and take the A69 towards Carlisle. After a mile the ground is on your right. The club car park (cost £1.50) can be found by taking the first right immediately after Brunton Park into Victoria Place and then turn first right onto St Aidans Road. Otherwise street parking.

By Train
James Prentice informs me; 'Brunton Park is situated about a mile from Carlisle Citadel station, but is relatively easy to get to. Upon exiting the station's main entrance, walk the short distance around The Crescent until reaching Warwick Road. You will be able to see the old Main Stand and the strangely-shaped roofs of the Warwick Road end after walking for about twenty minutes. There are directions to the away supporters' turnstiles above the Carlisle United club shop'.

Local Rivals
Hartlepool, Darlington and from a little further afield Preston & Burnley.

Admission Prices

Home Fans: *

Cumberland Building Society Stand:
Adults £20, Over 65's £14, Under 18's £10, Under 11's £4

Main Stand Seating (Centre):
Adults £20, Over 65's £14, No Concessions for Under 18's

Main Stand Seating (Wings):
Adults £20, Over 65's £14, Under 18's £10, Under 11's £4

Main Stand Terrace:
Adults £16, Over 65's £12, Under 18's £9, Under 11's £3

Warwick Road End Terrace:
Adults £16, Over 65's £12, Under 18's £9, Under 11's £3

Away Fans: *

Cumberland Building Society Stand Seating:
Adults £20, Over 65's £14, Under 18's £10, Under 11's £4

Petterill End Terrace:
Adults £16, Over 65's £12, Under 18's £9, Under 11's £3

* The ticket prices quoted above are for matchday. Tickets purchased prior to matchday (excluding Under 11's tickets) qualify for a £2 discount.

Programme
Official Programme: £2.50

Record Attendance
Record Attendances:
27,500 v Birmingham City, FA Cup 3rd Round, January 5th, 1957.

27,500 v Middlesbrough, FA Cup 5th Round, February 7th, 1970.

Average Attendance
2006-2007: 7,860 (League One)

Did You Know?
During its history, the ground has been completely flooded on a number of occasions, when the nearby River Petteril has burst its banks. This recently happened again in 2005. The floods have been so deep that they have reached almost the top of the goal posts.

Cheltenham Town

Whaddon Road

Ground Name: Whaddon Road
Capacity: 7,066 (3,912 seated)
Address: Whaddon Road, Cheltenham, GL52 5NA
Main Telephone No: 01242-573-558
Fax No: 01242-224-675
Team Nickname: The Robins
Year Ground Opened: 1932
Pitch Size: 111 x 72 yards
Home Kit Colours: Red & White

Official Website:
www.ctfc.com

Unofficial Websites:
Cheltenham Town Mad - www.cheltenhamtown-mad.co.uk (Footy Mad)
Robins Nest Forum - www.robinsnestforum.co.uk
CTFC Talk - www.ctfctalk.com

What's The Ground Like?

At one end of the ground is the newest addition to the stadium. The Carlsberg Stand which was built by Barr Construction, was opened in December 2005 and has a capacity of 1,100 fans. This stand is given to away supporters and is particularly steep in its design. It has a perspex windshield to one side and perspex panels incorporated into its roof, to allow more light to reach the pitch. The stand is unusual in the respect that it has a couple of more rows of seats on one side of it. There is also a small electric scoreboard on its roof. On one side of the ground is another relatively new stand. The In2Print Stand was opened in November 2001 and was built by Barr Construction. This stand sits proudly at one side of the pitch and houses 2,034 supporters. It is a covered, all-seated, single-tiered stand, part of which is sometimes given to away supporters. The ground is now enclosed in one corner where the two new stands meet, although it is not used for spectators. On the other side of the pitch is the Stagecoach Main Stand, which has seating to the rear and terracing at the front. Straddling the halfway line, it does not extend the full length of the pitch, having open spaces to either side. At one end is the small, covered, Cheltenham & Gloucester Terrace, which is the home end of the ground.

What Is It Like For Visiting Supporters?

Away supporters are housed in one end of the ground, in the new Carlsberg Stand. As would be expected from a new stand, the view of the playing area and the facilities are good, plus the bonus is that it also has good leg room. Just over 1,100 supporters can be accommodated in this area. If demand requires it, then up to 1,500 seats can be allocated in the In2Print Stand at one side of the pitch. The food on offer within the ground is not bad; you can choose from burgers (including for those with a bigger appetite a half-pounder with cheese £3), hot dogs, pies (including the Pukka Chicken Balti Pie £2) and bacon baps (£2).

I found Cheltenham itself to be quite pleasant and the supporters friendly. The picturesque Cotswold Hills around Cheltenham can easily be seen from inside the ground. The atmosphere is also pretty good and there is a drummer in the home end. I did find the P.A. to be a bit deafening, though.

Neil Le Milliere, a visiting Exeter City fan, informs me 'I have found some of the stewarding to be over the top, and some supporters were ejected from the ground for little reason'. Peter Llewellyn adds 'Don't go on race day like I did - it's worse than getting away from Old Trafford!'

Where To Drink?

There is a club bar at the ground called the Robins Nest which allows in small numbers of away fans for a small admittance fee. The closest pubs that I found to the ground were the Fox & Hounds & The Greyhound, but they both have more of a home feel about them. Away fans are probably better heading to the Sudeley Arms or The Conservatory on Prestbury Road on the outskirts of town. There is even a decent fish & chip shop situated in between the two. To find these pubs, turn right out of the club car park, and then turn left at the end of the road. Go straight over the roundabout, and the Sudeley Arms is on your left and The Conservatory is further up on your right. It is no more than a ten-minute walk from the ground.

Otherwise there is the Parklands Social Club, where you can also park your car (£4). Simply go down Whaddon Road, passing the ground and the bowling club on your left. Take the first left hand turn and the entrance to the social club car park is a short distance down on the left.

How To Get There & Where To Park?

From The North

Leave the M5 at junction 10 and take the A4019 towards Cheltenham. Keep straight on through the traffic lights, until you come to large roundabout (there is a McDonalds on the left), at which you turn turn left. Continue up this road going over a double mini roundabout. Keep going for about 300 yards and then turn right into Swindon Lane. Go over the level crossing and straight over the next roundabout (signposted Prestbury) passing the race course on your left. Turn right into Albert Road (signposted Gloucestershire University) and at the bottom at the roundabout turn left into Prestbury Road, (the ground is signposted from here) and then further down Prestbury Road, turn right into Whaddon Road. The ground is down on the left.

From The South

Leave the M5 at Junction 11 turning right towards Cheltenham. Go across 1st roundabout - GCHQ is on your left. Turn left at the next roundabout, into Princess Elizabeth Way. Go straight over the next roundabout, (the exit is over at about "1 o'clock"). Keep on up this road, and you will come to a big roundabout, where you will see a McDonalds on the corner. Go straight across this roundabout and continue up this road going over a double mini roundabout. *Then as North.*

There is no usable car park at the ground and nearby street parking is limited. The Parklands Social Club does allow some parking at £4 per car (See Where To Drink). Otherwise there is a free 'Park & Ride' service to the ground operating from Cheltenham Racecourse, which is well signposted around the town. Journey time on the 'Park & Ride' service is obviously dependent on traffic, but is around ten minutes on average.

By Train

Cheltenham station is over two miles from the ground, so best to jump in a taxi. If you are going to embark on the 35-40 minute walk then thank Dave Lucas for the following directions; 'Turn right out of station car park and follow Queens Road for around half a mile. At end of Queens Road and turn left into Lansdown Road. At the next (Montpellier) roundabout, turn left into Montpellier Walk (which later becomes the Promenade). At the end of the Promenade, turn right into the High Street. Go along High Street for around 100 yards and then turn left into Winchcombe Street (by a branch of the Cheltenham & Gloucester Building Society). Continue straight along Winchcombe Street and into Prestbury Road. Straight across the next roundabout and then right into Whaddon Road. The entrance to the away end is on the left'.

Local Rivals

Swindon Town, Yeovil Town and from non-league days, Gloucester City.

Admission Prices

In2Print Stand:
Adults £18, Concessions £12, Under 16's £7.

Stagecoach West Stand:
Adults £17, Concessions £11, Under 16's £7.

Family Area:
Adults £13, Concessions £9, Under 16's £5.

Terrace:
Adults £13, Concessions £9, Under 16's £5.

Concessions apply to over 65's and students (who have first registered at the Club, to obtain a Student Membership Card).

Programme

Official Programme £2.50.

Record Attendance

At Whaddon Road:
8,326 v Reading,
FA Cup 1st Round, November 17th, 1956.

At The Athletic Ground:
10,389 v Blackpool,
FA Cup 3rd Round, January 13th, 1934.

Average Attendance

2006-2007: 4,072 (League One)

Did You Know?

Cheltenham Town changed to red and white in 1903, earning them the nickname 'The Robins'. They had previously played in a deep red playing kit, inspiring the nickname 'The Rubies'.

Crewe Alexandra

Alexandra Stadium

Ground Name: Alexandra Stadium (but still known to a lot of fans as Gresty Road)
Capacity: 10,066 (all seated)
Address: Gresty Road, Crewe, Cheshire, CW2 6EB
Main Telephone No: 01270-213-014
Ticket Office: 01270-252-610
Fax No: 01270-216-320
Pitch Size: 100 x 66 yards
Team Nickname: The Railwaymen
Year Ground Opened: 1898
Home Kit Colours: Red, White & Blue

Official Website:
www.crewealex.net

Unofficial Websites:
www.crewealex.co.uk (Rivals Network)
Crewe Mad - www.crewemad.co.uk (Footy Mad Network)

What's The Ground Like?

The opening of the £6m pound Air Products Stand (formerly known as the Railtrack Stand) in 1999 changed forever the look and feel of the ground. Before, it had always been small and homely, but the addition of the Air Products Stand has drastically changed the overall scene. The stand, which sits proudly along one side of the pitch, is a single-tier cantilever holding just under 7,000 people. It looks huge compared to the other stands and is probably three times the size of the old Main Stand. It is simply designed, sits well back from the pitch and has windshields to either side. Considering that the overall capacity of the ground is just over 10,000, one can understand how the Air Products Stand dominates Gresty Road, accounting for 70% of the available seating.

The other three stands are roughly of the same height, covered and all seated, but are rather small when compared to the Air Products Stand. So much so, that balls are regularly kicked out of the ground during a game. The newest of these smaller stands is the Advance Personnel Stand (previously known as the Gresty Road End), which is the home end of the ground. This replaced a former open terrace and seats around 900. Opposite is the Charles Audi Stand. This has some executive boxes at the rear, but the seating area is only opened for the bigger games. The Blue Bell BMW Stand at one side of the ground, has an unusual television/press gantry on its roof. It almost looks as if part of a portakabin was at some point bolted onto the roof and it looks a bit precarious. In the corner between the Blue Bell BMW & Charles Audi Stands is a large clock, whilst on the other side of the Blue Bell BMW Stand is a Police Control Box, keeping a close eye on the away contingent.

An unusual feature is the absence of dugouts; instead the teams are given a section of seating at the front of the Air Products Stand. You will also notice that the pitch is slightly raised above ground level. The ground is completed with a set of modern-looking floodlights. I noted that on the Air Products side of the stadium additional lighting is present half way up the floodlight pylons. One assumes that the height of the new stand prevented enough light getting to the pitch and hence additional lighting needed to be subsequently added.

Future Ground Developments

At some point in the future, the club hopes to replace the Blue Bell BMW Stand (formerly known as the Popular Side) with a new two-tiered stand, which will also contain executive boxes.

Crewe Alexandra

■ What Is It Like For Visiting Supporters?

Away fans are housed in the Blue Bell BMW Stand at one side of the ground. The whole of this stand is given to away supporters and houses 1,680 fans, though if required the Charles Audi Family Stand can also be allocated to away fans. Entrance to the away stand is by ticket only, (no cash is accepted at, ironically, some of the oldest turnstiles I have ever seen at a league ground). Tickets need to be purchased from the ticket booth next to the supporters club at the entrance to this stand. Please also note that alcohol is not available in this stand.

I found Crewe to be relaxed and friendly, making for a good day out. There was a large away support on my last visit which boosted the atmosphere of the ground; however I have heard reports that it can be a bit flat at certain games, even with the efforts of a drummer in the home end. There was a good range of Holland's pies (£2), pasties (£2) and sausage rolls (£1.50) from the refreshment kiosk, as well as hot dogs (£2.50). There are a couple of supporting pillars in the Blue Bell BMW Stand which if you are unlucky could affect your view of the playing action. There is a popular fish and chip shop just outside of the stadium, the smell of which, early in the game, wafts across the ground.

As an aside, this is the only ground when just sitting there minding my own business, during the first half, I suddenly get a big wet tongue in my ear! Now before you all starting thinking all sorts of connotations (and I should add that Mrs Adams wasn't with me), it was in actual fact a black Labrador dog that was the culprit. This was my introduction to Pebble the trainee guide dog, who had been brought to the match to get used to crowd situations. Now just when I thought I had experienced it all on my travels...

■ Where To Drink?

If you get there reasonably early before the game, the supporters club at the ground allows small numbers of away fans in. There are also a number of pubs within walking distance of the ground. The pick of these, is probably the Royal Hotel on Nantwich Road. As Barry Cutts, a visiting Coventry City supporter adds; 'I found the Royal Hotel to be a warm & welcoming drinking house. Turn left out of the railway station & the pub is 50 yards down this road on the right hand side. There is also a fantastic chippie opposite'. Although the pub does not look that welcoming, with a number of bouncers on the door, once inside you will find it okay. There are separate bars for home and away supporters. The away supporters bar is called Clancys and is decked out in an Irish theme. On my last visit it had a large screen showing Sky Sports and had a number of filled rolls for sale. For those who like their real ale then further down Nantwich Road on the left hand side just past the traffic lights is the British Lion. This comfortable small pub is listed in the CAMRA Good Beer Guide and has regular changing guest beers.

If you park on the industrial estate just off Weston Road, then on your way to the ground you will pass the Brocklebank Pub, a Brewers Fayre outlet, which is very popular with away fans. It is also has a large screen showing Sky Sports. You can also park in their own car park which costs £1 for three hours. The cost of parking is refundable off your bill if you use their restaurant.

■ How To Get There & Where To Park?

Leave the M6 at Junction 16 and take the A5020 towards Crewe. Follow this road right into Crewe. At the roundabout junction with the A534, Nantwich Road, turn left. Gresty Road is down past the railway station on the left. Just before you reach this island on Weston Road, you will see a sign pointing to the right, which displays; 'Away Supporters On Street Parking'. This directs you to an industrial estate on the right of the road (you will also see the Volkswagen dealership, L C Charles, on the front of it). It takes about 15 minutes to walk to the ground from here.

■ By Train

The ground is only a few minutes walk from the train station. As you come out of the railway station turn left and Gresty Road is down the road on your left.

■ Local Rivals

Stoke City & Port Vale.

■ Admission Prices

All Areas Of The Ground:*
Adults £19,
O.A.P.'s £15,
Under 16's £8.50,
Under 11's £4.50

* Club members can qualify for a discount on these ticket prices.

■ Programme & Fanzines

Official Programme £2.50
Super Dario Land Fanzine £1
Once In A Blue Moon £1

■ Record Attendance

20,000 v Tottenham Hotspur
FA Cup 4th Round, January 6th, 1960.

Modern All Seated Attendance Record:
10,103 v Manchester United
Carling Cup Round 3rd Round,
October 26th, 2004.

■ Average Attendance

2006-2007: 4,926 (League One)

■ Did You Know?

That the Club took their name after the town and the then Princess Alexandra.

Doncaster Rovers

Keepmoat Stadium

Ground Name:	Keepmoat Stadium
Capacity:	15,231 (all seated)
Address:	Stadium Way, Lakeside, Doncaster, DN4 5JW
Main Telephone No:	01302-764-664
Fax No:	01302-363-525
Ticket Office:	01302-762-576
Team Nickname:	Rovers
Year Ground Opened:	2007
Home Kit Colours:	Red & White

Official Websites:

www.doncasterroversfc.co.uk
Keepmoat Stadium - www.smc-doncaster.co.uk

Unofficial Websites:

YAURS - www.yaurs.com
Doncaster Rovers A New Era - www.doncasterrovers-mad.co.uk
Official Supporters Club - www.doncasterrovers-supportersclub.co.uk
Viking Supporters Cooperative - www.vikingsc.co.uk

What's The Ground Like?

After 84 years of playing football at their old Belle Vue ground, the Club have now moved to a new purpose-built stadium, which was opened on January 1st, 2007. The Keepmoat Stadium cost £21m to build and is also home to Doncaster Lakers Rugby League team as well as ladies football team Doncaster Belles. The stadium complex was built by, and is owned by, Doncaster Council.

To be honest the Keepmoat Stadium, in common with a number of new stadiums, looks far more interesting from the outside that it does on the inside. The stadium is situated next to a lake (which I believe makes Doncaster the only league ground to do so) and looks smart with four interesting looking floodlights, protruding at an angle from the stadium roof. However, on the inside the stadium is rather non-descript. Yes it looks tidy, the stadium is completely enclosed, and all the stands, which are of the same height and all seated are covered. But it lacks character and it is rather similar to other new stadiums that have been built, except that it is on a smaller scale.

On one side of the stadium is the West Stand. This contains the teams' dressing rooms and tunnel, from which the teams emerge onto the pitch. The primary television gantry is also housed on this side, along with press facilities, as well as the main areas that house disabled supporters. Opposite is the East Stand which contains a row of 16 executive boxes, outside which patrons can sit. Both ends are identical, with the North End of the ground being allocated to away fans.

Unusually the stadium has large access points in three corners of the ground, which can be used, if need be, by emergency services. In the North East corner of the stadium is a small electric scoreboard.

What Is It Like For Visiting Supporters?

Away fans are located in the North Stand at one end of the stadium, where around 3,344 fans can be accommodated. Clubs with a smaller following will be allocated around a third to two-thirds of that number meaning that on those occasions the end is shared with home supporters. The view of the playing action, leg room, and facilities in this stand are all good, although fans are set well back from the pitch as there is a substantial tarmac-looking track which surrounds it. The concourses are of a good size and there are a number of televisions on view to keep supporters entertained. Pies (including the Chicken Balti pie), pasties and vegetarian 'Pizza Pods' are supplied by Shire Foods and cost £2.30 each. Burgers and Hot Dogs are also available as well as alcohol.

I found the stadium to be more atmospheric than the Belle Vue ground which was largely open to the elements. This is a bit unusual as most clubs that move to new grounds usually complain that the atmosphere suffers in the new arena; however at the Keepmoat this is not the case. The stewarding was relaxed on my visit and no problems were experienced. The pitch also looked in top condition, although you could still see the lines of a previous rugby league game. The club have their own troupe of cheerleaders called the Vikettes, who provide entertainment before the game and half time.

Please note that cash is not accepted at the turnstiles, they are ticket only. Tickets can be purchased from the South Stand ticket office. The stadium is completely non-smoking.

Where To Drink?
The Stadium has its own Sports bar on the outside of the West Stand. Away fans are admitted (unless there is an objection to this by the local Police); however, the bar soon fills up prior to the match. Inside the stadium John Smith's bitter and Fosters lager are available at a cost of £2.70 a pint. David Rose adds; 'There is a bar in the bowling alley next to the Vue Cinema on the other side of the lake'.

Andy Liney informs me; 'It is possible to park at the Woodfield Farm, a large new pub at the back of B & Q and use their facilities. There is also a Beefeater Pub (imaginatively called "The Lakeside") which is directly adjacent to the southern entrance of Stadium Way, which you will see over the roundabout by the retail park, if approaching the stadium from the M18. The Salutation Inn on Bennetthorpe (the road that runs from the town centre to Belle Vue) operates a free matchday bus to the ground for patrons (and donates 10p from every drink purchased to the Rovers!)'.

How To Get There & Where To Park?
From the A1(M) join M18 Eastbound at Junction 35 (signposted Hull) or from the M1 and join the M18 Eastbound at Junction 32. Once on the M18, leave at Junction 3 and take the A6182 towards Doncaster (the stadium is well signposted from Junction 3 and is about one and a half miles away). You will pass a retail park on your left and then at the next island (which has the Lakeside Pub visible behind it) turn left onto White Rose Way. The Lakeside Shopping Centre is now on your right (the stadium is located directly behind it). At the next island turn right and after passing the Tesco distribution centre on your right, turn right at the bottom of the road and the stadium is further down on your left.

There are just 1,000 car parking spaces at the stadium, meaning that for the bigger games, parking will be at a premium. There are 60 spaces reserved for disabled fans, which must be booked prior to matchday. The stadium management are also giving preference for parking to those cars that are carrying more than one passenger, but apparently this won't be enforced. The cost of parking at the stadium is £5. A number of businesses on the nearby industrial park offer matchday parking at around £3-£4 per vehicle. If you happen to arrive a couple of hours before kick-off then there is also some free street parking in this area. There is no coach parking available at the stadium. Visiting supporters' coaches drop fans off at the stadium and park off site.

By Train
Doncaster station is around two miles away so you are probably best taking a taxi to the ground. If you do fancy the long walk (around 25-30 minutes) then the route from the railway station is as follows:

On coming out of the railway station, walk to the dual carriageway and turn to face to your right (i.e. away from the road tunnel under the Frenchgate shopping centre). You are now looking down a more or less straight line to the stadium. Provided you then use the appropriate places to cross roads as necessary you just follow the line of the dual carriageway to the roundabout adjacent to Vardy's Renault dealership. Then turn left into Middle Bank and follow the road round to the stadium.Thanks to John Molloy for providing the train information. Colin Barrett informs me; 'The bus service has been improved for matchdays. From around two hours before kick off there is a dedicated shuttle service from the Doncaster Interchange bus station, which is adjacent to the train station and under the Frenchgate Shopping Centre. This is Route 75X and runs every 10 minutes direct to the Stadium. It leaves Stand C6 and the journey takes less than 10 minutes depending on traffic. The bus stops in a lay-by at the Ground close to the Ticket Office and after the match leaves for Doncaster Interchange from the same place. Cost is £1.10 each way'.

Local Rivals
Rotherham, Barnsley, Scunthorpe United & Hull City.

Admission Prices
The Club operate a category system (A & B) for ticket prices, whereby the more popular matches cost more to watch. Category B prices are shown below in brackets.

Home Fans*:

West Stand and **East Stand (**Centre):
Adults £21, Concessions £15, Under 11's £15

West Stand and **East Stand** (Wings):
Adults £18, Concessions £12, Under 11's £5

North & South Stands:
Adults £18, Concessions £12, Under 11's £5

All corners of the stadium:
Adults £15, Concessions £8, Under 11's £5

Away Fans:

North Stand:
Adults £18, Concessions £12, Under 11's £5

Programme
Official Programme £2.50

Record Attendance
At the Keepmoat Stadium:
14,470 v Huddersfield Town,
League One, January 1st, 2007

At Belle Vue:
37,149 v Hull City
Third Division North, October 2nd, 1948

Average Attendance
2006-2007: 5,764 (League One)

Did You Know?
That the new stadium was originally to be called the Doncaster Community Stadium, until Keepmoat plc sponsored it for £1m.

Gillingham

KRBS Priestfield Stadium

Ground Name: KRBS Priestfield Stadium
Capacity: 11,582 (all seated)
Address: Redfern Avenue, Gillingham, Kent, ME7 4DD
Main Telephone No: 01634-300-000
Fax No: 01634-850-986
Ticket Office: 01634-300-000 (choose option 3)
Team Nickname: The Gills
Ground Opened: 1893
Pitch Size: 114 x 75 yards
Home Kit Colours: Blue & Black Hoops

Official Website:
www.gillinghamfootballclub.com

Unofficial Websites:
Gills World - www.gillsworld.co.uk
Gills Connect - http://gillingham.rivals.net/default.asp?sid=934 (Rivals Network)
West Country Supporters - www.geocities.com/wheres_the_tables
Up The Gills - www.geocities.com/upthegillsuk/
From The Terrace - www.fromtheterrace.co.uk/gillingham

What's The Ground Like?

Priestfield Stadium has been virtually rebuilt since the current Chairman Paul Scally took over in 1995. On one side of the ground is the impressive two-tiered Medway Stand, opened in 2000, with a row of executive boxes (the type which you can sit outside of) running across the middle. Opposite is the tidy all-seater Gordon Road Stand. Unfortunately though, it contains a number of supporting pillars, which may hinder your view. This also has an unusual TV gantry perched on its roof. The Rainham End has also been redeveloped, with a single-tier cantilevered stand which replaced a former terrace. An open, all-seated 'temporary stand' has been erected on what was the former Gillingham End terrace; it is hoped that this will be replaced with a permanent 3,200-seated stand at some point. This stand has been named the Brian Moore Stand in memory of the legendary commentator and lifelong Gills fan. In a corporate sponsorship deal with the Kent Reliance Building Society, the stadium has been renamed the KRBS Priestfield Stadium.

Future Developments

The Club have recently announced that they are embarking on a joint feasibility study with Medway Council, to look at possible suitable sites for a new stadium. If the Club were to move then Priestfield would be redeveloped for housing.

What Is It Like For Visiting Supporters?

Away fans are housed in part of the Brian Moore Stand where around 1,500 supporters can be accommodated. Like last season the stand is of the temporary variety, i.e. the type that you would see around the 18th hole at the British Open Golf Championship, although it is of a good size and height, plus the views of the playing action are fine. Unlike most temporary stands though the facilities are surprisingly good, being of a permanent nature behind the stand. However it is uncovered, so although the Club hand out free rain macs if it rains, still be prepared to get wet! One unusual aspect of visiting Priestfield Stadium is that away supporters have to walk down a very narrow terraced street to reach the away entrance, or if coming from adjacent streets down very tight alley ways. However, there are never normally any problems with this although after the game the Police sometimes close off some of the surrounding streets to keep fans apart.

Where To Drink?

The ground is walkable from the town centre, where there are a fair few pubs to be found. Paul Kelly, a visiting Preston fan, adds; 'we have used the Will Adams in the town centre. The pub is in the good beer guide and does good cheap food. Plus a very friendly crowd of football locals happy to indulge in friendly banter - the landlord is a Gill fan too!' Robert Donaldson recommends the Southern Belle opposite the railway station, which also has a cafe located next door. Robert Phipps, a Gillingham supporter, recommends The Ship public house on the

Lower Rainham Road. Away fans though should avoid 'The Cricketers' in Sturdee Avenue.

Michelle Dixon, the landlady of the Livingstone Arms on Gillingham Road, informs me; 'Our pub is known as an "Away Supporters" pub and is situated approximately 100 yards from the away turnstiles. The atmosphere within the pub is both warm and friendly and there is even complimentary bar food laid on for fans. Otherwise you can purchase a hot pie with your pint, or visit the local chip shop, situated across the road.' This pub which also has a beer garden, is popular with both away and home supporters and as you would expect it gets rather busy on matchdays.

How To Get There & Where To Park?

Leave the M2 at Junction 4 and take the A278 towards Gillingham, going straight across two roundabouts. At the 3rd roundabout turn left onto the A2 towards the town centre. At the traffic light junction with the A231, turn right into Nelson Road and passing the small bus station take a right turn into Gillingham Road; the ground is down on your right. Street Parking.

Alternatively Roger Blackman provides another route from the M2; 'At the start of the M2 keep left and follow A289 towards Gillingham. Continue towards Gillingham and go through the Medway Tunnel (Priestfield Stadium is signposted from here). Continue on the A289 ignoring the turn off for Gillingham town centre, until you reach the Strand roundabout after about a mile. Turn right at this roundabout and up the hill and over the level crossing. Take the second left past the level crossing into Linden Road and the ground is on the right'.

There is a residents-only parking scheme in operation around the ground, so if you want to street park, this will mean driving a bit further away to do so. Chris Bell, a visiting Northampton Town fan adds; 'There is a cheap pay and display car park (£1 for 3 hours) on Railway Street near Gillingham station, which is less than 10 mins walk from the ground'.

By Train

The ground is about a ten-minute walk away from Gillingham railway station, which is served by trains from London Victoria (every 15mins) and Charing Cross (Every 30mins). Robert Donaldson provides the following directions; 'Turn left out of the station and follow the road until you come to a crossroads. Go straight on into Priestfield Road. The visitors turnstiles are at the far end of Priestfield Road. Allow ten minutes to get from the station and into the ground'.

To get to the home areas, turn right at the crossroads and then first left into Gordon Road for the Gillingham End Terrace home area, the Gordon Road Stand and the Rainham End. For the Medway Stand or an alternative route to the Rainham End, turn left at the crossroads and then first right. At the far end the road turns right and then left.

Local Rivals

With a lack of other league clubs in the area, Gillingham fans have focused on Millwall.

Admission Prices

Home Fans*:

KM Medway Stand:
Adults £22,
OAP's £17,
Under 21's £15,
Under 16's £11,
Under 7's £7 (please note there are no concessions available in Blocks D, E & F)

Gordon Road Stand:
Adults £22,
OAP's £17,
Under 21's £15,
Under 16's £11,
Under 7's £7

Rainham End:
Adults £22,
OAP's £17,
Under 21's £15,
Under 16's £11,
Under 7's £7

Brian Moore Stand:
Adults £19,
OAP's £14,
Under 21's £13,
Under 16's £11,
Under 7's £7

Away Fans*:

Brian Moore Stand:
Adults £24 (£17) (£15),
OAP's & Students £20 (£15) (£13),
Juveniles £18 (£13) (£12),
Minors £12 (£11) (£10)

* Please note that discounts of up to £4 per ticket are available if the ticket is purchased prior to matchday.

Programme & Fanzine

Official Programme: £2.50
Brian Moore's Head Fanzine: £1.50

Record Attendance

23,002 v Queens Park Rangers,
FA Cup 3rd Round, January 10th, 1948.

Average Attendance

2006-2007: 6,182 (League One)

Did You Know?

The Club were originally formed as New Brompton in 1893. They changed their name to Gillingham in 1913.

Hartlepool United

Victoria Park

Ground Name: Victoria Park
Capacity: 7,629
Address: Clarence Road, Hartlepool, TS24 8BZ
Main Telephone No: 01429-272-584
Fax No: 01429-863-007
Pitch Size: 113 x 77 yards
Team Nickname: The Pool
Year Ground Opened: 1908
Home Kit Colours: Blue & White Stripes

Official Website:
www.hartlepoolunited.co.uk

Unofficial Website:
Never Say Die - www.neversaydie.org.uk
(Rivals Network)

What's The Ground Like?

The ground was greatly improved in the mid-1990s, with the construction of two new stands at one end and one side of the ground. The Cyril Knowles Stand is the newer of the two side stands. It is a small single-tier covered all seated stand, raised above the ground level. The other side, the Camerons Brewery Stand, has covered seating to the rear and open terrace to the front. This stand does not run the full length of the pitch and has an odd mix of orange and green seating, that clashes with the club colours. Both ends are small covered affairs. The newer end is the small Expamet Town End, a covered terrace, for home fans. The other end, the Rink End stand, is a small, covered all-seated stand which houses away supporters.

Derek Hall adds; 'All real Hartlepool fans nickname the club Pools (not The Pool). This goes back to the pre-1967 days when the boroughs of (old) Hartlepool and West Hartlepool became amalgamated as just Hartlepool. It was because of the existence of the two very separate towns that the club was actually called Hartlepools United in the first place. That said though, I'd prefer to see us called The Monkey Hangers!'

What Is It Like For Visiting Supporters?

Ben Fuggles advised me to 'bring a jumper even in August!'. He was right. The wind whipping the North Sea goes right through you, so wrap up well unless there is a heat wave. Away fans are in the Rink End Stand at one end of the ground, where up to 967 can be seated. Unfortunately there are a few supporting pillars in this stand, which may hinder your view, especially if there is a large away following. However acoustics are good even for small numbers. Look out for the biggest meat & potato pies you have ever seen being served within the ground; they are huge! Generally I found the Hartlepool supporters okay, but unfortunately my day was spoiled by some crowd trouble at the game. I prefer thinking about the opposition's culpability rather than the Pools fans, but as the saying goes 'It takes two to tango'.

If you wonder why Hartlepool are referred to as the 'Monkey Hangers' then it is because the residents of Hartlepool are famously said to have hanged a monkey that was washed up from a ship that had sunk during the Napoleonic wars, because they thought the monkey was a French spy. The Club take this to good heart and of course who else would they have as their club mascot? H'Angus the monkey of course!

Where To Drink?

The Victoria Suite near the entrance to the away end is for members only. At the same end but at the opposite corner is the 'Corner Flag Supporters Bar' that welcomes away fans. The entrance fee is 50p, but the bar has a good pre match atmosphere and SKY TV. Popular with away fans is the Jackson's Wharf Pub near the ground. It has good food and real ale on tap. This pub is over the road from the ASDA store, to the left of the old sailing ship. Otherwise the ground is not far from the town centre where there are plenty of pubs to be found.

Ronnie Chambers adds; 'I would recommend The Causeway, 15 minutes walk away from the ground. It is located just around the corner from the brewery near the church, real ale and very friendly. The Engineers Club five minutes from the ground opposite the police station, just off the town centre is okay, as is the Raglan Club just behind the visitors end. Usual club rules apply regarding entry for these'.

How To Get There & Where To Park?
From the A19 take the A689 signposted Hartlepool. Follow the A689 towards the Town Centre. Follow Town Centre signs for 2.8 miles, over two roundabouts. Go straight over the next two sets of lights, passing Hartlepool College on your right. The next left takes you to the stadium. If you miss the turning (as I did), go past ASDA on your left, left at the next roundabout and then left at the next traffic lights for the ground. There is a fair sized car park at the ground. Otherwise there is plenty of street parking to be found behind the away end.

By Train
Hartlepool train station is a ten-minute walk from the ground. Leave the station and go straight up a short approach road. At the end of the approach, turn right and head up Church Street towards the large church. At the end of this road is a bridge and junction with the A689. Go straight across the junction and the ground is in front of you on the left hand side of the road. Thanks to Richard Brackstone for providing the directions.

Local Rivals
Darlington

Admission Prices

Home Fans:

Cyril Knowles Stand (Seats)
Adults £20,
Over 65's/Under 16's £10

Camerons Brewery Stand (Seats)
Adults £20,
Over 65's/Under 16's £10

Camerons Brewery Stand (Terrace)
Adults £18,
Over 65's/Under 16's £9

Expamet Town End (Terrace)
Adults £18,
Over 65's/Under 16's £9

Family Enclosure:
Adults £20,
Over 65's/Under 16's £8

Away Fans:

Rink End (Seats)
Adults £20,
Over 65's/Under 16's £10

Students can also qualify for a concessionary price in the home areas, providing that the ticket is purchased from the ticket office and a valid student identity card is produced on purchase.

Programme & Fanzine
Official Programme £2.50.
Monkey Business Fanzine £1.

Record Attendance
17,426 v Manchester United,
FA Cup 3rd Round, January 5th, 1957.

Average Attendance
2006-2007: 4,489 (League Two)

Did You Know?
The Victoria ground was a former rubbish tip made into a sports ground in 1886 and named after the Queen, who celebrated her Golden Jubilee in the following year.

Huddersfield Town

Galpharm Stadium

Ground Name:	Galpharm Stadium
Capacity:	24,500 (all seated)
Address:	Galpharm Stadium, Huddersfield, HD1 6PX
Main Telephone No:	0870-444-4677
Fax No:	01484-484-101
Ticket Office:	0870-444-4552
Team Nickname:	The Terriers
Year Ground Opened:	1994
Home Kit Colours:	Blue & White

Official Website:
www.htafc.com

Unofficial Websites:
HuddersfieldNet - www.thehuddersfield.net
Huddersfield Town Down Under - http://home.primus.com.au/jthorpe/huddersfield_town.htm
Terrier Bytes - www.terrier-bytes.com
Down At The Mac - www.downatthemac.com (Rivals Network)

What's The Ground Like?

This stadium was opened with three sides in 1995, the last stand being added a season later. The club previously played just down the road at the Leeds Road ground, now the site of a B & Q Superstore. Most new stadiums in this country are rather boring affairs with little character, but the Galpharm (I don't think I'll ever get used to that new name!) does not fall into this category. Each stand is semi circular rather than rectangular, and is further enhanced with large white steel tubing above the contours. In fact from the car park I first thought it looked like a new ride at Alton Towers! It is good to see something different from the architects for a change. The ground has won many design awards and is well worth a visit. The only disappointment is that the corners of the ground are open. The Panasonic North Stand at one end and the Riverside Stand at one side are both two-tiered stands, each with a row of executive boxes running across the middle. The other two sides of the ground are large single-tiered affairs. There is an electric scoreboard at the back of the away end.

What Is It Like For Visiting Supporters?

Away fans are located at one end of the ground in the Pink Link (South) Stand, where up to 4,000 supporters can be accommodated. The facilities in this stand and the view of the playing action are both good. There is also a Ladbrokes outlet and a bar serving alcoholic drinks at the back of the stand, which if you can't bear to watch your team during the game, you can always escape to, as the bar remains open during the first half and half time. They even serve draught Guinness, which makes for a pleasant change.

I had an enjoyable evening at the Galpharm Stadium. I was thoroughly impressed with the stadium and the general set-up.

Where To Drink?

The ground is walkable from the town centre, albeit a long one! (20 minutes). Robert Smith recommends the Peacock, Rickys Bar and the Bradley Mills Working Mens Club. They are all located on Leeds Road, about five to ten minutes walk from the Stadium. There is also a cinema and entertainment complex behind the North Stand, where there is the Rope Walk pub. However on my last visit all of the above bars were not allowing in away fans, although I did manage to get into the Rope Walk Pub (I was not wearing colours), where I enjoyed an excellent pint. Dougie Hames recommends the Gas Club on Gasworks Street; 'all fans and families are welcome. Bass beers, food available and you can also park in the patrolled club car park at a cost of £2. The club is easy to find as it is right by the large gas holder'. Otherwise alcohol is served in the away end.

Otherwise it is probably best to drink within the ground itself, as there are open bars at the back of the away end.

How To Get There & Where To Park?

The stadium is just off the A62 Leeds Road. It can be easiest reached from Junction 25 of the M62, simply follow the signs for Huddersfield (A62) and you will come to the stadium on your left. Alternatively, if approaching from the South, then leave the M1 at Junction 38 and take the A637 towards and then the A642 into Huddersfield. As you approach the town centre try to keep to the right hand lane as you will turn right at the island and go onto the A62 Leeds Road. The stadium is a short distance down this road on the right. For the car parks turn right at the traffic lights, where the Market Pub is on the corner. The stadium is generally well signposted around Huddersfield town centre.

There is a fair sized car park located at the ground (£5) and a number of unofficial car parks nearby (expect to pay around £3-£4).

By Train

The ground is walkable from Huddersfield train station, albeit a long one (15-20mins). After coming out of the railway station, turn down past the front of The George Hotel. Go straight over the crossroads into Northumberland Street and walk down across the Ring Road straight on into Leeds Road. Turn right down Gasworks Street. Straight over crossroads to the ground.

Local Rivals

Bradford City, Leeds United.

Admission Prices

Home Fans:

Riverside Stand (Upper Tier):
Adults £22
OAP's £13
Juniors £10

Riverside Stand (Lower Tier):
Adults £20.50
OAP's £11
Juniors £8

Antich Stand:
Adults £19
OAP's £10
Juniors £7

Panasonic Stand:
Adults £19
OAP's £10
Juniors £7

Away Fans*:

Pink Link Stand:
Adults £19,
OAP's £10,
Juniors £7

* The prices quoted are those charged on matchday. Tickets bought prior to matchday qualify for a discount of up to £2.50 per ticket.

Students can also qualify for a concessionary price in the home areas, providing that the ticket is purchased from the ticket office and a valid student identity card is produced on purchase.

Programme

Official Programme £3

Record Attendance

At Leeds Road;
67,037 v Arsenal,
FA Cup 6th Round, February 27th, 1932.

At the Alfred McAlpine:
23,678 v Liverpool,
FA Cup 3rd Round, December 12th, 1999.

Average Attendance

2006-2007: 10,401 (League One)

Did You Know?

That Town's old Leeds Road ground had in the 1950s the first electric scoreboard to be sited at a football ground in Britain.

Leeds United

Elland Road

Ground Name: Elland Road
Capacity: 40,204 (all seated)
Address: Elland Road, Leeds, LS11 0ES
Main Telephone No: 0113-367-6000
Main Fax No: 0113-367-6050
Ticket Office: 0845-121-1992
Pitch Size: 117 x 76 yards
Club Nickname: United
Year Ground Opened: 1919
Home Kit Colours: White With Blue & Yellow Trim

Official Website:
www.leedsunited.com

Unofficial Websites:
To Ell And Back - www.toellandback.com (Rivals Network)
Leeds Fan Club Message Board - www.leedsunitedfanclub.com
Leeds United Mad - www.leedsutd-mad.co.uk (Footy Mad Network)

■ What's The Ground Like?

The ground is dominated by the East Stand on one side of the stadium. This huge stand, which holds 17,000 supporters, was opened in the 1992-93 season, and is at least twice the size of the other three stands at Elland Road. The East Stand is a two-tier stand which has a large lower tier of seating with a smaller tier above. In between the two tiers is a row of executive boxes. The stand is completed by a large imposing roof. The good thing about the rest of the stadium is that it is totally enclosed, with the corners of the ground being filled with seating. The downside is that compared to the East Stand the other stands are looking rather tired and old in comparison. All the remaining stands have a number of supporting pillars and at the back of the West Stand (which was renamed in March 2004 the 'John Charles Stand' in honour of their former great player), there are a number of old wooden seats, which look as if they have been there since the stand was first opened in 1957. This stand also houses the team dugouts and television gantry. There is an electric scoreboard in one corner of the ground between the South & John Charles Stands.

■ What Is It Like For Visiting Supporters?

Apart from the visit of Manchester United and the odd cup tie or local derby, Leeds is a fairly enjoyable place to watch your football. However, if you are attending one of the former games, then exercise caution around the ground and the adjacent car parks. Away fans are located in the South East corner of the South Stand at one end of the ground, where up to 1,800 fans can be accommodated. This allocation can be doubled by giving away fans the whole of this stand. Facilities within are basic, the leg room sparse, plus I saw a number of fans being ejected (without warning) for swearing. So be on your best behaviour.

■ Where To Drink?

The nearest pub is the Old Peacock, situated behind the South Stand. It is a home supporters pub which really should be avoided. A far better bet is the Dry Salters pub which is about a ten-minute walk away from the ground. On my last visit it had a good mix of home and away supporters, good priced real ale and large screen SKY TV. To find this pub; with the Old Peacock pub behind you turn left and follow the road down to the very end. Pass the entrances to a number of car parks and go under a railway bridge. At the end of the road, turn left along the dual carriageway and the pub is a short way down 'tucked in' on the left. Otherwise alcohol is served within the ground.

Just a few doors down is the United Fisheries chippy, which does brisk business on matchdays. There is also a McDonalds outlet across the road from the East Stand. Inside the ground the delicious 'Football's Famous Chicken Balti Pie' is available (£2.20).

How To Get There & Where To Park?

Elland Road is well signposted around the Leeds area and is situated right by the M621.

From The North:
Follow the A58 or A61 into Leeds city centre, then follow signs for the M621. Join the M621 and after one and a half miles leave the motorway at the junction with the A643. Follow the A643 into Elland Road for the ground. Go down Elland Road past the ground on your right and the Old Peacock pub on your left, you will come to a couple of entrances to a couple of very large car parks (£3).

From The South:
Follow the Motorway M1 and then onto the M621. You will pass the ground on your left and then you need to take the next exit from the motorway and turn left onto the A6110 ring road. Take the next left onto Elland Road for the ground. Just as you go under a railway bridge there are entrances on either side to a couple of very large car parks (£3).

Surprisingly the traffic coming out of the car parks seemed to disperse quite well after the end of the game. Richard Drake informs me; 'a good tip for Elland Road is to park in Car Park A. They normally put away fans coaches here. From here we were back on the M621 within 10 minutes of coming out of the ground'.

By Train

Leeds train station is around a 35-minute walk from the station. Probably best to either take a taxi or one of the shuttle buses that run from just outside the station to the ground. Tom Whatling adds; 'The shuttle buses cost £2.50 return. As you come out of the station main entrance, cross the road and take the stairs down to the street below. Turn right and cross the road and you will see the double-decker buses lined up. The first bus in the queue also sells the tickets for all the other buses. The buses drop off and pick up at the corner of the North and East stands. It's best to get a return ticket as then you don't have to queue up after the match to get a ticket back to the station, you just walk straight onto the bus'.

Nicholas Small, a visiting Wolverhampton Wanderers supporter, provides the following directions if you decide to walk; 'It is best to leave the station from the rear exit, from where you can walk down the short hill out of the car park and follow the road around to the left. At the traffic lights go ahead (the road bears slightly left) and follow Whitehall Road for just shy of half-a-mile, passing under a railway bridge and then forking left down Springwell Street, to cut off a corner. At the end of Springwell Street, you come to a roundabout exit road with a zebra crossing in front of you. Cross at the zebra crossing, taking the next exit road clockwise around the roundabout. This is the A58 Domestic Road. This road becomes Domestic Street after about 400 yards (Domestic Road turning right and heading up to an overpass) and continues slightly uphill for about another 400 yards, passing under another railway bridge. There is a zebra crossing up here, which you should use to walk up the right-hand pavement. Upon reaching the top of the hill, you come to a garage, and some small shops, where you should turn right onto Shafton Lane. At the end of Shafton Lane, turn left onto Ingram Road and follow this until you see a pedestrian bridge ahead, as the road bears left, becoming Tilbury Road. By now, you should have seen the football ground over to your right. Cross the M621 via the footbridge, turning right at the bottom, and head down Elland Road towards the stadium'.

Local Rivals

Bradford City, Huddersfield Town, Sheffield United, Sheffield Wednesday and from a little further afield Manchester United & Chelsea.

Admission Prices

The Club operate a category system, so that ticket prices vary with the opposition being played. The categories are A, B and C. Category C prices are shown in brackets:

Home Fans

East and John Charles (West) **Stands:**
Adults £30 (£22), No Concessions

Revie (North) **& South Stands:**
Adults: £25 (£15), Over 60's: £15 (£11),
Under 16's: £12 (£8)

Family Area*:
Adults: £23 (£17), Over 60's: £18 (£13),
Under 16's: £10 (£10)

* Members of the Club can qualify for further discounts on the family area ticket prices quoted above.

Away Fans

South Stand:
Adults: £25 (£15), Over 60's: £15 (£11),
Under 16's: £12 (£8)

Programme & Fanzines

Official Programme: £3
The Square Ball Fanzine: £1
To Ell And Back: £1

Record Attendance

57,892 v Sunderland,
FA Cup 5th Round Replay, March 15th, 1967.

Modern All Seated Attendance Record:
40,287 v Newcastle United,
Premier League, December 22nd, 2000.

Average Attendance

2006-2007: 19,570 (Championship)

Did You Know?

That the South Stand was known commonly as the Scratching Shed until improvements in 1974 saw an impressive new £500,000 stand built, complete with 16 executive boxes.

Leyton Orient

Matchroom Stadium

Ground Name: Matchroom Stadium
Formerly known as Leyton Stadium, but still referred to by many fans as Brisbane Road.
Capacity: 9,271 (all seated)
Address: Brisbane Road, Leyton, London, E10 5NF
Main Telephone No: 0870-310-1881
Fax No: 0870-310-1882
Ticket Office: 0870-310-1883
Team Nickname: The O's
Year Ground Opened: 1937
Pitch Size: 115 x 80 yards
Home Kit Colours: Red & Black

Official Website:
www.leytonorient.com

Unofficial Websites:
LOFC Online - www.lofconline.com (Rivals Network)
O-Net - www.brisbaneroad.com

■ What's The Ground Like?

The ground has seen a lot of redevelopment in recent years, with the construction of three new stands. Finance for this has chiefly come from the proceeds of selling part of the Brisbane Road site to a property developer. In this groundbreaking development, the corners of the ground have been filled with blocks of residential apartments, which certainly gives the stadium a unique look. Some other clubs are looking at the scheme with interest and I wouldn't be surprised to see something similar take place at another league ground at some point in the future.

At one end is the single tiered, South Stand (capacity 1,336 seats), that was opened in 1999. This stand replaced a former open terrace. An interesting feature of this covered area is that it is raised above pitch level, meaning that you have to climb a small set of steps at the front to reach the seating area. The old Main (East) Stand, which was originally opened in 1956, has been reduced in length, but is still a fair size. This partly covered stand is now all seated after having seating installed on the former front terrace. Unfortunately, it has several supporting pillars and the roof doesn't quite cover all of the front seating. It does though have an interesting gable on its roof which has 'Leyton Orient' proudly emblazoned across it and gives a nice link to the Club's history.

Opposite is the new West Stand which was opened for the 2005/06 season. This all-seated stand, which has a capacity of 2,872, has an unusual look about it, as above the seating area is a tall vertical structure that houses the Club offices. In fact to be honest it looks more like an office block that has some seats installed on a large viewing gallery, rather than a football stand. It also has some corporate hospitality areas, which look a little precarious, as the outside seating area of these overhang the lower tier. If you carry on with the office theme, then you can almost imagine these being used by the window cleaners to clean the office windows. At the very top of the stand is a fair sized viewing gallery for television cameras and press and the roof of the stand contains a lot of perspex panels to allow more light to reach the pitch.

At the North End is the ground is the most recent addition to the stadium. The North Stand was opened at the beginning of the 2007/08 season and replaced a former open terrace. This simple-lookinq covered all-seated stand, has space for 1,351 spectators and looks similar to the South Stand. The ground also has a set of four modern-looking floodlight pylons.

Future Ground Developments

The Club have expressed an interest to move to the proposed Olympic Stadium, which will be built for London to host the Olympics in 2012. The stadium, which will be built in Stratford in East London, will have its capacity reduced from 80,000 to 25,000 after the games have finished. Whether this possible move for Orient will materialise remains to be seen.

What Is It Like For Visiting Supporters?

Currently away supporters are housed in one side (towards the South End) of the Main Stand, where there are a couple of supporting pillars that may impede your view. Around 1,000 fans can be accommodated in this area.

I have been to Orient a number of times and have always been impressed by the state of the pitch. Even in January it is immaculate and at the start of the season you could almost play snooker on it! The delicious 'Football's Famous Chicken Balti Pie' (£2) is available inside the ground.

Where To Drink?

The nearest pub to the ground is the Coach & Horses. To get there take a right out of Leyton station and walk down for about half-a-mile. It is on your left, within sight of the floodlights. The Three Blackbirds has been recommended to me and that is a bit further up Leyton High Road, on the right. Stephen Harris adds; 'the best pub near to the ground is the Birkbeck Tavern in Langthorne Road, behind the tube station'.

How To Get There & Where To Park?

Thanks to O-Net for the following directions: Approaching London you will at some point hit the M25. Use this to get to the M11 (unless you're coming from Cambridge, in which case you'll already be on it) take the southbound carriageway for about 6 miles and take the right fork signposted for the North Circular.

At the bottom of the flyover where the roads merge, move into the left-hand lane and turn left at the roundabout on to the A104. After about 1 mile at the next roundabout take the right exit - still the A104 (a landmark here is the quaintly-decorated Lamb's Cafe). Half a mile further on, turn left into Leyton Green Road (signposted to Leyton and Stratford), and left again into a short slip-road past the bus garage entrance and left into Leyton High Road - you'll see the Leyton Leisure Lagoon opposite as you wait to make the turn. Continue until you see the floodlights and then find a side turning to park in the back-streets. Street Parking.

By Tube

The nearest tube station is Leyton (about a quarter of a mile away) which is on the Central Line. Come out of the station and turn right down Leyton High Road. Cross over the road to the other side and continue down it. You will come to Coronation Gardens on your left and the floodlights of the ground can be clearly seen behind them. Take the next left past the gardens into Buckingham Road for the ground.

Local Rivals

West Ham United and from further afield, Brighton, Boston & Southend.

Admission Prices

West Stand:
Adults £22
Concessions: £14

South Stand:
Adults £20
Concessions: £13

North Family Stand:
Adults £20
Concessions: £13
Under 16's £5
Under 11's (when accompanied by an adult) Free

East Stand:
Adults £18
Concessions: £12

Concessions apply to Over 65's, Under 16's, students and unemployed (proof of status must be produced).

Programme

Official Programme: £3

Record Attendance

34,345 v West Ham United,
FA Cup 4th Round, January 25th, 1964.

Modern All Seated Attendance Record:
7,206 v Nottingham Forest,
League Two, April 28th, 2007.

Average Attendance

2006-2007: 5,049 (League One)

Did You Know?

That for 48 years the Club were known as Clapton Orient. They changed their name to Leyton Orient in 1946.

Luton Town

Kenilworth Road

Ground Name: Kenilworth Road
Capacity: 9,975 (all seated)
Address: 1 Maple Road, Luton, LU4 8AW
Main Telephone No: 01582-411-622
Ticket Office: 01582-416-976
Fax No: 01582-405-070
Pitch Size: 110 x 72 yards
Team Nickname: The Hatters
Home Kit Colours: White & Black

Official Website:
www.lutontown.co.uk

Unofficial Websites:
Hatter Net - www.hatternet.com (Rivals Network)
Supporters Trust - www.trustinluton.com
Luton Town Mad - www.lutontown-mad.co.uk (Footy Mad Network)

■ What's The Ground Like?

The club have been talking about moving to a new stadium for sometime now and hence investment in Kenilworth Road in recent years has been neglected. One side of the ground and one end are small and covered. A Luton fan once told me that the council would not let the club build any higher than the surrounding houses. The small end, The Oak Road Stand, is given to away supporters and this has a simple electric scoreboard on its roof. The other end is a large covered all seated stand, which was originally a terrace. The small side of the ground (called the Bobbers Stand as entrance once cost a Bob!) is predominantly filled with a row of executive boxes and is so small that you can clearly see the houses behind it. Netting has been suspended between the floodlight pylons on its roof to reduce the number of footballs being kicked out of the ground. The other side, the Main Stand, is an older two-tiered covered stand. This stand is mostly wooden (therefore no smoking allowed) and is really beginning to show its age. The Main Stand only runs around two-thirds of the length of the pitch, with another newer structure 'bolted' onto one end. This area is known as the 'New Stand' and is used as a family area. An odd feature is the dugouts being located opposite the players tunnel, resulting in quite a procession across the pitch. Also you will notice that rather than having floodlight pylons at each corner of the ground, as most older grounds have, they are instead featured along each side of the ground. This is a legacy of when floodlights were first installed at Kenilworth Road in the 1950s; there was no room in the corners of the ground to incorporate floodlight pylons and hence they had to go down the sides.

■ Future Ground Developments

The Club are looking to relocate to a new 20,000-seat stadium, possibly to be built somewhere near to Junction 12 of the M1. However, the scheme is facing opposition from local residents as well as some supporters who feel that the Club should stay within Luton itself.

■ What Is It Like For Visiting Supporters?

The entrance to the Oak Road Stand must be one of the most unusual in the country. After going down a rather small alleyway, the impression is of queuing to go into someone's house! Just over 2,000 supporters can be accommodated in this stand and even a small number of fans can really make some noise. The Luton fans who like to sing tend to congregate in the Main Stand immediately to the right of the away end, which can make for a good atmosphere. On the downside, there always seems to be a large Police presence, which seems unnecessary for the majority of games. Also there are a number of supporting pillars in this stand, which may hinder your view, plus the leg room is tight. The refreshments are not bad though, with a good selection of pies and burgers available, although I should add that the Pukka-Pies were a whopping £3 a go!

■ Where To Drink?

Josephine Kingston recommends the Bedfordshire Yeoman on Dallow Road near to the ground. Josephine adds 'all away supporters are welcomed, except those from Watford!'. To get to this pub, continue down Oak Road towards the official car park and then bear left following the road that goes behind the Main Stand. Continue to follow the road away from this stand and over a little bridge. On the left hand side you will see a chip shop (which always seems to do good business on matchdays) and over on the right you will see an alleyway. Go down this alleyway to the end and as you come out of it the pub is on your right. It is medium sized, popular with home and away supporters. Please note that alcohol is not served to away supporters within the ground.

■ How To Get There & Where To Park?

Leave the M1 at Junction 11 and take the A505 towards Luton. Go through one set of traffic lights and at the 1st roundabout, turn right into Chaul End Lane. At the next roundabout turn left into Hatters Way; whilst continuing down Hatters Way the ground will be seen on your left, although it is not accessible from this road. At the end of Hatters Way turn left and start looking for street parking from here on (the ground will now be on your left).

Please note that there is a residents-only parking scheme in operation near to the ground, so you will have to park somewhat further away. Simon House, a visiting Bristol City fan informs me; 'I managed to park at the Conservative Club which cost £2'. Dave and Karen Warner visiting Norwich fans add; 'There is also parking to be found in the Sainsbury's complex on the right after you have turned left from Hatters Way. Go under the bridge and turn first right after the casino and follow the road around. The ground is across the main road, about 5-10 minutes walk from there. It costs £5, but was easy to get out of and there was plenty of space'.

■ By Train

Luton train station is a good 15 minutes walk away from the ground. From the station, turn left along the railway bridge, down the steps, and turn right along Bute Street which runs through the Arndale Shopping Centre. At the top of the centre, bear right along Dunstable Road. Kenilworth Road and the ground is on the left.
Thanks to Tom Hunt for providing the directions.

■ Local Rivals

Watford.

■ Admission Prices

Home Fans*

Main Stand** (Upper Tier):
Adults £28, OAP's £23, Young Persons £17, Under 16's & Students £14

Main Stand** (Lower Tier):
Adults £23.50, OAP's £21.50, Young Persons £16, Under 16's & Students £13

Kenilworth Road End:
Adults £23.50, OAP's £21.50, Young Persons £16, Under 16's & Students £13

Family Areas:
Adults: £19.50, Under 16's £10 (minimum purchase of 1 adult & 1 child)

Away Fans

Oak Road Stand:
Adults £23.50, OAP's £21.50, Under 16's & Students £13.

* Ticket prices quoted are those for purchased on matchday. Discounts of around £2 are available if the ticket is purchased prior to matchday.

** There are a number of restricted view tickets also available for this stand which are offered at a discount on the prices quoted.

Young persons are aged 16-21; students must be in full time education.

■ Programme & Fanzine

Official Programme: £3 (away fans purchase them from inside the ground, from sellers on the pitch perimeter).
Mad As A Hatter Fanzine: £1

■ Record Attendance

30,069 v Blackpool,
FA Cup 6th Round Replay, March 4th, 1959.

Modern All Seated Attendance Record*:
10,248 v Wolverhampton Wanderers
Championship League, September 10th, 2005.

* This record has subsequently been equalled.

■ Average Attendance

2006-2007: 8,564 (Championship)

■ Did You Know?

The central section of the Main Stand was originally purchased from Kempton racecourse and was erected at Kenilworth Road in 1922.

Millwall

The Den

Ground Name: The Den
Capacity: 20,146 (all seated)
Address: Zampa Road,
London SE16 3LN
Main Telephone No: 020-7232-1222
Ticket Office: 020-7231-9999
Fax No: 020-7231-3663
Pitch Size: 105 x 68 yards
Team Nickname: The Lions
Year Ground Opened: 1993
Home Kit Colours: Blue & White

Official Website:
www.millwallfc.co.uk

Unofficial Websites:
House Of Fun - www.hof.org.uk
Millwall Online - www.millwallonline.co.uk
(Rivals Network)
Independent Supporters Association -
www.independentmillwall.com
Antwerp Lions - www.antwerplions.be

What's The Ground Like?

The ground is a dramatic improvement from the dank and foreboding 'Old' Den and is quite smart looking. The new Den is made up of four fair sized two-tiered stands that are of the same height. The corners of the ground are open, apart from one corner where there is a large video screen. Steve Armstrong informs me; 'the stadium is used to film the Sky One Channel TV show; Dream Team, which features an imaginary team called Harchester United.'

What Is It Like For Visiting Supporters?

Away fans are located at one end of the ground in the North Stand (usually in the upper tier only). Around 4,000 away fans can be accommodated in this end. Like the general improvement in football, a trip to Millwall is not as threatening as it once was. However, it is hardly a relaxing day out and I found the Den to be quite intimidating. The large police presence at the match I attended did nothing to dampen this feeling. I would advise that you exercise caution around the ground and not wear club colours. The most popular method of travel for away fans to the Den is by official club coach.
The Police are well drilled in dealing with the coaches and once inside the ground you will generally find the stewards helpful & friendly.

Where To Drink?

I wouldn't recommend drinking around the ground, so best instead to grab a beer around London Bridge before moving onto the ground. There are bars at the back of the stands that serve alcohol as well as some decent food such as chicken and chips.

How To Get There & Where To Park?

There are number of ways of getting to the ground, but the most straightforward, if not the shortest in distance is to follow the A2 into London from Junction 2 of the M25. The A2 actually passes the ground. Once you go past New Cross Gate tube station on your right the ground is about a mile further on. The only awkward bit is about half way in-between New Cross Gate and the ground where the road splits into two. Keep to the right following the signs A2 City/Westminster. You will come to the ground on your right. Street parking can be found on the small estate on your left just past the ground. There are no sizeable car parks around the ground (typical British planning!).

Millwall

By Tube/Train

There are two tube stations that are about 15-20 minutes walk away from the ground. Surrey Quays & New Cross Gate, both on the East London Line.

However, it is probably best to go by rail as South Bermondsey railway station is only a few minutes walk from the ground and there is now a direct walkway specifically built for away fans which takes you directly to the away end and back to the station afterwards. This has made the Police's job of keeping rival supporters apart so much more manageable. If your team brings a sizeable following, an 'away fan' football special may be laid on from London Bridge. In these instances the police are well drilled in getting away fans into the ground from the special train and safely away afterwards.

Local Rivals

West Ham United, Crystal Palace & Charlton Athletic.

Admission Prices

Like a lot of Clubs Millwall operate a category policy (1, 2, 3) whereby the most popular games cost more to watch.

Home Fans*:

West & East Stands (Upper Tier):
Adults £27
Over 65's £17
Under 16's £14
Under 12's £12

West Stand (Lower Tier):
Adults £25
Over 65's £15
Under 16's £11
Under 12's £8

Cold Blow Lane (South) **Stand:**
Adults £20
Over 65's £13
Under 16's £11
Under 12's £8

East Stand (Lower Family Enclosure):
Adults £20
Over 65's £13
Under 16's £10
Under 12's £7

Away Fans:

North Stand:
Adults £20
Over 65's £13
Under 16's £11
Under 12's £8

* Millwall Club members can obtain further discounts on these home ticket prices if tickets are bought in advance.

Programme & Fanzines

Official Matchday Programme £3
No One Likes Us (NOLU) Fanzine £1
The Lion Roars (TLR) Fanzine £1.50

Record Attendance

At the 'Old' Den; 48,672 v Derby County, FA Cup 5th Round, February 20th, 1937.

At the 'New' Den, 20,093 v Arsenal FA Cup 3rd Round, January 10th, 1994.

Average Attendance

2006-2007: 8,632 (League One)

Did You Know?

That Millwall called their ground 'The Den' as it is the home of 'The Lions', the nickname of the Club.

Northampton Town

Sixfields Stadium

Ground Name: Sixfields Stadium
Capacity: 7,653 (all seated)
Address: Sixfields Stadium, Northampton, NN5 5QA
Main Telephone No: 0870-822-1997
Fax No: 01604-751-613
Ticket Office No: 0870-822-1966
Ticket Office Fax No: 01604-589-138
Pitch Size: 116 x 72 yards
Team Nickname: The Cobblers
Year Ground Opened: 1994
Home Kit Colours: Claret & White

Official Website:
www.ntfc.co.uk

Unofficial Websites:
The Cobblers - http://web.ukonline.co.uk/ntfc/
Vital Northampton - www.northampton.vitalfootball.co.uk (Vital Football Network)
Sixfields Boys Message Board - www.ntfc.org.uk/phpBB2/

What's The Ground Like?

The Club moved from their old County Ground to the new stadium in October 1994. This neat, all-seater stadium is located on the outskirts of Northampton. Sixfields has three small covered single-tier stands, and another larger single-tier covered West Stand (capacity 4,000), at one side of the pitch. Away supporters are housed at the South Stand end. The club has received awards for the facilities provided for disabled supporters. A large hill overlooks the ground, where small numbers congregate to watch the game free, even though they can only see half the pitch!

Future Ground Developments

Kevin Dunn informs me; 'Following the Club's successful bid to buy a 150-year lease on Sixfields Stadium, they have announced that the stadium is to be further developed so that the overall capacity will rise to 15,000. This will mean new North, East & South Stands as well as executive boxes being added to the West Stand. Part of the development will also the feature the building of a hotel behind the South Stand of the stadium. The home end at Northampton's old County Ground was called the Hotel End, so it is quite apt that the new stadium will also feature its own Hotel End. It is believed that it will take five years for the plans to be fulfilled.'

What Is It Like For Visiting Supporters?

Away fans are located in the South Stand at one end of the pitch, where 850 supporters can be accommodated. If demand requires it, an additional 300 seats can be made available in the Alwyn Hargrave Stand. One slight pain about Sixfields is that you can't pay at the turnstiles. You have to buy your ticket first from a Portakabin and then you have to queue again. Some away fans have got caught out by this when arriving late. However, I have received a number of reports complementing the standard of stewarding, other club officials and the Northampton fans themselves.

Having lived in Northampton for a year and watched Northampton Town win the old fourth division, I have a soft spot for them. The fans themselves are quite passionate and this makes for a great atmosphere especially at cup games. Robert Dunkley informs me; 'outside the West Stand there is a used programme stall stocking a wide range of programmes from different clubs and seasons'.

Where To Drink?

The ground is built on a leisure complex on the outskirts of Northampton. This consists of a couple of fast food establishments, a cinema and the ground itself. There are two pubs on this site, the Magic Tower (formerly called Chevys), which is for home supporters only and The Sixfields Tavern (no away colours). I managed to get into the Magic Tower when I went to see Northampton play Gillingham. The bouncers on the door asked me which club I supported. When I replied "Birmingham City", they were totally confused as they had obviously not been programmed for this response. Nevertheless they still let me in.

Steven Jones informs me; 'a couple of other bars have opened recently opened on the Sixfields complex, both of which are better than the Sixfields Tavern and the Magic Tower in terms of service, space, atmosphere etc. Old Orleans is one (a restaurant & bar) and the Sports Bar is the other (bowling alleys, 9-ball tables, big screens for post-match scores round-ups etc, equally popular with home and away fans)'. Whilst Carl Brown adds; "I found myself drinking in a 'T.G.I. Friday's' outlet opposite the Main Stand. Maybe not your stereotypical pre-match watering hole but very convenient for a drink, plus there was a wonderful array of fine waitresses on display, serving the goods!"

If you are coming into Northampton from the M1, via the A45, you will pass the Turnpike Pub, which is okay for away fans. Otherwise if you have a bit of time on your hands then you can continue to walk along the A45 towards the town centre, where you will soon reach the Northampton Saints Rugby ground. Opposite is a pub called The Rover which is family friendly and has been recommended to me.

■ How To Get There & Where To Park?

From The South:
Leave the M1 at Junction 15A and take the A43 towards Northampton and you will come to the ground on your right.

From The North:
Leave the M1 at Junction 16 and take the A45 towards Northampton and you will come to the ground on your right.

The Sixfields stadium is well signposted around the area. There is a fair sized car park located at the ground, which costs £2. Make sure though that you arrive early as it has been known for it to get full for the more popular games. There is also a council-owned car park situated behind the away stand which costs £3.50. Also parking in the nearby cinema and restaurant car parks is not allowed, and parking there may result in your car being clamped!

■ By Train

Northampton train station is over two miles from the ground, so it is probably best to hire a taxi. However if you feel like braving the 25-30-minute walk then Phil Spokes provides the following directions; 'Turn right from the station and follow the road past the express lift tower (you can't miss it, a tall tower that was once used for testing lifts), passing the Wickes store on the left. Continue down to the Leisure Centre, turn left down the path beside it and then turn right onto the road. You will see the stadium in the distance in front of you.

Dave Stuttard, a visiting Bury fan adds; 'From the railway station it is possible to get a bus to take you most of the way to Sixfields stadium. The buses go from the bridge over the railway at the south end of the station. The number 40 and the more frequent 1/1A will get you near to the stadium (around half a mile away)'.

■ Local Rivals

Rushden & Diamonds & Peterborough United.

■ Admission Prices

The Club operate a category system, so that ticket prices vary with the opposition being played. The categories are Gold and Normal. Normal game prices are shown in brackets.

Home Fans*:

West Stand
Adults £22 (£19), Concessions £18 (£15),
Under 16's £15 (£12), Under 7's Free

Dave Bowen Stand
Adults £22 (£19), Concessions £18 (£15),
Under 16's £15 (£12), Under 7's Free

Alwyn Hargrave Stand
Adults £21 (£18), Concessions £16 (£13),
Under 16's £13 (£10), Under 7's Free

Away Fans:

Paul Cox Panel & Paint South Stand -
Adults £22 (£19), Concessions £18 (£15),
Under 16's £15 (£12), Under 7's Free

* Further discounts can be offered if multiple tickets are being purchased. Plus a number of family tickets packages are also available.

Concessions apply to over 60's and students (with current NUS card, or letter from school).

■ Programme & Fanzine

Official Programme £2.50.
Hotelenders £1

■ Record Attendance

At Sixfields Stadium;
7,557 v Manchester City,
Division Two, September 26th, 1998.

At the County Ground;
24,523 v Fulham,
Division One, April 23rd, 1966.

■ Average Attendance

2006-2007: 5,766 (League One)

■ Did You Know?

In 1978-79 Northampton Town's central defender Stuart Robertson was voted Player of the Year by the club's supporters. A week later he was given a free transfer.

Nottingham Forest

City Ground

Ground Name: City Ground
Capacity: 30,602 (all seated)
Address: City Ground, Nottingham, NG2 5FJ
Main Telephone No: 0115-982-4444
Fax No: 0115-982-4455
Ticket Office: 0871-226-1980
Team Nickname: The Reds
Year Ground Opened: 1898
Pitch Size: 115 x 78 yards
Home Kit Colours: Red & White

Official Website:
www.nottinghamforest.co.uk

Unofficial Websites:
Blooming Forest - http://nottinghamforest.rivals.net (Rivals Network)
Forest@Bugcafe - www.btinternet.com/~bugcafe/
Alternative Forest - www.alternativeforest.co.uk
The City Ground In 3D - www.3dcityground.com
Talk Forest - www.talkfNorest.com

What's The Ground Like?

The ground from a distance looks quite picturesque, sitting on the banks of the River Trent. Both ends have been redeveloped during the 1990s, much improving the overall appearance. At one end, the Bridgford Stand houses away fans in the lower tier; it is odd because one third of this stand was built lower then the rest, due to a local Council planning requirement to allow sunlight through to the houses in nearby Colwick Road. Opposite, the Trent End, is the most recent addition. It is a large two-tiered stand that looks quite smart. One unusual feature of the stand, is that running across the middle are a number of rows of seating enclosed within a covered shaded glass area. On one side there is a similarly impressive two-tiered stand, with executive boxes in between, which was built in 1980. Once called the Executive Stand, it was recently renamed the Brian Clough Stand in honour of their greatest manager. Facing this is a smaller and much older Main Stand that now looks quite tired in the company of its shiny new neighbours.

Future Ground Developments

The Club have announced ambitious plans to move to a new stadium on the outskirts of Nottingham. The stadium, which would be built in the Clifton area, would cost around £40m-£50m to construct and would house around 50,000 supporters. If the scheme comes to fruition then the stadium could be open by 2014.

What Is It Like For Visiting Supporters?

Up to 4,750 away fans can be accommodated in the lower tier of the Bridgford Stand, where the facilities and view of the action are good. I personally did not have any problems at the City Ground, but I have heard of away fans getting some hassle; for example it has not been unknown for the odd object to be thrown down on away fans from so-called Forest fans seated above. Don't be surprised also if the stewards keep asking you to sit down if you stand in the seated areas, which can get annoying. There is also an element of Forest supporters in the 'A' Block of the Main Stand nearest to the away supporters,who feel it is their duty to continually berate away fans during the game, which can be unsavoury.
It is also advised to keep colours covered around the ground, especially if you support another Midlands team. The good news, though, is that away fans can really make some noise from this stand, so make the most of it!

Where To Drink?

Michael Whitaker recommends the Larwood & Voce which is about five minutes walk from the away end, on a street called Fox Road (off Radcliffe Road). As Michael says, 'The place is an all round good pre match pub. Every time I've been there it's well occupied by away and Forest fans'. Michael adds that the Southbank, very near to the ground and the King John in the city centre, should be avoided by away supporters. Paul Stevens adds; 'The Trent Bridge Inn (TBI) beside the cricket ground is another pub the away fans are advised to steer clear of. They have doormen at the entrance checking matchday tickets to make sure you are a home supporter'. Simon Phillips recommends the Stratford Haven, just down the road from the Larwood & Voce, 'it has great beer and food, it bustles and is used by both home and away fans'. Tim Cooke, a travelling Millwall fan, has a different angle (so to speak); 'definitely one for the lads! Hooters (on the main road A6011, on the outskirts of the city centre, you can't miss it!) has very nice waitresses wearing just enough to cover things up, serves lovely beer, and great food. Take my advice, make a weekend of it, Nottingham is a top city!' Otherwise, alcohol is available inside the ground, including Fosters, John Smiths & Guinness.

If you are arriving by train and have a bit of time on your hands, then I would suggest that you check out the 'Olde Trip To Jerusalem'. This historic pub dates back to the 12th century and some of the rooms are 'cave like', having been carved out of the rock that Nottingham Castle is situated upon. Add real ale, food and a small beer garden, then it is certainly worth a visit. It is about a five-minute walk away from the train station. As you come out of the station turn right. At the top of the road turn left and then take the second right into Castle Road. Just tucked away on the left is the pub.

■ How To Get There & Where To Park?

From The North:
Leave the M1 at Junction 26 and take the A610 towards Nottingham and then signs for Melton Mowbray. Cross the River Trent and you will see the ground on your left. Alternatively as you approach Nottingham on the A610 you will pick up signs for 'football traffic'. Although following these seems to take you all round the outskirts of Nottingham you do eventually end up at the City Ground, along the A6011.

From The South:
Leave the M1 at Junction 24 and take the A453 towards Nottingham. Then take the A52 East towards Grantham and then onto the A6011 into Nottingham. The ground is situated by the A6011.

Rowland Lee informs me; 'There is an alternative route to the ground from the South; Leave the M1 at Junction 21a (Leicester East) and follow the A46 dual carriageway towards Newark. After around 20 miles take the A606 towards Nottingham. At the first roundabout that is the junction with the A52, take the 4th exit onto the A52, signposted towards Grantham. At the next roundabout turn left onto the A6011 towards Nottingham.
The ground is about a mile down this road.

There is a large car park at the ground, otherwise there is some street parking to be had. Steve Barratt informs me; 'regarding the parking at Forest, the council operate a car park on match days on the Victoria Embankment. They charge £3 but it is only a two-minute walk to the ground. The car park is right on the banks of the River Trent, on the ground side of the river, but on the other side of the dual carriageway from the ground'. Gerry Toms adds 'bear in mind that as the one end of the ground backs onto the River Trent, you cannot drive around it, so it is probably best to park at the first available opportunity, or you may find yourself crossing the River Trent and having to come back on yourself again'.

■ By Train
The ground is walkable from Nottingham railway station (20mins). As you come out of the main station entrance, turn left and then left again. Follow the road down to the dual carriageway and then turn right. The ground is about three-quarters of a mile down the dual carriageway on the left, just over Trent Bridge.

■ Local Rivals
Derby County, Leicester City.

■ Admission Prices
The Club operate a category system (AA & A) whereby the most popular matches (category AA) cost more to see.

All Areas Of The Ground (Except Family Area):
Adults*: £26,
Senior Citizens*: £20
Students & Under 18's: £10
Under 12's: £5

Family Area:
Adults*: £19,
Senior Citizens*: £15
Under 18's: £8 (£8)
Under 12's: £4 (£4)

* A £2 discount is available on this ticket price, if it is purchased prior to matchday.

■ Programme & Fanzine
Official Programme £2.50.
Blooming Forest Fanzine £1
LTLF Fanzine £1

■ Record Attendance
49,946 v Manchester United
Division One, October 28th, 1967.

Modern All Seated Attendance Record:
30,025 v Manchester United
Premier League, February 6th, 1999.

■ Average Attendance
2006-2007: 18,962 (League One)

■ Did You Know?
That innovative Forest were the first team ever to use shinguards in 1874.

Oldham Athletic

Boundary Park

Ground Name: Boundary Park
Capacity: 13,624 (all seated)
Address: Boundary Park, Oldham, OL1 2PA
Main Telephone No: 0871-226-2235
Fax No: 0871-226-1715
Pitch Size: 106 x 72 yards
Team Nickname: The Latics
Year Ground Opened: 1906
Home Kit Colours: Blue With White Trim

Official Website:
www.oldhamathletic.co.uk

Unofficial Websites:
Oldham Athletic E-Zine - www.oafc.co.uk (Message Board)
Latics Supporters Club Canada - http://latics.cjb.net/

■ What's The Ground Like?

At one end is the comparatively new Rochdale Road End, a good-sized all-seater covered stand with an excellent view of the pitch. It has windshields to either side of it and an electric scoreboard on its roof. Part of this stand is given to away supporters. The other end, the Chadderton Road Stand (also known as the 'Chaddy End'), is a medium sized all seater covered stand. Again there are windshields to either side, but the elderly nature of this stand is apparent from the supporting pillars running across the front of it. On one side there is an old two-tiered Main Stand. This used to have terracing in front, since filled with seating. There is still some old unused terracing on one side of this stand. On the other side is the small Broadway Stand. This is a covered seated stand that doesn't quite run the full length of the pitch. Again there are a number of pillars in the upper tier, where there is also a television gantry suspended beneath its roof. The stand is unusual in giving the impression of being on a slope - the lower tier has more seats on one side than the other. Part of this stand has a Police Control Box, whilst on the other side there is a strange single storey executive box-like structure, built on stilts. The ground also benefits from four large floodlight pylons, leaving the visitor in no doubt that this is a football ground. The Club has a mascot called 'Chaddy The Champion Owl'.

■ Future Ground Developments

The Club have announced plans to redevelop Boundary Park into a new 16,000 all seater stadium, the project of which is being referred to as the 'Oldham Arena'. This will include the building of three new stands (the present Rochdale Road End will remain) including a new 5,200 capacity Main Stand. As part of the redevelopment a 130-room hotel and separate living accommodation will also be built. However, no formal time scales have been announced as to when this might take place.

■ What Is It Like For Visiting Supporters?

Away fans are housed in the Rochdale Road Stand at one end of the ground, where the normal allocation is 1,800 seats. This can be increased to over 4,000 if required. Dependent on numbers the Rochdale Road End is either given totally to the away support or is shared with home fans. If the latter applies, away fans are kept separate from the home fans by a large moat-like gap, which certainly makes for a lot of banter. The facilities in this newish stand are fairly good, as are the acoustics. If you get the chance, make sure to try a Pukka pie (£1.50). Some fans reckon that this is the best part of a visit to Boundary Park.

This club I found to be particularly friendly. They have an unofficial motto that 'the only club we hate is Man United', everyone else is very welcome. The only complaint that I had about visiting the ground was that it always seems to be cold, with a biting wind that goes right through you. This is due to Oldham being on the edge of the Pennines.

Where To Drink?

There is a pub 'The Clayton Arms' on one corner of the ground. This small comfortable pub serves Lees beers, reasonably priced food and has a large screen to show SKY Television. It gets extremely busy on matchdays.

Chippy Lees, an exiled Latics fans in Cornwall, recommends the following; 'The Old Grey Mare on Rochdale Road is worth a visit. If you walk to the top of Sheepfoot Lane and turn left at the newspaper shop, the pub is about 100 yards down the road on the right. There's a varied selection of beers available, and again a warm welcome is assured. Further down on the right is The White Hart. If you turn right at the top of Sheepfoot Lane, you'll eventually come to The Queens. It's on the corner of a junction. It was frequented by several West Ham fans one night, who found the beer to be so good, and cheap compared to London prices, that they decided to stay there for the rest of the evening. It was just as well, as it was the usual bone chilling night, and they lost! Across the road from there is The Royal, which is a cosy little local, and next door is a larger more modern one, the Brook Tavern'.

Bill Harris adds; 'I went for a drink in the Rifle Range pub on Burnley Road, which is about a ten minute walk away from the ground. I found it to be a very friendly accommodating pub, with a family room, TV screens, good food and local ale. There is also a beer garden outside, which you can take advantage of, when the weather is good. There is also parking at the back of the pub and is easy to get away after the game onto the A627 which connects to the M62'.

How To Get There & Where To Park?

Leave the M62 at Junction 20 and take the A627(M) towards Oldham. Take the second slip road off the A627(M) following the signs for Royton (A663). At the top of the slip road you will find a large roundabout with a McDonalds and a KFC. Turn left onto the A663 towards Royton (beware though of 30mph speed cameras on this stretch). You will be able to see Boundary Park over on your right. Take the next right hand turn into Hilbre Avenue which will take you up to the large Club car park, situated behind the Lookers Stand. The cost of the car park is; cars £2, minibuses £5, coaches £10.

If you want to go straight to the Club main entrance, then at the roundabout take the second exit onto A627 Chadderton Way (signposted Oldham). After around 300 yards take the first left into Boundary Park Road and at the end of the road turn right into Sheepfoot Lane.

By Train

There are three stations that you could use to get to Boundary Park. Oldham Mumps, Oldham Werneth or Mill Hills. However Oldham Mumps and Mill Hills are both around a 45-minute walk away from the ground and are not really practical. Therefore it is best to use Oldham Werneth, which is served by North West Trains on the Oldham-Rochdale loop. Trains for Oldham depart from Manchester Victoria platforms 1 or 6. If you buy a ticket to Oldham and arrive from the South at Manchester Piccadilly your fare includes travel on the Metrolink to Victoria station. As you exit the platforms at Piccadilly turn left for the Metrolink station. Take the tram for BURY only to get to Manchester Victoria.

Oldham Werneth station is around a 15-minute walk away from the ground. Exit the station and turn right onto Featherstall Road South and walk for about 3/4 mile through one set of traffic lights and a small roundabout at Tesco until you come to a large roundabout. Turn left onto Chadderton Way (cross over at the underpass as Chadderton Way is a dual carriageway) and follow for another quarter of a mile until you come to Boundary Park Road (by the B&Q Warehouse) turn right and Boundary Park is ahead. You will be approaching the ground from the home supporters end, so at the end of Boundary Park Road turn right up Sheepfoot Lane past the main stand to the other end of the ground. It is extremely unusual for any taxis to be at Werneth station.

Chippy Lees adds; 'As you walk along Featherstall Road away from Werneth station, you will encounter quite a few Indian restaurants and pubs, which are worth a

visit. Turn right from the station and walk until you come to Tesco's at the top of the road. Turn left at the dual carriageway, and Boundary Park is on the right. Again, there are several pubs on the way, the best being The Spinners across from the dual-carriageway'.

Jon Brierley adds; 'Alternatively, rather than getting a train from Manchester to Oldham, you may find it easier to take a bus from Manchester Piccadilly bus station. Services operate every 15 minutes or so on Saturday afternoon. Numbers 24, 181 & 182 make the 25-minute trip to Oldham and go past the ground. Doing this would allow you to nip into the Rifle Range pub on Burnley Lane, where the beer is both good and cheap'.

Local Rivals

Manchester United, Manchester City & Stockport.

Admission Prices

Home Fans*:

Main Stand (Upper)
Adults £20,
OAP's/Under 16's £11,

Main Stand (Lower)
Adults £19,
OAP's/Under 16's £11,

Broadway Stand (Upper)
Adults £20,
OAP's/Under 16's £11,

Broadway Stand (Lower)
Adults £16,
OAP's/Under 16's £10,

Chadderton Road Stand
Adults £20,
OAP's/Under 16's £11
Under 12's £3,

Rochdale Road End
Adults £22,
OAP's/Under 16's £12,
Under 12's £3.

Away Fans:

Rochdale Road End
Adults £22,
OAP's/Under 16's £12,
Under 12's £3.

* A discount of £2 is available on these ticket prices, if the ticket is purchased prior to matchday (except Under 12's in the Chadderton/Rochdale Road Ends).

Programme & Fanzines

Official Programme £2.50

Record Attendance

47,671 v Sheffield Wednesday
FA Cup 5th Round, January 25th, 1930.

Modern All Seated Attendance Record:
13,171 v Manchester City
FA Cup 3rd Round, January 8th, 2005.

Average Attendance

2006-2007: 5,143 (League One)

Did You Know?

The club when formed in 1895 were called Pine Villa. They changed their name to Oldham Athletic in 1899.

Port Vale

Vale Park

Ground Name:	Vale Park
Capacity:	23,000 (all seated)
Address:	Hamil Rd, Burslem, Stoke On Trent, ST6 1AW
Main Telephone No:	01782-655-800
Main Fax No:	01782-834-981
Ticket Office:	01782-655-832
Team Nickname:	The Valiants
Year Ground Opened:	1950
Pitch Size:	114 x 77 yards
Home Kit Colours:	White & Black

Official Website:
www.port-vale.co.uk

Unofficial Websites:
One Vale Fan – www.onevalefan.co.uk
North London Valiants - www.northlondonvaliants.co.uk

■ What's The Ground Like?

At one end of the ground is a fair-sized single-tiered all seated stand, complete with an electric scoreboard on the roof. This stand, the Phones4U Stand, houses the away supporters and it replaced a former open terrace. Opposite is the Big AM Stand, covered and all seated. The corners on either side of this stand have been filled. The Tricell Stand (also known as the Railway Stand) on one side is fair sized, covered and all seated. All three of these stands have a small number of supporting pillars, halfway up them, which may restrict your view. The other side, the Lorne Street Stand, is a relatively new smart-looking 5,000 all seated stand, complete with 48 executive boxes, which so far has been half built. To keep some sense of history the original clock from the old stand has been incorporated into the new construction. Unfortunately it is unclear when this stand will be completed as building work has been suspended due to lack of finance. A pity, as the empty 'predominantly concrete' area really brings the ground down. Still, if this stand does get completed, it will look superb. On the opposite corner is a Police Control Box keeping a watchful eye over the crowd. The pitch is one of the widest in the League and the crowd are further set back from the playing action by the surrounding cinder track.

■ Future Ground Developments

During the 2007/08 season, the Club hope to eventually complete the currently half-built Lorne Street Stand. This would vastly improve the overall look of the ground.

■ What Is It Like For Visiting Supporters?

Up to 4,500 away supporters can be accommodated in the Phones4U Stand, where the view and facilities located on the concourse behind the stand are good. Even a relatively small number of away fans can really make some noise from this stand, as the acoustics are excellent. However, the slope is quite shallow, which might affect your view should a tall person be seated in front. Normally though, you could still move to another seat if necessary.

I've been to Port Vale on a number of occasions and always found it be a good day out. However the experience has sometimes been a little intimidating, not due to the Port Vale supporters but more because of the huge Police presence in and around the ground. One Police Officer said to me as we left the ground five minutes early, as my team were losing 4-0. "Leaving already? there's still five minutes to go!". Now who said that Police Officers don't have a sense of humour? Still, on the plus side the pasties on offer within the ground are among the best I've eaten at any football ground, so much so that I found myself going back for a second. The P.A within the ground is quite deafening at times and there is no escape, even in the toilets, as it is piped through!

If you wonder at half time why the Port Vale fans seem transfixed with staring at the away end, it is not intimidation, but the electric scoreboard perched on the roof of this stand! (which the away fans can't see). Also at half time the Vale fans in the Railway Stand tend to transfer from one side to another so that they can be nearer the goalmouth that Port Vale are attacking. Vince Smith, a visiting Northampton Town fan adds; 'I must say it was an enjoyable day out at Vale Park, with very friendly stewards, turnstile operators and very good food served by friendly staff. All in all a very pleasant experience and far more enjoyable than a visit to their near neighbours.'

■ Where To Drink?

Bernie Mountford informs me; 'The Vine near to the ground, on Hamil Road, is certainly a good bet for away supporters. A good pint is on offer coupled with an enjoyable pre-game atmosphere'. This pub is certainly the main away fan pub, but is not for claustrophobes, as this small pub packs the fans in like sardines. Still, it was friendly enough, with a range of real ales on offer.

The town centre is only a short walk away where there are a number of pubs to be found. I visited the New Inn (just along from Kentucky Fried Chicken), which was friendly, served real ale and reasonably priced food. Another pub worth visiting is the Bull's Head in St John's Square. This pub is the local outlet for the nearby Titanic Brewery which is located in Burslem. It is friendly for away fans and has good number of real ales on offer. To find this pub: From the outside of the away end, turn right and go down to the bottom of Hamil Road (passing the Vine Pub on your left). Turn right at the T-junction and then go straight across the traffic lights at the crossroads. Proceed past KFC, Wades and the New Inn on the right and then if you look over to your left you will see Woolworths at the bottom of the square. The Bull's Head is on the right of this square.

Also recommended to me is the Red Lion on Moorland Road (coming from the ground, at the bottom of Hamil Road turn right into Moorland Road B5051 and the pub is down on the right). This is a good sized pub that serves real ale and bar snacks.

■ How To Get There & Where To Park?

The ground is located in the town of Burslem, one of the six towns comprising Stoke On Trent. Leave the M6 at junction 15 or 16 and take the A500 towards Stoke on Trent. Follow A500 until the A527 Tunstall/Burslem exit, where you take the A527 towards Tunstall/Burslem. At the next island just past the Price Kensington factory turn right for Burslem town centre. Continue on this road up the hill, crossing another island and into Burslem town centre. Continue straight on over the traffic lights at the crossroads and then take the first road on the left which takes you down to the ground. Outside a superstore next to the ground there is a large car park located which costs £4; otherwise street parking.

■ By Train

Longport station is the closest to the ground, but is a good 30-minute walk away and is not well served. Most fans end up at Stoke On Trent railway station, which is over four miles away and take a taxi (about £6) up to the ground. Ian Bannister adds; 'You can catch bus service number 29 to Burslem. As you go out of the entrance to Stoke station the bus stop is a short way down on the left. The destination of the bus is Bradeley (the 29 going the opposite way from across the road goes to Keele) and you can get off in Burslem town centre for the ground. The bus costs adults £1 single or £1.90 return'.

Local Rivals

Stoke City.

■ Admission Prices

Home Fans*:

All Areas Of The Ground (except Family Stand & Directors Area):
Adults £18,
OAP's £12,
Under 16's £8

Family Stand:
Adults £18,
OAP's £10,
Under 16's £6

Family Tickets:
1 Adult + 2 Under 16's £30,
2 Adults + 2 Under 16's £44

Away Fans:

Hamil Road Stand
Adults £19.50,
OAP's £13,
Under 16's £6

Family Tickets:
1 Adult + 2 Under 16's £33, ,
2 Adults + 2 Under 16's £48

* Concession priced tickets are available to those who first become members of the club.

■ Programme

Official Programme £2.50 - Sold from booths within the ground.

■ Record Attendance

49,768 v Aston Villa,
FA Cup 5th Round, February 20th, 1960.

Modern All Seated Attendance Record:
15,582 v Chesterfield
Division Two, April 17th, 2004

■ Average Attendance

2006-2007: 5,221 (League One)

■ Did You Know?

Dave Seddon, a visiting Brentford supporter, informs me; 'the roof of the Caudwell Stand was originally that of the Main Stand at Chester City's old Sealand Road ground'. Stephen Wood adds; 'The roof of the away end was indeed bought by Bill Bell back in 1991-92 for £300,000 as Chester were moving grounds. It was installed during the 1992-93 season and the first team we played when the roof was fully constructed was, you guessed it, Chester!'

Southend United

Roots Hall

Ground Name: Roots Hall
Capacity: 12,392 (all seated)
Address: Victoria Ave, Southend-On-Sea, SS2 6NQ
Main Telephone No: 01702-30-40-50
Fax No: 01702-304-124
Ticket Office: 08444-77-00-77
Team Nickname: The Shrimpers
Year Ground Opened: 1906
Pitch Size: 110 x 74 yards
Home Kit Colours: Blue With White Trim

Official Website:
www.southendunited.co.uk

Unofficial Websites:
The Little Gazette (Footy Mad Network) - www.thelittlegazette.com
The Shrimpers Online - www.theshrimpers-online.co.uk
Shrimper Zone - www.shrimperzone.com
Southend United News (Vital Football Network) - www.southend.vitalfootball.co.uk

What's The Ground Like?

At one end of the ground is the relatively new South Stand. This stand replaced a former open terrace and greatly improved the overall look. It is a small 'double decker' type of stand, the upper tier hanging over the lower. It is all seated and covered, but unfortunately has a few supporting pillars. On its roof is a small clock, dedicated to former player, Director & Chairman, Frank Walton. There are a couple of blocks of flats that overlook the ground from behind this stand. Away fans are now housed in what was originally the home end, the North Stand, which is a covered seated stand at the other end of the ground. This stand, like the West Stand at one side of the pitch, are both single-tiered and have old-looking 'barrel' shaped roofs, with the West Stand having a unique double-barrel roof. The West Stand extends around to the North Stand so that one corner is filled with seating. It has a number of supporting pillars right at the front, which may hinder your view of the action. It also has the most precarious-looking TV gantry that stands on stilts and is accessed by a long ladder. On the other side the East Stand is another single-tiered, covered stand that has a row of executive boxes running across the back of it. At the front are some strange-looking dugouts, which has the management team standing at the front leaning on a wall, with the players sitting behind. The club have an unusual-looking club mascot called 'Elvis J Eel', the 'J' standing for jellied!

Future Ground Developments

The Club have received planning permission for a new 22,000-seat stadium at Fossetts Farm, just behind the club's training ground in Eastern Avenue. The Club hoped to have the stadium open in time for the 2008/09 season, however the scheme has suffered a couple of setbacks. Firstly the stadium is now subject to a public enquiry and secondly the Club have yet to receive planning permission for the residential redevelopment of Roots Hall, the proceeds of which are needed to finance the new ground. Although these hurdles are not insurmountable, it will mean that the £25m scheme may be delayed for some time yet.

What Is It Like For Visiting Supporters?

Away fans are housed in the North Stand, which is now all seated after being a former terrace. Like most former terraces that have had seats bolted onto them, the leg room and height distance between each row is less than desirable. The large number of supporting pillars will probably also impede your view; although this does not make for a great experience at least the Stand is covered. Up to 2,000 away fans can be accommodated in the North Stand, although the initial allocation is 1,200. One good thing for away fans in the North Stand is that comparatively few numbers of fans can really make some noise from it. On my last visit there was quite a good atmosphere and I experienced no problems around the ground.

Refreshments within the away area are served from a 'Transport Cafe' type establishment, complete with tables and chairs. The usual range is available such as Pukka Pies (£2.20), cheeseburgers (£2.80) and hot dogs (£2.80). Bear in mind that getting your drinks in one piece back to your seat can be quite a challenge. The front of the stand is below pitch level, with stairs leading up to each pitch access point where the stewards stand. Going up and down these flights of stairs, with a cup of coffee in each hand, can present a problem.

Even though Roots Hall is an older ground it has some rather modern electronic turnstiles. Each match ticket has a bar code printed onto it and fans insert their ticket into a bar code reader at the turnstile to gain entrance to the stadium. I did notice once inside the stadium, that the stewards were alerted when a concession or junior ticket was being used, so that they could check that it was for the appropriate person.

■ Where To Drink?

The main away fans pub is the Golden Lion, which is situated on the A127, just up from from the car park entrance to the Main Stand. On my last visit this pub was very busy, but the staff served people relatively quickly. This pub which serves drinks before the game in plastic glasses, also had a large screen television, showing Sky. The nearby Spread Eagle pub is for home fans only. There is also a good fish and chip shop located across the road by the traffic lights, called the 'Fish House', which I found to be excellent. Judging by the amount of fans standing outside eating fish and chips (there is some seating inside as well), then I'm not the only one that thinks it is good.

Henry Willard, a visiting Yeovil fan adds; ''The Blue Boar' pub which is at the crossroads (where the traffic lights are) is a very good place for away fans to congregate before the game, it was friendly and relaxed.'

A little further away are two more pubs, 'The Bell' which you pass on your way into Southend on the A127 and 'The Nelson' in North Road. The Bell is a large 'Toby Carvery', whilst The Nelson is a basic pub with a beer garden and is probably only worth a visit if you arrive early and want to kill time. It is five minutes walk from the Spread Eagle. Just go past the Spread Eagle on your right, turn right at the lights and then turn left into North Road, opposite the petrol station. The pub is on the right.

The 'Shrimpers Bar' at the ground itself is now for members only. Please note that alcohol is not served to away fans within the stadium.

■ How To Get There & Where To Park?

From M25 take Junction 29 and follow the A127 to Southend. Continue towards the town centre, through the lights near to the Bell Pub. At the next roundabout turn right (3rd turning), continuing on the A127. The ground is on the right just past the next traffic lights. If you turn right as you reach the ground, this will put you behind the away end where there is plenty of street parking to be found. Otherwise there is a car park at the ground, behind the Main Stand which costs £5.

Bear in mind that in the fair weather months Aug/Sep/April/May, if the weather is at all sunny the whole of East London seems to head down the A127 on a Saturday afternoon, so allow an extra 30 mins if the temperature is above 65F.

■ By Train

The closest station to the ground is Prittlewell, served by trains from London Liverpool Street. As you exit the station turn right towards to a crossroads with traffic lights. Pass the Fish House fish and chip shop and turn right. Walk 100 yards and the ground is tucked away on your left.

Southend Central station (served by trains from London Fenchurch Street), is about a 25-minute walk from the ground. The main bus station is close to Southend Central, and therefore it may be an idea to get a bus to the ground.

■ Local Rivals

Colchester United, Leyton Orient & West Ham.

■ Admission Prices

Home Fans*:

Southend Echo East Stand:
Adults £20, Concessions £12, Juniors £10

Hi-Tec South Stand:
Adults £20, Concessions £12, Juniors £10

Toomey Vauxhall West Stand:
Adults £20, Concessions £12, Juniors £10

Royal Bank Of Scotland Family Enclosure:
1 Adult + 1 Child £20,
Additional Adults £16, Additional Child £4

Away Fans*:

North Stand:
Adults £20, Concessions £12, Juniors £10

* Please note that these prices are for tickets purchased prior to matchday. Tickets purchased on the matchday itself can cost up to £2 more per ticket.

■ Programme

Official Programme £2.50.
All At Sea Fanzine £1.

■ Record Attendance

31,090 v Liverpool,
FA Cup 3rd Round, January 10th, 1979.

Modern All Seated Attendance Record:
11,735 v Yeovil Town, League Two, April 30th, 2005.

■ Average Attendance

2006-2007: 9,822 (Championship)

■ Did You Know?

That although Southend United played their first game at Roots Hall in 1906, they moved to the Kursaal Ground in 1919 and then subsequently played at Southend Greyhound Stadium. They returned to the Roots Hall site, to construct the present ground in 1953.

Swansea City

Liberty Stadium

Ground Name:	Liberty Stadium
Capacity:	20,500 (all seated)
Address:	Morfa, Swansea, SA1 2FA
Main Telephone No:	01792-616-600
Fax No:	01792-616-606
Ticket Office:	08700-400-004
Team Nickname:	The Swans or Jacks
Year Ground Opened:	2005
Pitch Size:	105 x 68 metres
Home Kit Colours:	White & Black

Official Website:
www.swanseacity.net

Unofficial Websites:
Jack Army - www.jackarmy.net (Rivals Network)
This Is Swansea - http://www.aardvarkcymru.co.uk/swansrd.htm
Vital Swansea - www.swansea.vitalfootball.co.uk/ (Vital Football Network)
A Touch Far Vetched - www.atfv.co.uk
Vital Swansea - www.swansea.vitalfootball.co.uk/ (Vital Football Network)
SCFC.co.uk - www.scfc.co.uk

■ What's The Ground Like?

After spending 93 years at their former Vetch Field home, Swansea have moved into the 21st Century, with a new stadium near to the former site of the Morfa Athletics Stadium on the West side of the River Tawe. The stadium was christened White Rock by the Swansea residents, but is now called the Liberty Stadium under a five-year corporate sponsorship deal.

Built by Interserve for a cost of around £27m, the stadium saw its first game in July 2005. Although fairly conservative in its design, the stadium is still impressive. It is completely enclosed with all four corners filled with seating. Each of the four stands is two-tiered and three are of the same height. The West Stand at one side of the pitch is slightly taller, having a row of 28 corporate hospitality boxes, situated above the upper tier. The Club's offices are also located behind this stand. An unusual feature is the great use of transparent roofing towards the South End of the stadium. This allows more natural light into this area, making for an interesting effect. Both ends have an electric scoreboard situated on the front of their roofs, although for some reason the scoreboard at the North End is larger than the one at the South End. The stadium is shared with Neath-Swansea Ospreys Rugby Union Club.

■ What Is It Like For Visiting Supporters?

Away fans are housed in the North Stand at one end of the stadium, where (if demand requires it) up to 3,500 fans can be accommodated. The views of the playing action from this area are excellent as there is a good height between rows and the legroom is probably the most generous of any stadium that I have visited.
The concourses are spacious, complete with television sets, for pre-match and half-time entertainment. As you would expect from a new stadium,the facilities are good. Away fans are separated from home fans by black netting spread over a block of seats to either side of the away section, with a line of stewards also in attendance.

Interestingly, the main singing contingent of home fans, have, in the traditions of the Vetch Field, situated themselves along one side of the pitch in the East Stand, rather than at the South end of the stadium. The catering facilities offer the delicious 'Football's Famous Chicken Balti Pie', pasties (£1.80), cheeseburgers (£2.30) and hot dogs, plus beer is also available. Please note though that the stadium is a completely non-smoking one; even on the concourses smoking is not allowed.

Surprisingly the Club have made the decision not to sell tickets or provide cash admission to the stadium for away fans on the day of the game. Away supporters are advised to purchase a ticket from their own Club's ticket office, before travelling to the stadium. It is also worth bearing in mind that the Swansea fans are passionate about their club and this can make for an intimidating atmosphere. Exercise caution around the ground.

Steve Griffiths adds; 'On the nearby retail park, there is a KFC & Pizza Hut – within 5 minutes walk. Opposite the stadium is a very nice chippy called 'Rossi's'. As well as the usual chips with fish, pies, sausages, etc., they also do salads and jacket potatoes'.

David McNeil informs me; 'As a West Brom fan on holiday in Swansea I visited the new stadium for the first League game against Tranmere. The stadium is very impressive and the facilities inside the stadium are excellent. Large concourse and great views from the stands. The atmosphere generated by the Swansea fans was excellent throughout the 90 minutes and it will become an intimidating place just as the Vetch used to be. Pre-match entertainment was enjoyed by my kids, especially the antics of Cyril the Swan. Great day out, would love to visit the ground as a Baggie playing the Swans in the FA cup. This stadium and their support deserve to have football played at a higher level'.

■ Where To Drink?

There are a few pubs within walking distance of the stadium, but with the stadium being new it is unclear yet as to which (if any) will become the favourite amongst away fans. Around a five-minute walk away from the visiting supporters turnstiles is the Station Inn pub in Hamilton Street, which is located in the area across the A4067 (Neath Road), opposite to the stadium. Go up Station Link Road (crossing over the railway line) and then turn left into Hamilton Street and this smallish pub, with a large screen showing Sky Sports, is on the right. A little further on is the larger Globe pub, which was welcoming to Fulham supporters in a pre-season friendly. This bar serves real ale and snacks and is located in Mysydd Road. Again go up Station Link Road, passing Hamilton Street on the left. Station Link Road runs into Mysydd Road. Follow Mysydd Road around to the left and the pub is situated further down on the left hand side. There is also the Coopers Arms which is around a ten-minute walk away from the stadium. This is located near to a roundabout on the A4067, going back towards the M4. The Railway pub in Siloh Road is best avoided by away fans.

Those arriving by train may find it better to drink in the city centre. Merv Williams informs me; 'There are a number of pubs on Wind (pronounced wine) Street in the centre of town, such as SA1, Yates, the Bank Statement and the No Sign Bar (the latter being listed in the CAMRA Good Beer Guide. Ask for Castle Gardens, and you'll see Wind Street'. There is also a large Wetherspoons outlet situated on the Kingsway.

Alcohol in the form of Carling and Worthington is served within the stadium, all costing £2.50 per pint. The Club open the turnstiles 90 minutes before kick-off, so that fans have the option to eat & drink within the stadium itself.

Thanks to Steve Griffiths for helping me out with the pub information near to the stadium.

■ How To Get There & Where To Park?

Leave the M4 at Junction 45 and take the A4067 towards the city centre (signposted A4067 South). Stay on the A4067 for around two and half miles and you will reach the stadium on your left. Car parking at the stadium is for permit holders only and most of the immediate residential areas around the stadium now have 'residents only' parking schemes in place. Away supporters are being encouraged to use the Park & Ride Facility located at Swansea Vale, which is signposted off the A4067, shortly after leaving the M4. The cost of parking there including transport by bus to and from the stadium is £5 per car (away coaches and mini buses are parked at the stadium itself at a cost of £10 per vehicle. Away supporters have their own separate buses to the ground, with the buses waiting outside the away stand at the end of the game to take supporters back to the car park. Don't be tempted to park on the nearby Retail Park as you may well end up with a ticket for your trouble!

■ By Train

Swansea High Street station is on the main line route from London Paddington. It is about two miles from the stadium. Regular local bus services (every ten minutes: routes 4, 4a, 120, 122, 125, 132) and taxis (around £3.50) are available from the train station to the stadium. Otherwise if you have time on your hands and wish to embark on the 25-30-minute walk, then as you come out of the station turn right and go up the High Street. At the traffic lights turn right into Neath Road. Proceed straight along Neath Road and you will eventually reach the stadium on your right. Thanks to Tom Evans for providing the directions.

■ Local Rivals

Cardiff City and from a little further up the M4, Bristol City.

■ Admission Prices

Home Fans:

West Stand
Adults £18,
OAP's/Students £13,
Under 16's £10

East Stand + North & South West Corners:
Adults £15,
OAP's/Students £11,
Under 16's £8

South Stand:
Adults £15,
OAP's £10,
Under 16's £7.

Family Tickets (South Stand):
1 Adult + 2 Children £25,
1 Adult + 3 Children £30,
2 Adults + 2 Children £38,
2 Adults + 3 Children £43.

Away Fans*:

North Stand:
Adults £15,
OAP's £10,
Under 16's £7.

* Please note that tickets for the away section are not on sale on the day of the game, but must be purchased in advance from the visiting club.

■ Programme

Official Programme £3
A Touch Far Vetched! Fanzine £1

■ Record Attendance

At The Liberty Stadium:
19,288 v Yeovil Town,
League One, November 18th, 2005.

At The Vetch Field:
32,796 v Arsenal,
FA Cup 4th Round, February 17th, 1968.

■ Average Attendance

2006-2007: 13,731 (League One)

■ Did You Know?

The Club were known as Swansea Town, up until 1970, when they changed their name to Swansea City.

Swindon Town

County Ground

Ground Name: County Ground
Capacity: 15,728 (all seated)
Address: County Road, Swindon, SN1 2ED
Main Telephone No: 0870-443-1969
Main Fax No: 01793-333-703
Ticket Office: 0870-443-1894
Ticket Office Fax: 01793-333-780
Team Nickname: The Robins
Year Ground Opened: 1896
Pitch Size: 110 x 70 yards
Home Kit Colours: Red & White

Official Website:
www.swindontownfc.co.uk

Unofficial Websites:
This Is Swindon - www.thisisswindontownfc.co.uk
Swindon Town Mad - www.swindontown-mad.co.uk (Footy Mad Network)
Supporters Trust - www.truststfc.co.uk
The Town End Fans Forum - http://thetownend.com/forum/index.php

What's The Ground Like?

At one end is the Stratton Bank Stand, a former terrace with rows of seats bolted on to it. This area is uncovered and has a clock above it as well as a small electric scoreboard. Opposite is the small, covered Town End, with several supporting pillars across the front.

An unusual feature is that the supporting legs of one of the floodlight pylons are actually in one side of the stand; there are even some seats situated behind them!

The sides are larger, two-tiered covered stands towering above the two ends. The newest of these is the attractive Nationwide Stand, while on the other side is the older Arkells Stand. The latter has windshields on either side and a few supporting pillars.

The ground also benefits by a striking set of four floodlight pylons. Once a feature across the country, floodlights are slowly but surely disappearing from the landscape, being replaced by rows of lights across the stand roofs. It's a shame really, if only because the floodlight pylons made it a lot easier to locate a ground in a town or city and were always synonymous with a football ground.

What Is It Like For Visiting Supporters?

Away fans are located in the Arkells Stand at one side of the pitch, where up to 1,200 fans can be housed. This is an older stand with facilities to match, but at least you are under cover. If you are at the back of this stand there is one supporting pillar which may impair your view of the goal, otherwise it is fine. You even get a view of some of the rolling Marlborough Hills beyond one corner of the ground! There is a small kiosk at the back of stand serving, amongst other refreshments, the delicious 'Football's Famous Chicken Balti Pie' (£2.20), but be careful when taking them back to your seat. The entrances to the seating areas are through large solid doors, and to compound matters they open out towards you!

Teams with a larger away following can also be allocated the Stratton Bank End if required. A further 2,100 fans can be accommodated in this area, but the end has no cover and is open to the elements. Fine on a nice sunny day, but on a cold wet, winter's day, it can be grim. I found Swindon to be a relaxed and fairly friendly day out, although the size of the police presence on my last visit seemed excessive. On a previous visit I managed to talk my way into the players lounge & bar after the game; quite an experience!

Where To Drink?

The County Hotel, right by the ground, did not allow entrance to away supporters on my last visit. Best to continue down County Road and seek out the Cricket Club that sits behind the Arkells Stand. As Mark Osborne from Swindon adds; 'On match days home and away fans can park on the cricket ground (for a small fee) and then have access to a drink in the cricket club. This is a very friendly (as well as cheap) club that always welcomes away fans'. I would echo these comments but also add that you can still get into the cricket club (there is no charge) even if you have not parked there.

Audrey MacDonald, a visiting Hartlepool United fan, recommends The Merlin on Drove Road, near to the Magic Roundabout. 'Away fans are welcome, but no team colours are allowed. They have Sky Sports showing on 12 television screens and even in the gents (according to my husband). Alcohol is available within the ground to away fans in the Arkells Stand (but not in the open Stratton Bank End), otherwise if you arrive early Swindon town centre is a 15-minute walk away.

How To Get There & Where To Park?

The ground is well signposted in and around Swindon town centre. Just follow signs for 'The County Ground'. From The M4:

Leave at junction 15 and take the A345 (Queens Drive) towards Swindon. At Drake's roundabout, turn left towards the Magic Roundabout, The County Ground is on the corner of this roundabout.

From the North A419 from Cricklade/Cirencester/M5:

This must be the easiest route - follow Cricklade Road down the hill. It becomes Cirencester Way about halfway down. At Transfer Bridges roundabouts turn left at the first and then straight over the second. The County Ground is on the left after the mini-roundabout.

If you survive the Magic Roundabout then there is some street parking. Otherwise park at the cricket club (take County Road off the Magic Roundabout, go past the County Hotel on your right and you will see a small sign further down on your right for football parking, just before the mini roundabout).

By Train

The ground is walkable from Swindon train station and will take you around 10-15 minutes. Leave the station, cross the road and proceed up the road between the two pubs (Great Western and Queen's Tap), continue to end of road. Turn left, proceed along Manchester Road, through traffic lights as far as you can go. At the junction turn right. The County Ground is about 300 yards up this road on the left. Thanks to John Bishop for providing me with the directions.

Local Rivals

Oxford United, Bristol Rovers & Bristol City and from further afield Gillingham.

Admission Prices

Home Fans:

Arkells Stand & Nationwide Stands*:
Adults £20,
Concessions £15,
Juniors £9

Town End:
Adults £15,
Concessions £12,
Juniors £7**

Family Area:
Adults £18,
Concessions £12,
Juniors £4

Away Fans*:

Arkells Stand*:
Adults £20,
Concessions £15,
Juniors £9

Stratton Bank:
Adults £15,
Concessions £12,
Juniors £7

* A reduction of up to £2 on these ticket prices is available if the ticket is purchased prior to matchday (excludes Junior tickets).

** Juniors must be accompanied by an adult in the Town End.

Programme

Official Programme: £2.50

Record Attendance

32,000 v Arsenal
FA Cup 3rd Round, January 15th, 1972.

Modern All Seated Attendance Record:
14,697 v Stockport County
Division Two, May 4th, 1996.

Average Attendance

2006-2007: 7,109 (League Two)

Did You Know?

During the Second World War, the County Ground was used as a prisoner of war camp, with wooden accommodation being situated on the pitch area.

Tranmere Rovers

Prenton Park

Ground Name:	Prenton Park
Capacity:	16,587 (all seated)
Address:	Prenton Rd West, Birkenhead, CH42 9PY
Main Telephone No:	0870-460-3333
Main Fax No:	0151-609-0606
Ticket Office:	0870-460-3332
Team Nickname:	Rovers
Year Ground Opened:	1912
Pitch Size:	112 x 72 yards
Home Kit Colours:	White With Royal Blue Trim

Official Website:
www.tranmererovers.co.uk

Unofficial Websites:
Rovers Rearguard - www.roversrearguard.com (Rivals Network)
Vital Tranmere - www.tranmere.vitalfootball.co.uk (Vital Football Network)
White Review - www.whitereview.co.uk

What's The Ground Like?

During 1994-95 the Club replaced three sides of the ground with new stands. Only the Main Stand on one side of the pitch was left intact. This stand is a fair sized, all seated, covered stand that was opened in 1968. It is two tiered and contains a couple of supporting pillars. The ground though is dominated by the Kop Stand at one end of the stadium. This stand, that has a capacity of around 5,500, dwarfs the rest of the ground and replaced a former open terrace. This end used to house both home & away supporters, but has now been changed to home fans only. At the opposite end, away fans are housed in another relatively new stand called the Cowshed. This single-tiered stand looks a little strange as one side of it has more rows than the other, giving a sloping effect. It has an electric scoreboard on its roof. On the other side is the John King Stand (formerly the Borough Road Stand), which is small covered stand that runs the entire length of the pitch.

What Is It Like For Visiting Supporters?

After a long campaign by Tranmere fans, the large Kop End is now purely for home fans. Away fans are housed in the opposite end, the affectionately named Cowshed. However, you will be relieved that the only connection with a real cowshed is the name, as the fairly new covered, all seated stand, has good facilities and unhindered views of the playing action. It can hold up to 2,500 fans.

I found Prenton Park to be one of those unremarkable away visits, not made any better by the smallish crowd in attendance. However, I experienced no problems around the ground and found it to be a fairly relaxing day out.

Where To Drink?

Jim Ennis informs me; 'The Prenton Park Hotel, which is situated about 20 yards away from the visiting supporters turnstiles, is popular with away fans. Otherwise alcohol is available in the away end'.

There are also a number of other pubs in walking distance of the ground. The Mersey Clipper, behind the Main Stand, and The Sportsmans Arms on Prenton Road East are recommended for away fans. A little further away is the Swan Pub on Woodchurch Road, Prenton, a good 20-minute walk away. Away fans are welcome and it has the added advantage of having 96 car parking spaces available, which are either free or have a small charge levied that can be redeemed against a drink at the bar.

All fans please note it is a criminal offence to drink alcohol on the streets of Birkenhead; you may find yourself being arrested if you do.

How To Get There & Where To Park?

From M6/M56 join the M53 and exit at Junction 4 and take the B5151 Mount Road from the fourth exit of the roundabout (the ground is signposted from here). After two and a half miles when Mount Road becomes Storeton Road, turn right into Prenton Road West and the ground will be visible on the right hand side.

Sue Warwick adds; 'An easier route to the ground is to leave the M53 at Junction 3 and take the A552 Woodchurch Road towards Birkenhead. You will pass a Sainsburys and then as you reach the Half Way House pub turn right at the traffic lights onto the B5151 Mount Road. Take the first left for the ground'.

There is a car park at the ground, otherwise, street parking, but beware that there is a strict local residents parking scheme in operation around the ground.

I got hopelessly lost trying to find the ground and did actually end up at the Mersey admiring the views of Liverpool across the river. My frustrations were not eased, when on asking a local chap for directions to the football ground the guy replied 'Liverpool or Everton?' After asking about another three locals I finally found the ground after going round most of Birkenhead.

By Train

The closest railway stations are Rock Ferry and Birkenhead Central, both served by Liverpool Lime St. Both stations are a fair walk from the ground. (15-20 minutes). Philip Jackman provides directions from Rock Ferry station; 'Upon leaving Rock Ferry turn right and walk up the road for a fair distance until you reach a roundabout. At the roundabout, turn right again and walk straight up until you are close to the Sportsman pub. Then turn left down Everest Road and walk straight down to the bottom where you will be standing opposite the turnstiles for the Cowshed Stand'. Craig Skyrme informs me; 'If you get off the train instead at Hamilton Square, there is a football bus laid on just outside the station. It runs about every 10-15 minutes and if you show your train ticket you can get aboard for free of charge, otherwise it costs 50p.

Local Rivals

Liverpool, Everton, Chester, Wrexham and from a little further afield, Bolton Wanderers.

Admission Prices

Home Fans:

Main Stand
Adults £18,
Young Persons £13,
Seniors £10,
Juniors £5

John King Stand
Adults £16,
Young Persons £11, Seniors £8,
Juniors £5

Kop Stand
Adults £15,
Young Persons/Seniors £8,
Juniors £5

Away Fans:

Cowshed Stand
Adults £17,
Young Persons £12,
Seniors £9,
Juniors £5.

Please note that tickets for young persons and senior citizens must be purchased from the ticket office and proof of age will be required.

Programme

Official Programme £2.50

Record Attendance

24,424 v Stoke City,
FA Cup 4th Round, February 5th, 1972.

Modern All Seated Attendance Record:
14,697 v Stockport County
Division Two, May 7th, 1995.

Average Attendance

2006-2007: 7,291 (League One)

Did You Know?

That the Club were originally formed in 1881 as Belmont FC.

Walsall

Banks's Stadium

Ground Name: Banks's Stadium (but still known to many fans as the Bescot Stadium)
Capacity: 11,300 (all seated)
Address: Bescot Crescent, Walsall, WS1 4SA
Main Telephone No: 0870-442-0442
Fax No: 01922-613-202
Ticket Office: 0870-442-0111/0222
Ticket Office Fax: 0870-787-1966
Team Nickname: The Saddlers
Year Ground Opened: 1990
Pitch Size: 110 x 73 yards
Home Kit Colours: White & Red

Official Website: www.saddlers.co.uk

Unofficial Websites:
Up The Saddlers - www.upthesaddlers.com/wp/
The Saddlers - www.thesaddlersfc.tk (Sport Network)
NMFE - http://walsall.rivals.net/default.asp?sid=931 (Rivals Network)

What's The Ground Like?

The Saddlers moved to the Bescot Stadium in 1990 from Fellows Park. With the opening of the now named Floors 2 Go Purple Stand in 2003 the Club are finally getting a ground to match their ambitions. This new stand is for home fans and is a large two-tiered affair that completely dwarfs the rest of the ground. It is smart-looking, with a glassed area running across its middle, which houses the concourse. Unusually, it has a slightly larger upper than lower tier. This end before it was redeveloped was previously called the Gilbert Alsop (a former Walsall playing great) Stand, but in a commercial sponsorship deal, has been renamed the Floors 2 Go Stand. Similarly the H. C. Fellows stand has been renamed the Txt 64446 Heath Stand. A sign of the times I guess...

The rest of the stadium is totally enclosed with three of the stands being roughly the same height, giving it a 'box-like' feel. These stands are not particularly big, around 15 rows high. The corners are filled, but only for advertising hoardings. Above the Homeserve (William Sharp) stand there is a small electric scoreboard, whilst on one side there is a small television camera gantry precariously perched on the roof. One unusual feature are the strange-looking floodlights, which sit on the roofs of the side stands. The main disappointment is the large number of supporting pillars in each of the older stands. As Walsall unfortunately very rarely fill the stadium, this is not a huge problem. There is also a small electric scoreboard on top of the Homeserve (William Sharp) Stand.

In a corporate sponsorship deal with Marstons Brewery, the stadium has been renamed the Banks's Stadium.

Future Ground Developments

The Club have been granted planning permission to redevelop the William Sharp end of the ground. The new stand would look similar to the Floors 2 Go Stand and add 2,300 seats to the stadium, raising the overall capacity to 13,500. It would also mean that up to 4,000 away supporters could be accommodated at that end. The back of the stand will also feature a giant advertising hoarding, clearly visible from the M6. The Club are seeking a suitable sponsor for this proposed development.

What Is It Like For Visiting Supporters?

Away supporters are housed in the Homeserve (William Sharp) Stand at one end of the ground, where around 2,000 away supporters can be accommodated. There are a few supporting pillars at the front which could impede your view. The good news though, is that even a small amount of away fans can really make some noise and make a good atmosphere. A trip to Walsall can be disappointing in terms of trying to get there and the stadium itself, but is more than countered by the relaxed atmosphere around the ground and the friendliness of the Walsall fans themselves.

Neil Harding, a visiting Hull City fan provides his thoughts on the stadium; 'In my opinion The Bescot has to be one of the poorest grounds in the country. It has a strange look to it with three covered stands all the same size, but one large stand that towers over the rest of the ground, giving it a somewhat lopsided feel.

I found the away end to be rather cramped and the view distorted by one of the four pillars that run across the front. The only good thing is that if the stand is covered, which means a good away following can create a lot of noise. The away end is served by a food kiosk stuck in each corner, and near to the toilets which created a bit of a bottle neck at half time, especially as a large away following was present. The food though, if you are prepared to wait, was excellent, especially the chicken balti pies. The home fans didn't appear to be threatening in anyway and the stewards came across as a friendly bunch of people. The amount of police on duty though did seem a little excessive for what was a bit of a nothing game'.

■ Where To Drink?

The King George V in Wallowes Lane is okay, but as the nearest pub to the ground it gets rather busy. It is 15 minutes walk away, opposite Morrisons. If you are walking from the stadium, go out of the official car parks and down towards McDonalds on your right, then turn left into Wallowes Lane. At the end go left onto the main road and the pub is set back on the left. Away fans should avoid the Fulbrook pub near the ground.

Gary Cotterill informs me; 'at the stadium there is the Saddlers Club, which normally allows small numbers of away fans in at a cost of £1, but you need to arrive there early'. Alcohol is not served inside the stadium. There is a McDonalds on the adjoining retail park, that you pass on the way in to the stadium.

Neil LeMilliere, a visiting Exeter City fan, adds; 'Couldn't get into the Saddlers Club at 2.10pm. It is then a long way to go to get a drink anywhere else if you don't know where you are going - in fact too far!'

■ How To Get There & Where To Park?

The ground is right next to the M6, in fact you can see it from the motorway just north of the RAC Control Centre. Unfortunately, this stretch normally has a large traffic jam on both Saturday lunchtimes and early weekday evenings, so allow extra time.

From M6 South:
Leave the M6 at Junction 7 and take the A34 towards Walsall (beware of speed cameras). At the end of the dual carriageway turn left at the Bell Inn pub into Walstead Road (sign posted Bescot Stadium, Bescot Station Park & Ride). Continue straight on this road for two miles, passing another pub called the Tiger on your left. You will come to Bescot Stadium and entrance to the away end on your right.

From The M6 North:
Leave the M6 at Junction 9 and take the A461 towards Walsall. Bear right on to the A4148 (Wallowes Lane) and turn right at the second set of traffic lights. You will see the ground on your left.

Car Parking:
There is a good sized car park located at the ground (£3) and behind the away stand, for a quick getaway after the match. Bescot Railway Station also offers car parking for £2. Ian Stevens advises, 'avoid parking on the nearby Morrisons car park (built on the site of the old Fellows Park), as unless you can prove you are shopping there, you run the risk of being clamped'.

■ By Train

Note that if you go by train, Bescot Stadium has its own station, situated behind the away end only a few minutes walk from the turnstiles. Trains run there on a local line from Birmingham New Street and the journey time is around 20 minutes. There is a regular service on Saturdays along this line and you should not have too many problems getting away after the game.

■ Local Rivals

Wolverhampton Wanderers, West Bromwich Albion, Birmingham City, Aston Villa & Shrewsbury Town.

■ Admission Prices

Home Fans*:

Floors 2 Go Stand (Upper Tier)
Adults £18, Senior Citizens/Juniors £12
Floors 2 Go Stand (Family Tickets)
1 Adult + 1 Junior £21,
Extra Junior on family ticket £6
Floors 2 Go Stand (Lower Tier)
Adults £14, Concessions £10
Txt 64446 Health (H.L. Fellows Stand)
Adults £18, Concessions £13
Banks's Stand
Adults £18, Senior Citizens £12. Juniors £10.
Banks's Stand (Family Tickets)
1 Adult + 1 Junior £20,
Extra Junior on family ticket £6

Away Fans*:

Homeserve (William Sharp) **Stand**
Adults £18, Concessions £12

* Discounts of up to £2 are available on most of these prices when tickets are purchased prior to matchdays.

■ Programme & Fanzine

Official Programme £2.50
Ninety Minutes From Europe (NMFE) Fanzine 50p
There is also an excellent programme shop behind the William Sharp Stand.

■ Record Attendance

11,049 v Rotherham United
Division One, May 9th, 2004.

Record Attendance At Fellows Park:
25,453 v Newcastle (Div 2), August 29th, 1961.

■ Average Attendance

2006-2007: 5,639 (League Two)

■ Did You Know?

That the Club are nicknamed the 'Saddlers' as Walsall was once well known for its leather industry.

Yeovil Town

Huish Park

Ground Name:	Huish Park
Capacity:	9,400 (Seating 5,212)
Address:	Lufton Way, Yeovil, Somerset, BA22 8YF
Main Telephone No:	01935-423-662
Fax No:	01935-473-956
Pitch Size:	115 x 72 yards
Team Nickname:	Glovers
Year Ground Opened:	1990
Home Kit Colours:	Green & White Hoops

Official Website:
www.ytfc.net

Unofficial Websites:
Cider Space - www.ciderspace.co.uk
The Dutch Glover - www.dutchglover.tk
Official Supporters Club - www.gwsc.net

What's The Ground Like?

Yeovil is predominantly remembered for some classic 'giant killing' deeds in the FA Cup and the famous slope of the pitch. With the move to a new ground in 1990, that slope has gone, but the team have continued to impress. Generally the ground is a tidy-looking one, in a pleasant setting, with lots of trees visible behind the stands. Both sides of the ground are similar-looking stands and are of the same height. They are both cantilevered, covered single-tiered stands that are all seated. Each stand has windshields to either side. The only differences between these stands, is that the Yeovil College Stand has some executive boxes running across the back of it, plus the dugouts and players' tunnel, whilst the Bartlett Stand has a press box suspended from beneath its roof and a small simple-looking electric scoreboard. At one end is the medium sized Westland Terrace, which is covered and for home supporters and again has windshields to either side. Opposite is the Copse Road Terrace, which is given to away fans. This is smaller and uncovered. Oddly the steelwork is in place at the back of this stand to incorporate more terrace space, but the concrete rows have so far not been added. Perched above the rear of this stand is a large electric scoreboard. The ground is completed with four modern floodlight pylons, one in each corner of the ground.

What Is It Like For Visiting Supporters?

Away fans are situated in the Copse Road open terrace at one end of the ground. This is uncovered, so hope for a dry day. Up to 1,750 supporters can be housed in this area. Additionally a small number of seats are allocated to away fans in the Yeovil College Main Stand. As this stand is covered, this may be a better bet, especially if the weather is bad. Normally a visit to Huish Park is enjoyable, and the atmosphere good. This is boosted by a very vocal crowd in the home terrace as well as the presence of a drummer and trumpeter in that end (on my last visit the trumpeter was even imitating an ambulance siren as the trainer ran on to treat an injured player!). If Yeovil score then 'Glad All Over' by the Dave Clark Five blasts out around the ground. It is worth noting though that the local fans are passionate about their club and caution around the ground may be required for some of the bigger games.

On my last visit I was five minutes late getting to the game and had missed the kick off. Unbelievably the turnstiles had already closed at the away end and myself and a number of other away fans had to run around the ground to try and find someone who could get us in. We managed this, and I have to say that the stewards were particularly helpful and friendly. I found the large police presence in and around the ground perturbing. In my mind I was not at a high profile game, so I was somewhat surprised at the amount of local constabulary there. To make matters worse they started on my pet hate, the videoing of away fans during the game. The catering offered was the usual assortment of pies, pasties and burgers (£2), but let's just say they were not the best I or my wife have ever had.

Where To Drink?

I was pleasantly surprised to find a large marquee outside of the ground, that had been set up as a makeshift beer tent. There was a large sign outside the marquee which announced that 'Everyone Is Welcome!' Just a pity that wasn't quite correct as any away fans in colours were turned away at the entrance by a couple of burly-looking bouncers. Some visiting fans did refer the bouncers to the said sign, but to no avail.

There are three pubs within about 10-15 minutes walk of the ground, 'The Bell', 'The Arrow' and 'The Airfield Tavern' (formerly 'Brewsters', which according to Stephen

Pugsley also has a handy fish and chip shop next door called Palmers). I could only find the Arrow pub and in efforts to locate it, ended up joining up with a number of other away fans who were also looking lost in our quest to find beer! The pub itself when located was quite a spacious estate type pub, which on my visit was fine and I was served quickly, although it was predominantly home support with only a small number of away fans present (in colours). Richard Reardon, a visiting Carlisle fan adds; 'The Archers is only 10-15 minutes walk away. The weather was excellent so most of our substantial following sat outside at a number of picnic tables. Not a wide choice of beers but one real ale available. Both sets of supporters mixed well, Sky TV for those that like that sort of thing. Police presence outside but it was all very friendly'. I have since received mixed reports about this pub so use your discretion.

To find this pub, from the ground car park, walk back up the road past the ground to the top of it and turn right. At the end of this road, turn left onto the main road and after a short distance take the first right. Go straight down this road through the new-looking residential area and after about ten minutes of walking, you will see a clearing on your right and just beyond this there are some shops and the Arrow pub in the middle.

Colin Jordan, a visiting Exeter City fan, adds; 'We found The Bell on Preston Road (towards the town centre from the A3088 roundabout, rather than turning left towards Huish Park). It's a very large Greene King "Hungry Horse" pub, with a great deal of outside seating, and as with most of Yeovil it seems to be away fan friendly. Usual Greene King beer fayre (IPA, Abbot, Morland OSH), plus good quality food. It is though at least a 15-20-minute walk away from the ground'.

How To Get There & Where To Park?

The ground is located on the very outskirts of Yeovil and is signposted from the A303. Leave the A303 at the Cartgate roundabout and take the A3088 towards Yeovil. Follow the road for approximately 8-9 miles until you reach a roundabout on the outskirts of Yeovil with the Westlands Airfield directly in front of you. Turn left at this roundabout and then continue straight on, crossing a number of roundabouts. As you pass the entrance to an Asda superstore, take the next left for the ground, which can be seen from the road.

There is a fair sized car park at the ground, which costs £2. Otherwise there is plenty of street car parking to be had on the roads leading down to the ground. Tim Porter, a visiting Torquay United fan, informs me; 'make sure you arrive at the official car park, early in winter as otherwise you will end up in the overspill car park, which actually is a field which doesn't drain nearly as well as the pitch!' Richard Reardon adds; 'Getting away from the ground was a bit of nightmare as there is only one road out of the official car park. It took 35 minutes to travel the half mile to the Preston Road roundabout'.

By Train

Yeovil has two railway stations, Yeovil Junction is 2-3 miles out of town and Pen Mill junction about a mile from the town centre. Both are on the opposite side of town to the ground. From both stations it is advised to get a taxi to the stadium or alternatively if you arrive at Yeovil Junction, then you can catch the 'Hopper' minibus to the bus station in the town centre.

On Saturday matchdays there is one shuttle bus which leaves the bus station at around 1.50pm (returning from Huish Park at 17:05). Otherwise there is the First Traveller Bus Service No 1 that leaves from the town centre (stop outside Lloyds TSB in the High Street) and drops you at the Abbey Manor Housing Estate near to the stadium.

Local Rivals

From non-league days Weymouth and from a little further afield Bristol Rovers and Bristol City. The nearest league club is Bournemouth.

Admission Prices

Home Fans*:

Main Stand:
Adults £16, Concessions £13, Under 16's £7

Bartlett Stand:
Adults £15, Concessions £11, Under 16's £7

Westland Terrace:
Adults £15, Concessions £10, Under 16's £7

Away Fans*

Bartlett Stand (Seating):
Adults £15, Concessions £11, Under 16's £7

Copse Road Terrace:
Adults £14, Concessions £9, Under 16's £7

* A £2 discount is available on the above ticket prices, if the ticket is purchased prior to matchday. Members of the Junior Glovers Club can obtain further discounts on the Under 16's ticket price.

Programme & Fanzine

Official Programme £2.50
Onto Victory Fanzine £1.

Record Attendance

At the original Huish Park:
16,318 v Sunderland,
FA Cup 4th Round, January 29th, 1949

At the current Huish Park:
9,348 v Liverpool
FA Cup 3rd Round, January 4th, 2004.

Average Attendance

2006-2007: 5,728 (League One)

Did You Know?

That the Club was formed as Yeovil Casuals in 1895.

Accrington Stanley

Fraser Eagle Stadium

Ground Name:	Fraser Eagle Stadium (But still known to many fans as the Crown Ground)
Capacity:	5,057 (1,200 seated)
Address:	Livingstone Rd, Accrington, Lancashire, BB5 5BX
Main Tel No:	01254-356-950
Fax No:	01254-356-951
Pitch Size:	111 x 72 yards
Team Nickname:	The Reds, Stanley
Year Ground Opened:	1968
Home Kit Colours:	Red & White

Official Website:
www.accringtonstanley.co.uk

Unofficial Websites:
Vital Accrington Stanley (Vital Football Network):
www.accrington.vitalfootball.co.uk
Accrington Stanley History: www.accringtonstanley.has.it

What's The Ground Like?

Although the ground is on the smallish side, it is set in a picturesque area, with views over fields and hills behind the Coppice Terrace at one end of the ground. On one side of the ground is the Main Stand, which at first glance looks like one stand, but in fact it is comprised of two small stands; the Main & Thwaites Stands. They sit on either side of the halfway line, with an open gap between the two. Both are all seated covered stands and have a row of floodlights at the back of them. To compensate for the fair slope of the pitch which runs up along the ground from the Coppice Terrace to the Clayton Terrace, the Thwaites Stand has fewer rows of seats than the Main Stand. Both these stands also have an usual array of tubular steelwork, running across the top of them. Opposite is a very small covered terrace, called the Whinney Hill Terrace. This comprises only three rows of terrace and has a row of supporting pillars running across the middle of it. Behind this stand is a relatively new housing development which overlooks the ground, meaning that some residents can see the game for nothing. Both ends are fairly new-looking open terraces. One unusual aspect of the ground is that it has a total of eight floodlight pylons, with three on either side of the ground and another being located at one end.

What Is It Like For Visiting Supporters?

Away fans are housed in the Coppice Terrace at one end of the ground, where around 1,500 fans can be accommodated. Unusually the Club have taken the decision not to provide away fans with any additional seating in the Main Stand, so only the terrace is available. The Coppice Terrace is an open end and with the location of the ground, somewhat exposed, so it pays to be wrapped up well, especially in the winter months. Han van Eijden adds; 'The burgers were excellent, although this did lead to long queues for refreshments'. Otherwise in the Coppice Terrace the facilities are basic with some rather old toilets (which have known to flood from time to time). There are supplemented with some portaloos.

John Schmidt, a visiting Darlington fan adds; 'The away end is totally exposed and on our visit it started chucking it down with rain. Fortunately someone at the Club showed some common sense and allowed the small contingent of away supporters to go into the Winney Hill covered terrace'.

Shirley Lawrence, a visiting Swindon Town supporter tells me; 'We had a pleasant day at the Crown Ground. Before the game we went to the Crown Pub which was crowded, but as they had six staff serving, we were able to get our drinks relatively quickly. Inside the ground there was not much atmosphere due to the away end being uncovered. Although we had over 800 supporters who were in good voice, the noise just wasn't carried around the ground'.

Accrington Stanley

■ Where To Drink?

There is a Club Bar at the ground, however this is for home fans only. The nearest pub is the Crown, which is just behind the ground on the main Whalley Road. This pub welcomes all fans, has some Accrington Stanley memorabilia, and displays scarves and pennants given by visiting fans. A little further down Whalley Road (five minutes walk in the direction of the motorway), is the Greyhound pub, which is a Sam Smith's house.

John Schmidt adds, If you go from the ground to the main road and head towards the town centre, then a five-minute walk away, down on the right is the Grey Horse pub; it is only a small pub but served decent real ale. Opposite is a small row of shops that contains an excellent chip shop. This area also seemed to be good for street parking'.

If you arrive early and have a bit of time on your hands then you may consider visiting the 'Peel Park Hotel' in Turkey Street. This pub serves food and is listed in the CAMRA Good Beer Guide. It also overlooks Peel Park, the site of Accrington Stanley's old ground. Go along Whalley Road (A680) towards the town centre. Before reaching the town centre turn left onto the B6237 Queens Road (if you miss this turning proceed into the town centre and turn left onto the A679 Burnley Road). Continue along Queens Road into Penn House Lane. At the end of this road you will reach a T-junction with the A679 Burnley Road. Turn left onto the Burnley Road and then go almost immediately right into Alice Street. The Peel Park is down on the right in Turkey Street.

■ How To Get There & Where To Park?

Leave the M6 at Junction 29 and take the M65 towards Blackburn. Continue past Blackburn towards Accrington and leave the M65 at Junction 7. Then take the left hand exit at the roundabout onto the A6185 towards Clitheroe (this is in the opposite direction to Accrington). At the first set of traffic lights turn right onto the A678, towards Padiham, and then at the next traffic lights, turn right onto the A680 towards Accrington. After about half a mile along the A680 you will pass the Crown pub on your left. Take the next left into Livingstone Road and then an immediate left for the Club car park. The car park is of a reasonable size and is free, however as you would expect it fills up pretty quickly. Otherwise street parking.

■ By Train

Accrington station is about a mile away from the ground. Leave the station and travel down the slope towards the large viaduct roundabout in the centre of town.
Take the Milnshaw Lane exit at the opposite side of the roundabout alongside the Perry's Peugeot dealership. After approximately 100 metres this road then joins Whalley Road. Bear left up the hill and follow Whalley Road for about a mile, passing the hospital, a set of traffic lights and then a mini roundabout. Take the next right after the mini roundabout junction into Livingstone Road. The football club is approximately 100 metres on the left on Livingstone Road. Thanks to Rob Heys for providing the directions.

■ Local Rivals

Blackburn, Burnley and from a little further afield, Morecambe, Southport & Barrow.

■ Admission Prices

Seats:
Adults £15,
Concessions £10,
Under 12's £5.

Terrace:
Adults £13,
Concessions £8.

Concessions apply to OAP's, Students & Under 18's.

Programme
Official Programme £2.50

■ Record Attendance

At The Crown Ground:
4,368 v Colchester United
FA Cup 3rd Round, January 3rd, 2004.

■ Average Attendance

2006-2007: 2,260 (League Two)

■ Did You Know?

When Accrington Stanley resigned from the league in 1962, they were replaced in the league by Oxford United. 24 years later when the re-formed Accrington Stanley gained promotion back to the Football League, it was at the expense of Oxford who were relegated to the Conference.

Barnet

Underhill Stadium

Ground Name: Underhill Stadium
Capacity: 5,500
Address: Barnet Lane, Barnet, EN5 2DN
Main Telephone No: 020-8441-6932
Fax No: 020-8447-0655
Ticket Office: 020-8449-6325
Team Nickname: Bees
Year Ground Opened: 1907
Pitch Size: 115 x 75 yards
Home Kit Colours: Black & Amber

Official Website:
www.barnetfc.com

Unofficial Website:
Supporters Association - www.bfcsa.co.uk

What's The Ground Like?

Unfortunately the ground has not seen any major investment for some years. Only one side of the ground, the East Terrace, is completely covered and this is over terracing. Part of this stand is given to away supporters. The Main Stand on the other side of the ground is quite small and straddles the halfway line, running barely half of the pitch. This stand, which was built in 1964, is seated with a capacity of 800. On the North side of the Main Stand is a small terrace, whilst on the other side is a small all seated Family Stand. This stand at one time was a small covered terrace, that has now had seats installed. At one end is the North Terrace. This end is so small that it has a large mesh fence at the back of it, to prevent footballs hitting the houses that sit on the other side of Westcombe Drive. At the other end, the South Stand is a 'temporary' stand, which has been there for a few years now. This end has a bank of green seating, around five rows high, that is open to the elements. The most striking feature of the ground is the relatively new club office building which sits at one corner of the ground, beside the South Stand. Although the slope of the pitch is not as bad as it once was, it is still fairly noticeable, running down the length of the pitch from North to South.

Future Developments

The Club for some years now have signalled their intention to leave Underhill and move to a new stadium, as it is felt that the capacity of Underhill cannot be expanded any further. However, they have encountered numerous obstacles in trying to find a suitable location in the Barnet area and at present it is still unclear whether they may have to look further afield for a new home.

What Is It Like For Visiting Supporters?

Away fans are housed on one side of the covered East Terrace, towards the North End of the ground. This area accommodates around 1,000 supporters. If demand requires it then the open North Terrace can also be allocated, increasing the allocation to 1,500. Normally a relaxing and enjoyable day out, although when you view the slope of the pitch, you almost think that it must be an optical illusion, as it is at quite an angle. As a matter of interest you may hear the home fans singing that Beatles classic 'Twist & Shout' from time to time!

Where To Drink?

Jim Prentice informs me; 'there are a number of good pubs around Underhill. A favourite with away fans is The Old Red Lion, just behind the north entrance to Underhill. Situated up in the town at the top of Barnet Hill are the Moon Under Water and the King John, and down the bottom of the hill (under the Underground bridge) are the Queen's Arms and The Weaver. Away fans are welcome in all of these pubs on the whole - Barnet fans are generally friendly and welcoming'. Steve Smith adds: 'if you come into New Barnet railway station, then opposite is a Wetherspoons pub called the Railway Bell, which has a good selection of beer'. There is a supporters' club at the ground, but this is for home fans only.

How To Get There & Where To Park?

Leave the M25 at J23. Take the A1081 towards Barnet. Follow this road for about three miles. Continue towards Barnet as the road becomes the A1000. The the ground is at the foot of Barnet Hill near to the junction with Station Road (A110). Street Parking or there is a car park at High Barnet Underground station (£2).

By Train/Tube

The nearest tube station is High Barnet which is on the Northern Line. There is only five minutes walk down Barnet Hill to the ground (although it is a fair hike back up the hill after the game!). Alternatively you can take a quicker train to New Barnet railway station, which is around fifteen minutes walk away from the ground. This station is served by trains from London Kings Cross and is a shorter journey time than the tube, taking around 20 minutes from Central London.

Anthony Hammond adds; 'Coming out of New Barnet station turn right and then left into Station Road. Walk up to the traffic lights opposite the Odeon Cinema and turn right onto Barnet Hill (A1000). After going under a railway bridge, you will be able to see the ground behind the Old Red Lion pub on your left. Alternatively you can get a bus from New Barnet Station; the 84, 384 or 107 buses run every 15 minutes or so from New Barnet to Underhill'.

Local Rivals

Enfield are the traditional rivals. The nearest Club in the league is Leyton Orient.

Admission Prices

Home Fans:

Main Stand:
Adults £20,
Concessions £16

East Terrace:
Adults £15,
Concessions £11

Family Stand (Seating):
Adult £16,
Concessions £12

North & North West Terraces:
Adults £13,
Concessions £9

In addition Under 12's can gain admission to league games for just £5, providing that a voucher has first been obtained from the ticket office.

Away Fans:

East Terrace
Adults £15,
Concessions £11

Concessions are available to home and away supporters, who are over 60, under 18, or are full time students. However to qualify for the discount you must first obtain a voucher from the Barnet ticket office prior to paying at the turnstiles. Home supporters who qualify for a concession can also obtain a further discount, providing they have become Club members.

Programme

Official Programme £2.50

Record Attendance

11,026 v Wycombe Wanderers
FA Amateur Cup, February 23rd, 1952.

Average Attendance

2006-2007: 2,195 (League Two)

Did You Know?

After playing over 100 years in non-league football, Barnet finally joined the ranks of the Football League in 1991, after gaining promotion from the Conference.

Bradford City

Intersonic Stadium

Ground Name:	Intersonic Stadium (But still known to a number of fans as Valley Parade)
Capacity:	25,136 (all seated)
Address:	Bradford, West Yorkshire, BD8 7DY
Main Telephone No:	0870-822-0000
Fax No:	01274-773-356
Ticket Office:	0870-822-1911
Club Nickname:	The Bantams
Year Ground Opened:	1903
Pitch Size:	113 x 70 yards
Home Kit Colours:	Claret & Amber

Official Website:
www.bradfordcityfc.co.uk

Unofficial Websites:
City Gent - www.citygent.yorks.com
Boy From Brazil - www.boyfrombrazil.co.uk
Independent Supporters Club - www.bcisc.net

■ What's The Ground Like?

The term 'a game of two halves' is often applied to a football game; in the case of Valley Parade, a stadium of 'two halves' comes to mind. The ground has now been completely rebuilt since the mid-80s, but the initial impression is that one side is twice as big as the other. The Kop End (now known as the Carlsberg Stand), is a relatively new two-tiered stand that is simply huge and looks quite superb. It once towered over the rest of the ground, but the addition of another tier to the Sunwin Stand during 2001 has led to it meeting its once larger neighbour. With the corner between these stands also being filled, one has a truly impressive spectacle. The rest of the ground now looks rather out of place in the shadow of its shiny neighbours. Away fans are housed in a small 'double decker' type stand at one end, called the TL Dallas Stand. The other side, the Yorkshire First (East) Stand, is a single-tiered stand. There is also an electric scoreboard in one corner of the ground.

■ What Is It Like For Visiting Supporters?

Away fans are housed in the TL Dallas Stand where 1,130 supporters can be accommodated. If possible try to get tickets for the upper tier as the view of the action is far better. On the downside there are a number of supporting pillars which could well impede your view. If demand requires it then a section of the Yorkshire First (East) Stand can also be made available to away supporters. The delicious 'Football's Famous Chicken Balti Pie' (£2) is available inside the ground. Roger Mulrooney, a visiting Barnsley fan, adds; 'On my last visit I found the home crowd friendly and non-threatening. The stewards were particularly good-natured and helpful. Still a very good away day for a visiting fan'.

Having been a student in Bradford and having watched them win the old Third Division, I have a bit of a soft spot for this club. Pleasingly I have found Bradford to have become rather more friendly towards away supporters in recent years. It is quite an enjoyable day out especially if you enjoy what the city has to offer. Make sure that you wrap up well unless the weather forecast is 80 degrees. This is because Bradford is situated at the bottom of a valley, down which a rather cold wind normally prevails.

■ Where To Drink?

There is the Carlton pub which is only a few minutes walk from behind the Kop Stand. It does allow in away fans, but the pub is quite a basic one. There are also a couple of hotels with bars, all about a ten-minute walk away. They are the Park & Cartwright hotels. Just continue to walk on the main road by the ground away from the town centre and at the traffic lights where the entrance to the park is, turn right and you will see them in a row on your right. Also about a ten-minute walk away is the Corn Dolly, a good real ale pub on Bolton Road, but this has more of a home fan feel about it. Otherwise it is probably wise to drink in the centre, or if you are feeling adventurous jump in a taxi and visit the Fighting Cock in Preston St which serves excellent real ale and is quite a mecca for CAMRA members. Darren Middleton recommends Haigys Bar on Lumb Lane whilst Jamie Morgan adds; 'a new pub/curry house has just opened called The Valley. It is on Manningham Lane, only a short distance past the ground'.

■ How To Get There & Where To Park?

Leave the M62 at Junction 26 and take the M606 for Bradford. At the end of the motorway, keep to the right hand lane and Valley Parade (Bradford & Bingley) is well signposted. Mostly street parking around the ground.

■ By Train

If going by train into Bradford Interchange, it is quite a walk to the ground (25 minutes). Either take a taxi (£3.50) or alternatively the bus station is located next to the train station (Bus Nos 622, 623, 626 or 662). Chris Hawkridge suggests; 'supporters travelling via Leeds should catch the Leeds - Bradford Forster Square service (two trains per hour during the day) rather than those to Bradford Interchange. Forster Square is only 10 minutes walk from the ground'.

■ Local Rivals

Leeds United & Huddersfield Town.

■ Admission Prices

Home Supporters*:

Sunwin Stand:
Adults £20,
Students £15,
OAP's £14,
Juveniles £12

Sunwin Stand (Family Area):
Adult £16 (when accompanied by a junior),
OAP £11, Juvenile £5

East Stand:
Adults £20,
Students £15,
OAP's £14,
Juveniles £12

Carlsberg Stand:
Adults £20,
Students £15,
OAP's £14,
Juveniles £12

Carlsberg Stand:
Adults £18,
OAP's £12,
Juveniles £10

Away Supporters:

TL Dallas Stand:
Adults £20,
OAP's £14,
Juveniles £12.

* Club Members can receive additional discounts on these prices.

■ Programme & Fanzine

Official Programme: £2.50
City Gent Fanzine: £1.50

■ Record Attendance

39,146 v Burnley,
FA Cup 4th Round, March 11th, 1911.

Modern All Seated Attendance Record:
22,057 v Liverpool
Premier League, May 1st, 2001.

■ Average Attendance

2006-2007: 7,925 (League One)

■ Did You Know?

That Bradford City is the only league club in England to wear claret and amber.

Brentford

Griffin Park

Ground Name: Griffin Park
Capacity: 12,763
Address: Braemar Road,
Brentford, TW8 0NT
Main Telephone No: 08453-456-442
Fax No: 020-8380-9937
Team Nickname: The Bees
Year Ground Opened: 1904
Pitch Size: 110 x 73 yards
Home Kit Colours: Red, White & Black

Official Website:
www.brentfordfc.co.uk

Unofficial Websites:
Brentford Mad - www.brentford-mad.co.uk
(Footy Mad Network)
Brentford Supporters Trust - www.beesunited.org.uk
Griffin Park Grapevine - www.griffinpark.org
Brentford Always - www.brentfordalways.org

What's The Ground Like?

The ground is rather compact and certainly has an individual feel. On one side is the recently christened Bill Axbey Stand (formerly the New Road Stand), which is named after a long time supporter who watched the Bees for an incredible 89 years before passing away in 2007. This stand is a single tiered, covered all seated stand, which has a number of supporting pillars running across the front of it. The roof of the stand is painted with a large advert, designed to catch the eye of passengers flying into Heathrow Airport. Currently this is an advert for Qatar Airways, but in the past amongst others, it has been for KLM and easyJet. Opposite is the Braemar Road Stand that is now known as the 'The Refreshing Solutions Stand' under a corporate sponsorship deal. Again this stand is single tiered, all seated and has a number of supporting pillars. It has a very low roof, which makes you wonder what the view would be like from the very back row of the stand.

At one end is the Ealing Road Terrace, which up to 2007, was an open terrace that was given to away supporters. However the Club have now erected a roof on this end and decided to give it to the home fans. This should really help boost the atmosphere within the stadium. Opposite is the Brook Road Stand. This stand which was opened in 1986, is a strange affair; a small double decker stand that has seating on the first tier and terracing below. It is known affectionately by the Brentford fans as the 'Wendy House'. The ground is complete with a set of four imposing floodlights.

What Is It Like For Visiting Supporters?

After being housed in the Ealing Road Terrace for the past few seasons, away fans now find themselves back at the other end in the Brook Road Stand. This stand has 600 seats in its upper tier and room for around 1,000 fans below in the terrace. This stand is covered, but there are a couple of prominent supporting pillars that may affect your view from the terraced area. There is a good selection of refreshments on offer including a selection of Wright's Pies & Pasties (£2.20), Herta Hot Dogs (£2.60), Cheeseburgers (£2.80), Chips (£1.20) and even Curry & Rice (£4). I had an enjoyable visit to the ground and didn't experience any problems.

Tim Porter, a visiting Torquay United supporter adds; 'The home fans were the most friendly I've come across for a long time - before kick-off, the stadium announcer asked all the home fans to put their hands together for the Torquay fans who had made such a long journey. I expected indifferent silence or abuse, but there was almost universal clapping!'

Where To Drink?

Brentford is famous for being the only ground in England that has a pub at every corner. If you are feeling thirsty, get there early and have a pint in all four. They are the Royal Oak (a small locals pub), The Griffin (serves Fullers real ale), The Princess Royal & The New Inn. The New Inn is the favoured pub for away supporters. Derek Hall, a visiting Hartlepool United fan adds; 'Probably the best pub out of the four is the Griffin, with the New Inn a fairly close second. On my visit the New Inn became so packed that we left in search of another pub and found the Potters Arms, which is a nice quiet little place for a beer, plus it has a large screen showing Sky Sports. This pub was just a couple of minutes walk away across the road from the New Inn'.

Jim Prentice informs me; 'besides the corner pubs, another favourite is the Waggon and Horses. This pub is in easy reach of the ground, especially by alighting at Kew Bridge station, just before Brentford on the Waterloo - Reading line'. Whilst Roger Stamp adds; 'Probably the best real ale pub in Brentford is the Magpie & Crown which is only five minutes walk away from the ground, on Brentford High Street. The pub has four real ales on tap and welcomes both home and away supporters'.

Phil Hodgin adds; 'There is also a pub called Stripes, which although being predominantly a home fans pub, is probably worth a visit if only to check out the pictorial history on the walls and the "Bees Knees Ale" from Fullers. Fans not wearing colours should be okay there'.

■ How To Get There & Where To Park?

Leave the M4 at junction 2 and take the A4, going around the Chiswick Roundabout so that you end up coming back on yourself. Continue along the A4 and at the first roundabout take a left onto the B455 (Ealing Road). The ground is located about half a mile down this road on your right. Street parking.

■ By Train/Tube

The nearest train station is Brentford, which is around five minutes walk away from the ground. This station is on the London Waterloo to Reading line, which normally runs every 15 minutes on Saturday afternoons. To get from the station to the ground, exit onto Station Road. Take the first right into Orchard Road, right again into Windmill Road and then first left into Hamilton Road which leads into New Road and the ground.

Caleb Johnstone-Cowan informs me; 'The nearest Underground station to the ground is South Ealing, which is on the Piccadilly Line. This tube station is around a 15-minute walk from the ground, down Ealing Road'. Mick Hubbard adds; 'Finding the ground is easy enough though - you simply turn right out of the tube station and just go straight down Ealing Road, then taking your life in your hands to cross the A4 at the bottom! Otherwise as you come out of the station cross over to the other side of Ealing Road and catch a number 65 bus down to the ground'.

■ Local Rivals

Queens Park Rangers & Fulham.

■ Admission Prices

Home Fans:

Refreshing Solutions Stand:
Adults £20,
OAP's & Students £14,
Juniors £5

Bill Axbey Stand:
Adults £19,
OAP's & Students £13,
Juniors £5

Ealing Road Terrace
Adults £15,
OAP's £8,
Juniors £5

Away Fans:

Brook Road Stand (Seating)
Adults £19,
OAP's & Students £13,
Juniors £5

Brook Road Stand (Terrace)
Adults £15,
OAP's & Students £8,
Juniors £5

* Students and the unemployed can buy adults tickets for the home areas at a discounted rate providing that they are purchased prior to matchday and that the necessary proof is shown (i.e current NUS card/UB40/photographic ID). This must be purchased in advance of matchday.

■ Programme & Fanzines

Official Programme £2.50
Thorne In The Side Fanzine £1
Hey Jude Fanzine £1
Beesotted £2

■ Record Attendance

39,626 v Preston North End,
FA Cup 6th Round, March 5th, 1938.

■ Average Attendance

2006-2007: 5,778 (League One)

■ Did You Know?

That the surrounding land was formerly owned by the Griffin Brewery, hence the ground name; Griffin Park.

Bury

Gigg Lane

Ground Name: Gigg Lane
Capacity: 11,669 (all seated)
Address: Gigg Lane, Bury, Lancashire, BL9 9HR
Main Telephone No: 0161-764-4881
Main Fax No: 0161-764-5521
Ticket Office: 0161-705-2144
Ticket Office Fax: 0161-763-3103
Team Nickname: The Shakers
Year Ground Opened: 1885
Pitch Size: 112 x 73 yards
Home Kit Colours: White & Blue

Official Website:
www.buryfc.co.uk

Unofficial Website:
Bury Mad - www.bury-mad.co.uk (Footy Mad Network)

What's The Ground Like?

The ground was completely re-built in the 1990s with the last 'new' stand, the Cemetery End, completed in 1999. The new stands have vastly improved the overall look of the ground, whilst at the same time making it an all seated one. The Manchester Road End is a fair-sized stand that is covered and has an electric scoreboard; however it does not run the full width of the pitch, one side ending with the edge of the penalty box. The other end, the Cemetery End, is a former terrace that has been demolished and replaced with a relatively new all seater stand. This stand extends around one corner to the South Stand and looks quite smart. There is a small police control box suspended beneath the roof in this corner of it.
On one side is the Main Stand, with raised seating meaning that supporters have to climb a small set of steps to enter it. Part of the front has a small box like structure, with a number of windows running along the front.
It particularly caught my eye, as with the windows being almost at pitch level, I wondered just how many broken windows they get each season. Opposite is the South Stand, similar in design to the ends with a TV gantry suspended below its roof. The one open corner of the ground has a small block of flats situated behind it, but the rest of the ground has a number of trees visible behind and above the stands, making the ground more attractive.

Jeff Johnson informs me; 'Le Stade de Gigg' as the locals call it, is now shared with FC United of Manchester'.

What Is It Like For Visiting Supporters?

After taking account of an online poll amongst home fans, the Club have decided to relocate away supporters from the Manchester Road End to the opposite end, the Cemetery End. This area holds 2,500 fans and it could be argued that this is the best area within Gigg Lane to watch a game as there are no supporting pillars to hinder your view. The end is covered and has good acoustics, meaning that even a small amount of fans can really generate some noise. The catering is quite good, with a range of burgers and hot dogs (£2.20) and the delicious 'Football's Famous Chicken Balti Pie' (£2.20). On the whole Bury is normally a relaxed and enjoyable day out.

Where To Drink?

There are plenty of pubs around the ground and along Manchester Road in particular. There is also a supporters club at the ground, which sometimes allows in small numbers of away fans. My pick of the pubs on Manchester Road is the Swan & Cemetery, around a ten-minute walk from the ground. This Thwaites pub is quite comfortable, serves good hand-pulled beer and has a separate restaurant area. Nearer to the ground are the Pack Horse & the Staff Of Life. The Pack Horse on my last visit seemed to be the main pub for away fans and has a conveniently situated chippy around the corner from it. The Staff Of Life is a stone's throw from the Park and is a basic pub serving hand-pulled Lee's. Also recommended on Manchester Road, is the Waterloo, nearer the town centre.

Bury

How To Get There & Where To Park?

Leave the M66 at Junction 3. Take the left hand exit at the junction and follow this road until you come to the junction with the A56 Manchester Road. At this T-junction which has traffic lights, turn right towards Bury. You will pass the Swan & Cemetery pub on your left and then some playing fields. At the end of the playing fields just before the traffic lights and a couple of pubs, turn right into Gigg Lane for the ground. However please note that Gigg Lane is normally closed on matchdays and the ground itself is not easily seen from the A56. Street parking.

By Train/Metro

Bury Metrolink is served by trams from Manchester Victoria & Piccadilly mainline railway stations. Bury Metrolink station is about a 15-minute walk from the ground. Turn left out of the station along a pedestrian walkway going underneath the dual carriageway. On the other side of the dual carriageway turn right towards the Town Hall. Just before the Town Hall turn left into Knowsley Street and at the bottom of Knowsley Street turn left onto the main A56 Manchester Road. It is then a case of going straight along Manchester Road for about half a mile and you will reach Gigg Lane on your left. Thanks to Andy Grainger for supplying the directions.

Jon Hall adds; 'Alternatively bus numbers 90, 92, 135 and 137 run every ten minutes down Manchester Road past the end of Gigg Lane'.

Local Rivals

Bolton Wanderers & Rochdale.

Admission Prices

Home Fans:

Main & South Stands
Adults £16,
Under 21's £10,
Concessions £7

Manchester Road Stand
Adults £14,
Under 21's £10,
Concessions £7

Away Fans:

Cemetery End
Adults £14,
Under 21's £10,
Concessions £7

Concessions apply to juniors, senior citizens, disabled and the unemployed.

Programme

Official Programme: £2.

Record Attendance

35,000 v Bolton Wanderers,
FA Cup 3rd Round, January 9th, 1960.

Modern All Seated Attendance Record:
9,115 v Burnley, December 26th, 1999.

Average Attendance

2006-2007: 2,534 (League Two)

Did You Know?

The Club are nicknamed 'The Shakers' due to their first chairman, John T Ingham who, before a Lancashire Cup game, said "We will shake them. In fact, we are the Shakers." The local press picked up on this quote and the nickname stuck.

Chester City

Saunders Honda Stadium

Ground Name: Saunders Honda Stadium (but still known to many fans as the Deva Stadium).
Capacity: 6,012 (3,284 seated)
Address: Bumpers Lane, Chester, CH1 4LT
Main Telephone No: 01244-371-376
Fax No: 01244-390-265
Team Nickname: The Blues
Year Ground Opened: 1992
Home Kit Colours: Blue & White

Official Website:
www.chestercityfc.net

Unofficial Website:
Unofficial Chester City - www.chester-city.co.uk
Deva Chat Message Board - www.devachat.com

■ What's The Ground Like?

The ground was opened in 1992. All four sides are covered and are roughly the same height, making the stadium look quite tidy. Each stand has perspex windshields to each side, whilst the corners of the ground are open. The stadium is a small, fairly simple affair with two sides being seated and the two ends being terrace. The East Stand is slightly taller than the facing West Stand, having a few more rows of seating and some enclosed glassed viewing areas at the back of it. The home North Terrace was during the 2006/07 renamed the Harry Mcnally Terrace after a former manager. The stadium is completed with a set of four thin modern floodlight pylons.

■ What Is It Like For Visiting Supporters?

Away fans are mostly housed in the South Terrace at one end of the ground, where around 1,200 supporters can be accommodated. 600 seats are also made available to away supporters in part of the West Stand. On my one visit when Birmingham played there, the Blues fans were allocated the whole of the West Stand as well as the South Terrace, which made for a great atmosphere. It was a friendly and relaxed day out.

■ Where To Drink?

Unfortunately the Social Club at the ground no longer admits away supporters and as there are no pubs close to the ground, it means a 15-minute walk into the city centre to find a local hostelry. Lee Wilcox recommends 'the Coach and Horses and the Dublin Packet near the Town Hall. The latter was once owned by ex-Everton striker Dixie Dean. Near to the train station down by the canal is the excellent Old Harkers Arms which also serves good food'. Whilst Mark Pilling adds; 'Also worth a visit are the 'Ship Victory' on George Street and the Mill Hotel. The latter serves a large selection of real ales'.

■ How To Get There & Where To Park?

The ground is located out of town on an industrial estate. Stay on the M56 until you reach a roundabout at the end of the motorway. Follow the signs to North Wales & Queensferry A5117. After around one and a half miles you will reach a set of traffic lights where you need to bear left on to the A550 (signposted North Wales & Queensferry). Then from the A550, take the A548 towards Chester. Head straight through the first set of traffic lights and after passing a Vauxhall and then a Renault garage on your left, turn right at the next lights (there is a Volvo Garage on the corner) into Sovereign Way. Continue to the end of Sovereign Way and then turn right into Bumpers Lane and the entrance to the Club car park is just down on the right.

There is plenty of car parking available at the ground (£3), however if you use the club car park, it can be quite difficult to get away easily after the match. Henry Willard, a visiting Yeovil fan adds; 'It may be an idea if you can plan an appropriate route, to stay in the left hand lane as you leave the car park and head westwards away from the city centre, as most of the traffic after the game seems to go towards town'.

■ By Train

Chester railway station is over two miles from the ground, so it is probably best to jump in a taxi.

Local Rivals
Wrexham, Tranmere Rovers.

Admission Prices

Executive Area:
Adults £29, Concessions £24

East & West Stands:
Adults £16, Concessions £11, Under 16's £5

South & Harry Mcnally North Stands:
Adults £14, Concessions £9, Under 16's £4

Concessions apply to over 65's or students with a valid NUS card.

Programme
Official Programme £2.

Record Attendance
At Sealand Road:
20,500 v Chelsea
FA Cup 3rd Round, January 15th, 1952.

At Deva Stadium:
5,987 v Scarborough
Conference League, April 17th, 2004.

Average Attendance
2006-2007: 2,700 (League Two)

Did You Know?
That most of the ground (apart from half the East Stand and the club offices) is actually situated in Wales.

Chesterfield

Recreation Ground

Ground Name: Recreation Ground
Capacity: 8,504
Address: Saltergate, Chesterfield, S40 4SX
Main Telephone No: 01246-209-765
Ticket Office No: As Above
Fax No: 01246-556-799
Pitch Size: 113 x 71 yards
Team Nickname: The Spireites or Blues
Year Ground Opened: 1884
Home Kit Colours: Blue & White

Official Website:
www.chesterfield-fc.co.uk

Unofficial Websites:
Spirezine - www.spirezine.co.uk (Rivals Network)
Compton Street - www.chesterfield-mad.co.uk (Footy Mad Network)

What's The Ground Like?

At one end is the Spion Kop, a covered terrace for home supporters. Opposite is the small, open Cross Street End terrace. The covered Main Stand is medium sized, and unusual in having its seating area raised above the pitch, thus there are a number of stair wells at the front of the stand leading up to the seats. There are a number of supporting pillars in this stand, which could restrict your view. This stand dates back to 1936 and could really do with at least a lick of paint, as from the outside it looks very rusty in parts. The other side, the Compton Street Side, had a lot of work carried out on it during 2002 and this former terrace has now been made all seated. This stand is partly covered (to the rear) and has a row of supporting pillars. It has an unusual television gantry perched on its roof. It was originally constructed in the early 1920s.

Future Ground Developments

Following a public enquiry the Club have received the green light to build a new 10,600 capacity stadium at the disused Dema glass factory site, next to the Chesterfield-Sheffield bypass/Sheffield Road, about one mile from the town centre. The club though are still awaiting formal planning permission to be granted. If this is given this Summer, then building work could begin in October/November this year, with the stadium being completed in October/November 2008. Dema Glass have been awarded the contract to build the stadium, with Saltergate to be redeveloped for housing. Andy Ford adds; 'The good news for supporters is that the Dema Glass site is easy to get to and there are plenty of pubs & chip shops near by!'

What Is It Like For Visiting Supporters?

Away fans are primarily housed in the Cross Street Terrace at one end of the ground, where 1,400 fans can be accommodated. This area is uncovered and open to the elements so be prepared to get wet. Additionally away supporters are also given 450 seats in the covered Main Stand. Please note that the 'seats' allocated to away fans in the Main Stand are in fact wooden benches and the facilities in this stand are pretty poor and like the ground are showing their age. On the plus side Chesterfield is a pleasant town with plenty of eating and drinking places within easy walking distance of the ground. Although normally a relaxed and friendly day out, the local constabulary often have a high presence and regularly film supporters before, during and after games, which I found to be intrusive.

Chesterfield

Where To Drink?

The Barley Mow in Saltergate is worth a visit as they have scantily-clad barmaids serving the beer. For once it was a pleasure to wait at the bar to be served! There is also 'The County' pub which is across the road from the Barley Mow. Tricia Hastings recommends the Market Tavern in the town centre, which apparently is a good real ale outlet. Derek Hall, a visiting Hartlepool United fan adds; 'Another cracking pub for away fans is the appropriately named Chesterfield Arms. Coming out of the away end, it is a right turn, then turn first left. No more than a five minute walk away. It also next door to a pub called The Industry, which is also popular with away fans'.

How To Get There & Where To Park?

Leave the M1 at Junction 29 and take the A617 towards Chesterfield. On reaching the edge of the town centre go straight across the first roundabout and then the next, passing the famous Chesterfield Church with the crooked spire on your left. As the road divides, keep to your left, going around an open car park. This road leads into Saltergate, where you will pass the Barley Mow pub on your left and the Town Hall car park, before reaching the ground on your right.

I parked in the Town Hall council car park on Saltergate (£2.40 for four hours) and walked the relatively short distance (five minutes) to the ground. There seemed to be plenty of other car parks in the town centre to choose from.

By Train

Chesterfield railway station is walkable from the ground and takes around ten minutes. Just follow the road out of the station (Corporation Street), and go straight across a big roundabout and you will find yourself on Saltergate. The ground is on your right. Thanks to Kevin Finney for providing the directions.

Please note that I have received reports of Police 'rounding up' away fans arriving at the station and escorting them to the ground. So you may want to bear this in mind if you intend travelling by rail. Chris Rudd, a visiting Millwall fan, adds; 'The Police do indeed keep the visiting fans at the station, but at timely intervals escort groups of them to the local pubs; The Chesterfield Arms & The Industry. The Police I spoke to were friendly and their approach low key. The downside is that the pubs close 30 minutes before kick-off to allow time for the Police to get you into the ground.

Local Rivals

Mansfield Town, Sheffield Wednesday & Sheffield United.

Admission Prices

Home Fans:

Main Stand (Executive Area):
Adults £25,
No Concessions

Main Stand (centre):
Adults £19,
Over 65's/Under 18's £13
Under 14's £13

Main Stand (wings):
Adults £17,
Over 65's/Under 18's £12
Under 14's £11

Compton Street Stand:
Adults £17,
Over 65's/Under 18's £12,
Under 14's £7

Family Area:
Adults £17,
Over 65's /Under 18's £12,
Under 14's £3

Graysons Kop Terrace:
Adults £17,
Over 65's/Under 18's £9,
Under 14's £5

Away Fans:

Main Stand (wings):
Adults £17,
Over 65's/Under 18's £12,
Under 14's £11

Cross Street Terrace:
Adults £15,
Over 65's/Under 18's £9,
Under 14's £5

Programme

Official Programme £2.50.

Record Attendance

30,986 v Newcastle United,
Division Two, April 7th, 1949.

Average Attendance

2006-2007: 4,406 (League One)

Did You Know?

That Chesterfield were the last League Club to install floodlights. They were switched on in October 1967.

Dagenham & Redbridge

Glyn Hopkin Stadium

Ground Name:	Glyn Hopkin Stadium (but still known to many fans as Victoria Road)
Capacity:	6,000
Address:	Dagenham, Essex, RM10 7XL
Main Telephone No:	0208-592-1549
Fax No:	0208-593-7227
Team Nickname:	Daggers
Year Ground Opened:	1917
Pitch Size:	112 x 72 yards
Home Kit Colours:	Red, White & Blue

Official Website:
www.daggers.co.uk

■ What's The Ground Like?

On one side of the ground is the new Main Stand that was constructed during 2001 and is now sponsored by Carling. The stand is all seated and covered and has a press area at the back of it. The stand is elevated above pitch level which means that supporters have to climb small sets of steps at the front of it, to gain access to the stand. The stand though, only runs for three quarters of the length of the pitch and at one end another separate stand exists.
This small covered, seated stand, was previously reserved for families, but promotion to the Football League now means that it has been allocated to away supporters.
The rest of the ground is terracing, with small open terraces behind each goal, and a small covered North Stand terrace running down the other side of the pitch. This North Terrace is known affectionately by the Dagenham fans as 'The Sieve' as apparently at one time it was famed for its leaking roof. The home end, the Bury Road End, has a small digital clock sitting amongst the advertising hoardings at the rear of it and is known as the 'Clock End'.

■ What Is It Like For Visiting Supporters?

The majority of away fans are housed in the Pondfield Road terrace at one end of the ground. This area accommodates 1,200 fans. It is a small terrace, being around 10 rows high and is open to the elements, so be prepared to get wet. However, the view from this part of the ground isn't bad and the refreshments are excellent. A small section of seats is also allocated, in a small stand adjacent to the Carling Stand. Although this stand does have cover, it does have a number of supporting pillars that may impede your view. There is normally a good atmosphere within the ground and there are normally no problems for visiting fans.

■ Where To Drink?

Neil Le Milliere, a visiting Exeter City fan, informs me; 'There is a fair-sized social club at the ground, which allows in away supporters for a nominal fee. Otherwise there are three pubs in walking distance of the ground. The nearest is The Eastbrook, which is down the hill towards Golds Gym. There is also The Railway which is down the road beside the station. A ten minute walk away is the Bull, which is down Rainham Road (going past the Jet Garage), by a large roundabout'.

■ How To Get There & Where To Park?

Leave the M25 at Junction 27 and take the M11 towards London. At the end of the M11 continue onto the A406 towards Docklands (A13) and London City Airport. At the intersection with the A13, turn onto this road towards Dagenham/Dartford Tunnel. As you near Dagenham, you will see a cinema complex on your left. At this point you leave the A13 and join the A1306 towards Dagenham. At the third set of traffic lights turn left at the McDonalds into Ballards Road. At the end of this road you will come to a large roundabout, (known as the Bull roundabout, after the public house of the same name) at which you turn left, into Rainham Road. Proceed up Rainham Road passing Dagenham East tube station on the left and Victoria Road is a quarter of a mile further on, on the same side of the road. There is a fair sized car park at the ground which is free, but is normally full 45 minutes ahead of kick off. Otherwise street parking.

■ By Tube/Train

Take the District Line to Dagenham East (and not Dagenham Heathway). Turn left as you come out of the station and the ground is clearly sign posted and only five minutes walk away. Please note that the journey by tube from Central London can take around 45 minutes. Neil Le Milliere adds; 'The tube journey out there can be a bit of a nightmare and it's probably better to get a train from Fenchurch Street to Barking station and then a tube to Dagenham from there'.

■ Admission Prices

Home Fans:

Seating*:

Carling Stand (Centre):
Adults £19, Concessions £13.

Carling Stand (Victoria Road Wing):
Adults £18, Concessions £12.

Carling Stand (Family Area):
Adults £12, Concessions £7.

Away Fans:

Terrace*:
Adults £15, Concessions £10.

* Apart from the Family Area, the prices quoted above are for matchday. Tickets bought prior to matchday are offered at a discounted price, typically £2 on an adult ticket and up to £4 on a junior (under 16) terrace ticket.

■ Programme & Fanzine

Official Programme £2.50.

■ Record Attendance

Record Attendance:
5,949 v Ipswich Town,
FA Cup 3rd Round, January 5th, 2002

■ Average Attendance

2006-2007: 1,756 (Conference National League)

■ Did You Know?

That the present Club came into being in 1992 when Redbridge Forest FC merged with Dagenham FC. The new club decided to play at Dagenham's Victoria Road Ground, which Dagenham had previously played in since 1955.

Darlington

96.6 TFM Darlington Arena

Ground Name:	96.6 TFM Darlington Arena
Capacity:	25,000 (all seated)
Address:	Neasham Road, Darlington, DL2 1DL
Main Telephone No:	01325-387-000
Fax No:	01325-387-050
Ticket Office:	0870-0272-949
Pitch Size:	110 yards x 74 yards
Team Nickname:	The Quakers
Year Ground Opened:	2003
Home Kit Colours:	Black & White

Official Website:
www.darlington-fc.net

Unofficial Websites:
Darlo Uncovered - www.darlofc.co.uk (Rivals Network)
The Tin Shed - www.the-tinshed.co.uk
DAFTS - www.dafts.co.uk
Vital Darlington - www.darlington.vitalfootball.co.uk (Vital Football Network)

■ What's The Ground Like?

The stadium, which was opened in 2003, is impressive-looking and is of a good size. It is completely enclosed with all the corners filled with seating. All the stands are single-tiered and of an equal height. There is a perspex strip that runs around the stadium, beneath the roof, to allow more light to reach the pitch. The stands look virtually identical apart from the South Stand, which has a row of executive boxes running across the back of it. In the South East corner of the stadium is a Police Control Box, whilst in the North East corner there is a large video screen.

■ What Is It Like For Visiting Supporters?

Away fans are housed in the East Stand at one end of the stadium, where around 3,000 supporters can be accommodated. Martin Redfern, a visiting Scunthorpe fan informs me; 'It's a nice stadium and there seems to be plenty of parking (although I heard several grumbles about the £5 charge!). The usual food and drink are on offer inside from well-run & well-staffed outlets and the view from the away end is very good. I hardly noticed the stewards (which is good), but the atmosphere was a little subdued on my visit. No surprise really with just over 3,600 fans sitting in a stadium that can seat over 20,000'. Peter Llewellyn adds; 'Although I'm not that tall at six foot, I found the leg room to be one of the tightest that I have come across at a new stadium. I was so uncomfortable that I seriously thought about leaving before the end'.

Although the stadium is conservative in its design and shows little character, the acoustics inside are very good as well as the facilities on offer. It also has the best display of pies that I have ever come across at a football ground. Like going into your local bakers, glass cabinets display the rows of different hot pies that are available. These included pork pies (served hot), minced beef & onion and steak and kidney all at £1.30 each, plus as Tim Porter informs me they also now offer 'a steak and gravy pie with mushy peas and mint sauce for £2'. This 'Aladdin's Cave' of pies certainly had the desired effect on myself and my colleagues as we promptly ate a pie before the game started and another (or two) at half time (it did help our appetite though, that it was a bitterly cold day!). However the downside was that teas and coffees were only available from a vending machine (which also had soup, crisps & chocolate), which meant queuing for a second time. The atmosphere was boosted somewhat by the presence of a drummer in the home end.

■ Where To Drink?

The stadium is located on the outskirts of Darlington and there are not that many pubs in the vicinity. Steve Duffy informs me; 'There is the Copper Beech Pub on Neasham

Road, a ten-minute walk towards the town centre. Otherwise there is the Tawny Owl Pub, a Vintage Inn which is about a quarter of a mile the other side of the A66 roundabout. This though is more of a restaurant than pub, but decent enough for lunch'.

It may therefore be an idea to drink in the town centre, where there are plenty of pubs to be found. For the real ale buffs there is the Number Twenty 2 in Coniscliffe Road, a large spacious pub that offers food as well as a good range of beers. Mick Hubbard, a visiting Aston Villa fan adds; 'We ducked down a side street called Mechanic's Yard (which is opposite the indoor market, near the big train sculpture) and discovered a gem of a pub called the Quaker House. The small bar was an Aladdin's Cave of real ales, having ten on tap. It was a fantastic place and also has a separate cafe upstairs'. There is also a Wetherspoons outlet situated on Skinnersgate.

At the stadium itself there are two bars; one called 'Bar 66' and the other called the 'Corner Bar'. Both admit away fans, however, as you would expect, they get very crowded. Otherwise alcohol is available on the concourses inside the stadium in the form of Fosters Lager & John Smiths Bitter.

■ How To Get There & Where To Park?

From The South:
Leave the A1 (M) at Junction 57 and take the A66 towards Darlington/Teeside. Continue straight along the A66 going across two roundabouts. At the third roundabout you can clearly see the stadium just over on your left. Turn left at this roundabout into Neasham Road for the stadium.

From The North:
Leave the A1(M) at Junction 59 and take the A167 towards Darlington. Then take the A1150 towards Teesside. Turn onto the A66 towards Darlington and you will come to the stadium on your right. Although this route is not the shortest it does avoid driving through Darlington town centre.

■ Car Parking

There is a fair sized car park at the stadium which costs £5 per car. Although the stewards do their best to let the cars get away quickly at the end of the game, it is almost an impossible task, with supporters also walking through car parks to leave the area, so expect some delay. If you continue on past the stadium towards Darlington, then there is some street parking to be found, although this can be quite a walk from the stadium as there is a residents only parking scheme in operation on matchdays in the streets nearest to the ground.

■ By Train

Darlington train station is around one and a half miles away from the stadium. Either get a taxi, a bus (see below) or walk it; leave the station and turn right past the taxi rank and towards the car park. Cross the covered footbridge back over the railway into Albert Road. Go right down this road and then take a right into Neasham Road. The stadium is about a mile further on down this road on your left. It should take about 25 minutes in total to walk it.

Simon Brodie informs me; 'The Club now pay for a subsidised bus which runs every 15 minutes from Tubwell Row in the town centre to the ground. It costs just £1 for a return ticket. On Saturday afternoons the first bus departs at 1.15pm and the last at 2.30pm. The first bus back is at 4.45pm from outside the ground, with last leaving at 5.30pm. Away fans will be welcomed on this service as long as they are well behaved'.

■ Local Rivals

Hartlepool United.

■ Admission Prices

All areas of the stadium*:
Adults: £16,
OAP's/Students £11,
Under 16's £7,
Under 11's £5,
Under 7's Free.
Family Ticket (2 adults + 2 children) £40**

* A £1 discount is available on these ticket prices providing that the ticket is purchased prior to matchday.

** A £5 discount is available on this ticket price providing that the ticket is purchased prior to matchday.

Concessions apply to over 60's, under 16's and students.

■ Programme

Official Programme £2.50.

■ Record Attendance

At The New Stadium:
11,600 v Kidderminster Harriers
Division 3, August 16th, 2003.

At Feethams:
21,023 v Bolton Wanderers,
League Cup 3rd Round, November 14th, 1960.

■ Average Attendance

2006-2007: 3,559 (League Two)

■ Did You Know?

That even though the stadium has only been open for four years it has already had four different names. First it was simply known as the 'New Stadium', then it was christened the 'Reynolds Arena', before being renamed the 'Williamson Motors Stadium' and now more recently the '96.6 TFM Darlington Arena'.

Grimsby Town

Blundell Park

Ground Name:	Blundell Park
Capacity:	9,546 (all seated)
Address:	Blundell Park, Cleethorpes, DN35 7PY
Main Telephone No:	01472-605-050
Fax No:	01472-693-665
Team Nickname:	The Mariners
Year Ground Opened:	1899
Pitch Size:	111 x 75 yards
Home Kit Colours:	Black & White

Official Website:
www.gtfc.co.uk

Unofficial Websites:
Electronic Fishcake - www.grimsby.org (Rivals Network)
Cod Almighty - www.codalmighty.com
Supporters Trust - www.gtst.net

■ What's The Ground Like?

At one side of the ground is the Carlsberg Stand, which is the tallest stand and is two tiered and covered. However this stand only runs half the length of the pitch, straddling the half way line. Opposite is the old Main Stand, which is small covered all seated stand and has a large number of supporting pillars running across the front of it. Both ends are small covered affairs. Home fans are located in the Pontoon Stand at one end, away fans at the opposite end in the Osmond Stand. The corner between this stand and the Main Stand is also filed, as the stands are joined at this point. For big games the Club increases the capacity of the ground by 500 by installing blocks of temporary seating in the open corners of the ground.

It is interesting to note that the Pontoon Stand gets its name from the fish docks in Grimsby and as at one time many of the crowd would have worked on 'the pontoon', it is an apt name. Grimsby fans still identify with their town's fishing heritage, with the chant 'We only sing when we're fishing!

■ Future Ground Developments

After a lengthy process, the Club have received outline planning permission to build a new stadium at the Great Coates Interchange of the A180 and A1136. The new stadium has a proposed final capacity of 20,100, although initially the first phase of the scheme will see around 12,000 seats being put in place. The stadium will be called the ConocoPhillips Stadium, following a corporate sponsorship scheme. The development, which will cost around £14m, will also include a retail park. Formal time scales have yet to be announced as to when construction will begin, but the Club hope that they will be kicking off in their new home for the start of the 2008/09 season.

■ What Is It Like For Visiting Supporters?

Away fans are located in the Osmond Stand, at one end of the ground, where 2,200 supporters can be accommodated. One downside of this stand is that there are a number of supporting pillars which could impede your view of the game. Blundell Park is a rather small ground and sometimes gets over criticised by visiting fans. But there is normally always a passionate crowd, which contributes to a good atmosphere. Remember though to wrap up warm as there can be a biting wind coming off the North Sea.

■ Where To Drink?

Dave Peasgood has informed me that the unofficial away fans pub is the Leaking Boot (formerly Darley's Hotel) which is halfway between Cleethorpes and Blundell Park on the north side of Grimsby Road. To get there head down the A180 and drive past the ground. It's about 400 yards further up the road on the left. It is a large pub and car park and allows in children. The fish & chips in

Cleethorpes are legendary and there are some good outlets located near to the ground. Josh's fish and chip shop near the Leaking Boot comes recommended. Other recommendations by Dave include the Blundell Park Hotel, which if you arrive early serves some good food at reasonable prices (expect to pay around £5 for a good portion of fish and chips). The Rutland Arms is also recommended for both home and away fans to mingle, however this is some distance from the ground and doesn't allow in children. (it is about about half a mile before Blundell Park; turn left at Ramsdens superstore and left again, and you'll see the pub at the opposite end of their car park. If in coaches, then from where you will be parked, head back the way you came, along the sea wall for 5 minutes and you'll see the pub). The Imperial pub by the ground is not recommended for away fans. There is also a McDonalds situated right by Blundell Park.

■ How To Get There & Where To Park?

First thing to remember is that the ground is not actually in Grimsby, but the neighbouring town of Cleethorpes. The ground is on the A180 which runs between Grimsby & Cleethorpes. Cleethorpes is well signposted from Grimsby town centre.

There is no car park at the ground, therefore only street parking. As you drive along the A180 towards the ground, the home end appears first, then after the McDonalds is the away end. From there, continue towards Cleethorpes and try any of the side streets to the left or preferably the right and you should find a parking spot okay.

■ By Train

Cleethorpes railway station is about a mile from the ground and takes around 15-20 minutes to walk. Exit the station and turn right; then turn left onto Station Road. At the end of Station Road turn right onto the High Street. Follow this road down to the roundabout; where you turn right onto the Grimsby road (A180). Continue straight for approximately half a mile and you will see the floodlights of the ground on your right. Turn right into Neville Street and then left onto Harrington Street; entrance to the Osmond Stand for away fans is on the left. Thanks to Andy Cowling for providing the directions.

■ Local Rivals

Scunthorpe United, Hull City & Lincoln City.

■ Admission Prices

Home Fans:

Upper Carlsberg Stand
Adults £17,
OAP's £11,
Juniors £7

Lower Carlsberg Stand
Adults £15,
OAP's £11,
Juniors £7

Pontoon Stand
Adults: £15,
OAP's £11,
Juniors £7

Main Stand
Adults: £17,
OAP's £11,
Juniors £7

■ Away Fans:

Osmond Stand
Adults: £17,
OAP's £11,
Juniors £7

■ Programme

Official Programme £2.50.

■ Record Attendance

31,651 v Wolverhampton Wanderers,
FA Cup 5th Round, February 20th, 1937.

Modern All Seated Attendance Record:
9,528 v Sunderland,
March 13th 1999

■ Average Attendance

2006-2007: 4,027 (League Two)

■ Did You Know?

Part of the Main Stand dates back to 1901, possibly making it the oldest surviving stand in league football.

Hereford United

Edgar Street

Ground Name: Edgar Street
Capacity: 8,843 (1,761 Seated)
Address: Edgar Street,
Hereford, HR4 9JU
Main Telephone No: 01432-276-666
Fax No: 01432-341-359
Team Nickname: Bulls
Year Ground Opened: 1924*
Home Kit Colours: Black & White

Official Website:
www.herefordunited.co.uk - www.herefordunited.co.uk

Unofficial Website:
Bulls Online - www.bolsa-hufc.com

■ What's The Ground Like?

On one side is the Floors 2 Go (Edgar Street) Stand, which is a strange-looking covered, two-tiered affair. The upper tier is all seated and overhangs the lower terrace, which has a number of supporting pillars. Part of this stand which was built in 1974 is given to away supporters. Opposite is the Merton Meadow Stand, which is a raised, covered single-tier, all seated stand. This stand which was opened in 1968, is used as a Family Stand. At the front of this are the team dugouts and a number of windows belonging to offices and Club Bar. On my last visit I wondered just how many of these get broken during the season, by balls that have gone astray. The home end, the Merton Meadow Terrace, is a classic-looking, partly covered (to the rear) stand. This stand is semi circular in shape, going out around the back of the goal and has a number of supporting pillars. Opposite is the Blackfriars End, which is another partly covered terrace. This end is normally only used for larger games, where it can house both home and away fans. The ground also has some large, unusual-looking floodlights.

The pitch is the largest in the top five divisions and only the former Wembley had a larger playing area. There are plans to relocate in the future as the club are in negotiations about a move with the local council and developers. Fans will find it hard to leave Edgar Street as it has been the ground which has seen many a cup upset, most famously Newcastle who lost 2-1 here in 1972. It is intended to have Edgar Street redeveloped as part of a regeneration of the area, including the cattle market and Merton Meadow car park area. The football ground will be part of a new leisure, administration and retail centre in the city'.

Special thanks to Terry Goodwin for providing a lot of the information for this page.

■ What Is It Like For Visiting Supporters?

Away fans are housed on one side (towards the Blackfriars End) of the Floors 2 Go (Edgar Street) Stand at one side of the pitch. This stand has an upper tier of seating that overhangs a lower tier of terracing.
Going to Hereford is usually a happy and relaxed occasion, however unfortunately there have been some recent incidents around the ground, so exercise caution. On the whole though, away fans often mingle in the pubs with United fans before and after games and a visit to Edgar Street should be an enjoyable one. Cup days are also great occasions, as a live 'Prize' Bull is paraded around the ground and the Swede is blessed. This often gives the team the incentive to upset the odds. Facilities within the ground are basic, but there are a good range of refreshments available, including the delicious 'Football's Famous Chicken Balti Pie' (£2).

■ Where To Drink?

There is a club bar at the ground, called Legends, which is open before and after the game. This small bar enjoys views across the ground. Scott Lyndon adds, 'We found the Oxford Arms on the edge of the main car park friendly. It has a beer garden and Sky sports'. As the stadium is in the city centre, there are many pubs and chip shops around the stadium within walking distances which serve good food and have a friendly atmosphere. Not too far from the ground (five minutes walk) is the Newmarket Tavern, which has a large screen and was quite comfortable. I have had mixed reports about this pub, so use your discretion. To find it; with the Club Shop behind you, turn right and walk up to the end of the stand and out of the car park. Turn left at the end of the ground, and at the end of this road turn right, towards the town centre. As you get to the ring road, the pub is on your right. If you arrive at the ground early, then by turning left instead and following the ring road to its end, you will come to the Victory Tavern. A selection of real ales and a bar which resembles half an old sailing ship, complete with cannons!

■ How To Get There & Where To Park?

From The North
Leave the M5 at Junction 8 and take the M50 towards South Wales. At Junction 2, take the A417 towards Ledbury and then the A438 towards Hereford. Keep on the A438 into Hereford and after passing the Victory pub on the left, bear right onto the inner ring road that goes around the town centre. At the large roundabout, turn right onto the A49 Edgar Street and then right again into Blackfriars Street. The ground and car park entrance are down on the left.

From the South & London
Exit the M4 at Junction 15 and take the A417 to Gloucester. Then follow the A49 to Ross-on-Wye and onto Hereford. At the roundabout, take the Grayfriars Bridge/Victoria Street road. At Steels Garage, keep left into Edgar Street. Take Blackfriars Street (right) immediately before the football stadium. Turn left for parking.

From the South West
M5 until Junction 18a to take the M49. Join the M4 at Junction 22 and turn left over the New Severn Bridge. At Junction 24 take the A449 and follow until the Raglan roundabout. Take the Monmouth (A49 east) road and follow through first roundabout. At the roundabout, take the A4137. Join the A49 (left) and follow the signs for Hereford. At the second roundabout, take the Grayfriars Bridge/Victoria Street road. Then As South.

There is a large pay and display car park at the ground, which costs 80p for four hours.

■ By Train

Hereford Station is under a ten-minute walk away. Carl Brace provides directions to the ground; 'Come out of the station and turn left and down the road towards the Safeway supermarket. Cut through the Safeway car park (heading left) and follow the pedestrian walkway out of the store out onto Commercial Road. Go left down Commercial Road, where you will pass the Merton Hotel on your right and a Wetherspoons pub on your left. At the top of the road at the traffic lights, turn right (against the direction of the traffic) into Blueschool Street. Keep walking along here until you come to a set of lights and a multi storey car park opposite and to the right (this is Widemarsh Street). Cross over and bear slightly right and cut up a walkway between the car park and Garrick House (council offices) where you come into a car park (if you head left you will find the Newmarket Pub) head right and walk out the car park. Turn left and you can't miss the ground, it's on your right'.

Fabrinelli provides these alternative directions which avoid the town centre; 'Follow the road out from the station until you get to Rockfield DIY. At this crossroads take a left turn so that you are looking up a big hill. Walk for about 2 minutes and take the first left turning (before the hill). Walk to the end of this road (Barrs Court Road) where you will see a mini roundabout. Take the left turning and walk across the bridge footpath. Stay on this winding pavement for about 2 or 3 minutes until you see two car sales rooms on the other side of the road - there is a gap between the two garages and this leads into the Merton Meadow car park (footy ground car park) where you will see the ground'.

■ Local Rivals

Shrewsbury Town & Kidderminster Harriers.

■ Admission Prices

All Areas:

Seating:
Adults £15,
Concessions £13*

Terrace:
Adults £13,
Concessions £10*

* Club members can qualify for a £1 discount on these concession ticket prices. Concessions apply to Over 65's and Under 16's.

■ Programme

Official Programme £2

■ Record Attendance

18,114 v Sheffield Wednesday,
FA Cup 3rd Round, January 4th, 1958.

■ Average Attendance

2006-2007: 3,374 (League Two)

■ Did You Know?

That the Club have a rousing motto - Our greatest glory lies not in never having fallen but in rising when we fall.

* Hereford United moved into Edgar Street when the Club was formed in 1924. However the ground was already being used prior to that date by Hereford City Football Club.

Lincoln City

Sincil Bank

Ground Name:	Sincil Bank
Capacity:	10,130 (all seated)
Address:	Sincil Bank Stadium, Lincoln, LN5 8LD
Main Telephone No:	0870-899-2005
Fax No:	01522-880-020
Team Nickname:	The Imps
Year Ground Opened:	1895
Pitch Size:	110 x 73 yards
Home Kit Colours:	Red, White & Black

Official Website:
www.redimps.com

Unofficial Websites:
The Imps - www.sportnetwork.net/main/s261.php (Sport Network)
Planet Imp - www.lincolncity-mad.co.uk (Footy Mad Network)
The Forgotten Imp - www.theforgottenimp.co.uk

What's The Ground Like?

On one side is the large all seater CO-OP Community Stand. This large single-tiered covered stand opened in 1995 and has a capacity of 5,700. Opposite is the Lincolnshire Echo Stand, a small, old-looking covered stand (although in fact it is comparatively modern, being built in 1987). It is seated, but only runs half the length of the pitch, straddling the halfway line and hence there are gaps at either side. One gap has now been partly filled by a tiny covered Family Stand. Both ends are small covered affairs. The IMPS Stand is all seated and has a row of executive boxes running across the back. This stand has a couple of supporting pillars at the front. The other end is the 'Stacey West' all-seated, covered stand for home supporters.

Future Ground Developments

The club are looking into the possibility of extending the Lincolnshire Echo Stand, so that it widens along the side of the pitch. This is still in the feasibility stage.

What Is It Like For Visiting Supporters?

Away fans are housed in part of the CO-OP Community Stand at one side of the pitch. The normal allocations for away fans is 1,900 and this stand is divided between home and away supporters. The facilities and view of the pitch are good, and there is also a great range of food available, including the delicious 'Football's Famous Chicken Balti Pie', burgers, Lincolnshire sausage and bacon rolls. I had an enjoyable day at Lincoln. There was a good atmosphere at the ground, with plenty of noise being created by the local band in the CO-OP Stand.

Jason Adderley, a visiting West Brom supporter adds; 'Lincoln's small band of fans are passionate about their team and are one of the friendliest bunches I've met on my travels. The atmosphere was great and the drums were rousing, leading the chants of the Lincoln supporters'.

Where To Drink?

Neil Le Milliere, a visiting Exeter City fan, adds; 'away supporters are admitted to the Supporters Club (called the Centre Spot) behind the South Park Stand. The Mansfield Smooth beer and the hot pork rolls were excellent'. There are plenty of good pubs to be found if you head along the High St towards the town centre. John Bennett a visiting Bristol Rovers supporter recommends the Golden Eagle on the High Street, which is listed in the CAMRA Good Beer Guide. Jon Morley adds; 'The Portland pub down Sincil Bank about 800 yards from the ground and the Wetherspoon's pub 'Ritz' on the High St both serve reasonably priced food and ales'. Whilst Alex Karpasitis informs me; 'I would recommend the Anchor which is virtually next door to the Wetherspoons pub and the Millers Arms which is further up the High Street'.

How To Get There & Where To Park?

Lincoln is not the easiest place to get to, as it is not conveniently situated next to a motorway. I had great difficulty in finding the ground and two people that I asked for directions were unaware that Lincoln had a football team! However I have been recently informed that the ground is now well signposted around Lincoln. Otherwise follow the A46 into Lincoln (which leads onto the High St) and the ground is indicated from there. If you follow the signs for 'away coaches' then this leads you onto the A158 South Park Avenue, where there is plenty of street parking to be found (although it is a ten-minute walk around to the ground). Otherwise the signs lead you to the ground, where if you arrive early then you can park behind the Stacey West Stand (cost £4), otherwise, street parking. Ian Gibson adds; 'On matchdays the South Common is open for parking, this can be found at the beginning of South Park Avenue when coming in from either the A46 or from the High Street. It's free to park and only about 5/10 mins from the ground'.

■ By Train

Lincoln Central train station is around a 15min walk to the ground. Turn 'left out of the train station and walk up to the traffic lights next to St. Mary's church. Turn left at these traffic lights onto the High Street, walking over the railway level crossing. Walk along the High Street (passing many good pubs) for approx 10 minutes before turning left into Scorer Street. Walk along Scorer Street until you come to a bridge across the Sincil Drain river. Turn right immediately after crossing the bridge onto Sincil Bank, the ground is straight ahead. Thanks to John Smalley for providing the directions.

Alternatively there is a shorter route (but you miss those fine pubs!): 'Come out of the station and turn right to go down the road. About 30 yards ahead on your right you will see some steps and a bridge over the railway. Go over the bridge and once on the other side follow the road down to the ground'. Thanks to Ben Schofield for providing these directions.

■ Local Rivals

Scunthorpe United, Mansfield Town, Hull City, Grimsby Town, Peterborough & Boston United.

■ Admission Prices

Like a number of clubs, Lincoln operate a category system for games (A & B) whereby the most popular games cost more to watch.

Home Fans*:

Echo & CO-OP Community Stands:
Adults £15,
Concessions £11,
Under 15's £5

Stacey West, IMPS & Family Stands:
Adults £13,
Concessions £9,
Under 15's £5

Away Fans:

CO-OP Community Stand
Adults* £15,
Concessions £11,
Under 15's £5*.

* The adult prices quoted above are for tickets purchased prior to matchday. Tickets purchased on matchday will cost £2 more.

Concessions apply to under 20's, over 60's and the disabled.

■ Programme & Fanzine

Official Programme £2.50.
The Deranged Ferret Fanzine £1.20

■ Record Attendance

Record Attendance:
23,196 v Derby County,
League Cup 4th Round, November 15th, 1967.

Modern All Seated Attendance Record:
9,202 v Huddersfield Town,
Division Three Play Off, May 15th, 2004.

■ Average Attendance

2006-2007: 5,280 (League Two)

■ Did You Know?

That the Stacey West Stand was named in memory of the two Lincoln City supporters who lost their lives in the Bradford City Fire at Valley Parade in 1985.

Macclesfield Town

Moss Rose

Ground Name:	Moss Rose
Capacity:	6,335 (2,599 seats)
Address:	London Road, Macclesfield, SK11 7SP
Main Telephone No:	01625-264-686
Fax No:	01625-264-692
Team Nickname:	The Silkmen
Year Ground Opened:	1891
Pitch Size:	100m x 60m
Home Kit Colours:	Blue & White

Official Website:
www.mtfc.co.uk

Unofficial Website:
Silkweb - www.thesilkweb.com (Rivals Network)

What's The Ground Like?

Even with the recent developments at the ground, it is still on the smallish side, with a bit of a non-league feel about it. One side is predominantly uncovered terracing, with the small, seated Silk FM 'Main' Stand sitting in the middle. This type of stand is a classic design, once common across the country, but many have since disappeared with redevelopment. It is though unusual to see a stand of such age, that doesn't have any supporting pillars running across the front of it. On the other side is the covered, single-tiered Alfred McAlpine Stand, which was opened in March 2001. This smart-looking all-seated stand, with a row of executive boxes to its rear, has greatly improved the overall look of the ground. The Star Lane End is a relatively new covered stand that is a strange mix of seating and terracing; strange and unusual in having a terrace area behind the seating area. Apparently seating was added to the terrace in this way, so that the Club could fulfil the then Football League's rules concerning the number of seats that a club ground needed to be admitted into the Football League. Opposite is the open terraced Silkman End, which is given to away supporters. In one corner of the ground there is a basic-looking electric scoreboard which sits on top of the Police Control Box, next to the Star Lane End. The ground also has a set of unusual-looking floodlights.

Future Ground Developments

The Club have outlined proposals to redevelop the Silkman End. The existing terrace will remain much the same but behind it will be a tier of seating and behind this a new four storey building containing offices and a gym. There will also be a roof over both the new seats and the terrace. However, no firm time scales have been announced as to when this will take place.

What Is It Like For Visiting Supporters?

Away fans are primarily located in the open Silkman End, where up to 1,500 fans can be accommodated. Additionally, 403 seats are made available in the new Alfred McAlpine Stand, which sits at one side of the pitch. The seating may well be a better bet, as this stand is covered and the facilities new. On my last visit I opted for an away supporters seat in the Alfred McAlpine Stand. Oddly you gain access to this relatively new stand by going through a rather old-looking turnstile. However, once inside you should be impressed with the excellent facilities on offer. From your seat you can also enjoy the views of the rolling countryside stretching away behind the Main Stand. The view of the playing action and the atmosphere within the ground are both pretty good, with some enjoyable banter between the two sets of supporters. Food inside the ground included cheeseburgers (£2.80), hot dogs (£2.60) along with pies and pasties. Macclesfield is generally a good ground to visit and an enjoyable day out as well, being hassle free and friendly on both my visits.

Macclesfield Town

■ Where To Drink?

The ground is located on the outskirts of Macclesfield and therefore there is not a tremendous choice of pubs or even a handy chippy. The Golden Lion is the only close pub, about a ten-minute walk from the away turnstiles. I found the pub warm and friendly, although it didn't do any food which was surprising. There was a 50-50 mix of home and away supporters in this pub on my last visit. To find the Golden Lion, simply head down Moss Lane, behind the away terrace, and then turn left at the corner of the ground and walk down behind the new stand. Keep straight on and you will come to the pub on the left.

If you like your real ale then I would suggest taking the 10-minute walk to The Railway View pub on Byrons Lane. This smallish pub has around six ales on offer including a number of guest beers. They also sell homemade pies and if the weather is good then there is a small beer garden. To find this excellent pub follow the A523 from the ground towards Macclesfield town centre. You will pass a pub, The Albion, and then at the next set of traffic lights turn right into Byrons Lane. Just go over the railway bridge and the pub is on the right. Paul Petty, a visiting Colchester United fan, adds; 'I went to the Railway on Byrons Lane before (and after) the game. I am not sure if it is a annual event but I was lucky enough to hit their mini-spring beer festival. I would highly recommend the pub for both the quality of the beer and the friendliness of both the landlord and clientele. My only regret was that I didn't book a later train back to London!'

Steve Bennett recommends 'The Albion' on London Road towards the town centre from the ground. As Steve says; 'The pub serves first class real ales, has a great beer garden and is welcoming towards away fans'.

■ How To Get There & Where To Park?

From the South:
Leave the M6 at Junction 17 and turn onto the A534 towards Congleton. On reaching Congleton town centre follow the signs for A54 Buxton. Stay on the A54 for around 5 miles and then turn left on to the A523 towards Macclesfield. You will see the ground on your left after entering the outskirts of Macclesfield. Mostly street parking around and behind the ground and on the A523 itself.

From The North:
Leave the M6 at Junction 18 and take the A54 towards Congleton. On reaching Congleton town centre follow the signs for A54 Buxton. Then as South.

■ By Train

Geoff Knights informs me; 'Macclesfield railway station is about 1¼ miles from the Moss Rose ground, about a 20-minute walk away. As you leave the station, at the bottom of the station approach, turn left onto Sunderland Street and follow until the traffic lights at Park Green (War memorial and gardens). Turn left onto Mill Lane (it is probably better to cross the road here at the traffic lights) and follow this road which becomes London Road. Just after passing the Catholic Church on the right the ground comes into sight ahead.

Chris Dale adds; 'You can also catch a bus up to the ground from the new bus station in the town centre.

To reach the bus station from Macclesfield railway station, cross the main road outside the station, turn right and then left by the car showroom into Waters Green and follow this road up the hill (Queen Victoria Street) to the bus station on the left. Buses returning from the ground stop on the main road outside the railway station.

■ Times and Routes:-

Service 9 Moss Rose circular - every 30 minutes (hourly at night and on Sundays)
Service 14 Langley - hourly all day and evening (no Sunday service)

Further information is available on Traveline: Telephone number 0870 608 2608.

■ Local Rivals

Altrincham & Stockport County.

■ Admission Prices

Home Fans:

Silk FM Main Stand
Adults £13, Concessions £10

Alfred McAlpine Stand
Adults £13, Concessions £10

HFS Loans Stand (Star Lane End)
Adults £10, Concessions £7

Away Fans:

Alfred McAlpine Stand (Seating)
Adults £13, Concessions £10

Silkman Terrace
Adults £10, Concessions £7

All Areas Of The Ground:
Under 16's £5
Under 12's Free

■ Programme

Official Programme £2 (on sale within the ground).

■ Record Attendance

9,003 v Winsford United,
Cheshire Senior Cup 2nd Round, February 4th, 1948.

■ Average Attendance

2006-2007: 2,086 (League Two)

■ Did You Know?

That during last season's FA Cup tie with Walsall, play had to be suspended for a short time. This was because around 20 footballs were propelled from outside the ground and onto the pitch at the Star Lane End!

Mansfield Town

Field Mill

Ground Name: Field Mill
Capacity: 10,000 (all seated)
Address: Quarry Lane, Mansfield, NG18 5DA
Main Telephone No: 0870-756-3160
Fax No: 01623-482-495
Team Nickname: The Stags
Year Ground Opened: 1919
Shirt Sponsors: Perry Electrical
Home Kit Colours: Amber & Blue

Official Website:
www.mansfieldtown.net

Unofficial Websites:
Ollerton Stags - www.ollertonstags.co.uk
Supporters Association - www.stagsnet.net

What's The Ground Like?

During the past few years and at a cost of £6.5m, Field Mill has been transformed into a modern stadium, with the building of three new stands. Both ends, the North Stand & Quarry Lane End plus the West Stand on one side of the pitch have been redeveloped. The ends are almost identical single-tiered stands, each accommodating just under 2,000 supporters. The latest addition to the ground is the West Stand, opened in February 2001. This is a cantilevered two-tiered stand, with a capacity of 5,500. On the other side of the ground is the rather small Bishop Street Stand, a covered seated stand that only runs half the length of the pitch. This now looks rather dowdy alongside its new shiny neighbours.

Future Ground Developments

There are plans to redevelop the small remaining Bishop Street Stand, but no formal time scales have been announced as to when this might take place.

What Is It Like For Visiting Supporters?

To confuse matters, away fans are now housed in the opposite end from last season. Away fans are now housed in the North Stand, a move that has been unpopular with a number of home fans, as the North End of the ground has been the traditional home end for many years. As you would expect from a relatively new stand the views of the playing action and facilities are pretty good. Around 1,800 supporters can be accommodated. I had a fairly uneventful trip to Mansfield and did not encounter any problems. It seemed to be a friendly place that was quite relaxed. However Alistair Wright, a visiting Bristol City supporter, adds; 'I found the standard of stewarding at Field Mill to be particularly poor and at times they seemed almost hostile towards the away support'.

Rob Ferguson adds 'for those away fans arriving by coach, please note that buses should drop off at Portland Street and pick up at Portland Street at the end of the match.'

Where To Drink?

The 'Early Doors' pub next to the ground is popular with both home and away supporters, although it can get rather crowded. It does quite good food and has an outside seating area. Pete Smith recommends 'The Talbot' on the A60 near to the Sainsburys Supermarket. Chris Patrick adds; 'The Sir John Cockle pub is on the A38 going into Mansfield from the M1 and again serves good food'. Terry Gospel advises that away fans should avoid the Victoria and Red Lion Pubs.

Mansfield Town

How To Get There & Where To Park?

From The North:
Leave the M1 at Junction 29; take the A617 to Mansfield. After 6 miles turn right into Rosemary Street. Follow road for 1 mile and turn right into Quarry Lane.

From The South:
Leave the M1 at Junction 28, take A38 to Mansfield and after 6.5 miles turn right at the crossroads into Belvedere St, then turn right into Quarry Lane.

Peter Llewellyn informs me; 'You can park at the ground at a cost of £2. Otherwise it is street parking'. Malcolm Dawson, a visiting Sunderland supporter adds; 'I parked in the retail park (PC World, Currys, B&Q) behind the North Stand. I assumed that there would be unlimited free parking, but when I got back after the match I had a parking ticket for £50. Be warned!'

By Train

The ground can be seen from Mansfield railway station which is no more than ten minutes walk away.
The station is on a local line and is served by trains from Nottingham. To get to the ground from the station; Leave the station and turn left along the dual carriageway, (away from the town centre, you should see a retail park on the right. Go straight ahead at the first set of traffic lights, along Portland Street and then right at the next lights and into Quarry Lane. The ground is a short distance down this road on the right hand side.

Martin Monk adds; 'for away fans using the trains take note that for mid-week matches the last train leaves from Mansfield - Nottingham at 9.45 pm and the last train leaves from Mansfield - Worksop at 9.38 pm, please check with your train operators as both of these times fall before a 7.45 KO match finishes. Away fans have been known to have been left stranded in Mansfield, and have struggled to get home. Also note the Robin Hood Line does not run on a Sunday'.

Local Rivals

Chesterfield, Notts County & Lincoln City.

Admission Prices

Home Fans:

West Stand (Upper Tier):
Adults £16,
OAP's £11,
Under 16's £8

West Stand (Lower Tier):
Adults £15,
OAP's/Students £10,
Under 16's £ £7

South (Quarry Lane End) **Stand:**
Adults £16,
OAP's £10,
Under 16's £7

Family Enclosure:
Adults £15,
Under 10's £5

Bishop Street Stand:
Adults £16,
OAP's £10,
Under 16's £7

Away Fans:

North Stand:
Adults £16,
OAP's £10,
Under 16's £7.

Programme

Official Programme: £2.50

Record Attendance

24,467 v Nottingham Forest
FA Cup 3rd Round, January 10th, 1953.

Modern All Seated Attendance Record:
9,243 v Northampton Town
Division Three Play-Off, May 20th, 2004.

Average Attendance

2006-2007: 3,542 (League Two)

Did You Know?

The Club's origins can be traced back to the 1890s to a team called Mansfield Wesleyans. The team's colours were then brown and blue stripes.

Milton Keynes Dons

stadium:mk

Ground Name: stadium:mk
Capacity: 22,000 (all seated)
Address: Denbigh,
Milton Keynes, MK1 1SA
Main Telephone No: 01908-607-090
Main Fax No: 01908-209-449
Ticket Office: 01908-609-000
Team Nickname: The Dons
Year Ground Opened: 2007
Home Kit Colours: All White

Official Website:
www.mkdons.co.uk

Unofficial Websites:
New Stadium Website - www.stadium-mk.co.uk
Bucks Fizz Fanzine - www.thebucksfizz.com
MK Dons R Us - www.mkdonsrus.com
Trust in MK Dons - www.trustinmkdons.com
Supporters Association - www.mkdsa.com

What's The Ground Like?

After four years at the National Hockey Stadium, the Club have now moved to a new purpose-built stadium on the outskirts of Milton Keynes. At a cost of around £50m, the 22,000 all-seated stadium certainly looks a quality one and one that does look a bit different to other new stadiums that have been built. It was designed by HOK, the same firm of architects responsible for the Emirates & Wembley stadiums. From the outside it has a modern look, with good use of silver coloured cladding and a large amount of glass on view. The most striking feature of the stadium is its roof, which sits high up above the football ground with a large gap between it and the back row of seating. This allows more natural light to reach the pitch. The stadium is totally enclosed and has a bowl like design.

It is two-tiered, with on three sides having a large lower tier being over hung by a smaller upper tier. The West side of the stadium is slightly different, with the seating areas in the upper tier being replaced by the Director's Box and executive and corporate hospitality areas. Unusually the concourse areas at the back of the lower tier see directly into the stadium, so there is what seems a noticeable gap between the lower and upper tiers, where the concourse is located.

Future Developments

At some point the upper tier of seating will be installed, which will raise the capacity to 30,000 and should have a big impact on the overall look of the stadium. Also as part of the development there will be attached to the south end of the stadium a 6,500 capacity indoor arena, in which the MK Lions basketball team will play and a hotel.

What Is It Like For Visiting Supporters?

Well, the stadium promises such creature comforts as big 'Emirates Style' comfy seats and the ability to continue to watch the game in progress, whilst at the same queuing on the concourse for a burger. There is no doubt that the views of the game will be great, but with only the lower tier of seating being installed and open for the new season, then it may well have an odd unfinished look. Like a number of new stadiums though, its main drawback is location. It is located adjacent to the A5, but well away from the centre of Milton Keynes, so there is little on offer in the way of pubs or eateries. There is, though, a cafe in the Asda next door! The stadium will also have electronic turnstiles, so expect to put your ticket into a bar code reader to gain entrance.

In keeping with the infamous concrete cows of Milton Keynes, the Club have a mascot called Mooie, whilst the South Stand is called the 'cowshed'. '

Where To Drink?

There doesn't appear to be many pubs in the vicinity of the stadium, although alcohol is served inside. There is, though, one pub called The Beacon, which is on Mount Farm about a ten-minute walk away. Otherwise, if you have time on your hands then you can embark on the 20-25 minute walk into Bletchley, where there are a few pubs to be found, but none of which you would 'write home about'. The nearest is probably the Enigma Tavern on Saxon Street. Just follow the signs for Bletchley by Asda and you will reach the pub on your left.

There are a number of bars located in Milton Keynes itself, adjacent to the main shopping centre, or in walking distance of Milton Keynes Central station. If coming out of the station you go straight up Midsummer Boulevard in front of you, then after around five minutes walk you will find a Wetherspoons outlet located on the left. Further up Midsummer Boulevard is another Wetherspoons outlet called the 'Secklow Hundred', plus a 'Bar Med' and 'All Bar One'. These three pubs are a ten minute walk away.

■ How To Get There & Where To Park?

The stadium is situated at Denbigh North, just off the A5, south of Central Milton Keynes and just north of Bletchley. It is adjacent to a Retail Park with Asda and IKEA, so expect some traffic congestion. For those familiar with MK's grid road system the ground is on V6 Grafton Street on the junction with H9 Groveway.

Central Route from North or South:
This is the best route if you wish to use the central facilities bar areas/ shopping centre. Leave the M1 at Junction 14 and head towards Central Milton Keynes. At the first roundabout take the third exit H6 Portway, go straight over the next 9 roundabouts past the City Centre and the old Hockey Stadium ground. At the next roundabout take the first left onto the A5, take this road until the next junction get in the right hand lane and take the fourth turning, V6 Grafton Street, the stadium will be in front of you, then turn left at the traffic lights.

Potential alternative/quicker routes:

From the North:
Leave the M1 at Junction 15 and turn right on to the A508. Follow this road for 14 miles, until you come to a roundabout at the A5, take the left turn heading south, leave the A5 at the third roundabout, take the fourth turning (V6 Grafton Street), the stadium will be in front of you, then turn left at the traffic lights.

From the South
Leave the M1 at junction 13 and take the second exit (A421). After 3 miles take the second exit on ther roundabout, called H9 Groveway. Stay on this road going straight over 4 roundabouts, and the stadium is in front of you slightly to the left; take the second exit. The entrance to the stadium is first left at the traffic lights.

Alternative Parking
No designated parking has been approved yet. After passing the stadium entrance on your left, turn right at Granby roundabout, and then take the next turn left, and immediately left again onto an industrial estate called Denbigh West. Pedestrian crossings towards Asda will allow access back towards the ground.
Thanks to Matthew Day for providing the above directions.

■ By Train

The nearest station is Bletchley, just over a mile away from the stadium. There is a taxi rank outside, a bus station in the town centre, or you can embark on the 25-minute walk to the stadium past a couple of pubs.

Milton Keynes Central is around four miles away. There is a taxi rank and bus station located outside. However, it is unclear as to which services will go to the stadium. You can also get a train to Bletchley from here.

■ Local Rivals

Luton Town.

■ Admission Prices

Home Fans:

West & East Stands (Centre):
Adults £22, Concessions £18, Juniors £14

West & East Stands (Wings):
Adults £19, Concessions £15, Juniors £11

Cowshed South Stand:
Adults £17, Concessions £13, Juniors £9

Stadium Corners:
Adults £15, Concessions £11, Juniors £7

West Stand Family Wing*:
Adults £17, Concessions £13, Juniors £7

Family Corner*:
Adults £15, Concessions £11, Juniors £5

Away Fans:

North Stand:
Adults £17, Concessions £13, Juniors £9

Under 7's are admitted free to all areas (except the corporate executive areas) as long as they are accompanied by an adult and proof of age can be shown.
* A minimum of one adult and one junior ticket must be purchased. Maximum of two adults/concessions tickets per junior.

■ Programme & Fanzines

Official Programme - £2.50
Bucks Fizz Fanzine - £2

■ Record Attendance

8,306 v Tottenham Hotspur
League Cup 3rd Round, October 25th, 2006.

■ Average Attendance

2006-2007: 5,848 (League Two)

■ Did You Know?

That the locals have christened the stadium 'The MooCamp.'

Morecambe

Christie Park

Ground Name:	Christie Park
Capacity:	6,400 (seating 1,200)
Address:	Lancaster Road, Morecambe LA4 5TJ
Main Telephone No:	01524-411-797
Fax No:	01524-832-230
Team Nickname:	Shrimps
Year Ground Opened:	1921
Home Kit Colours:	Red & White

Official Website:
www.morecambefc.com

Unofficial Websites:
Official Supporters Club - www.morecambefc-supporters.org.uk
MegaShrimps - www.megashrimps.co.uk
Gazetta de la Shrimp - www.gazzettaonline.co.uk

What's The Ground Like?

On one side of the ground is the Main Stand, which is a classic old-looking stand. It runs in length for around half the size of the pitch and straddles the halfway line. It is a covered stand, with a seating area which is elevated above pitch level, so that spectators need to climb a set of stairs to enter the stand. On each side of the stand there is a windshield, to help protect fans from the sea breeze. The stand is slightly set back from the pitch and hence there is a small terrace area in front of the seated area. The only disappointment is that there are a couple of modern-looking floodlight pylons which are situated directly in front of the stand at the side of the pitch. Opposite is a very small uncovered terrace, which is only a few steps high. This area is known affectionately as the 'car wash terrace', as it is the only uncovered area of the ground and has a car wash situated behind it. It has a set of four floodlights located along the front of it. At one end is the impressive-looking North Stand. This good sized terrace is covered and has windshields to either side. Opposite is the smaller Umbro Stand, also a covered terrace with several supporting pillars in front. The ground is also used for Blackburn Rovers reserve games.

Future Ground Developments

The Club are shortly to embark on redeveloping the South East part of the ground, at the corner of the car wash and Umbro Stands. The £1m development will see construction a three storey stand, that will also incorporate a pub and hospitality suite. The pub is scheduled to open shortly after the new season starts, with the new stand being ready for the start of the 2008/09 season.

What Is It Like For Visiting Supporters?

Fans are primarily housed in the Umbro Stand at one end of the ground. This covered terrace can accommodate around 1,500 fans. A small number if seats are also made available in the Main Stand. Unfortunately there are a number of supporting pillars running across the front of this stand which may impede your view. Catering is provided by the obligatory burger van, although there is a handy chip shop located near the entrance to the away end, which you may care to visit before or after the game. The covered ends contribute to a good atmosphere at the ground and Christie Park is normally a pleasant and relaxed day out.

Where To Drink?

Inside the ground under the Main Stand, is the club's own bar called JB's. However with the Club now gaining league status, then for most games it is unlikely to admit away fans. This is simply because of the increased numbers of away supporters that the Football League will bring. However a new pub is being constructed at the south east corner of the ground and hopefully this will admit away fans this season.

A better bet would be the popular York Hotel on Lancaster Road, which is about a ten-minute walk away from the ground, going towards the town centre. It has Sky television, serves food and has a selection of Everards real ale on offer. If you have a bit more time on your hands then there are plenty of bars to be found along the sea front.

How To Get There & Where To Park?

Exit the M6 at junction 34, then take the A683 towards Lancaster and the A589 towards Morecambe. Go straight across two roundabouts passing a McDonalds outlet on your left. At the next roundabout take the second exit into Lancaster Road. The ground is down this road on your left. The main car park at the ground is for pass holders only. However there is another small car park behind the Umbro Stand which is free. Otherwise street parking.

The town of Lancaster can often be a bottleneck for traffic, so allow a little extra time for your journey from the motorway.

By Train

Morecambe railway station is about a ten minute walk away from the ground. As you come out of the station turn right going straight down Central Drive and then alongside Euston Road. This leads into Lancaster Road where the ground is located. Morecambe is served by trains from Lancaster.

Local Rivals

Lancaster, Southport

Admission Prices

Seating:
Adults £13,
Concessions £10,
Under 16's £5

Terrace:
Adults £12,
Concessions £9,
Under 16's £4

Concessions apply to over 65's, Students with NUS card and disabled.

Programme & Fanzine

Official Programme £2.20.

Record Attendance

9,234 v Weymouth
FA Cup 3rd Round, 1962.

Average Attendance

2006-2007: 1,598 (Conference National League)

Did You Know?

The ground was originally called Roseberry Park, but was renamed Christie Park in the 1920's in honour of the Club's then President Mr J B Christie.

Notts County

Meadow Lane

Ground Name: Meadow Lane
Capacity: 20,300 (all seated)
Address: Meadow Lane, Nottingham, NG2 3HJ
Main Telephone No: 0115-952-9000
Fax No: 0115-955-3994
Ticket Office: 0115-955-7204
Pitch Size: 114 x 76 yards
Club Nickname: The Magpies
Year Ground Opened: 1910
Home Kit Colours: Black & White

Official Website:
www.nottscountyfc.co.uk

Unofficial Websites:
Notts County Supporters Trust - www.nottscotrust.org.uk
Notts County Mad - www.nottscounty-mad.co.uk (Footy Mad Network)
1862.net - www.1862.net
You Pies - www.youpies.co.uk

■ What's The Ground Like?

During the early 1990s the ground was completely rebuilt, creating an attractive all-seater stadium. Although the ground comprises four separate stands, it is quite smart looking. Both sides are single-tiered stands, the larger of which is the Derek Pavis (Main) Stand. Opposite the Jimmy Sirrell Stand has a gable on its roof reminiscent of those old grounds, where they were once a common sight. Away fans are housed in the large Kop End, containing 5,400 supporters. Again this is a newish stand with excellent facilities. The other end is the smaller, covered Family Stand. This stand has one sizeable solitary supporting pillar, which may affect your view as it is situated right of the front of the stand in the middle. This stand also has a small electric scoreboard on its roof.

■ What Is It Like For Visiting Supporters?

I was very impressed with the new stands at the ground and had a pleasant day out. The view from the away end was excellent as were the catering facilities. The local fans seemed friendly enough. The only disappointments were that the substantial supporters club didn't allow in away supporters and that the ground generally lacked atmosphere, although away fans can really make some noise in the Kop Stand. Christopher Bushe, a visiting Brentford supporter adds; 'the Notts County stewards were a bit over the top in terms of numbers and in attitude'.

■ Where To Drink?

There are a few pubs around the ground that let away supporters in and are quite friendly and serve good real ale. Steve from the Pie Fanzine informs me; 'On the main London Road, just across from the humpback bridge over the canal, is the newly refurbished and renamed Globe. A comfortable open-plan pub with good food and 5 ever-changing real ales (children can use the upstairs room). Just the other side of Trent Bridge (although mercifully facing away from that rusting monstrosity with a red tree painted on the side!) is the Southbank, the Globe's sister pub. It also serves excellent food and has sport on the numerous televisions; three real ales are offered here including one from the tiny local Mallards brewery. Just across from the front of the station down Queensbridge Road is the "Vat and Fiddle" situated next door to the Castle Rock micro-brewery. It offers ten real ales and hot and cold food. Children are welcome. At the far end of Meadow Lane away from the ground, you will find the Magpies pub. Named after Notts County's nickname it is of course painted red and depicts two magpies on its sign - testimony indeed that national brewers have lost touch with their customers! It offers well-kept real ales and excellent but inexpensive meals. Get there early enough and you can even park in their car park'.

Chris Rhoades recommends the Trent Navigation (parking also available there at £1.50) and the Trent Bridge Inn. Chris claims 'The food is locally renowned, especially the pies!' Whilst Tim Cooke, a travelling Millwall fan has a different angle (so to speak); 'definitely one for the lads! Hooters (on the main road A6011, on the outskirts of the city centre, you can't miss it!) has very nice waitresses wearing just enough to cover things up, serves lovely beer, and great food. Take my advice, make a weekend of it, Nottingham is a top city!' Alcohol is also available within the ground.

If you are arriving by train and have a bit of time on your hands, then I would suggest that you check out the 'Olde Trip To Jerusalem'. This historic pub dates back to the 12th century and some of the rooms are 'cave like' having been carved out of the rock that Nottingham Castle is situated upon. Add real ale, food and a small beer garden, then it is certainly worth a visit. It is about a five-minute walk away from the train station. As you come out of the station turn right. At the top of the road turn left and then take the second right into Castle Road. Just tucked away on the left is the pub.

■ How To Get There & Where To Park?

Leave the M1 at Junction 26 and take the A610 towards Nottingham and then signs for Melton Mowbray. Turn left before the River Trent in to Meadow Lane. You can park at the Cattle Market (opposite the away end £2) or in the club car park (opposite the club offices in Meadow Lane £2.50). Otherwise there is plenty of street parking.

■ By Train

The ground is ten minutes walk from Nottingham railway station. As you come out of the main station entrance, turn left and then left again. Follow the road down to London Road and then turn right. The ground is about a quarter of a mile down the dual carriageway on the left.

■ Local Rivals

Nottingham Forest, Mansfield Town, Chesterfield & Derby County.

■ Admission Prices

Home Fans:

Derek Pavis (Main) **Stand**
Adults £18,
Senior Citizens £11
Students/Young Adults
£9, Under 16's £5

Jimmy Sirrell Stand
Adults £16,
Senior Citizens £10
Students/Young Adults £9,
Under 16's £5

Family Stand
Adults £16,
Senior Citizens £10
Students/Young Adults £9,
Under 16's £5

Away Fans:

Kop Stand
Adults £16,
Senior Citizens £10
Students/Young Adults £9,
Under 16's £5

■ Programme

Official Programme £2.50.

■ Record Attendance

47,310 v York City
FA Cup 6th Round, March 12th, 1955.

Modern All Seated Attendance Record:
16,952 v Tottenham Hotspur,
October 26th, 1994.

■ Average Attendance

2006-2007: 4,612 (League Two)

■ Did You Know?

That Notts County are recognised as the World's oldest league club, having been formed in 1862.

Peterborough United

London Road

Ground Name: London Road
Capacity: 15,314
Address: London Rd, Peterborough, PE2 8AL
Main Telephone No: 01733-563-947
Fax No: 01733-344-140
Pitch Size: 112 x 76 yards
Team Nickname: The Posh
Year Ground Opened: 1934
Home Kit Colours: Blue & White

Official Website:
www.theposh.com

Unofficial Websites:
Posh Net – www.posh.net
Up The Posh– www.uptheposh.com

What's The Ground Like?

On one side of the ground is the South Stand, which was opened in 1996 and replaced a former open terrace. Encased in supporting tubular steelwork, the 5,000 capacity stand is an impressive sight. The two-tiered stand, is covered and all seated. There is also a row of executive boxes running across its middle. The other side, the Main Stand, is a two-tiered covered stand that is all seated. Both ends are covered terracing that look almost identical. They were given white roofs a couple of seasons back, in an effort to brighten up their appearance. However they both have a number of supporting pillars at the front of them, which could impede your view of the game. They do though give some charm to London Road, as these types of terraces are quickly disappearing from the football landscape in this country. Interestingly, there is an open air gap at the back of these terraces between the roof and the back supporting wall, which must mean that they can get a bit draughty in winter. In one corner of the ground, between the South Stand and the London Road Terrace, is a Police Control Box. On either side of the Main Stand are two tall, old fashioned-looking floodlights. The ground had a set of four at one time, but two were taken down when the new South Stand was built.

What Is It Like For Visiting Supporters?

Just under 4,000 away fans can be accommodated in the Moyes Terrace, with a further 800 seats being made available to away fans in the Main Stand. If, however, only a small away following is expected, then the terrace is kept closed and away supporters are housed just in the Block A seats of the Main Stand. The Moyes terrace has several supporting pillars, which may obstruct your view, but the acoustics of the covered terrace are good, leading to a good atmosphere. There are a good range of pies available including the delicious 'Football's Famous Chicken Balti Pie' (£2.20), plus rollover hot dogs (also £2.20). I found London Road to be a good and fairly relaxed day out.

Where To Drink?

Michael Howard, a visiting Reading supporter informs me; 'The Cherry Tree pub on Oundle Rd is quite popular with away fans. Although small it is a friendly pub. It costs £2 to park in their car park but you get £2 off a beer if you present the parking ticket at the bar'. Alun Thomas, a visiting Wrexham supporter, adds; 'We found a better bet than the Cherry Tree was the Palmerston Arms. It is away fan friendly and has around 10 real ales on on offer. This pub is situated around 100 yards further along Oundle Road on the opposite side'. Whilst Gordon Pearson recommends the Peacock, which can be found 'as you come over the River Nene, proceed down London Road past the ground on the left and the pub is situated on the right at the traffic lights next to a KFC drive through'.

Near to the ground is Charters, which is certainly worth a visit. This former Dutch barge is moored on the River Nene, just a few minutes' walk away from London Road, on the left hand side of the bridge, going towards the town centre. Upstairs is a Chinese restaurant, but downstairs there is a bar, which had on my last visit 12 real ales on tap. It was friendly enough and fans were able to take their drinks out onto the river bank, which makes it quite pleasant when the weather is good. Alternatively, the ground is within walking distance (10 minutes) of the town centre (which is very pleasant and complete with a cathedral) where there are plenty of good pubs to be found. If you are arriving by train then the Brewery Tap near to the station on Westgate, is worth a visit. The home of Oakham Ales, this spacious bar serves good beer, Thai food and allows you views into the brewery itself.

■ How To Get There & Where To Park?

The ground is located on the outskirts of the town centre, on the A15 London Road. The ground is fairly well signposted around the town centre.

■ From the North/West:

Drive into the town centre, follow signs for Whittlesey (A605) which will lead you to the London Road. The new stand is quite visible from some distance away, so keep a lookout.

From the South:
Leave the A1 at the junction with the A15. Take the A15 towards Peterborough, you will eventually come to the ground on your right.

There is a car park at the ground, or otherwise there is a council pay & display car park just off London Road (on your left as you pass the ground going towards the town centre).

■ By Train

Peterborough station is around a mile away from the ground. Turn right out of the station and follow the main road, passing an Asda store on your right. At the traffic lights near to Woolworths, turn right. Go over the bridge and you can see the floodlights of London Road, over on your left. It takes about 20 minutes to walk from the station to the ground. Thanks to Andrew Dodd for providing the directions.

■ Local Rivals

Cambridge United, Northampton Town,
Rushden & Diamonds.

■ Admission Prices

Home Fans:

Norwich & Peterborough South Stand Seating:
Adults £20,
OAP's/Students £12,
Under 16's £9,
Under 10's Free*

Main (North) Stand Seating:
Adults £20,
OAP's/Students £12,
Under 16's £9,
Under 10's Free*

London Road Terrace:
Adults £15,
OAP's/Students £12,
Under 16's £9

Away Fans:

Main (North) Stand A Wing Seating
Adults £20,
OAP's/Students £12,
Under 16's £9,
Under 10's Free*

Moyes Terrace:
Adults £15,
OAP's/Students £12,
Under 16's £9

* When accompanied by an adult or senior citizen. One free child per adult.

■ Programme

Official Programme £2.50

■ Record Attendance

30,096 v Swansea City,
FA Cup 5th Round, February 20th, 1965.

■ Average Attendance

2006-2007: 4,570 (League Two)

■ Did You Know?

The Club nickname 'The Posh' is believed to have come from a former manager Pat Tirrell, who early in the 1920's is attributed with saying that he needed; 'posh players for a posh team'.

Rochdale

Spotland

Ground Name: Spotland
Capacity: 10,249
Address: Sandy Lane, Rochdale, OL11 5DS
Main Telephone No: 0870-822-1907
Fax No: 01706-648-466
Team Nickname: The Dale
Year Ground Opened: 1906
Pitch Size: 114 x 76 yards
Home Kit Colours: Blue With White Trim

Official Website:
www.rochdaleafc.co.uk

Unofficial Website:
RochdaleAFC.com - www.rochdaleafc.com (Rivals Network)

What's The Ground Like?

The ground has benefited greatly with the construction of three new stands over the last ten years and is quite picturesque, with a number of trees being visible behind the stands. The latest addition is the smart-looking Westrose Leisure Stand at one side of the pitch, which was opened during the 2000/01 season. This single-tiered stand replaced a former terrace and has a capacity of 3,650. On the other side is another single tier, the all seated Horners Main Stand. This has a number of supporting pillars and some executive boxes at the back. At one end the W.M.G (Pearl Street) Stand is the third of the new stands. This is also all seated and serves as a Family Stand. It has a couple of supporting pillars that are right at the front of the stand. The Thwaites Beer (Sandy Lane) end is the only terraced area remaining. This small terrace has in recent seasons had a roof erected. There is a Police Control Box located in one corner, between the Main & Pearl Street Stands. Spotland is shared with the Rochdale Hornets rugby league team.

What Is It Like For Visiting Supporters?

Away supporters are housed in the Willbutts Lane Stand (recently renamed the Westrose Leisure Stand), where the view of the action and the facilities are pretty good. Up to 4,000 supporters can be accommodated in it and normally away fans are confined to the centre of the stand. If required, then this stand can be split between home and away fans. The acoustics are excellent, so away fans can really make some noise from within it. This, coupled with both home ends singing and the obligatory drummer, makes for a good atmosphere. If Rochdale do score then 'Tom Hark' by the Piranhas blasts out around the ground from the p.a. system.

I would say that Spotland, in my book, is one of the best footballing days out in the country. Friendly & knowledgeable fans, good stewards, good facilities, three pubs located at the ground, a great range of pies on offer and not a bad atmosphere to boot. In other words, all the right elements to make for a great day out. Add a pretty lady on my arm, my team winning six-nil and I'll think that I have been transported to heaven!

Where To Drink?

At the ground there are two bars to choose from, Studds & the Ratcliffe Arms. Studds is located underneath the Pearl Street Stand and is worth a visit, if only to sample the large range of tasty pies & pasties on offer at £1.50 (which are also available inside the ground). You can even have a pie and peas for £1.80. No real ales here, but the bar has some lovely-looking barmaids which softens the blow. The Ratcliffe Arms is located at the car park entrance to the ground, on Sandy Lane. This pub has Sky TV and on my last visit had a mixture of home and away fans. A couple of minutes walk along Willbutts Lane, is the Church Pub, which seemed to be the favoured haunt of away fans. Also on Willbutts Lane, is a small chip shop, with lengthy queues.

If you arrive early, the Cemetery Hotel, located at the bottom of Sandy Lane and on the corner with Bury Road, is also worth a visit. This comfortable historic pub has a range of real ales on offer and again friendly clientele.

Otherwise alcohol is available inside the ground, although it is cans poured into plastic glasses.

■ How To Get There & Where To Park?

Exit the M62 at Junction 20 and take the A627(M) towards Rochdale. At the end of the A627(M) you should be in the left hand lane to turn left at the traffic lights. Go straight on over the roundabout (approach in the middle lane) into Roch Valley Way. At the next crossroads (where the Cemetery pub is on the corner) go straight onto Sandy Lane, where the ground can be found on the right after approx 3/4 mile.

Car parking at the ground is now for permit holders only, so it is a case of either street parking or using the matchday parking facility at Oulder Hill School. The school is located on the way up to the ground, on the left hand side, along Sandy Lane (it is then a 10-minute walk uphill to the ground). If you do elect to park on the street then be wary of the "residents only" parking scheme, as otherwise you could end up with a parking ticket for your trouble.

■ By Train

Rochdale is served by trains from Manchester & Leeds, and is around two miles away from the ground
So I would recommend taking a taxi, but if you do decide to walk it will take you around 30-35 minutes to do so. Immediately as you leave the station there is a roundabout in front of you. Cross it, keeping to the left and take the second left into Lower Tweedale Street. Follow this street until its end where it meets Manchester Road. Turn right along Manchester Road (which is a dual carriageway). Pass Drake Street and then cross the Manchester Road via the pedestrian crossing. On the left hand side of the dual carriageway, carry on in the same direction as before. Turn left into Dane Street (where you will see a large Asda store) and this leads into Mellor Street (A6060). At the end of Mellor Street turn left along Spotland Road (A680) and then left again into Willbutts Lane for the ground. Thanks to Björn Sandström for providing the directions.

■ Local Rivals

Bury, Burnley, Oldham, Manchester United & Manchester City.

■ Admission Prices

Home Fans:

Horners Main Stand
Adults £17,
Concessions £10

W.M.G Stand
Adults £15,
Concessions £8

McDonalds Family Stand
Adults £15,
OAP's £8,
Under 16's £7,
Under 12's £5,
Under 7's Free

Thwaites Beer Stand (Terrace)
Adults £12,
Concessions £8

Away Fans:

Westrose Leisure Stand (Willbutts Lane):
Adults £17,
Concessions £10.

■ Programme

Official Programme - £2.50

■ Record Attendance

24,231 v Notts County
FA Cup 2nd Round, December 10th, 1949.

■ Average Attendance

2006-2007: 2,712 (League Two)

■ Did You Know?

That Rochdale haven't been out of the bottom division since 1974/75, the longest consecutive run of any team in the bottom league.

Rotherham United

Millmoor

Ground Name: Millmoor
Capacity: 7,500 (capacity reduced due to building work)
Address: Millmoor Ground, Rotherham, S60 1HR
Main Telephone No: 01709-512-434
Main Fax No: 01709-512-762
Ticket Office: 0870-443-1884
Pitch Size: 110 x 72 yards
Team Nickname: The Millers
Year Ground Opened: 1925
Home Kit Colours: Red & White

Official Website:
www.themillers.co.uk

Unofficial Websites:
Supporters Trust - www.rufctrust.co.uk
Millers Net - www.millersnet.co.uk (Rivals Network)
Rotherham Mad - www.rotherhamunited-mad.co.uk (Footy Mad Network)

What's The Ground Like?

During 2005 the Club embarked on building a new Main Stand at one side of the pitch. However part way through the building the club experienced severe financial difficulties and were unable to complete the work. So what should have been a smart looking, 4,500 capacity, single tiered stand, has instead ended up as a half finished shell of a stand, that is only partly used. The roof of the stand has been completed and some seats have been installed towards the Tivoli End, but the rest of it looks a mixture of grey concrete and exposed steelwork. It remains to be seen whether the Club will be able to complete the stand in the foreseeable future.

On the other side of the ground is the Millmoor Lane Stand, which has a mixture of covered and open seating. Roughly each section on this side is about a third of the length of the pitch. The covered seating in the middle of this stand looks quite distinctive, with several supporting pillars and an arched roof. Both ends are former terraces, with several supporting pillars and have now been made all seated. The larger of the two is the Tivoli End, used by home fans. It was noticeable that the pitch slopes up towards this end. The ground also benefits from a striking set of floodlights, the pylons of which are some of the tallest that I have come across (approximately 124 feet high, I've since been told).

What Is It Like For Visiting Supporters?

Away fans are housed in the Railway End where normally just over 2,000 fans can be accommodated. This end is covered and all seated and it doesn't take a lot of away fans to really make some noise. On the downside there are a couple of supporting pillars which could impede your view. An unusual feature is that away fans can only access this end via a small, narrow alleyway. If demand requires it then part of the Millmoor Lane Stand can also be made available to visiting supporters.

I enjoyed my last visit to the ground. I found the Rotherham fans fairly friendly in the pub that I visited before the game and the standard of stewarding within the ground to be relaxed. There is a range of Pukka Pies on offer inside the ground, including Chicken Balti Pies (£2.20) and even hot pork pies are available.

Where To Drink?

I had an enjoyable pre-match drink in the Butchers Arms in Midland Road. The pub had a warm welcome and a good mix of home and away supporters. There is on street parking to be had in the surrounding streets and the ground is about an eight minute walk away. To find this pub; as you proceed along the A629 from the A6109, turn right at the first island that you reach on the A629 which appears to lead into a small industrial estate and then take the second left into Midland Road. The Butchers Arms is situated down this road on the left, opposite the bus depot.

Stuart Abbs recommends the Tivoli Club at the ground. whilst Wayne Hopkins gives the thumbs up to the Millmoor Pub on the corner of Millmoor Lane next to the ground. 'This is a great place for both home and away fans to meet before a match and is also the HQ for the Rotherham United Supporters Club'. There is also the Prince Of Wales Hotel in Princes Street (from the ground go over the railway bridge and turn right) which has an upstairs bar for home fans and a cellar bar for away fans.

Neil Uttley adds; 'The Moulders Rest on Masbrough Street occasionally let away fans in depending on the opposition. Otherwise there are a good selection of pubs in the town centre, however many employ door staff on match days and police presence is high; some pubs operate a no club colours policy. Recommended is the Rhinoceros (a Wetherspoons pub) on Bridgegate (across the road from McDonalds) and one to avoid is the County Borough opposite the bus station on the corner of Corporation St and Bridgegate'.

I have also been advised that 'Shooters' (formerly known as Queens) is best avoided by away supporters. Please note that alcohol is not available in the away end.

■ How To Get There & Where To Park?

Leave the M1 at Junction 34 and take the A6109 towards Rotherham. At the large roundabout which is the junction with the A629 turn right. Proceed along the A629 crossing a small roundabout and then at the second much larger roundabout turn right and you will see the ground over on your right. You can see the floodlights of the ground for some distance away. Either street parking or there is a car park behind the Main Stand which costs £2.

There is a handy unofficial car park that away fans can use behind the Zone nightclub on Main Street. Access to the car park, which costs £2, is by a slip road off the dual carriageway and is well signposted near to the ground. From the car park a subway takes you down the back of the scrap yards to Millmoor Lane and the away end turnstiles.

■ By Train

The ground is walkable from Rotherham train station, about a five to ten-minute walk. Steve Orton adds; 'To get to the ground, turn left out of the railway station and walk towards the roundabout. Then follow the blue tourist type signs directing pedestrians to Rotherham United F.C.'

■ Local Rivals

Barnsley, Sheffield Wednesday, Sheffield United & Doncaster Rovers.

■ Admission Prices

Tickets Bought In Advance:

Main Stand:
Adults £20,
Senior Citizens/Students £12,
Under 16's £10*,
Under 6's £3

All Other Areas Of The Ground:
Adults £18,
Senior Citizens/Students £10,
Under 16's £8*,
Under 6's £1

Matchday Prices:

Main Stand:
Adults £22,
Concessions £14

All Other Areas Of The Ground:
Adults £20, Concessions £12

* Children who become members of the Junior Millers can qualify for a £2 discount on these ticket prices.

■ Programme

Official Programme: £2.50.

■ Record Attendance

25,170 v Sheffield United,
Division 2, December 13th, 1952.

■ Average Attendance

2006-2007: 4,951 (League One)

■ Did You Know?

That Rotherham United were formed in 1925, when Rotherham Town & Rotherham County amalgamated into one club.

Shrewsbury Town

New Meadow

Ground Name: New Meadow
Capacity: 10,000 (all seated)
Address: Oteley Road, Shrewsbury, SY2 6QQB
Main Telephone No: 01743-360-111
Fax No: 01743-236-384
Team Nickname: The Shrews
Year Ground Opened: 2007
Pitch Size: 114 x 74 yards
Home Kit Colours: Blue & Amber

Official Website:
www.shrewsburytown.com

Unofficial Websites:
Blue & Amber - www.blue-and-amber.co.uk (Rivals Network)
Talk Of The Town - www.themightyshrew.co.uk
News Of The Shrews - www.newsoftheshrews.com
New Meadow - www.newmeadow.com

What's The Ground Like?

After 97 years at playing at their Gay Meadow ground, the Shrews have moved to a new stadium on the outskirts of the town. The New Meadow as it is currently called, has a capacity of 10,000 seats. It is comprised of four separate stands and at first glance looks similar in design to some of the stands at the Kassam Stadium in Oxford. Each of the stands are simple single tiered stands, that are covered. Below the roof at the back of the stands is a sizeable strip of perspex that runs along the length of the stands. This is to allow more light into the stadium to facilitate pitch growth. Four small floodlights pylons are present on the roofs of the side stands.

What Is It Like For Visiting Supporters?

Away fans are located in the North Stand at one end of the ground.

With a new stadium you would hope that the facilities on offer and views of the playing action would be good. Plus I'm sure that the atmosphere will be better at the new stadium, as the old Gay Meadow ground was largely open and therefore not conducive for generating atmosphere. However, the main drawback with the stadium is its location. Literally built on a field on the very edge of town, there is little in the way of facilities around it. There is a Retail Park nearby, which has some eating outlets such as a McDonalds, Pizza Hut and a supermarket cafe, but there seems to be little else.

Personally I was sad to see the old Gay Meadow ground go. A great traditional ground, a breed of which now seems to be dying out in this country. Still, I don't visit the ground every week so I can understand the need for better facilities and the feel-good factor that a new stadium can bring. However, I look at the bland new stadium and do I think that I'll be rushing there to see a game? Probably not, although obviously for the Guide, I will do so. With so many non-descript new stadiums popping up all over the country, then I can see why probably fewer and fewer fans will want to visit all 92 grounds. At one time grounds were very different, no two being alike, but now with so many grounds being similar and located in remote outskirts of towns, the incentive to visit them all has greatly diminished.

Where To Drink?

David Matthias informs me; 'There are a couple of pubs within walking distance of the new stadium. Firstly there is the 'Brooklands Hotel', just off Meole Brace Island - about 5 minutes walk away and an official "park and walk" pub with about 100 spaces costing £5 each. Big screens & catering on matchdays. There is also the Charles

Darwin Pub - 10 minutes walk away from new Meadow with 70 free parking spaces & a good chippy opposite'.

The Brooklands Hotel is situated on Mill Street. From the stadium turn left along the B4380 Oteley Road. Head around the large roundabout towards Shrewsbury Town Centre. Then turn left into Roman Road and then left again into Mill Street. The hotel is down on the right.

The Charles Darwin Pub is in the opposite direction. From the stadium turn right along the B4380 Oteley Road. Take the second left into Sutton Road and the pub is down on the right.

Gareth Hopkins adds; 'There are some other pubs and some off-street parking to be had along the Hereford Road (A5191) going towards Shrewsbury Town Centre'. Please note that alcohol is not served to away fans within the stadium.

■ How To Get There & Where To Park?

At the end of the M54 continue onto the A5. After about seven miles, there is a traffic island which is at the junction with the A49. Bear left at this island still following the A5 (ignore the signs for Shrewsbury Town Centre signposted A5064 town centre/crematorium). At the next roundabout turn right towards Shrewsbury on the A5112 (signposted town centre/park & ride). You will pass a Retail Park on your right and then at the next roundabout you take the 4th exit onto the B4380 towards Oteley (also signposted golf course). The stadium is a short way down this road on the right, just as you go over the railway bridge.

There is a large car park at the stadium. However, this is for permit holders only and street parking is prohibited in the nearby residential area and retail park. The Club will operate a number of Park & Ride schemes on matchdays at a cost of £2 per person, starting at 12.30pm on Saturdays & 5.30pm for evening matches. These operate from various locations including Shire Hall & Shrewsbury Business Park. These park & ride schemes are located near to the A5, just take the A5064 towards the town centre from the A5.

■ By Train

Shrewsbury train station is around two miles away from the stadium. So it should take around 35 minutes to walk. Otherwise you can grab a taxi up to the ground, or take a bus from the town centre bus station (service numbers 16, 23, 25 & 544/546 all stop near to the stadium). There are also plans to introduce a dedicated bus service on matchdays. Shrewsbury train station is served by trains from Birmingham New Street & Crewe.

What is a shame is that the new stadium is situated right next to a railway line and so it does beg the question as to a why a station has not been built too? Okay, I probably know that the answer will have something to do with a lack of money, but it is just annoying when Governments & Local Authorities continually harp on about leaving the car at home and using public transport instead. Well, the next time I visit the stadium, I'll just have to use my car, won't I? (even though I won't be allowed to park at the stadium!)

■ Local Rivals

Hereford United, Wrexham & Walsall.

■ Admission Prices

Home Fans*:

West Stand (Centre)
Adults £18,
Concessions £12

West Stand (Wings)
Adults £15,
Concessions £10

East Stand
Adults £18,
Concessions £12

South Stand
Adults £15,
Concessions £10

East Stand (Family Area)
1 Adult + 1 Under 16 £18,
1 Adult + 1 Under 11 £16,
Additional Adult: £16,
Additional OAP/Student £11,
Additional Under 16 £2,
Additional Under 11 Free (if a Club member)

Away Fans:

South Stand
Adults £15,
Concessions £10.

* Please note that the prices quoted above are for tickets purchased in advance of matchday. Tickets purchased on matchday will cost £1 more.

Concessions apply to OAP's, Students & Under 16's. Under 16's can obtain further discounts on these prices if they become Club Members. In addition disabled and accompanying carer are admitted free.

■ Programme

Official Programme £2.50

■ Record Attendance

18,917 v Walsall,
Division 3, April 26th, 1961.

■ Average Attendance

2006-2007: 4,499 (League Two)

■ Did You Know?

Although formed in 1886, it was not until 1950 that the Club were admitted into the Football League. They still remain as Shropshire's only league club.

Stockport County

Edgeley Park

Ground Name: Edgeley Park
Capacity: 11,000 (all seated)
Address: Hardcastle Road,
Stockport, SK3 9DD
Main Telephone No: 0161-286-8888
Fax No: 0161-286-8900
Team Nickname: The Hatters
Year Ground Opened: 1902
Pitch Size: 111 x 71 yards
Home Kit Colours: Blue & White

Official Website:
www.stockportcounty.com

Unofficial Websites:
Hatters Matters - www.hattersmatters.com
(Rivals Network)
Stockport County Trust - www.stockportcountytrust.com

What's The Ground Like?

At one end is the large Cheadle End Stand, which is the newest addition to the ground and is the home end. This stand towers over the rest of the stadium, which looks rather small in comparison. Opposite, the Railway End is a former open terrace converted to a seating area. It is usually unused on matchdays and has a small electric scoreboard above it. Both sides are quite old-looking stands, that are both covered and all seated. The Main stand is only about two-thirds the length of the pitch and straddles the halfway line. On the other side is the Popular Side Stand, allocated to away supporters. The football club is now owned by the Stockport County Supporters Trust and the ground is shared with Sale Sharks Rugby Club.

Future Ground Developments

Paddy Dresser informs me; 'The Club still hope to re-develop the Railway End, with a two-tier, 5,200-seater stand, which will be similar in design to the existing Robinsons Brewery Stand. However no time scales have been announced as to when this will take place".

What Is It Like For Visiting Supporters?

Away fans are predominantly housed on one side of the Popular Side Stand, where the normal allocation is 800 seats. This stand is covered, however, there are a number of supporting pillars which may impede your view. If this happens, the stewards do allow you to stand at the back of the stand to get a better view. You can access the entrance to this stand by walking behind the large Cheadle End and through the car park. Strangely, then you have to walk across the front of the home fans section to reach the away area; however I have not received any reports of this causing problems.

The Railway End, where most of the away fans used to be housed, is now normally not open for most games. It can still be allocated to away fans if demand requires it, increasing the allocation by another 1,500 seats. However, this end is uncovered, so if you do end up in there, be prepared to get wet.

The facilities within the ground are pretty good, with modern toilets, whilst the refreshment kiosk, staffed by friendly faces, offers a good range of pies, including the delicious 'Football's Famous Chicken Balti Pie' (£2).

Stockport is another club that has become tolerant towards away supporters in recent years and is now a more pleasurable away trip than it used to be. If you are a plane spotter, then this is your ground, as during the game many large aircraft fly over the ground, having taken off from nearby Manchester Airport!

Matthew Jones, a visiting Darlington fan, adds; 'On my recent visit, the away fans were not allowed to stand up to see around the supporting pillars of the stand. When fans did stand up, the stewards were onto us straight away and we faced being kicked out if we did not sit down. This meant that for most of the game, I could not see most of the one goal, due to a supporting pillar being in the way. Also flags were not permitted to be put on seats in case fans needed them, even once the game had started. I noticed that home fans were able to do so!'

Mark White, a visiting Northampton supporter adds; 'The segregation is a bit odd, you can use the home toilets and pie stall prior to the match, and you walk in front of the home fans to get to your expensive seats, but not at half time or after the match when you are directed in front of the former open terrace and out of the ground'.

Where To Drink?

There is a small Labour Club (C.I.U. Affiliated) right by the entrance to the Railway End, that allows visitors in, for a small entrance fee. It is a small club that could do with modernising, but I found it both comfortable & welcoming. Otherwise there are a number of pubs along a shopping area, across the main road from the away end. Probably the best is the Royal Oak just at the end of Castle Street. Very friendly, away supporters are welcomed and there's always a bit of good natured banter flying about.

John Keane adds; 'away fans will get a warm welcome in the Sir Robert Peel half way up Castle Street. One pub to avoid is John Jo Greens'. Steve Johnson recommends The Armoury, a Robinsons pub situated by the roundabout at the top of Castle Street, 'is excellent for away fans. The Landlord is very friendly, the Robbies beer is excellent and the home fans there are very welcoming'. Whilst Vaughan Skirrey, a visiting Sheffield Wednesday supporter recommends The Grapes. As you come up the hill from the station, the pub is on the left at the top of Castle Street.

Please note that alcohol is not available in the away end. If you choose to drink in Stockport town centre, it is worth looking out for a Robinsons pub, as the beer is excellent and is actually brewed in Stockport itself.

How To Get There & Where To Park?

From The North/South:
M6 to Junction 19. Take the A556 towards Manchester/Altrincham. Then join the M56 towards Manchester Airport. After a few miles leave the M56 and join the M60 towards Stockport. Leave the M60 at Junction 1 and head towards Stockport. Turn right at the second set of traffic lights to go onto the A560 towards Cheadle. Then turn left into Edgeley Road (there is a pub on the left hand corner at the lights at this junction). The ground is down this road on the right.

From The East:
M62 to Junction 18. Take the M60 towards Stockport. Leave the M60 at Junction 1 and head towards Stockport. Turn right at the second set of traffic lights to go onto the A560 towards Cheadle. Then turn left into Edgeley Road (there is a pub on the left-hand corner at the lights at this junction). The ground is down this road on the right.

The ground is well sign posted around the area. Street parking.

By Train

Stockport railway station is in walking distance of the ground (around half a mile). Come out of the station and turn left up Station Road, and continue up the hill towards the roundabout. Go straight over the roundabout and turn left into Caroline Street for the ground. Thanks to Andy Harris for the directions.

Mark White adds; 'Stockport station's entrance has recently been modernised, and now has a new main entrance that you are signposted to from the platforms. This is on the opposite side of the station from the ground. If you find yourself in the ticket hall with a taxi rank in front of you, go back into the station through the subways under the platforms, then follow the directions above'.

Local Rivals

Manchester City, Crewe Alexandra, Oldham, and a little further afield, Burnley.

Admission Prices

Home Fans:

Stockport Express Main Stand:
Adults £18, Concessions £11, Juniors £5

Stockport Express Main Stand:
Family Ticket 1 Adult + 1 Junior £24,
1 Adult + 2 Juniors £29, 2 Adult + 2 Juniors £48

Popular Side Stand:
Adults £18, Concessions £11, Juniors £5

Popular Side Stand:
Family Ticket 1 Adult + 1 Junior £20,
1 Adult + 2 Juniors £22, 2 Adult + 2 Juniors £38

Cheadle End Stand:
Adults £16, Concessions £11, Juniors £5

Printerworks Cheadle End Stand:
Family Ticket 1 Adult + 1 Junior £20,
1 Adult + 2 Juniors £24, 2 Adult + 2 Juniors £40

Away Fans:

Popular Side Stand:
Adults £18, Concessions £11, Juniors £5

Railway End:
Adults £16, Concessions £11, Juniors £5

Programme

Official Programme £2.50

Record Attendance

27,833 v Liverpool,
FA Cup 5th Round, February 11th, 1950.

Modern All Seated Attendance Record:
10,006 v Carlisle United,
League Two, May 6th, 2006.

Average Attendance

2006-2007: 5,026 (League Two)

Did You Know?

Following the success of Argentina in the 1978 World Cup, Stockport County adopted sky blue and white striped shirts, until the Falklands war caused them to rethink.

Wrexham

Racecourse Ground

Ground Name: Racecourse Ground
Capacity: 15,500 (10,500 seated)
Address: Mold Road,
Wrexham, LL11 2AH
Main Telephone No: 01978-262-129
Fax No: 01978-357-821
Team Nickname: Red Dragons
Year Ground Opened: 1905*
Pitch Size: 111 x 74 yards
Home Kit Colours: Red & White

Official Website:
www.wrexhamafc.co.uk

Unofficial Websites:
Red Passion Fanzine - www.red-passion.com
Supporters Trust - www.wst.org.uk/wst/index.php
One Nil To The... - www.onttss.co.uk

■ What's The Ground Like?

The Racecourse is a classic-looking football ground with four prominent floodlight pylons and a large home terrace. The stadium also has a great blend of the old and the new, with the Mold Road Stand, having a modern interesting design. To show how times have changed and the amount of all seated stadiums that there are now, Wrexham now boasts the largest terrace in the league, with the Kop Terrace having a capacity of 4,000. This stand is a throw back to when every ground had a similar kind of terrace and even the crowd barriers are painted in the club colours of red & white (rather than those dull metallic coloured barriers present in modern stands). The terrace, which is located at one end of the ground, is partly covered (to the rear).

At the other end is the Roberts Builders Stand. This stand when it was opened in 1978 was called the Plas Coch (Red Hall) Stand. This two tiered stand is covered and all seated. It has a couple of supporting pillars, situated between the two tiers. It also has an electric scoreboard on its roof. On one side is the Yale Stand. This stand was opened in 1972 and got its name from the Yale College, which was situated behind this stand. It is a fair sized two tiered covered stand, which is now all seated, having previously had terracing at the front. The team dugouts are located in front of this stand. Opposite is the Mold Road Stand that was opened in 1999. This side of the ground had been unused for a number of years so its construction greatly improved the overall ground appearance. It is semi circular in design with a capacity of 3,500 seats and features an unusual roof design. The ground is also used for Liverpool FC Reserve team games.

■ What Is It Like For Visiting Supporters?

Away fans are housed in the upper tier of the Roberts Builders Stand, holding just over 2,000. If demand requires it a further 1,000 can be accommodated in the lower tier. There are a couple of small supporting pillars in the upper tier of this stand, however the acoustics are good. On my last visit I found Wrexham to be relaxed and friendly, with both sets of supporters mixing freely in the pubs beforehand. The atmosphere was generally good; however there was a section of Wrexham supporters in the Pryce Griffiths Stand who seemed to be permanently baiting the away fans. Inside the ground the delicious 'Football's Famous Chicken Balti Pie' (£2.20) is available.

Tim Porter, a visiting Torquay United supporter, adds; 'The signs around the ground directing visiting fans to the appropriate entrance are poor. We followed the signs from the Sainsburys Stand for 'Visiting Supporters' which took us to one end of the ground. There were no signs here and so we paid our £13 /£7 and went in. We were just a bit surprised to walk up the bank and find ourselves on the Wrexham Kop! I explained our mistake to a steward who said it was always happening! He kindly led us through the ground to the away end. It wasn't until I was looking at the notes I'd made from the guide at the services on the way home, that I realised it was £16 for adults and £11 for juniors in the away end, so I'd inadvertently saved £7!'. The Guide doesn't recommend that you do this to save money, of course, so take time to make sure you are at the proper end first before parting with your cash.

■ Where To Drink?

There is one pub right on the corner of the ground at the Kop End called 'The Turf'. It is a Marstons pub which does allow in away supporters, but only in small numbers. It can get extremely busy, so arrive early. Before the new Pryce Griffiths Stand was built, this pub used to have a balcony that overlooked the ground. Otherwise the town centre is about a ten-minute walk away, where there are plenty of good pubs to be found. A favourite haunt of away supporters is the Wetherspoons pub in the town centre, called the Elihu Yale (named after a local man who founded Yale University in the USA). To find it, walk along the road from the ground towards the town centre. After about half a mile go through the double set of traffic lights. After the next road junction it is in the row of buildings on your left, in Regent Street. Apparently Wrexham has more pubs in ratio to the population than any other town in Britain, sounds a good place to me!

■ How To Get There & Where To Park?

From The North:
Take the A483 towards Wrexham (this is the Wrexham by-pass). Leave the A483 with at the junction of the A541 Mold road. The ground is 300 yards from this junction (on the A541) towards Wrexham town centre.

From The South:
Take the M54 from the M6 (Junction 10A Northbound). Follow the M54 to the end of the motorway and join the A5 towards Shrewsbury. Continue on the A5 past Shrewsbury and Oswestry and then join the A483 towards Wrexham. Stay on the A483 as you reach Wrexham (this is the Wrexham by-pass). Then as above. Street parking. If you arrive early (around 1-1.15pm) there is some street parking to be had, on the other side of the road from the car showroom by the Turf pub. Otherwise there a couple of private car parks, charging in the region of £2.

■ By Train

Wrexham General train station is located next to the ground.

■ Local Rivals

Chester City, Cardiff City, Swansea City, Tranmere Rovers, Crewe Alexandra & Shrewsbury Town.

■ Admission Prices

Home Fans*:

Directors' Box
Adults £40,
No Concessions

Sainsbury's Stand Executive Area
Adults £25,
No Concessions

Sainsbury's Stand
Adults £16,
OAP's £10,
Juniors £5

Pryce Griffiths Stand
Adults £17,
OAP's £10,
Juniors £5

Kop Terrace
Adults £14,
OAP's £7,
Juniors £5

Family Tickets (all stands):
1 Adult & up to 2 Children £20
1 Adult & 3 Children £25

Away Fans:

Roberts Builders Stand
Adults £16,
OAP's £10,
Juniors £5

* In addition young adult home supporters under the age of 21 can qualify for reduced admission prices provided that they first register with the club and buy match tickets in advance.

■ Programme & Fanzine

Official Programme £2.50
Dismal Jimmy Fanzine £1.50

■ Record Attendance

34,445 v Manchester United,
FA Cup, 4th Round, January 26th, 1957.

■ Average Attendance

2006-2007: 4,132 (League Two)

■ Did You Know?

In 1962 the Club built a small covered stand at the back of the Kop, which became known as the 'pigeon loft'. This stand was dismantled and sold to Wrexham Rugby Club in 1980 and the present roof was then constructed.

* In 1905 the Club took up permanent residence at the Racecourse. However, the ground had hosted many football matches previous to that date, including the first ever Wales international v Scotland in 1876.

Wycombe Wanderers

Adams Park

Ground Name: Adams Park
Capacity: 10,000
Address: Hillbottom Road, High Wycombe, HP12 4HJ
Main Telephone No: 01494-472-100
Fax No: 01494-527-633
Ticket Office: 01494-441-118
Pitch Size: 115 x 75 yards
Team Nickname: The Chairboys
Year Ground Opened: 1991
Home Kit Colours: Navy & Light Blue

Official Website:
www.wycombewanderers.co.uk

Unofficial Website:
Chairboys On The Net - www.chairboys.ndirect.co.uk

■ What's The Ground Like?

On one side of the ground is the impressive-looking Frank Adams Stand, opened in 1996. This was named in memory of the man who originally donated to the club their previous ground at Loakes Park. It is a large two-tiered stand, complete with a row of executive boxes and it dwarfs the rest of the stadium. The other three stands are smaller affairs, but are at least all covered. Only the Valley Stand at the home end remains as terracing. Opposite is the Dreams Stand, housing away supporters, a medium-sized single-tiered stand, with windshields to either side. Along the other side of the ground is the Seymour Taylor Main Stand. This single-tiered stand has a raised seating area, meaning that fans access it by climbing a small set of stairs in front of it.

Jon Wood adds; 'As the local council have stipulated that the capacity of Adams Park cannot rise above 10,000, the additional seats have meant that certain areas of terracing, such as the paddock area of the Seymour Taylor Stand, have been made 'out of bounds' to fans'. The ground is currently shared with Wasps Rugby Club.

■ Future Ground Developments

William Vince informs me; 'the club is looking at the possibility of increasing the current capacity to around 12,500-15,000. This would include the rebuilding of the main stand and replacing it with a mirror image of the existing Frank Adams stand. To do this another access road would need to be built and approval from the local council'.

■ What Is It Like For Visiting Supporters?

Away fans are mostly located at one end of the ground in the Dreams Stand, where just over 2,000 supporters can be accommodated. I personally had an enjoyable day at Wycombe. The Club has a relaxed friendly feel about it. The ground is situated in a nice setting with a wooded hill overlooking the ground (this normally has a small contingent of supporters watching the game for nothing) and with green fields surrounding the other sides.
The standard football ground fayre of burgers (£2.30), pies (£2), pasties and hot dogs are available from the refreshments area.

David Abbott, a visiting Northampton Town supporter, informs me; 'I have to say what an excellent ground Adams Park is. Good signposting around the ground, good organisation, good atmosphere, excellent view from the away end and friendly fans. It was a very pleasant visit and if all grounds and supporters were as welcoming and well-behaved as Wycombe the game would be all the better for it'.

Toby Hillier, a visiting Brentford fan, adds; 'The ground is absolutely splendid and set in wonderful surroundings. Although the atmosphere was pretty flat on my visit, the beating of a drum in the home end often rallied the home fans behind the team. The home fans are a friendly bunch and all of the staff that we encountered were also very friendly. You can park at the ground itself, however it is a nightmare trying to get out at the end of the game.

It took us 50 minutes to do the 2 miles back to the motorway. My suggestion would be to park a mile or so away from the ground and walk. This should provide you with a quicker route away from the game'.

Mike Jordan, a visiting Torquay United fan tells me; 'I found the home fans, stewards and staff of Wycombe to be friendly & welcoming towards away supporters. Also, for visitors interested in wildlife, at half time or during dull moments, look out for Red Kites drifting over the ground!'

■ Where To Drink?

As the ground is on the edge of an industrial estate, there aren't many pubs around. Neil Young informs me 'The nearest pub to the ground is the Hourglass in Sands (about a 15-minute walk, from the end of the road up to the ground). Away fans are normally okay in small groups except for big games or local derbies'. Martin Redfern, a visiting Scunthorpe United fan, informs me; 'we arrived early at the ground and were able to go into the Supporters Club at the ground, which cost £2 to enter. The Club is one of the suites at the far end of the Main Stand. It was a spacious room with 2 bars and food. The atmosphere was extremely relaxed and friendly with both home and away supporters'.

■ How To Get There & Where To Park?

The stadium is located on the outskirts of Wycombe on the Sands Industrial Estate. Leave the M40 at Junction 4 and take the A4010 towards Aylesbury. Turn left at the 4th roundabout into Lane End Road and then continue straight down this road. Cross another roundabout and into Hillbottom Road. The ground is down at the very bottom of this road. On my last visit I noticed that there were a number of AA road signs labelled 'London Wasps' which were helpful in pointing the way to the ground.

There is a fair-sized car park located at the ground which costs £3 per car, or some of the industrial units provide matchday parking (also at around £3). As there is only one road that leads from the stadium, I have heard that it can be a nightmare leaving the official car park at full time. I would recommend therefore, parking in one of the industrial units that line Hillbottom Road towards the ground. I did this and got away alright.

■ By Train

If coming by train into Wycombe station, then either take a taxi (costs about £5) or get the football special bus that runs from the station to the ground on match days. The Football Special (No.501) departs the railway station for the stadium at 13.55 on Saturday matchdays and 18.40 for midweek games (cost about £2.50 return). The Special returns 10 minutes after the final whistle. Paul Willems, a visiting Bristol City supporter, adds; 'If you have got the energy, then a walk from the station to the ground along the West Wycombe Road takes in several pubs and can make the three quarters of an hour or so walk seem a lot less!! Those in the know will cut across a park just after the last pub on the West Wycombe Road and be there ten minutes sooner'.

■ Local Rivals

Oxford & from a little further afield Colchester United.

■ Admission Prices

Home Fans:

Frank Adams Stand (Upper Tier Centre):
Adults £20, Concessions £16, Students/Young Adults (Under 22yrs) & Under 16's £15

Frank Adams Stand (Upper Tier Wings):
Adults £18, OAP's £15, Students/Young Adults (Under 22yrs) & Under 16's £14

Hypnosis Family Enclosure:
Adults £16, OAP's £14, Students/Young Adults (Under 22yrs) £13, Under 16's £6

BCUC Main Stand (Centre):
Adults £20, Concessions £16, Students/Young Adults (Under 22yrs) & Under 16's £15

BCUC Main Stand (Wings):
Adults £18, OAP's £15, Students/Young Adults (Under 22yrs) & Under 16's £14

Valley Terrace:
Adults £16, Concessions £16, Students/Young Adults (Under 22yrs) £10, Under 16's £6

Away Fans*:

Dreams Stand:
Adults £18, Concessions £15, Under 16's £14

* A £2 discount is available on these tickets prices, providing that the ticket is purchased prior to matchday. A further £1 discount is available if the ticket is bought online.

■ Programme

Official Programme: £2.50

■ Record Attendance

At Adams Park:
10,000 v Chelsea
Friendly, July 13th, 2005.

At Loakes Park:
15,850 v St Albans
FA Amateur Cup, 4th Round, February 25th, 1950.

■ Average Attendance

2006-2007: 4,983 (League Two)

■ Did You Know?

That Wycombe Wanderers Football Club, originally called North Town Wanderers, was founded around 1884 by a group of young furniture trade workers. Hence the club nickname 'The Chairboys'.

Wembley Stadium

Capacity: 90,000 (all-seated)
Address: Empire Way,
Wembley, Middlesex HA9 0DS
Main Telephone No: 0208-795-9000
Fax No: 0208-795-5050
Year Ground Opened: 2007

Official Website:
www.wembleystadium.com

What's The Stadium Like?

Well, it may have been late in opening and over budget, but the new stadium has certainly been worth the wait and the extra expenditure. To say that it looks superb is really an understatement. 'Fantastic', 'tremendous', such words probably still don't do it enough justice. But what is really great about the stadium is that it has its own individual identity and character. From the moment you see the Arch towering over the stadium in the distance, then you know that this is going to be something special, and special it is. Plus, unlike a number of other stadiums around the world that host a number of sporting events including football, Wembley is primarily for football and is the home of the England team. No wonder that it is labelled the 'Home of Football'.

The old Wembley closed its doors in 2000 and was due to re-open in August 2005, but delays meant that the new stadium was not ready until March 2007. Designed by Foster & Partners and HOK Sport, the stadium which was built by Multiplex cost £737m to construct.

The stadium is totally enclosed and comprises three tiers, with both sides of the stadium being slightly large larger than the ends. These sides are semi-circular in construction and although on a larger scale are reminiscent of the similar designs at the Emirates and City Of Manchester Stadiums. Both these side stands have large upper and lower tiers, with a smaller middle tier sandwiched in-between. This middle tier overhangs the large lower tier and has a row of executive boxes at the back of it. At each end there is a large video screen, which is moulded into the third tier and hence is an integral part of the stadium. The stadium has a complicated looking roof that looks at first glance that it is retractable and could if necessary be used to enclose the stadium from the outside elements. However in reality, just over one third of it can be moved, so that the pitch will always be open to the elements. The parts of the roof that can be moved are for the benefit of spectators in inclement weather and to ensure that television broadcasters won't suffer from poor images, when there is a vivid contrast between sunlight and shaded areas of the pitch as seen at some other stadiums, when it is a particularly sunny day. Unlike the old stadium whereby the players would enter the field of play from a tunnel at one end, the players now enter the field in the conventional way, onto the half way line from the North Stand, where the Royal Box is situated.

The most striking external feature of the stadium is 'The Arch', towering some 133 metres above it. It is comprised of white tubular steel that can be seen for many miles across London and looks particularly spectacular at night when it is lit up. Oddly you can't see much of the Arch from inside the stadium. It does, though have a practical use in being a load-bearing support frame for the roofs of the stands. It reminds me of some sort of theme park ride and I half expect to see people being propelled over it.... now that would be interesting to watch at half time!

A bronze statue of Bobby Moore is situated in front of the stadium. The legendary England World Cup winner gazes down on fans coming up Wembley Way.

What Is It Like For Visiting Supporters?

Seeing Wembley for the first time, you can't help but be impressed with the sheer quality of the place. From escalators to transport fans up to the top tier, to the landscaped concourse areas, you can see that no expense has been spared. Although not the most generous of leg room that I have come across, it is still more than adequate and there is good height between rows. Add to this that there literally is not a bad seat in the house (even seats at the very top of the upper tier have excellent views) and with the roofs of the stadium being situated very close to the crowd, then a full house should generate an excellent atmosphere. The top tier (Level 5) is particularly steep, which may cause a few to be a bit short of breath as they reach the top, but at least this angle ensures that the spectators are kept as close to the playing action as they possibly can be.

Whereas most concourses in new stadiums so far built in this country are normally rather drab affairs, with a combination of breeze blocks and cladded piping, being predominantly on view, at Wembley it is different. For once someone has had the vision to hide these ugly features with timber rafting and well positioned lighting, giving a modern stylish look. Apparently there is one refreshment till per 100 spectators in the stadium. Whether that is a good or bad ratio, in terms of queuing times, remains to be seen. The catering is provided by the same American company who also supply and run the catering at Arsenal. Prices have always been historically expensive at Wembley and the new stadium certainly follows in the tradition here; various pies £4.50, jacket potato £4, pizza baguette £4.20, hot dog £4, soup £3.50, pint of lager or bitter £3.50, red or white wine (miniature bottle) £4. The caterers claim that the price reflects the quality of the product. Well, at those prices I decided not to put that statement to the test, opting instead to eat and drink outside of the stadium. The concourses themselves are mostly fairly spacious, have betting facilities provided by BetFred, a number of flat-screen televisions, as well as programme and merchandise outlets.

Where To Drink?

As you would expect, pubs near the stadium are almost dangerously crowded. I have tended to either drink in the centre of London before the game, or have drunk around Harrow-On-The-Hill, which is three stops away from Wembley Park on the tube. Alternatively, alcohol is sold within the stadium.

How To Get There & Where To Park?

The stadium is labelled as a 'public transport' destination. There is little parking available at the stadium itself and there is also a residents-only parking scheme in operation in the local area. The stadium is well signposted from the end of the M1 & M40. Basically the stadium is just off the A406 North Circular Road.

I would recommend parking at one of the tube stations at the end of the Metropolitan Line such as Uxbridge, Hillingdon or Ruislip or at Stanmore on the Jubilee Line and then take the tube to Wembley Park.

Wembley Stadium

By Tube/Train

The nearest tube station is Wembley Park which is around a ten minute walk from the stadium. This is served by both the Jubilee & Metropolitan lines, although it is best to take the latter as it has fewer stops. Wembley Central is slightly further away from the stadium and has both rail & Underground connections. This Underground station is served by the Bakerloo line, whilst the railway station is on the London Euston-Milton Keynes line. The nearest train station is Wembley Stadium which is on the London Marylebone-Birmingham line.

Record Attendance

126,047* West Ham United v Bolton Wanderers
FA Cup Final, April 28th, 1923.

Modern All Seated Attendance Record:
89,826 Chelsea v Manchester United
FA Cup Final, May 19th, 2007.

* This was the official recorded attendance. But as so many more people had got into the stadium without paying, it is estimated that the crowd was nearer 200,000.

Did You Know?

At 133 metres high and with a span of 315 metres, the Arch is the longest single roof structure in the world.

* Wembley Stadium was originally opened in 1924. That stadium was demolished in 2000.